I0042402

THE JACOBITE CESS ROLL FOR
THE COUNTY OF ABERDEEN IN 1715

John Forbes of Upper Boyndlie, Collector of the Cess.

From painting in possession of J. C. M. Ogilvie-Forbes, Esq., of Boyndlie.

THE
JACOBITE CESS ROLL
FOR THE
COUNTY OF
ABERDEEN IN 1715

FROM THE MS. OF JOHN FORBES OF
UPPER BOYNDLIE, NOW IN THE
POSSESSION OF J. C. M. OGILVIE-
FORBES OF BOYNDLIE

EDITED WITH INTRODUCTION,
NOTES AND GENEALOGICAL TABLES
BY

Alistair and Henrietta Tayler

Joint Authors of "The Book of the Duffs," "Lord Fife
and his Factor," "Jacobites of Aberdeenshire and
Banffshire," "Jacobite Letters of Lord Pitsligo," etc., etc.

HERITAGE BOOKS
2012

HERITAGE BOOKS

AN IMPRINT OF HERITAGE BOOKS, INC.

Books, CDs, and more—Worldwide

For our listing of thousands of titles see our website
at
www.HeritageBooks.com

A Facsimile Reprint
Published 2012 by
HERITAGE BOOKS, INC.
Publishing Division
100 Railroad Ave. #104
Westminster, Maryland 21157

Originally printed in Great Britain by the
Aberdeen University Press Limited
for
The Third Spalding Club
1932

— Publisher's Notice —

In reprints such as this, it is often not possible to remove blemishes from the original. We feel the contents of this book warrant its reissue despite these blemishes and hope you will agree and read it with pleasure.

It was not possible to reprint the original over-sized map of the shires of Aberdeen and Banff in this edition as a single map; however, the map has been included as six sections which span six individual pages.

International Standard Book Numbers
Paperbound: 978-0-7884-2844-9
Clothbound: 978-0-7884-9212-9

CONTENTS

LIST OF ILLUSTRATIONS

EDITORS' NOTE

THE editing of this Cess Roll for the Third Spalding Club has been a work of great interest, and has involved much research into both printed and manuscript records. The most fruitful source of information not hitherto printed has been, of course, the *Particular Register of Sasines for Aberdeenshire*, the Register House, Edinburgh.[1] All available documents in Aberdeen and Edinburgh have also been consulted, and so many books bearing on the subject that it would be tedious to enumerate them. A list of the more important will be found on page 250. As is said by Michelet in his monumental history of France, "Nous supprimons généralement les citations de livres imprimés que tout le monde a dans les mains. Nous ne citerons guère que les manuscrits."

Assistance has been sought from all those learned in particular families. Dr. J. M. Bulloch on the Gordons; the late A. M. Mackintosh, Esq., on the Farquharsons; Lieut.-Colonel James Forbes, D.S.O., and J. C. M. Ogilvie-Forbes, Esq. of Boyndlie, on the Forbes family; Thomas Innes, Esq. of Learney, Carrick Pursuivant, for that of Innes, etc., while every one, without exception, who has been asked for permission to examine family papers has generously accorded it.

Our personal thanks are due, as well as to the above, to

Miss Mabel D. Allardyce.   James Cruickshank, Esq.
J. G. Burnett, Esq. of Powis,   Douglas Davidson, Esq.
    M.P.   Lord Forbes.
Lord Clinton.   Dowager Lady Forbes.

---

[1] *Page* references are *not* given for the Sasines quoted, as they can easily be found under their dates by those anxious to consult the originals.

The late J. A. Henderson, Esq.

Charles Leith-Hay, Esq. of Leith Hall.

Rear-Admiral Walter Lumsden of Pitcaple.

John Paton, Esq. of Grandhome.

Sidney Russell, Esq. of Aden.

David Sampson, Esq.

Major Francis Skeet.

W. Middleton Stewart, Esq.

Sir John Burnett-Stuart of Crichie.

Falconer L. Wallace, Esq. of Candacraig.

ALISTAIR N. TAYLER.

HENRIETTA TAYLER.

Christmas, 1931.

PREFACE

It was at first proposed to issue the Cess Roll of 1715 in one Volume, together with the Valuation of the County in 1667 (from a contemporary MS.), with Introduction and Notes by the same editors.

It was found, however, that the two together would make a cumbersome volume, and the Club decided to issue the *later* document for the present year, 1932, reserving the Valuation Roll to form the volume for 1933.

A few of the genealogical tables prepared for the Valuation, to which reference could have been made had both documents been printed together, are given in this volume and will be repeated in that for next year (along with the map).

As Professor Sanford Terry has pointed out, much of Scottish history is difficult of comprehension without the assistance of such tables. The editors of the present document felt, therefore, fully justified in including many family trees to elucidate the connections between the Aberdeenshire lairds of the period, and in making this a special feature of their work.

Biographical details are given in the case of every individual mentioned, as far as possible, with his or her progenitors and immediate descendants; besides any interesting historical or personal events in which they took part, and occasional longer accounts, especially where these can be drawn from unpublished or not easily available sources.

A few historical notes are added dealing with the state of the country at the period covered by this document, which was a time of great political and religious ferment in Scotland. Constant changes occurred throughout the 17th and 18th centuries in the government and constitution of the Church in Scotland. Presbyteries, however (themselves grouped under Synods, which were first instituted by the General Assembly at Glasgow in 1580), had definitely been established as the units of Church government, instead of bishoprics, and in their main outlines and nomenclature have remained to the present day. There were about nine hundred parishes in Scotland, sixty-eight presbyteries, and fourteen synods—Aberdeenshire had one synod, eight presbyteries, and in 1715 ninety-seven parishes.

INTRODUCTION

THE year 1715 saw a great upheaval in the North-East corner of Scotland. The establishment on the throne of Great Britain (in the previous year) of the Hanoverian family, which had taken place with such surprising ease in London, was viewed with disfavour by a large party in Scotland. The banished Stuarts were Scottish kings, gifted by Scotland to the southern kingdom ; the final, if un-successful, attempts for the cause of Charles I (1645–1650), and of that of his younger son, James II (1689), had both taken place in Scotland,[1] and love for the family lingered long.[2]

Cromwell, that able administrator, fully realised this fact when he temporarily crushed the Scots at Dunbar,[3] and knew that, but for the ill-advised passing of the Scots army into England to its final defeat at Worcester, his so-called " crowning mercy " might never have occurred (21st September, 1651). It is often forgotten that, following on this, Cromwell evolved and brought into being for a short time a complete Union of the two Kingdoms, political and

---

[1] The attempt in the reign of Queen Anne, 1708, when James II's son failed even to set foot in Scotland, was also exclusively the work of the Scots and their allies the French.

[2] Montrose wrote to Charles from Scotland in 1641 :—" Ye are not lyk a trie lately planted which oweth the fall to the first wind. Your ancestors have governed here, without interruption of race 2,000 years or thereabout, and taken such deep root as it can never be plucked up by any but yourselves," which latter circumstance did, in fact, occur, since the throne of Charles was lost for the family in 1688, and neither *his* son, James, nor his grandson, James, nor even his great-grandson, Charles Edward, was able to recapture it.

[3] The Covenanting army which faced him had been almost ludicrously weakened by the purging from its ranks of all officers and men not of extreme Presbyterian views, and David Leslie's own military knowledge over-ridden in the matter of giving instant battle by the fanatic members of Committee, so that he had to abandon his strong position and come downhill to certain defeat.

fiscal. The Act (published in his name) "For the Incorporating of Scotland into one Commonwealth and Free State with England and for abolishing the Kingly office in Scotland" was passed in 1652, and the ordinance of Incorporation bears date 12th April, 1654. All the Scottish governing bodies, the Privy Council, the Committee of the Estates, the Court of Session, and even the General Assembly of the Church were abolished. Thirty Scots members were summoned to the English Parliament (though received at Westminster with a very poor welcome), while the actual administration was in the hands of a Commission of seven. This body, composed of four Englishmen and three Scots, sat in Edinburgh, and in conjunction with the army under General Monk kept order in Scotland (undoubtedly very good order too), while industry improved by free trade with England, and in spite of heavier taxation the country was on the whole better off. But on the death of Oliver, 4th September, 1658, after his five years of Dictatorship or Protectorate, the organisation fell to pieces like a pack of cards, and Scottish loyalty to the Royal House showed itself still very much alive.

There was technically no "Restoration" in Scotland in the year 1660, for Charles always was the King; he had been proclaimed King at Edinburgh Cross within a week of his father's execution (5th February, 1649, the moment the news arrived), and crowned at Scone, 1st January, 1651 (before Worcester); and, though a section of the West Country Whiggamores wished to uphold "the Covenant, without the young man Charles Stuart," the country, as a whole, believed it could combine allegiance to both, while the North and the East, with which the present document is solely concerned, certainly placed loyalty to the King first of all.

When Charles, and even more his brother James had strained this loyalty to breaking point, it was some months before the Estates of the Realm, in Edinburgh, decided that James had forfeited the Crown of Scotland and agreed to offer it to William and Mary—the reigning sovereigns in England ; and it will be remembered that William, while tacitly at least permitting such outrages on human decency as the massacre of Glencoe, had in the end abandoned the attempt to bring Scotland entirely into line, and turned to the more congenial occupation of fighting the foes of Holland with English arms ! Under Queen Anne (who was after all a Stuart, though in the opinion of some a usurping daughter) affairs in Scotland were quieter, but the final political and fiscal Union of 1707 roused fierce opposition, especially in the North, where the possible benefits were less understood, while the objections were patent to every one. When, seven years later, the Stuart queen died and George, Elector of Hanover, quietly assumed the throne, in virtue of the Act of Settlement passed by William's subservient Parliament of 1701 (and *not* confirmed by the Scottish Estates, the Parliament of the day), there were many prominent Scots who took up the perfectly legal position that this Act was not binding upon Scotland, and that the *de jure* King of Scotland at the moment was Anne's half-brother, the Chevalier de St. George, otherwise " his gracious Majesty King James VIII," who, as explained in a manifesto printed by Fairbairn in 1715, had been banished the country from his birth, and, on account of this banishment, termed an alien.[1]

The party for King James in Aberdeenshire and the North was composed of many and various elements. Not only were there the true loyalists and legitimists, such as George, Earl Marischal ; Lord Fraser, Lord Panmure, Irvine of Drum, " Black Jock " Forbes of Inverernan (in whose house all the leaders stayed after raising the Standard in September,

---

[1] Extract from proclamation addressed "To all true hearted Scotsmen, whether soldiers or others :—They forced the King's son to France without reason and then made a pretended law to disinherit him for being bred there." Then with a sly hit at the parentage of George I's own son, the proclamation enquires : " Whether has a native child of a country, owned by both parents, . . . or a foreign child, born of a woman whose husband was jealous of her, separated from her, and who confined her, the best title to legitimacy ?"—*S.P.* 54.10.173.

1715), and a host of smaller lairds ; there were also the less convinced adherents who wished to support the Stuart cause *if* it were going to be successful. Among these must be numbered the Marquis of Huntly, Erskine of Pittodrie, Farquharson of Invercauld, Gordon of Abergeldie, and, somewhat surprisingly, John Gordon of Glenbucket. He has long been held to be the type *par excellence* of the sturdy Jacobite, and the fact remains that he took a distinguished part in both Risings—1715 and 1745. He was, indeed, pronounced by no less an authority than the late Dr. W. B. Blaikie as, in some senses, the prime mover of the '45, but a study of the State Papers for the year 1716 shows him, along with the Marquis of Huntly (afterwards 2nd Duke of Gordon) as hand and glove with the representatives of the Hanoverian Government in what was called " the pacification of the Highlands," and as obtaining his release from Carlisle on those express grounds.

The letters of General Carpenter, who was in charge of Prisoners, show that Glenbucket surrendered to Brigadier Grant under some kind of guarantee. Carpenter says, " He had a pass, and it will be a great discredit to Government if he be brought to tryall. He came to Edinburgh and was with Huntly."[1]

The next stage is shown by the following letter from Lord Townshend, Secretary of State, to Brigadier Stanwix, Commanding Officer at Carlisle :—

" WHITEHALL, October 16, 1716.
" SIR,
" Application having been made to H.R.H. on behalf of John Gordon of Glenbucket, now in prison in Carlisle, there appear several circumstances, which render his case very favourable. I am commissioned to signify to you his R.H. pleasure that you give order for setting the said John Gordon att Liberty.
" TOWNSHEND."

After Glenbucket's release, Carpenter writes again that " Glenbucket has returned from Carlisle, deeply grateful,"

[1] *S.P.* 54.12.199.

and adds that he, Huntly, and Sir William Gordon of Inver-gordon, the Governor of Fort William (a noted Whig), are concerting schemes for the pacification of the Highlands, and that Glenbucket is to meet Carpenter at Inverness and report progress.[1]

Of Huntly, it is well known that early in the Rising he was half-hearted, and delayed declaring himself.

The Lord Justice-Clerk wrote to Lord Townshend on 1st September, 1715: " I am with impatience expecting the result of the meeting last Monday between the Marquis of Huntly and the Earl of Mar—'tis reported the former is not so forward since the latter came into this country. Whether the latter having chief direction, as is said he has, gives any discontent, I know not. A few days will clear the matter." [2]

Two days later, intelligence was sent to the Lord Justice-Clerk that " The Marquis of Huntly came to Strathdown [Strathavon] upon Tuesday, but refuses to raise any of his men under any Subjects command and is returned home." [3]

He did, however, subsequently raise his men, forcing out the greater part of his father's tenants, who afterwards laid on him the blame and looked to his influence to help them to escape the consequences. It was sparsely exerted, though he sent pecuniary help to many suffering prisoners in Carlisle.

Very shortly after the battle of Sheriffmuir he began to treat with Argyll, who reports on 30th November that " Huntly (and some others) are willing to return to duty and would come in now," if Argyll could promise them " they would not be confined." This he was not authorised to do, and Huntly surrendered on 27th February, 1716,[4] and became an ordinary prisoner in Edinburgh Castle, though released seven months later.

The third element among the Jacobites who rose in 1715 was composed of the disappointed Scots, typified by the Earl of Mar himself. He had been quite ready to serve the

[1] S.P. 54.12.194 passim.   [2] S.P. 54.8.5.   [3] Ibid.   [4] S.P. 54.10.96a.

Elector of Hanover as King, but on his rejection by King George (who turned his back on him at the first levée) he threw himself with all his energy into the opposite camp, and by his ill-timed precipitancy in raising the Standard, and later by his unaccountable delay in coming to blows with Argyll, undoubtedly wrecked all chance of success for the Rising. He was a politician but no soldier, and by the testimony of his enemies he shamefully misused his opportunities. Argyll wrote from " Burrowbridge " on 12th September, 1715, to Lord Townshend, complaining of the tardy arrival of the promised dragoons, etc., and adds, " If the Enemy think fitt to act with the vigour that men of common sense would in their circumstances, the handfull of Troops now in Scotland may be beat out of the country before reinforcements can join them." [1]

Mar took on himself to raise the King's Standard at Braemar on 6th September, 1715, and announced himself as the King's Lieutenant and Commander in Chief of the Forces in Scotland. As a matter of fact his Commission did not arrive until 3rd October, and James, at Commercy, was unaware of what had happened in Scotland until afterwards.

The enthusiasm for his cause was great, the men were numerous, even (in contradistinction to the circumstances of the '45) funds and weapons were available ; all that was wanting was a leader, and since the Duke of Berwick was not allowed by the French Government to champion the cause of his half-brother, and James himself, the timid and hesitating son of Mary of Modena, was no soldier, the best chance the Stuarts had of regaining their throne was lost for ever. Had Prince Charles Edward, whose Stuart blood was reinforced by the fiery strain of the Sobieskis, been in Mar's place, he would have made short work of Argyll, who himself allowed that quite half his army at Sheriffmuir " behaved scandalously."

The Cess Book of John Forbes is, however, concerned

---

[1] S.P. 54.8.49.

with Mar's proclamations at the *beginning* of the Rising, when all seemed hopeful, and the following orders were issued to the authorities of each shire in the North and East, and wherever Mar thought such orders had any chance of success.

Copies are to be found among the State Papers.

"John Earl of Mar, Commander of his Majesties forces in Scotland. 27th October, 1715.

"Our Sovereign Lord James the Eight having been pleased to intrust me with the direction of his affairs and the Command of his forces in Scotland, And it being absolutely necessary to raise money for their support and maintenance, These are therefore in his Majesty's name requyring and commanding that all men betwixt sixty and sixteen years of age within the Shyre do forthwith repair to the Camp at Perth or where the army shall be for the time, with their best cloaths, horses and arms and fforty days provisions on loan at six shillings Scots a day, or otherwwys that every heretor feuar or Wadsetter *pay 6 months cess.*

"Heretors and doers also requyred to give in lists of those deficient in payment.

"Payment to be made before 15th November next."

—*P.R.O.*

It was on this order that John Forbes acted, as well as on the more particular instructions, given in another paper, dealing with those unfavourable to the Rising, which runs as follows :—

"Instruction for the Collectors of the Shyre—To exact of all heritors the Cess.

"That forthwith you issue out coppies of the order for raising the Cess in the said Shyre and cause publish the same timeously.

"That you exact of all the heritors who do not attend the King's standard, twelve months Cess within the Shyre excepting the following cases, viz. Excepting all minors, factors upon bankrupt estates in creditors hands, women liferenters and superannuate heretors who are not able to serve, provided if they have sons, that one or more of them be in his Majesty's service.

"You are immediately to give notice of the Deficients that they may be quartered upon and poynded and their persons apprehended.

"You are likeways instructed to uplift from the respective collectors of the Burghs the several Quotas of moneys as their six months Cess payable by them, upon payment whereof you are hereby impowered to give your receipt which shall be sufficient to the Receivers." [1]

Peter Rae's *History of the Rebellion* gives the following account of Mar's methods of raising money :—

"The Earl of Mar, resolving to make use of the advantages he had by possessing so large an extent of country, thought next of raising more money for subsisting the Rebel army, by imposing a Cess upon such as were within the limits of his usurped Jurisdiction and for that end issued his general order :—

"'These are commanding and requiring every heretor, Feuer or Wood-setter now attending the King's standard or that may be excused, or their Factors or Doers in their absence and likewise all Life renters, immediately to proportion and raise among their tenants and possessors of their respective estates and Life rent lands, the sum of twenty shillings on each hundred pound Scots of valued rent ; and such heretors as do not immediately nor shall betwixt now and the 12th of Oct. inst., attend the King's Standard (if not excused by him the said Earl) immediately to proportion and raise out of their respective estates, *then* the sum of forty shillings sterling on each hundred pounds Scots of valued rent, which several proportions according to their respective cases aforesaid, he ordained to be paid by the persons above mentioned on the 12th day of that month. Dated at Perth the 4th of Oct. 1715.'"

It is worth noting that "teinds" and "vicarage dues" occur more than once in the Cess Roll, as a source of income which itself had to yield revenue. It is often forgotten that perhaps the only one of King Charles I's fiscal acts in Scotland which was both popular and able was embodied in the "Decreits arbitral," by which the complicated matter of the tithes was regulated and the lay owners made to contribute both to the support of the Parish Minister and to the National Exchequer. This was in 1629, eight years before the unfortunate affair of the attempted introduction of a new Liturgy and the riot in St. Giles, 23rd July, 1637, so well known to every one.

The Archbishop of St. Andrews and several of the clergy appear among the Cess payers. Thirty-six years had elapsed since the murder of James Sharp on Magus Muir,

[1] It is actually the Instruction for the Collector of " the Shyre of Banff " which is to be found, signed by Mar.—S.P. 54.12.344.

3rd May, 1679, and Episcopacy, which had been twice solemnly abolished by the General Assembly in 1638 and 1639, had come into its own in 1662, under Charles II, only to be abolished again by the General Assembly of 1689 ; but Bishops and Archbishops still existed as they do to this day (though not now as part of the *Established* Church of Scotland).

The members of the Episcopalian Church of 1715 and 1745, from the highest to the lowest, were almost exclusively Jacobites.

The County of Aberdeen itself had always been intensely Royalist : Catholic in the 16th century—under Huntly, " the Cock of the North," killed at Corrichie, 1562—Episcopalian and Jacobite in the 17th, and remained so, as is well known, till long after the '45.

John Forbes, who was the official collector of Cess for the County of Aberdeen, being a convinced Jacobite and recognising James Stuart as his lawful sovereign, naturally put all the machinery of his office at the disposal of Mar, and during the months of November and December collected the Single or Double amounts, that is six months' or twelve months' Cess, according to Mar's instructions. It is in some cases difficult to understand why certain people should have been made to pay double and others single, but the marking in his own list is unmistakable and has been faithfully reproduced here.[1] He appears to have employed certain other individuals as deputy collectors. On the other hand, many large landed proprietors pay Cess in many different parishes, and very often the names of estates or portions of estates are given without the proprietor's name. Diligent search has led to the identification of all these, with the single exception of Condryside, Strathdon.[2]

[1] Those from whom twelve months' Cess was demanded are marked with an italic *D*—all others were single.

[2] Of individuals who have *not* been traced, there are only four :—
James McMarquis, in the Parish of Tullich.
George Petrie, in the Parish of Premnay—a Messenger in Edinburgh.
William Smith, in the Parish of Longside.
Mr. Alex. Muir, in the Parish of Rathen.

Besides the accounts of his takings, John Forbes left a short account of moneys paid out by him, which will be found at pp. 27-28.

John Forbes, the collector of Cess, was the fourth son of Sir John Forbes, 3rd Baronet of Monymusk, eldest son of his second wife, Barbara Dalmahoy. He was twin with his sister, Agnes, who married Henry Elphinstone of Glack.

He was born at Monymusk, 1680, and married in 1704 Susanna Morison, daughter of Theodore Morison of Bognie. They had eleven children :—

1. Christian, born 1705, married her cousin, Sir William Forbes, the 5th Baronet, and became the mother of Sir William Forbes, the 6th Baronet and celebrated banker, ancestor of Lord Clinton.

2. John, born 1706, died young.

3. Barbara, born 1707, died unmarried, 1793.

4. Mary, born 1708, died unmarried, 1795.

5. William, born 1709, died young, 1713.

6. Agnes, born 1710, died young, 1714.

7. Theodore, born 1711, succeeded his father; died unmarried, 1737.

8. John, born 1712, succeeded Theodore, married Catherine Forbes of Echt.

9. Margaret, born 1714, married Charles Copland, of Aberdeen. *o.s.p.* 1751.

10. George, born 1715, died 1794. Married (1) Jane, daughter of William Keith of Bruxie, died 1763; (2) Christian Kerr, died 1807. He was great grandfather of Mr. Ogilvie-Forbes, the owner of the Cess Roll, and is buried in Boyndlie churchyard.

11. Elizabeth, posthumous child, born 1717, at Fraserburgh.

John Forbes bought Upper and Nether Boyndlie from Alexander, Lord Pitsligo, in 1711 (but there is nothing to show that he ever lived there, and almost all his children were born at Pitfichie).

The deed of purchase was signed by Sophia Erskine, Lady Pitsligo, mother of the Jacobite Lord.

A good deal of information can be gathered about John Forbes, collector of Cess, from papers preserved at Fettercairn House, including a Memorial by his widow, Susanna Morison, undated, but obviously written many years after his death, since the eight children were grown up, three (of the eleven) having already died in their father's lifetime. The Memorial is as follows :—

"Mr. Forbes had taken part in the publick troubles with which this kingdom was afflicted in 1715 and had joined himself to the standard set up at Perth, and as he had been collector of Cess in the Shire of Aberdeen for some time before, he not only levied the Cess for that year, imposed by Parliament but also, as far as the shortness of time would allow, by quartering and otherwise, he levied the double Cess imposed by authority from Perth, commonly called 'Lord Mar's Cess.'

"In 1716 after sculking about in the Country for some months he found himself obliged, as many others were, to go out of the Island for some time at least, that he should see in what shape matters would settle and accordingly he left Scotland about the middle of November that year and in a few days after was unluckily washed overboard and drowned in a storm upon the Coast of Scotland, leaving four daughters, Christian, Barbara, Mary and Margaret, and three sons, Theodore, John and George, and the Memorialist with child of a fifth daughter who was born after his death and named Elizabeth.

"Mr. Forbes had made no Testament, but as he had £3095 due him by a friend a little time before he left Scotland, he gave up that bond and took bonds to the extent of £4000 in the names of the four daughters he then had, viz. to Christian £1333.6.8, to Barbara and Mary £1000 each and to Margaret £666.13.4, by which means he came to be due that gentleman a ballance of £905, which was paid to him by the Memoralist soon after Mr. Forbes' death. . . .

"Mr. Forbes died possessed of a Land estate worth £600 yearly or thereby and liferented by the memoralist.

"In May 1717 the memoralist was confirmed executrix to her husband.

"The memoralist was never legally constituted Tutrix or Curatrix to any of her children, but still alimented all the eight suitably to their rank, and continued in virtue of her liferent of the Land to manage the whole effects left by her husband, and at the time of his death it was mighty uncertain how his affairs might turn out, whether he might not be forfaulted or whether the Gentlemen of Aberdeenshire might not repeat from his heir the Double Cess, etc., he had levied from them upon his own receipt, which would have entirely ruined him, she endeavoured as much as possible to keep the whole of his affairs concealed. . . .

"The same view of defeating in so far, either the Crown or the Shire in case they had inclined to take advantage of the Disasters that unlucky year had brought upon her husband as well as many others in that part of the country, made her not pay the £2000 due to Charles Forbes, her husband's nephew, but to keep it still on foot as what might be reckoned a debt preferable to either—there was likewise other reasons for not paying it, viz., one third part was liferented for 3 years and Charles Forbes was a minor and if he had died, her own children were his nearest heirs."

Susanna certainly brought up her children well—Theodore was " bred a doctor " and was in good practice in Banff, where he died in 1737. John was apprenticed to Mr. George Keith, the well-known advocate, and George also went to College. Two of the daughters married well, and two others lived to extreme old age. She claims that she " very genteely educated all the eight, of whom the eldest was not eleven when her father died."

On the marriage contract of John Forbes and Susanna Morison the lands are enumerated as " all and haill the lands of Upper Boyndlie and Nether Boyndlie[1] with the mill of Boyndlie, miln lands, multures, sucken, sequells and knaveships of the same. The town and lands of Tarmair, Ardequhan, Ladysfoord, and Skelmanae, with the haill houses, biggings yeards Tofts, crofts mosses, muirs meadows, parts pendicles and hail pertinents of the same lying within the parioches of Tyrie and Sheriffdom of Aberdeen."[2]

John Forbes was supposed by some to have met with foul play on his journey from Banff to Holland in 1716, after the collapse of the Rising, as sailors were seen wearing his clothes, but his grandson, Sir William Forbes, the banker, gives a different version in his " Account of the last sickness

[1] Middle Boyndlie was not included, but remained in the hands of another John Forbes, who was a Hanoverian.

[2] *Papers at Fettercairn.*

and death of Dame Christian " Forbes (his mother). He says :—

" My maternal grandfather died young, having been wrecked and drowned on the coast of Holland in the year 1715." It was actually 1716. Shipwreck and murder might, of course, have been part of the same plan.[1] His widow lived at Mill of Forgue (the property of *her* family), with her daughters, Barbara and Mary, who survived the Rising nearly 80 years !

The List of the Cess collected, and the manner of its disposal follow next.

Then the details of the individuals from whom it was collected.

---

[1] Susanna's memorial says " off the Coast of *Scotland*," which seems more likely, if sailors in Scotland were seen wearing his clothes. The fugitive was, no doubt, " making for Holland " where many Jacobites congregated both in 1716 and in 1746.

THE CESS ROLL
OF ABERDEENSHIRE 1715.

JOHN FORBES OF BOYNDLIE.

Collector of the subsidy imposed by the order of the Earl of Mar from the camp at Perth the 4th day of October, 1715.

Follows a Table how to proportion the subsidy of any summe of valued rent at £12 upon the £100.

Accompt of the Valuation of the Shyre of Aberdeen and of the Subsidy imposed thereon by order of the Earle of Mar, dated from the Camp at Perth the 4th day of October, 1715.

1. PRESBRITRIE OF KINCAIRDEN.

1. PARISH OF TARLAND.

			Valued Rent.			Subsidy.		
			£	s.	d.	£	s.	d.
Dec.	15.	The Laird of Drum for	966	13	4	107	10	10
Dec.	17.	Kincraigie for Drum for	233	.	.	25	18	6
Nov.	4.	Halhead for Westoun for	250	.	.	27	16	3
Dec.	30.	John Forbes of Invernan for	246	10	2	27	8	7
Nov.	16.	George Forbes of Skellater	92	.	.	10	4	9
,,	,,	Candycraig	18	.	.	2	.	.

2. PAROCH OF LOGIEMAR.

Dec.	25.	The Laird of Drum for	500	.	.	55	12	6
Nov.	11.	John Lumsden for part of Tille- foudie (liferent)	140	.	.	16	11	6
Nov.	10.	Mr. George Gordon of Logie for	280	.	.	31	3	.
Nov.	11.	The Laird of Blelack for	290	.	.	32	5	3

3. PAROCH OF MIGVIE.

			Valued Rent.			Subsidy.		
			£	s.	d.	£	s.	d.
Nov.	11.	John Innes of Sinnahard for Lord Elphinstone	300	.	.	33	7	6
Nov.	9.	The Laird of Finzean for Blelack for	300	.	.	33	7	6
Nov.	11.	Blelack for Old Lands for . .	215	.	.	23	18	5
Nov.	10.	Blelack for Eastermigvie . .	220	.	.	24	9	6
Dec.	23.	Pittentaggart	33	6	8	3	14	2
Nov.	9.	Smiddyhill for Blelack for . .	34	.	.	3	15	9
Nov.	30.	Fuedueties the Earl of Mar for .	100	.	.	11	2	6
Nov.	10.	Blelack for Isobel Og's Valuation for	27	.	.	3	.	1

4. PAROCH OF COLDSTANE.

			Valued Rent.			Subsidy.			
Nov.	10.	Invercauld for Pitallochie for .	691	4	.		76	18	.
Nov.	18.	Invercauld for Melgome for .	558	16	.		62	3	7
Nov.	2.	Whitehouse for . . .	136	6	8		15	3	5
Dec.	17.	Heirs of Robert Douglas for Blackmill	100	.	.	D	22	2	6
Nov.	9.	Blelack for Skeen for. . .	60	.	.		6	13	6
Nov.	9.	The Earle of Aboyn for George Anderson's valuation . .	26	13	4		2	19	4

5. PAROCH OF COULL.

			Valued Rent.			Subsidy.			
Nov.	14.	The Earle of Aboyn for . .	288	6	8		32	1	7
Dec.	5.	The Laird of Drum for Coul for .	466	13	4		51	18	4
Dec.	8.	Ditto for Auchtercoull for . .	345	6	8		38	8	5
Nov.	4.	The Laird of Craigyvar for. .	432	4	6	D	95	12	10

6. PAROCH OF ABOYN.

			Valued Rent.			Subsidy.			
Nov.	2.	The Earle of Aboyn for . .	1104	4	4		122	16	9
Nov.	3.	James Midltoun for Earle of Aboyn for	10	.	.		1	2	3
Nov.	9.	Auchinhove for. . . .	100	4	6		11	3	1
Nov.	7.	Kirktoun of Aboyn for . .	75	.	.	D	16	13	9
Dec.	10.	Finzean for	100	.	.	D	22	2	6
Nov.	8.	Dr. Gordon for Bennacraig for .	133	6	8		14	16	8
Nov.	2.	Bennacraig for Waterside . .	40	.	.		4	9	.

7. PAROCH OF BIRSS.

			Valued Rent.			Subsidy.			
			£	s.	d.		£	s.	d.
Dec.	10.	Laird of Finzean for . . .	786	.	.	D	173	16	3
Nov.	3.	Torwinlachie for . . .	33	6	8	D	7	8	4
Nov.	3.	Migstrath for	300	.	.	D	66	15	.
,,	,,	Earl of Aboyn for Kirktoun for .	189	.	.		21	.	7
Nov.	9.	Balfour Farquharson for . .	216	13	4		24	2	1
Nov.	2.	Birsbeg for	140	.	.	D	31	3	.
Nov.	2.	Birsmore for Inverebry for. .	153	19	.		17	2	3
Nov.	2.	Drumachie for . . .	110	.	.		24	9	6
Nov.	2.	Turners half of Kilminaty for .	53	6	8	D	11	17	4
Nov.	12.	Kirksession of Birss for ¼ of Kilmanaty for	26	13	4		2	19	4
Nov.	2.	James Malcom for ¼ of Kilmanaty for	26	13	4	D	5	18	8
Nov.	2.	Tillesnaught for . . .	300	16	.	D	66	18	7
,,	,,	Inverchatt for	115	.	.	D	25	8	11
Nov.	14.	Tillefroskie for	150	.	.	D	33	7	6
Nov.	3.	Easter-clune Jo. Forbes for .	250	.	.	D	55	12	6
Nov.	4.	Wester-clune for . . .	140	.	.	D	31	3	.
Jan.	25.	Glencatt for (serv) . . .	60	.	.		6	13	6
Nov.	15.	Mariewell for (Min) . . .	88	.	.		9	13	10

8. PAROCH OF KINCAIRDEN.

			Valued Rent.			Subsidy.			
Nov.	8.	Mill of Kincairden for (serv) .	90	.	.		10	.	3
Dec.	15.	Auchlossen for	130	.	.		14	9	3
Nov.	3.	Kirktoun of Kirkcairden for .	346	.	4	D	77	2	8
Dec.	20.	Dilhaikie for	470	.	4		52	5	9
Nov.	3.	Dors for Midbeltie for . .	516	13	.	D	114	19	2
Dec.	8.	Lord Forbes for Lands and Mercat for	500	.	.		55	12	6
Nov.	2.	Provost Mitchell for Easter Beltie for	300	.	.	D	66	15	.
Dec.	3.	Ballogie for Westerbeltie for .	224	.	8	D	49	11	5
Nov.	2.	Campbell Burnet for . . .	253	6	.	D	56	7	4
Dec.	9.	Ballogie for Lernie for . .	225	.	.	D	49	15	8
Nov.	28.	Relict of Craigmyle . . .	450	.	.		50	13	.
Nov.	9.	Heirs for Craigmyle for Craigour .	170	.	.		18	18	3

9. PAROCH OF LUMPHANNAN.

			Valued Rent. £ s. d.		Subsidy. £ s. d.
Dec.	15.	Auchlossen for Inverey	490 . .		54 10 3
Nov.	30.	Captain Forbes for a part of Auch-inhove for (Seq)	681 17 10		75 17 5
Nov.	9.	Robert Duguid of Auchinhove for his part thereof	126 15 6		14 2 3
Nov.	12.	Bannacraig Chalmers	200 . .	D	44 10 .
Nov.	3.	Fran. Fraser, Pitmurchie	100 . .⎫		18 10 10
,,	,,	Finlargue Fr. Fraser for	66 13 4⎭		
Dec.	23.	Camphill Forbes for	100 . .		11 2 6
Nov.	11.	Craigivar tor Kintocher for	136 . .	D	30 1 11
Nov.	11.	Burnside Charles McHardie for	35 . .		3 17 11
Nov.	30.	Ross of Cloack for	146 . .	D	32 6 2

10. PAROCH OF KINDROUGHT.

			Valued Rent.		Subsidy.
Nov.	18.	Inverey for	199 7 4		22 3 7
,,	,,	Dalmore for	140 . .		15 11 6
Nov.	18.	Invercauld for	333 6 8		37 1 8
Nov.	18.	Cambasnakist for	70 13 4		7 17 3
Nov.	18.	Earle of Mar for Fueduties and Lands for	500 . .		55 12 6
Nov.	18.	Auchindryne for	150 . .		16 13 9
Nov.	26.	Allanaquoich for	140 . .		16 11 6
		John Grewers, Elder and Ygr	41 16 .		4 13 3
		John Areskine for	40 . .		4 9 .

11. PAROCH OF GLENGAIRN.

			Valued Rent.		Subsidy.
Nov.	3.	Earle of Aboyn for	226 . .		25 2 11
Nov.	11.	Earle of Mar for Tambelly for	100 . .		11 2 11
Nov.	18.	Abergeldie for	140 . .		15 11 6
Nov.	19.	Cults Farquharson for	213 6 8		23 14 8
		Alexr. McGrigor for	160 . .		17 16 .
Dec.	8.	Invercauld for	66 . .		7 6 11
		Thomas and James Kiers for	80 . .		8 18 .

4

12. PAROCH OF CRATHIE.

			Valued Rent. £ s. d.			Subsidy. £ s. d.		
Nov.	18.	Tullochcoy for	90	.	.	10	.	3
Nov.	18.	Invercauld for	230	13	4	23	13	3
Nov.	22.	Monaltrie for	220	.	.	24	9	6
Nov.	18.	Balmurrell for	232	.	.	25	16	3
Nov.	18.	Abergeldie for	600	.	.	66	15	.
Nov.	18.	Ed and Robt Mchardies for	280	.	.	31	3	.
Nov.	18.	Lawsie, Donald Symond	280	.	.	31	3	.

13. PAROCH OF TULLICH.

Nov.	25.	Allanaquoich for	110	.	.	12	4	9
Dec.	1.	Inverey for	430	.	.	47	16	9
Dec.	6.	Donald Farquharson for	318	.	.	13	2	7
Dec.	6.	Edward Fleming for	16	.	.	1	15	8
Nov.	4.	Patrick Ogg for	40	13	4	4	10	6
,,	,,	Westermicras for	155	.	.	17	4	11
,,	,,	Robert McHardie for	44	9	.	4	19	1
Dec.	6.	James McMarquis for	22	4	4	2	9	7
Nov.	4.	John Morgan for	55	.	.	6	2	5
Nov.	2.	Earle of Aboyne for	262	.	.	29	3	.
Nov.	2.	Patrick Gordon for E. of Aboyne	24	3	4	2	14	.

14. PAROCH OF GLENMUICK.

Nov.	25.	Earle of Aboyn for	120	10	.	13	8	2
Nov.	18.	Abergeldie for	430	.	.	47	16	9
Nov.	18.	Braichlie for Lands and Tiends for	300	.	.	33	7	6
Nov.	3.	Belletrach for	100	.	.	13	8	2
Nov.	3.	Bellamore Robert Farqson for	51	10	.	5	14	8
Nov.	23.	Aucholzie for	120	.	.	13	7	.

15. PARISH OF GLENTANNER.

Nov.	2.	Earle of Aboyn for his old Lands	123	.	.	13	16	.
Oct.	28.	Ditto for Thos. Midltouns valuation for	21	10	.	2	7	11
Nov.	23.	Ballamore Wm. Gardon for	93	10	.	10	8	2
Nov.	1.	Bellastrine for	34	10	.	3	16	11
Nov.	2.	Candycraig Midltoun for	33	13	4	3	14	11

			Valued Rent.			Subsidy.		
			£	s.	d.	£	s.	d.
Nov.	2.	Earle of Aboyne for Waternadie and Newtoun for . . .	86	10	.	9	12	7
Nov.	1.	Ditto for Farquharson for · .	50	.	.	5	11	3

16. PAROCH OF KINERNIE.

Dec.	9.	Laird of Ballogie for . . .	650	.	.	D 143	16	3
Dec.	8.	Carnday for	210	.	.	23	7	5
Nov.	8.	Lord Fraser for . . .	260	.	.	28	18	6

17. PARISH OF MIDMAR.

Dec.	9.	Ballogie for	888	.	.	D 196	16	3
Nov.	8.	Cluny for little Sauchen for .	65	.	.	7	4	8
Dec.	8.	Shiels for	284	.	.	31	12	.
Dec.	9.	Lady Ballogie Liferentrix . .	500	.	.	55	12	6

18. PAROCH OF ECHT.

Jan.	23.	Laird of Echt Elder for . .	955	5	.	D 211	7	1
Jan.	21.	Laird of Echt Younger for .	674	4	8	D 149	3	10
Nov.	11.	Laird of Drum for . .	575	.	.	63	19	5
Nov.	15.	Easterecht for (minor) . .	160	.	.	17	16	.

19. PAROCH OF CLUNY.

Nov.	8.	Lord Fraser for . . .	560	.	.	62	6	.
Nov.	8.	Laird of Cluny for . . .	913	6	8	101	12	2
Dec.	8.	Shiels for	53	6	8	5	18	8
Nov.	4.	Sauchen for	310	.	.	34	9	9
Dec.	8.	Lord Forbes for . . .	26	13	4	2	19	4

2. PRESBITRIE OF GARRIOCH.

1. PARISH OF LESLIE.

Nov.	5.	The Laird of Leithhall for . .	833	.	·} D 228 12 .			
Nov.	5.	Ditto for his old Lands for .	200	.	.}			
Nov.	8.	The Laird of Whitehaugh for .	533	6	8	59	6	8

2. PARISH OF PREMNAY.

			Valued Rent.			Subsidy.		
			£	s.	d.	£	s.	d.
Nov.	5.	Licklehead for	400	.	.	D 89	.	.
Nov.	5.	Leithhall for Lesly for	166	13	4	18	10	10
Dec.	16.	Rothney for	266	13	4	59	.	.
Nov.	7.	Barnes for	366	13	4	40	15	10
Nov.	29.	George Petric for Newtoun for	100	.	.	11	2	6
Nov.	10.	Overhall for	428	.	.	47	12	4
Nov.	5.	Leithhall for Etherlick	50	.	.	D 11	1	3
Nov.	29.	Ditto for Part of Lesly	100	.	.	D 22	2	6

3. PAROCH OF INCH.

Nov.	3.	Balquhane for Miecle Wardhouse for	354	.	.	39	7	9
Nov.	3.	Ditto for E. of Mar's	304	.	.	33	16	6
Nov.	10.	Threefields Valuation for	116	13	4	12	19	7
Nov.	17.	Dunnydeer for	333	6	8	37	1	8
Nov.	8.	Wardhouse for	160	.	.	17	16	.
Nov.	3.	Balquhame for Kirktoun of Inch for	247	.	.	27	9	7
Nov.	3.	Overboddam for	200	.	.	22	5	.
Nov.	3.	Cairnstown for	36	10	.	4	1	4
Nov.	10.	Nether Boddam for	114	10	.	12	14	11
Nov.	10.	Drumrossie for	236	.	.	D 52	3	5
Oct.	31.	Lesmore for Jonesleyes for	66	13	4	8	6	11

4. PAROCH OF CULSALMOND.

Jan.	26.	Newtoun Davidson for	1500	.	.	166	17	6
Dec.	1.	Rothny for Wrangham for	300	.	.	D 66	7	6
Nov.	17.	Tillemorgan for	300	.	.	D 66	7	6

5. PAROCH OF RAIN.

Nov.	5.	Threefield and Newrain for	406	13	4	D 89	19	6
		Lonehead for (Seq)	70	.	.	7	15	9
Dec.	12.	Mr. John Elphinstone of Logie for	1070	.	.	D 236	14	9
Nov.	1.	Blackfoord for	45	.	.	5	.	2
Nov.	1.	Rotmais for (Sup)	140	.	.	15	11	6
Nov.	1.	Littlewartle for	364	.	.	D 80	19	10
Nov.	3.	Old Rain for	448	.	.	49	16	10

6. PAROCH OF MELDRUM.

			Valued Rent.			Subsidy.		
			£	s.	d.		£	s.	d.
Nov.	25.	The Earle of Aberdeen for . .	50	.	.	D	11	1	3
Jan.	31.	The Laird of Meldrum for Liferent Lands for	1096	15	6		122	.	6
,,	,,	Provost Ross for a part of Meldrum for	71	16	6		8	.	.
Nov.	7.	Town of Aberdeen a part of Meldrum for	119	19	6		13	7	.
Dec.	2.	Ditto for Ardforsk and Culblen .	200	.	.		22	5	.
Jan.	31.	The Laird of Meldrum for Lands unliferented	311	8	10	D	68	18	6

7. PAROCH OF OYN.

Nov.	7.	Tillefour for	186	13	4		20	15	4
Nov.	9.	Pitodry elder for . .	33	6	8		3	14	2
Nov.	25.	Westhall and Pitmedden for .	800	.	.		89	.	.
Jan.	11.	Gordonstoun for Ryhill for .	333	6	8		37	1	8
Nov.	25.	Westhall for part of Overhall for	60	.	.		6	13	6
Nov.	25.	Ditto for Buchanstown for .	133	6	8		14	16	8
Dec.	10.	Auchorsk for	40	.	.	D	8	17	.
Nov.	25.	Westhall for Newlands for . .	310	.	.		34	9	9
Nov.	9.	Pitodry Yr. for Kirktoun for Oyn for	133	6	8		14	14	8
Nov.	9.	Ditto for Torries for . . .	66	13	4		7	8	4
Nov.	3.	Cairden for (liferent) . . .	40	.	.		4	9	.
Nov.	9.	Pitodry Yr. for Old Harthill for .	75	.	.		8	6	11
Nov.	25.	Westhall for Mr. Pat Coupland's valuation for . . .	89	.	.		9	18	1

8. PAROCH OF DAVIOT.

Nov.	17.	Lumphard Lethenty for . .	320	.	.	D	70	16	.
Nov.	8.	Glack and for Daviot for . .	750	.	.		83	8	9
Dec.	9.	Sir John Ried of Barra for .	150	.	.		16	13	9
Dec.	9.	Barra Younger for . . .	150	.	.	D	33	3	9
Dec.	6.	Munie for.	900	.	.	D	199	2	6

9. PAROCH OF LOGIEDURNO.

Nov.	9.	Pitodry Elder for . . .	163	13	4		18	4	2
		Earl of Mar for Feuduties for .	200	.	.		22	5	.
Nov.	9.	Pitodry Younger for . . .	627	6	8		69	15	10

			Valued Rent.			Subsidy.		
			£	s.	d.	£	s.	d.
Nov.	8.	Balquhayn for old lands for .	466	13	4		51	18	4
Dec.	12.	Sir James Elphinstone for (Sup)	1151	6	8		128	1	9
Nov.	8.	Balquhayn for Fetternier . .	400	.	.		44	10	.
Nov.	17.	Lethenty for	433	6	8	D	95	17	6
Nov.	2.	Inveramsay for. . . .	438	.	.		48	14	7
Nov.	26.	Pitcaple for . . .	367	3	8		40	17	1
Nov.	9.	Pitodrie for Knochollachy for .	76	3	.		8	9	7
Dec.	10.	Auchorsk for	40	.	.	D	8	17	1
Nov.	25.	Earl of Aberdeen for . .	89	.	.	D	19	13	11
Nov.	29.	Blairdaff for	80	.	.		8	18	.
Nov.	9.	Pitodry elder for Alex. Anderson for	24	.	.		2	13	6
Nov.	5.	Harlaw for	158	.	.		17	11	7
Nov.	8.	Glack for	19	.	.		2	2	4

10. PAROCH OF KIETHHALL.

| Nov. | 8. | The Earle of Kintoir for . . | 1600 | . | . | | 178 | . | . |
| Nov. | 30. | Elrick for Newplace for . . | 90 | . | . | D | 19 | 19 | . |

11. PAROCH OF BOURTY.

Dec.	9.	Sir John Ried for Bara for .	530	.	.		58	19	3
Dec.	9.	Barra Younger for . . .	530	.	.	D	117	5	3
Nov.	8.	Bourty Anderson for ½ of Bourty for	200	.	.		22	5	.
Nov.	8.	Captain Anderson for the other half for	200	.	.		22	5	.
Nov.	17.	Auchortis for Colliehill for . .	200	.	.		22	5	.
Nov.	4.	Thorntoun for	320	.	.	D	71	.	.
Nov.	2.	Heirs of Blair for (DR Stewart) .	459	.	.		51	1	4
,,	,,	Blackhouse for	62	.	.		6	18	.

12. PAROCH OF KINKELL.

Nov.	8.	Earl of Kintoir for . . .	650	7	4		72	7	3
Nov.	7.	Balbithan for	409	12	10	D	90	13	.
Nov.	4.	Thainstown for . . .	666	13	4		74	3	4
Nov.	7.	The Lady Balbithan for . .	100	.	.		11	2	6

13. PAROCH OF KEMNAY.

| Nov. | 8. | The Earl of Kintoir for . . | 104 | . | . | | 11 | 11 | 6 |
| Nov. | 8. | The Laird of Kemnay for . . | 1500 | . | . | D | 331 | 17 | 6 |

14. PAROCH OF MONYMUSK.

			Valued Rent.			Subsidy.		
			£	s.	d.	£	s.	d.
Dec.	10.	The Lord Cullen for . . .	2543	.	.	D 563	17	11

15. PAROCH OF KINTOIR.

Nov.	8.	The Earle of Kintoir for . .	1028	19	6	114	9	6

16. PAROCH OF INVEROURIE.

Nov.	8.	The Earle of Kintoir for . .	224	.	.	24	18	6
Nov.	8.	Balquhayn for his old Lands for .	360	.	.	40	1	.
Nov.	8.	Ditto for a part of Fetternier for.	210	.	.	23	7	.
Nov.	9.	Pitodry elder for Conglass for .	204	.	.	22	14	.
Nov.	25.	The Earle of Aberdeen for Bracco	100	.	. D	22	2	6
Nov.	1.	Auchorsk John Lesly for (Ser) .	124	.	.	13	16	.
		Blackhall for	100	.	.	11	2	6
Nov.	8.	Ardtannies for (Sup) . . .	112	.	.	12	9	3
Nov.	8.	Badefurrow for (Lifer :) . .	200	.	.	22	5	.

3. PRESBITRY OF ALFORD.

1. PAROCH OF ALFORD.

Nov.	10.	Sir John Guthrie for Breda for .	449	10	.	50	.	3
Dec.	21.	Master Arthur Forbes for Asloun						
		and Dorsell	430	16	.	47	18	9
Nov.	11.	The Laird of Balfluig for . .	1233	6	8	137	4	2
Dec.	8.	Kinstair for (Min) . . .	276	13	4	30	15	7
Jan.	6.	Patrick Duguid for ⅓ of Kin-						
		stair for	138	6	8	15	7	10
Dec.	22.	Haughtoun for	300	.	.	33	7	6
Nov.	11.	Carneveran for	100	.	.	11	2	6
Dec.	16.	Tillechetly for	128	.	. D	28	7	.
,,	22.	Brainly for	70	.	. D	15	10	.

2. PAROCH OF TOUCH.

Dec.	2.	Kincraigie for (seq) . . .	640	.	.	71	4	.
Dec.	10.	Arrinbath for	590	14	.	65	14	5
Nov.	2.	The Lady Finzeach for . .	80	.	.	8	18	.

			Valued Rent.				Subsidy.		
			£	s.	d.		£	s.	d.
Nov.	4.	Tillechetly for a part of Campfield for	41	6	8	D	9	4	.
Nov.	11	Tilleriach Mr. Robt. Strachan for Ditto for	133	6	8	D	29	13	4
Oct.	27.	Tillefour John Coupland for Ditto for	135	6	8	D	30	2	4
Dec.	2.	Ardgous .	50	.	.		5	11	3

3. PAROCH OF LEUCHEL.

Nov.	11.	Craigyvar for	1238	13	4	D	274	1	2
Nov.	30.	Lenturk for (seq)	120	.	.		13	7	.
Nov.	2.	Lady Lenturk for	240	.	.		26	14	.

4. PAROCH OF CUSHNY.

Nov.	25.	Halhead for	166	13	4		18	10	10
Nov.	11.	The Laird of Cushny for	586	11	8		65	5	4
Nov.	11	Craigivar for	80	.	.	D	17	14	.
Dec.	21.	Brux for .	90	.	.		10	.	3

5. PAROCH OF KEARN.

Nov.	7.	The Lord Forbes for .	500	.	.		55	12	6

6 PAROCH OF FORBES.

Dec.	1.	The Lord Forbes for .	666	13	4		74	3	4

7. PAROCH OF KIEG.

Nov.	4.	Putachie for	420	13	4		46	16	.
Nov.	29.	Lesly for .	210	.	.		23	7	3
Nov.	5.	Finzeach for	252	6	8		28	1	6
Nov.	18.	Balgowan for	140	.	.		15	11	6
Nov.	11.	Terpersie for	370	.	.		41	3	3
Nov.	10.	Tulloch for ½ Liferenter for	182	11	4	D	30	9	6

8. PAROCH OF CLATT.

Nov.	8.	Knockaspock for	225	.	.	D	50	1	4
Nov.	7.	The Lord Forbes for .	290	.	.		32	5	3
Nov.	24.	Tilleangus for .	120	.	.		13	7	6
Nov.	8.	Auchlyn for (supr.) .	640	4	4		71	4	7

9. PAROCH OF TILLENESSEL.

			Valued Rent.			Subsidy.		
			£	s.	d.	£	s.	d.
Nov.	8.	Whitehaugh for . . .	810	13	4	90	3	9
Nov.	25.	Terpersie for	200	.	.	71	4	7

10. PAROCH OF KINETHMOUNT.

			Valued Rent.				Subsidy.		
Nov.	5.	Liethhall for	520	.	.		115	1	.
Nov.	8.	Law for	180	.	.		20	.	6
Nov.	1.	Kirkhill for . . .	133	6	8	D	29	13	4
Nov.	5.	Cults for	134	.	.	D	29	16	4
Nov.	5.	Craighall for . . .	190	.	.		21	2	9
Nov.	5.	Wardhouse for . . .	510	6	8		56	15	6
Nov.	5.	Leithhall for Leslie for . .	150	.	.	D	33	3	9

11. PARISH OF KILDRUMIE.

			Valued Rent.				Subsidy.		
Nov.	1.	The Earle of Mar for . .	563	13	4		62	14	2
		Brux	250	16	8		27	18	4
Nov.	11.	Cushny for	140	12	.		15	12	11
Nov.	8.	Midclova for . . .	80	13	4		8	19	6
		Glenkindy for	16	.	.	D	3	10	11

12. PAROCH OF AUCHINDORE.

			Valued Rent.			Subsidy.		
Nov.	16.	Auchmillen for . . .	70	6	8	7	16	8
Nov.	2.	Newmill for . . .	70	.	.	7	15	9
Nov.	7.	The Lord Forbes for . .	150	.	.	16	13	9
Nov.	12.	Craig for	720	.	.	80	2	.
,,	,,	Lesmore for (Min) . .	12	.	.	1	6	9
Nov.	2.	Bogsheads Jo. Lumsden for .	60	4	8	6	14	1
Nov.	2.	Terpersey Valuation Do. for .	180	.	.	20	.	6
Nov.	2.	Birkenbreul for (Ser) . .	60	.	.	6	13	4

13. PAROCH OF GLENBUCKET.

		Valued Rent.			Subsidy.		
Glenbuicket for . . .		785	.	.	87	6	8

14. PAROCH OF CABRACH.

		Valued Rent.			Subsidy.		
The Duke of Gordon for . .		454	2	10	50	10	7

15. PAROCH OF KINBETACK.

			Valued Rent.			Subsidy.		
			£	s.	d.	£	s.	d.
Nov.	5.	The Earle of Mar for . .	364	7	2	40	10	10
Nov.	11.	Balnaboth for Lord Elphinstone						
		one half to Skellater . .	125	.	.	D 20	17	3
,,	,,	Sinnahard and Sinnaboth for .	260	.	.	28	18	6
,,	,,	Glenkindy for . . .	140	.	.	D 30	19	6
Nov.	12.	Brux for	426	.	.	47	7	11
Nov.	1.	Kinclune for	160	.	.	17	16	.

16. PAROCH OF INVERNOCHTY.

		The Earle of Mar for . . .	384	9	.	42	15	7
		Glenkindie for	420	.	.	D 92	18	6
Nov.	25.	Buquham Inverernan for . .	90	.	.	10	.	3
Nov.	25.	Culquhunny Jo. Forbes for .	130	17	8	14	11	5
,,	,,	Condryside ditto for . .	43	11	.	4	18	1
Nov.	25.	Toldawhill Ditto for . .	74	.	.	8	4	9
Nov.		Ditto for Robert Moir's valuation						
		for	80	.	.	8	18	.
Nov.	25.	New for	250	.	.	27	16	3
,,	,,	Culquharrie for . . .	132	15	4	14	15	7
Nov.	22.	Invernochtie tor . . .	100	.	.	11	2	6
Nov.	22.	Corriebrech for . . .	50	.	.	5	11	3
Nov.	25.	Balnaboddach for . . .	50	11	6	5	12	8
,,	,,	Ballabeg for	150	.	.	16	13	9
,,	,,	Skellater elder for . . .	88	2	4	9	16	.
,,	,,	Oldergue for	36	14	8	4	1	11
Nov.	16.	Skellater for Tolloskink for .	188	.	.	20	18	4
Nov.	25.	Ludmacoy Jo. Forbes for . .	130	.	.	14	9	3
Nov.	22.	Invernetie for	200	.	.	22	5	.
		Candycraig for	340	.	.	37	16	6

6. PRESBITRY OF DEER.

1. PAROCH OF PETERHEAD.

Dec.	3.	The Earle Marischall for . .	1212	5	.	134	17	4
Nov.	1.	William Moir of Invernetie for .	550	.	.	61	3	9
Nov.	4.	Sir Wm. Keith for . . .	466	13	4	51	18	4
Nov.	18.	Balmuir for	466	13	4	D 103	3	.
Nov.	18.	Blackhouse for . . .	233	6	8	D 51	12	6

			Valued Rent.			Subsidy.		
			£	s.	d.		£	s.	d.
Dec.	2.	Collonell Ogilvie for Litle Cocklaw for	233	6	8	D	51	12	6
Nov.	1.	Faichfield for Miecle Cocklaw for.	800	.	.		89	.	.
Nov.	4.	Clerkhill for	200	.	.		44	10	.
Nov.	10.	Kinmundy Alex. Gordon for .	150	.	.		16	13	9
Nov.	1.	Dounyhills for . . .	133	.	.		14	16	8
Nov.	1.	Collelaw for Earle Marischall for.	80	.	.		8	18	.

2. PARISH OF LONGSIDE.

			£	s.	d.		£	s.	d.
Nov.	1.	The Earl Marischall for . .	472	.	.		52	10	3
Nov.	8.	Inverquhumrie for . . .	600	.	.		66	15	.
Nov.	17.	Auchmedden for . . .	144	.	.		16	.	6
Nov.	1.	Fortrie for liferented for . .	90	.	.		10	.	3
Nov.	18.	Andrew Arbuthnot for . .	266	13	4	D	59	.	.
Nov.	1.	Heirs of Mr. John Paton, Inverquhumry for	60	.	.		6	13	6
Nov.	8.	Heirs of Wm. Smith for . .	60	.	.		6	13	6
Nov.	8.	Auchtydonald for . . .	466	13	4		51	18	4
Nov.	17.	Ludquharn for	600	.	.	D	132	15	.
Nov.	10.	Alex. Gordon for Kinmundy for .	500	.	.		55	12	6
Nov.	1.	Faichfield for	600	.	.		66	15	.
Feb.	6.	Thundertoun for . . .	133	6	8		14	16	8
Nov.	1.	Cairngall for	400	.	.	D	89	.	.
Feb.	6.	Buthlaw for	200	.	.		22	5	.

3. PAROCH OF STRIECHEN.

			£	s.	d.		£	s.	d.
Nov.	17.	Adiell in Striechen for Pitfour .	125	.	.		13	18	2
Nov.	25.	Striechen for	1700	.	.		189	2	6
Nov.	7.	Heirs of Wm. Knox for Pitfour .	50	.	.		5	11	4

4. PAROCH OF REATHEN.

			£	s.	d.		£	s.	d.
Nov.	4.	Auchiries for	606	13	4		67	9	10
Dec.	19.	The Lord Saltoun and his vassals	693	6	8	D	153	8	.
Dec.	7.	Techmurie for	40	.	.		4	9	.
Nov.	1.	Collonell Buchan for . .	1133	13	4		126	2	5
,,	,,	Craigelie for	87	6	8	D	19	7	.
Dec.	2.	Collonell Ogilvie for . .	179	.	.	D	39	12	4
Nov.	18.	Inverallochie for . . .	600	.	.		66	15	.
Nov.	4.	Corthis for Auchiries . .	80	.	.		8	18	.
Nov.	10.	Mr. Alex. Muir for Reathen liferented	100	.	.		11	2	6

5. PAROCH OF DEER.

			Valued Rent. £ s. d.			Subsidy. £ s. d.		
Nov.	17.	Earl Marischall for . . .	860	3	4	95 14	.	
,,	,,	The Earl Marischall's Vicarage for	300		.	33	7	6
Nov.	29.	Troup for Elrick for . . .	200	.	. D	44	5	.
Nov.	17.	Auchmedden for . . .	366	13	4	40	15	10
Nov.	7.	Dudwick for Parcock for . .	233	6	8	25	19	2
Nov.	3.	Techmurie for	466	13	4	51	18	4
Jan.	3.	Pitlurg for Kinmundie liferented for	800	.	.	89	.	.
Nov.	17.	Pitfour for	600	.	.	66	15	.
Dec.	5.	Kininmonth for Knock . .	200	.	. D	44	5	.
Nov.	17.	Captain Stewart for Litle Crichie for	133	6	8	14	16	8
Nov.	5.	Coynach for	300	.	. D	66	7	6
Nov.	17.	Cuthill for	150	.	.	16	13	9
Nov.	17.	The Heirs of George Rankine for	100	.	.	11	2	6
Nov.	17.	Saplenbrae for . . .	50	.	.	5	11	3
Nov.	17.	Clackaich for	450	.	.	50	1	3
Nov.	1.	Crichie	320	.	.	35	12	.
,,	,,	Kidshill for	24	.	.	2	13	6
Nov.	17.	Bruntbrae for	40	.	.	4	9	.
Dec.	17.	The Heirs of Provost Ross for .	67	.	.	7	9	1
Nov.	4.	Troup for Anachie for liferented be Shives	200	.	.	22	5	.
Nov.	15.	Bithie for (Min) . . .	300	.	.	33	7	6
Nov.	17.	Captain Stewart for Denns and part of Marischall . . .	266	13	4	29	13	4

6. PAROCH OF LONEMAY.

Nov.	8.	Law for the heirs of Cummin for .	533	6	8	59	6	8
Dec.	2.	Collonell Ogilvie for Cairness for .	355	11	. D	78	13	8
Dec.	2.	Lonemay for	1000	.	. D	221	5	.
Dec.	5.	Kinimount	666	13	4 D	147	10	.
Dec.	2.	Milbog Coll Ogilvie for . .	258	17	6 D	57	5	9
Dec.	25.	Crimonmogat for (Seq) . .	215	2	.	23	18	8
Nov.	25.	Inverlochy for part of Cairness .	44	9	.	4	19	1
,,	,,	Craigelie for	293	12	.	65	.	6

7. PAROCH OF TYRIE

								Valued Rent.			Subsidy.		
								£	s.	d.	£	s.	d.
Nov	4.	Lord Pitsligo for	.	.	.		700	.	.		77	17	6
Dec.	21.	Boynlie for	.	.	.	.	100	.	.	D	22	2	6
Dec.	24.	Tyrie for .	.	.	.	.	360	.	.		40	1	.
Nov.	25.	Striechen for	.	.	.	.	310	.	.		34	9	9
,,	,,	pt Feddret, Bonykelly for		.			60	.	.		6	13	4

8. PAROCH OF ABERDOUR.

						Valued Rent.			Subsidy.		
Nov.	25.	Foveran for Lord Pitsligo .	.		950	.	.	D	210	3	9
Dec.	2.	Auchmedden for	.	.	666	13	4		74	3	4
Nov.	18.	Pittencalder for	.	.	80	.	.	D	17	16	.
,,	,,	Cowburty	.	.	266	13	4		29	13	4

9. PAROCH OF PITSLIGO.

						Valued Rent.			Subsidy.		
Nov.	10.	The Lord Pitsligo	.	.	.	1000	.	.	111	5	.
Nov.	4.	Pitulie for	.	.	.	1000	.	.	111	5	.
Dec.	19.	Lord Saltoun for Boghead .	.	100	.	.	D	22	2	6
Dec.	24.	Wester-Tyrie for	.	.	300	.	.		33	7	6

10. PAROCH OF FRASERBURGH.

				Valued Rent.			Subsidy.		
		The Lord Saltoun for	.	1300	.	.	D 287	12	6
		My Lady Dowager of Saltoun for	900	.	.	100	2	6
Dec.	24.	Tyrie for .	.	200	.	.	22	5	.
Dec.	21.	Boynly for his Lady's Jointure for	200	.	.	D 44	3	.
Dec.	7.	Techmuirie for .	.	400	.	.	44	10	.
Dec.	7.	Lord Saltoun in Fraserburgh Paroch (including my Lady Dowager) is of valued rent .		2200	.	.			
Nov.	18.	My Lady Dowager of Saltoun to account	.				61	18	10
Dec.	19.	My Lord Saltoun for £1200 valued rent .	.				265	10	.
		Lord Saltoun rests for £100 valued rent	.				22	2	6
		Lady Dowager of Saltoun rests .					38	3	8

11. PAROCH OF CRIMOND.

			Valued Rent.			Subsidy.		
			£	s.	d.	£	s.	d.
		Law for Mill of Crimond for	80	.	.	8	18	.
Nov.	1.	Laird of Crimond for	732	.	.	81	8	9
Oct.	31.	Brodland for	333	6	8	D 74	3	4
Nov.	22.	Heirs of Mr. John Barclay for	30	.	.	3	6	9
Dec.	21.	Logie Gordon for	400	.	.	D 88	10	.
Dec.	26.	Ratray Auchmacoy for	181	.	.	20	2	9
Oct.	31.	John Scott for	8	.	.	D 1	18	6
Nov.	9.	Haddo for	248	.	.	27	11	10
Nov.	8.	Alex. Dalgairdno, Millhill for	150	.	.	D 33	7	6
Oct.	31.	Jean Bisset for	10	.	.	D 2	9	8

12. PAROCH OF AUCHRYDIE.

Nov.	25.	The Earle of Aberdeen for	666	13	4	D 147	10	.
Oct.	31.	Niethermuir Elder and Younger for	839	6	8	94	2	6
Nov.	7.	Feddret for	900	.	.	100	2	6
Nov.	7.	Shives for Auchnagatt for	466	13	4	D 103	5	.
Oct.	27.	Whitehill, Stonywood for (Ser)	333	6	8	37	1	8
Nov.	17.	Ludquharn for Auchrydie for (seq)	133	6	8	14	16	8
Oct.	31.	Barrack for	133	6	8	14	16	9
Oct.	31.	Auchmunziel for	100	.	.	D 22	5	.
Nov.	2.	Cairnbanno liferented for	83	6	8	9	5	5
Nov.	2.	Mr. Adam Hay for Chiens and Keiths valuations	103	6	8	11	9	11
Oct.	31.	Auchinlech ¾ unliferented for	150	.	.	D 33	7	6
Jan.	12.	Ditto ¼ liferented for	50	.	.	5	11	3
Oct.	31.	Brucklaw and Ironside for	400	.	.	D 89	.	.
Nov.	8.	Ardtamford	233	6	8	25	19	2
Jan.	27.	Culsh for	266	13	4	D 59	.	.
Nov.	8.	Oldwhatt for (abroad)	166	13	4	18	10	10
Nov.	10.	Allathen for	133	6	8	D 29	13	4

7. PRESBITRY OF ELLON.

1. PAROCH OF CRUDEN.

		The Earl of Erroll for	4450	16	4	495	3	4
Nov.	8.	Auchleuchries for	324	.	.	36	.	.
Dec.	7.	Laird of Ellon for Muirtack	33	6	8	3	14	2
Nov.	17.	Ludquharn for Auquharnie	266	13	4	D 59	.	.

		Valued Rent.			Subsidy.		
		£	s.	d.	£	s.	d.
Nov.	12.	Sandend for (Lifrt) . . .	200	.	.	22	5	.
Nov.	2.	The Earl of Panmuir for . .	40	.	.	4	9	.
Dec.	5.	Earl of Erroll in part of his subsidy £66 sterling				792	.	.
		which pays all his subsidies in the Paroches of Turreff, Montquhitter, Slaines, Ellon and the Parsonage of Turreff and pays £121.2.1 Scots in part of Earl of Erroll's subsidy in Cruden and he rests				374	.	.

2. PAROCH OF SLAINES.

Dec.	5.	The Earl of Errol for. . .	2167	6	8	241	2	4
Dec.	15.	Seafield for	100	.	.	11	2	6
Nov.	17.	Birniss for Leask for . . .	500	.	.	D 110	13	6
Dec.	11.	Earnhill for	66	13	4	7	8	4

3. PAROCH OF FOVERAN.

Feb.	1.	Laird of Foveran for. . .	2132	4	8	D 471	15	3
Dec.	1.	Udny for	2211	4	4	246	.	.
Dec.	2.	Newtyle for . . .	249	10	6	27	15	3
Dec.	1.	Auchterellon for Cultercullen for .	133	6	8	14	16	8
Nov.	15.	Rickartoun for Auchnacant for .	200	.	.	D 44	5	.

4. PAROCH OF UDNY.

Dec.	6.	Lord Pitmedden for . . .	1266	.	.	140	16	11
Dec.	6.	Laird of Pitmedden for . .	911	13	4	101	8	6
Dec.	20.	Barron Maitland of Pitrichie for .	569	13	4	D 126	1	.
Dec.	20.	Liferented Lands of Pitrichie for	780	6	8	86	16	3
Dec.	1.	Udny for	500	.	.	55	12	6
Dec.	24.	Wattertoun for Bonaketle . .	200	.	.	22	5	.
Nov.	5.	Tillecorthy for . . .	120	.	.	13	7	.
Nov.	3.	Torrelieth for . . .	166	13	4	37	1	8
Jan.	16.	Knapernay for (I want receipt from Knapperay for Cesse Lamas 1715 which I've allowed)	1000	.	.	111	5	.
Feb.	1.	Foveran for . . .	266	13	4	D 59	.	.
Nov.	15.	Slagmagully	50	.	.	5	11	3

5. PAROCH OF METHLICK.

					Valued Rent. £ s. d.			Subsidy. £ s. d.		
Nov.	25.	Earl of Aberdeen for	.	.	1943	6	8	D 430	.	4
Dec.	20.	Pitrichie for	.	.	266	13	4	D 59	.	.
		Gight for .	.	.	490	.	.	54	10	3

6. PAROCH OF TARVES.

Nov.	25.	Earl of Aberdeen for	.	.	1680	.	.	D 371	14	.
Nov.	2.	Tolquhon for (Seq)	.	.	1500	.	.	166	17	6
Nov.	7.	Shives for	.	.	600	.	.	D 132	15	.
Jan.	3.	Cairnbrogie for	.	.	600	.	.	66	15	.
Dec.	17.	Kiethfield for	.	.	150	.	.	D 33	3	9
		Ditto for Liferented .	.	.	150	.	.	16	13	9
Nov.	17.	Auchortis for	.	.	200	.	.	22	5	.

7. PAROCH OF LOGIEBUCHAN.

Nov.	16.	Tartie for.	.	.	1120	.	.	D 247	16	.
Nov.	12.	Turnerhall for lands unmortified.			148	6	8	16	10	.
Nov.	8.	Mostoun for	.	.	100	.	.	11	2	6
Nov.	3.	Auchmacoy for	.	.	981	13	4	108	2	.
Nov.	9.	Mieckle Artrochy for	.	.	317	.	.	D 70	3	2
Nov.	17.	Birniss for	.	.	418	.	.	D 92	10	2
Nov.	5.	Rainistoun for	.	.	310	.	.	34	9	9
Jan.	24.	Turnerhall for Mortified Lands	.		366	13	4	40	15	10

8. PAROCH OF ELLON.

Dec.	5.	Earl of Errol for	.	.	1653	6	8	183	16	2
Nov.	25.	Earl of Aberdeen for	.	.	1033	6	8	D 228	12	6
Nov.	25.	Drumwhynle for	.	.	533	6	8	D 118	.	.
Nov.	17.	Arnage unliferented for	.	.	350	.	.	38	18	9
Dec.	17.	Liferented lands of Arnage.	.		350	.	.	38	18	9
Nov.	12.	Turnerhall for .	.	.	963	17	.	107	4	10
Jan.	24.	Ditto for Mortified Lands for	.		102	16	4	11	9	.
Nov.	8.	Coldwells unliferented for .	.		50	.	.	D 11	9	.
Nov.	8.	Ditto Liferented for .	.		50	.	.	5	11	3
Nov.	8.	Fortrie Liferented for	.	.	133	6	8	14	16	8
Nov.	7.	Dudwick for	.	.	716	13	4	79	14	7
,,	,,	Lady Auchterellon for	.	.	716	13	4	79	14	7
Dec.	2.	Fechill for	.	.	400	.	.	88	10	.
Dec.	24.	Watertoun for .	.	.	633	6	8	70	9	2
Nov.	7.	Laird of Ellon for	.	.	1266	13	4	140	18	.

5. PRESBITRY OF TURREFF.

1. PAROCH OF FYVIE.

			Valued Rent.			Subsidy.		
			£	s.	d.	£	s.	d.
Dec.	30.	Lop of Fyvie	1862	19	4	207	5	3
Dec.	30.	Cowhill and Kirktoun and half of						
		Ardlogie for	203	14	.	22	13	5
Dec.	2.	Tolquhon for (Seq) . . .	429	16	.	47	16	.
		Towie for	150	.	.	16	13	9
		Gight and Mains of Ardlogie .	996	13	4	110	17	7
Nov.	18.	Monkshill for	80	.	. D	17	14	.
Nov.	3.	Litlfolla for	155	12	.	17	6	4
Nov.	1.	Miecklefolla for	155	12	. D	34	12	6
Nov.	1.	Blackfoord for (Lifer) . .	100	.	.	11	2	6
Jan.	27.	Jackstoun for	100	.	.	11	2	6
Jan.	6.	Laird of Meldrum for . .	350	.	. D	77	8	9
Nov.	11.	Crichie for	666	13	4	74	3	4
Jan.	26.	Savock and Bogheads for . .	400	.	. D	88	10	.
Nov.	1.	Wartle for Midaple . . .	83	6	8 D	18	10	10
Nov.	8.	Law for Terpersies Valuation for	411	.	.	45	14	6

2. PAROCH OF DRUMBLADE.

Nov.	22.	Lesmore for	1200	.	.	133	10	.
Oct.	21.	Lessendrum for . . .	950	.	.	105	13	9
Oct.	31.	The Minister of Rhynie for ½ of						
		Camalegy	125	.	.	13	18	2
		Drumirs half of Camalegie for .	125	.	. D	27	13	2
		Dalmuie for	333	6	8 D	73	15	.
Nov.	18.	Cocklarachy	333	6	8	37	1	8

3. PAROCH OF KINEWARD.

Nov.	19.	Mountcoffer for . . .	586	13	4	65	5	4
Nov.	16.	Balmad mortified to Ye King's						
		College	366	.	.	40	14	5
Dec.	19.	Bracco for Iden for . . .	483	.	.	53	14	9
Nov.	11.	Byth for	400	.	.	44	10	.
Dec.	17.	Craigstown and Castletown for .	717	.	. D	158	12	10
Nov.	4.	Blacktoun for	236	13	4	26	6	7
Nov.	1.	Walkerhill for (Lifer) . .	66	13	4	7	8	4

			Valued Rent.				Subsidy.		
			£	s.	d.		£	s.	d.
Dec.	19.	Bracco for Fisherie for . .	444	13	4	D	49	9	6
Nov.	8.	Denlugas for—Peter Grant .	150	.	.		33	3	9
Nov.	11.	Tolquhon for Gairnistoun for .	366	13	4		40	15	10
,,	,,	Bracco for Braeside for . .	60	.	.		6	13	6
Dec.	19.	Bracco part of Fisherie . .	222	.	.		24	14	.

4. PAROCH OF TUREFF.

Dec.	5.	The Earl of Errol for. . .	1650	17	10		183	13	5
Dec.	17.	Craigstoun for	133	6	8	D	29	10	.
Oct.	31.	Muiresk for	400	.	.		44	10	.
,,	,,	Balquholly for Old Lands for .	833	6	8		92	14	2
,,	,,	Balquholly for Leask's valuation for	88	5	.		9	16	5
Feb.	1.	Woodend for	53	6	8		5	18	8
Dec.	17.	The heirs of Provost Ross for .	66	13	4		7	8	4
,,	,,	Towie for	300	.	.		33	7	6
Nov.	11.	Tolquhon for Fintray for . .	333	6	8		37	1	8
Nov.	2.	Gask for	300	.	.	D	66	15	.
Nov.	12.	The Fuers of Turreff for . .	100	.	.		11	2	6
Nov.	5.	Laithers for	800	.	.		89	.	.
Nov.	1.	Balmelie sequestrate for . .	100	.	.		11	2	6

5. PAROCH OF MOUNTQUHITAR.

Nov.	5.	Auchry for	733	6	8	D	162	5	.
Nov.	7.	John Brown Netherasleed for .	62	4	.	D	13	17	.
Nov.	11.	Tolquhon for Little Auchry and c. for	266	13	4		29	13	4
Nov.	5.	Tucker for	60	.	.		6	13	6
Dec.	5.	The Earl of Errol for. . .	260	.	.		28	18	6
Nov.	2.	Mr. Adam Hay for . . .	60	.	.		6	13	6
Feb.	1.	Foveran for Backlands of Balquoly	266	13	4	D	59	.	.
Feb.	1.	Thomas Mouat's Wadsett for .	74	9	.	D	16	11	2
Dec.	5.	Hairmoss for	66	13	4		7	8	4
Feb.	1.	Keathen for	40	.	.		4	9	.
Nov.	1.	Balquhynachy for . . .	30	.	.	D	6	13	6
Feb.	6.	Foveran for Greens of Allathen .	300	.	.	D	66	7	6
Feb.	1.	Brownhill for	55	11	2	D	12	6	1

6. PAROCH OF AUCTERLESS.

			Valued Rent.			Subsidy.		
			£	s.	d.	£	s.	d.
Dec.	17.	Hattoun and for William White for	1303	6	8	D 280	7	4
Nov.	11.	Badenscoth for . . .	566	13	4	63	.	4
Nov.	11.	The Lady Badenscoth for . .	283	6	8	31	10	5
Nov.	5.	Laithers for	283	6	8	25	19	2
Nov.	1.	Blackfoord for (lifert) . .	193	6	8	21	10	5
Nov.	11.	Templand and Kirktounhill for (Sup)	73	6	8	8	3	2
,,	,,	Towie for	500	.	.	55	12	6

7. PARISH OF FORGUE.

Nov.	8.	Bogny for	666	13	4	74	3	4
Nov.	8.	Ditto for ¾ of Conland for . .	150	.	.	16	13	9
Dec.	2.	Geo. Leslie of Northlesly for— ¼ of Conland for . . .	50	.	.	D 11	1	3
Nov.	8.	Bogny for Little Forgue for .	83	6	8	9	5	5
Nov.	8.	Frendraught for . . .	666	13	4	74	3	4
Nov.	8.	The Heirs of Thomas Cushny for	350	.	.	38	18	9
Oct.	31.	Crichtoun's half of Comistie for .	50	.	.	5	11	3
Nov.	15.	Shand's half of Comistie for .	50	.	.	5	11	3
Nov.	5.	Drmdollo Walter Leslie for .	266	13	4	D 59	.	.
Nov.	30.	Cornyhaugh for Robert Irving .	88	13	4	9	17	4
Nov.	8.	My Lady Frendraught for Glen-melan for	66	13	4	7	8	4
Nov.	4.	Ditto for Bogfontoun for . .	88	13	4	9	17	4
,,	,,	Auchintender for . . .	66	13	4	7	8	4
Nov.	2.	Pardargue Theo. Morison for .	140	6	8	15	12	3
Nov.	14.	Garriesfoord for . . .	152	.	.	16	18	3
Nov.	1.	Monelie Wischart for . .	133	6	8	D 29	13	4
Nov.	11.	Largue and Drumblair for . .	100	.	.	11	2	6
Dec.	2.	Northlessly for	666	13	4	D 147	10	.
,,	,,	Ashallon for	100	.	.	11	2	6

4. PRESBITRY OF STRATHBOGIE.

1. PAROCH OF DUMBENNAN.

Duke Gordon for . . .	1810	.	.	201	7	3

2. PAROCH OF KINOIR.

	Valued Rent.			Subsidy.		
	£	s.	d.	£	s.	d.
Duke Gordon for . . .	830	.	.	92	6	9
Avachie for	430	.	.	47	16	9

3. PAROCH OF RUTHEN.

4. PAROCH OF BOTARIE.

Duke Gordon for . . .	3610	17	.	401	14	5

5. PAROCH OF GARTLY.

Duke Gordon for . . .	1040	15	1	115	15	9

6. PAROCH OF RYNIE.

7. PAROCH OF ESSY.

Duke Gordon for . . .	1437	19	8	159	19	7
Lesmore for	265	.	.	29	9	8

8. PAROCH OF GLASS.

Bracco for Edenglassie for .	900	.	.	100	2	6
Bracco for Cairnburrow for .	600	.	.	66	15	.
Aswanly for	300	.	.	33	7	6

8. PRESBITRY OF ABERDEEN.

1. PAROCH OF PETERCULTER.
&
HALF OF BANCHORY.

Nov.	23.	Laird of Drum for . . .	700	.	.	77	17	6
,,	,,	The Laird of Coulter for . .	750	.	.	83	8	9
Nov.	11.	Pitfoddels for	500	.	.	55	12	6
,,	,,	Coulter for Glasterberrie for .	42	.	.	4	13	6
Oct.	31.	The Toun of Aberdeen for Murthill	335	13	4	37	6	6
Nov.	8.	Cults and Bieldside . . .	286	.	.	31	16	5

2. PAROCH OF DRUMEACK.

Nov.	23.	The Laird of Drum for . .	1000	.	.	111	5	.

3. PAROCH OF SKEEN.

						Valued Rent.			Subsidy.		
						£	s.	d.	£	s.	d.
Dec.	8.	Fornet for	.	.	.	260	.	.	D 57	10	6
Nov.	30.	Concraig for	.	.	.	200	.	.	22	5	.
Nov.	1.	Ye Town of Aberdeen for	.	.	1340	.	.	149	1	6	
Nov.	15.	The Laird of Skeen	.	.	.	700	.	.	D 154	17	6

4. PARISH OF KINELLAR.

Nov.	1.	The Town of Aberdeen	.	.	200	.	.	22	5	.	
Nov.	19.	Kinellar for	.	.	.	152	6	7	16	19	1
Nov.	8.	Mieckle Kinaldy for	.	.	127	13	5	14	4	1	
Nov.	30.	Concraig for Nether Auchorsk for	174	7	2	D 38	12	2			
Nov.	5.	Auchorsk for	.	.	.	133	6	8	D 29	10	.
Nov.	3.	Glasgowego for	.	.	.	133	6	8	14	16	8

5. PAROCH OF DYCE.

Nov.	1.	Kinaldy liferented for	.	.	76	13	4	8	10	7	
Dec.	2.	William Johnston of Craig for	.	221	7	.	24	12	8		
Nov.	8.	Sir John Johnstoun for	.	.	768	13	.	85	10	.	
Nov.	3.	Ye Laird of Dyce for.	.	.	550	.	.	D 122	7	6	
Nov.	17.	The Heirs of Provost Johnstoun for	.	.	.	.	.	90	.	.	10 . 2

6. PAROCH OF FINTRAY.

Nov.	11.	Craigivar for	.	.	.	.	1783	17	2	D 394	14	8
Nov.	3.	Dyce for .	.	.	.	.	25	.	.	D 5	11	3
Nov.	15.	Skeen for Westerfintray for	.	850	.	.	D 188	.	6		
Nov.	7.	Disblair for	.	.	.	.	288	17	6	32	3	4
Nov.	2.	William Reid for	.	.	.	59	13	4	D 13	5	7	

7. PAROCH OF BALHELVIE.

Nov.	2.	The Earl of Panmuir for	.	.	2932	.	.	326	3	6	
Nov.	23.	Blairtoun for	.	.	.	.	248	.	.	27	11	1
Oct.	31.	Menie for	.	.	.	.	500	.	.	55	12	6
Nov.	16.	Colpnay for	.	.	.	.	541	13	4	60	5	3
Nov.	8.	Town of Aberdeen for Pettans for	241	13	4	26	17	.			

8. PAROCH OF NEW MACHAR.

			Valued Rent.			Subsidy.		
			£	s.	d.	£	s.	d.
Nov.	2.	The Earl of Panmuir for . .	40	.	.	4	9	.
Nov.	15.	Mr. George Gordon for Rainieshill	366	13	4	40	15	10
Nov.	2.	Boddams for (seq) . . .	100	.	.	12	2	6
Nov.	17.	Hiltoun for	500	13	4	*D* 110	15	6
Nov.	2.	Kinmundie, sequestrate for .	366	13	4	40	15	10
Nov.	7.	Snalend for Liferented . .	103	4	.	11	12	9
Nov.	7.	Rosehall or Boghall for . .	346	16	.	38	11	11
Nov.	17.	Guovell for	80	.	.	*D* 17	14	.
Nov.	30.	Elrick for.	550	.	.	*D* 121	13	9

9. PAROCH OF OLD MACHAR.

Nov.	2.	The Earl of Panmuir for . .	300	.	.	33	7	6
Jan.	27.	The Town of Aberdeen for Gilkinstoun	501	1	2	55	14	11
Nov.	19.	The Town of Aberdeen for .	469	8	10	52	4	6
Nov.	12.	Lady Stonywood's jointure Lands for	200	.	.	22	5	.
Nov.	8.	Scotstoun for	150	.	.	16	13	9
Jan.	26.	Newtoun for Berryhill and Fishing for	400	.	.	*D* 88	10	.
Nov.	12.	Thomas Cassie for . . .	34	2	6	3	16	1
Nov.	19.	Kings College for Mortified Lands for	195	15	2	21	15	9
Nov.	12.	William Thomson for part of Cassie's Valuation . . .	8	14	.		19	8
Nov.	17.	Hiltoun for	283	6	8	*D* 62	13	10
Nov.	1.	Sunnyside for	45	.	.	5	.	2
Nov.	10.	Balgowny, Lord Gray for . .	720	.	.	*D* 159	6	.
Nov.	7.	Grandham and Densfield for .	600	.	.	66	15	.
Jan.	26.	Mr. Peacock, Pitmuckstoun for .	120	.	.	13	7	.
Jan.	26.	Whitestripes, John Anderson for.	110	.	.	12	4	9
Jan.	3.	Ruthrestoun mortified for . .	300	.	.	33	7	6
Nov.	12.	Stonywood for Salmond fishing for	100	.	.	11	2	6
Nov.	17.	Seatoun for .	166	13	4	*D* 36	17	6
		Mr. George Keith Writter for fishing for	166	13	4	*D* 36	17	6

			Valued Rent.			Subsidy.		
			£	s.	d.	£	s.	d.
Feb.	1.	Cottoun for	146	13	4	16	6	4
Nov.	19.	Mr. Allex. Fraser for Lands and						
		fishing	363	6	8	40	8	5
		William Moir for fishing for half						
		net	200	.	.	22	5	.
Nov.	16.	Kings College for fishing for half						
		net	166	13	4	18	10	10

10. PAROCH OF NEWHILLS (BECAME A PARISH IN 1660).

			£	s.	d.	£	s.	d.
Dec.	2.	William Johnstoun for Bishops						
		Clinterty	66	13	4	7	8	4
Nov.	8.	Stonywood Elder for . .	400	.	.	44	10	.
Nov.	8.	Stonywood Younger for . .	300	.	.	33	7	6
Nov.	1.	Crabstoun for . . .	240	.	. D	53	8	.
Nov.	5.	Auchmull for	166	13	4	18	10	10
Nov.	1.	Sclety for.	140	.	.	15	11	6

11. PAROCH OF NEW ABERDEEN.

			£	s.	d.	£	s.	d.
Nov.	25.	The Earl of Aberdeen for Fishing	266	13	6 D	59	.	.
Dec.	2.	Mr. Allex. Moir for Fishing .	166	13	4	18	10	10

CHURCH LANDS.

			£	s.	d.	£	s.	d.
		The Archbishoprick of St. An-						
		drews for	150	.	.	16	13	9
		The Bishoprick of Aberdeen for .	1666	13	4	185	8	4
Dec.	30.	The Parsonage of Auchterless for	100	.	.	11	2	6
		The Parsonage of Invernochtie for	100	.	.	11	2	6
Dec.	5.	The Parsonage of Turreff, Earl of						
		Errol for	300	.	.	33	7	6
		The Parsonage of Kincairden for	300	.	.	33	7	6

ABERDEEN SHYRE. *DR.*

For Subsidy equal to Six Moneths Subsidy, viz.

	Sterling.			Scots.		
	£	s.	d.	£	s.	d.
For the Subsidy of £236240.13.9 Scots valued rent	2036	8	.	24436	16	.
Ditto of £63953.19.10 valued Rent which pay double subsidy per Account	551	5	8¾	6615	8	9
	£2587	13	8¾	31052	4	9

CONTRA. *CR.*

		Sterling.			Scots.		
		£	s.	d.	£	s.	d.
NOV. 21.	By cash paid to the Committee for funds at Perth . . .	1000	.	.	12000	.	.
DEC. 5.	By ditto to Mr. James Forbes per Precept from Committee at Aber.	50	.	.	600	.	.
DEC. 8.	By ditto to Robert Lindsay pr Ditto	5	.	.	60	.	.
Ditto 20.	By ditto to Mr. James Forbes Commander of Independent Compy per ditto . . .	50	.	.	600	.	.
,, 20.	By ditto to the Marquis of Huntly per receipt . . .	400	.	.	4800	.	.
,, 20.	By ditto to George Maitland per precept from the Committee .	3	.	.	36	.	.
,, 22.	By ditto for Account of Wine, etc. sent to Perth per Acct. . .	23	4	5	278	13	.
,, ,,	By ditto for Acct of Paper sent to Perth for the Press . .	5	2	.	61	4	.
,, 28.	By ditto Payed John Duff for expenses going to Perth per receipt	20	7	8	244	12	.
1716 JAN. 2.	By ditto Baillie Simson for Meal by order from Committee . .	123	6	8	1480	.	.
Ditto 6.	By ditto to Allex. Midletoun per Precept from Committee at Abdn.	12	.	.	144	.	.
,, 10.	By ditto to Robert Lindsay per ditto	5	.	.	60	.	.

27

CONTRA. CR.

			Sterling.			Scots.		
			£	s.	d.	£	s.	d.
JAN.	11.	By ditto paid to the Committee at Perth per Receipt . .	200	.	.	2400	.	.
,,	17.	By ditto paid per precept from the Committee at Abdn. . .	10	.	.	120	.	.
,,	20.	By ditto paid Andrew Jaffray per Ditto	24	6	8	292	.	.
,,	,,	By ditto to Robert Lindsay per Ditto	20	.	.	240	.	.
,,	25.	By ditto to ditto . . .	20	.	.	240	.	.
,,	27.	By ditto to Mr. James Forbes per ditto	50	.	.	600	.	.
,,	,,	By ditto to Robert Lindsay per ditto	30	.	.	360	.	.
FEB.	1.	By ditto to John Cow per ditto .	10	.	.	120	.	.
,,	6.	By ditto to the Laird of Drum Younger per receipt . . .	10	.	.	120	.	.
		By account of Incident charges .	26	11	10	319	2	.
		By Account of Subsidie and Cesse Resting in the Shyre . .	377	12	3½	4531	7	7

NOTES ON THE CONTRA OF THE ACCOMPT.

These accounts are interesting, as showing that the greater part of the money collected, viz., £1210 sterling, was handed over to the authorities at Perth and used, presumably, to pay the troops. The only other large sum of £400 sterling was paid to the Marquis of Huntly for his contingent.

BAILLIE SIMSON received £123 to buy meal.

Three times £50 was paid out, to "Mr. JAMES FORBES, commander of an independent company." He was probably the Hon. James, afterwards the 16th Lord Forbes. ROBERT LINDSAY, who has not been identified, received by precept from the Committee at Aberdeen, £5, £5, £20, and £20, and finally £30. Wine and paper sent to Perth accounts for nearly £30.

JOHN DUFF, a King's Messenger of Aberdeen (that is one legally qualified to deliver letters of Horning, writs, decreets, etc.), received £20 7s. 8d. for "expenses in going to Perth."

John Duff was of the family of Muldavit, and when he died in 1718 "his fortune (according to a paper in the Lyon Office) went to Braco," i.e., William of Dipple and Braco, father of the first Lord Fife—who succeeded in 1718 to his nephew, William, who committed suicide at Balvenie (see page 224). "John Duff King's Messenger was made a Burgess of Aberdeen Sept. 22. 1684," his father having been a merchant of the town.

Many letters from John to William of Dipple and from Dipple to him exist, and are printed in the *Book of the Duffs* (William Brown, Edinburgh, 1914). He is also referred to in the Sheriff Court Book of Aberdeen, and in the Poll Book as "John Duff messenger for himself no wife nor child" (another John Duff messenger being already dead, leaving "a relict"). He subsequently married Anna Innes of Belhelvie, youngest daughter of Lord Panmure's factor.

After the failure of the Rising of 1715 John Duff (who had been an active Jacobite), in the quaint words of William Baird (first historian of the Duffs), "stepped over to Holland, in the beginning of the year 1716, where he soon fell into a large acquaintance and was treated by them all with the greatest civility and kindness. There he laid himself out to serve all his young countrymen who came over to the Continent. . . . He died at Rotterdam in 1718, universally regretted." According to an account given by William Rose, he was "drowned, returning with Taylor of Boyndlie, and both their bodies got clasped with a rope and an oak plank. Boyndlie in life got on the shore of Musselburgh, but Duff drowned." His wife had died in the previous year, as William Gordon of Farskane wrote to the Duke of Mar, Paris, Dec. 21, 1717—"Poor John Duff's wife is dead at Rotterdam, and her burial charges will be hard on him in this winter season, if his Majesty is not pleased to allow him something." [1] He left no issue. He himself describes, in a letter to William Gordon, how he "had the honour to be one of the last to serve our master in the field and garrison, and was taken out of the castle of Fedderat with Lord Frendraught, and suffered 12 months imprisonment." [2]

ALEXANDER MIDLETOUN received a small sum of £12 "per precept from the Committee at Aberdeen," but the purpose is not stated.

This was Captain Alexander Middleton, one of the "persons who came into Aberdeen with the Earl Marischal 20th September 1715," and was also present at the gathering at Mistress Hepburn's (see page 30). He was Comptroller of Customs in Aberdeen. He married, in 1705, Elizabeth Burnett, and died 26th October, 1751, "in an advanced age." He was the son of Principal George Middleton of King's College, Aberdeen, and his wife, Janet Gordon, daughter of James Gordon of Seaton. Brigadier-General John Middleton was his brother, and it is curious to

---

[1] *Calendar of Stuart Papers*, vol. v, p. 299.

[2] This must refer to the campaign of 1689, as obviously he did not suffer imprisonment after the collapse of the Rising in February, 1716.

note that he was *at the time* in King George's army, and also Member of Parliament for Aberdeen.[1]

ANDREW JAFFRAY, son of the Provost, was a merchant of Aberdeen and a Jacobite, being one of those who met at Mistress Hepburn's house.[2]

JOHN COW, who was entrusted with £10, has not been identified.

For ALEXANDER IRVINE, Laird of Drum, see page 31.

The INCIDENT CHARGES, £26 11s. 10d., are like the Sundries in every account, and the sum of £377 12s. 3½d., or its near equivalent, was long after claimed, as being due by the representatives of John Forbes to the next Collector, for according to papers at Fettercairn Mr. Arthur Forbes, the next Collector of Cess (relationship to John not stated), obtained a decreet against the Executors of John Forbes for the sum of £366 13s. 11d. as part of the Cess of 1715 uplifted and not accounted for to the Government.

The phrase "Subsidie and Cesse resting in the Shyre" looks as if John Forbes had not received it ; but in any case the sums are not exact and do not tally !

In his widow's memorial, already given, it is stated that Mr. John Forbes was due to Charles Forbes, his nephew, £2,000, but the reasons for the non-payment of that sum have already been given (Intro., page xxiii). The widow had made a gallant fight to bring up the Collector's family, and those in whose veins still runs the blood of their daughter, Christian, may well be proud of the inheritance.

---

[1] John Middleton of Seaton, also of Fettercairn by purchase, 5th son of Principal George Middleton. He was M.P. for Aberdeen burghs, 1713, until his death in 1739.
—Foster's M.P.'s for Scotland.

[2] "22nd Sept. 1715. The Magistrates having mett in the Council house about the towne's affairs, they were insulted by a mobb, who first mett at Mistress Hebburns and then came to the Council house and sequyred the arms and ammunitions belonging to the town with the keys of the Blockhouse, seeing they were not to regard the magistrates any longer as Magistrates."
—A Short Memorandum of quhat heath occurred in Aberdeen.

NOTES ON THE CESS ROLL.

PARISH OF TARLAND.

LAIRD OF DRUM.

Alexander Irvine, Laird from 1696 to 1720. He had formerly been "of Murthill," and before that of Crimond.[1]

Alexander Irvine, his predecessor, who succeeded in 1688, was of weak intellect. He married Marjorie Forbes of Auchredie. It is stated (in Colonel J. F. Leslie's *Irvines of Drum*) that he was induced to enter into this union by Mr. Robert Keith of Lentush, the lady's uncle by marriage, who himself celebrated the marriage ceremony according to Scottish usage. This was afterwards confirmed by the Court of Session. The only child died at birth, and Alexander himself having died 3rd January, 1696, was succeeded by his cousin, Alexander Irvine of Murthill, above. This branch owned the estate for 40 years.

Alexander married Jane Irvine, sister of the late laird, and left a son, Alexander, who succeeded, and two daughters. Alexander, the son, was "out" in the '15 and is said to have been wounded at Sheriffmuir. He escaped abroad, and on 19th February, 1718, a royal permission was granted by George I to "Alexander Irvine, only son of Alexander Irvine of Drum, Robert Gordon of Cluny and James Bisset of Lessendrum to return to Great Britain and remain unmolested." This document is preserved at Gordon Castle, the licence to return having been obtained by the good offices of the 2nd Duke of Gordon, who, as Marquis of Huntly, was prominent in the Rising, but early made his peace with Government. Numbers of his tenants hoped to benefit by his influence, but Irvine of Drum, as a friend, and Bisset of Lessendrum, as a follower, were the only ones for whom he exerted himself. Gordon of Cluny had already obtained a licence for himself to return, which now lies in the Public Record Office,[2] with a note to say it was "not used." It was dated 21 October, 1717.

---

[1] He was one of those Jacobites who carried the unwilling Lord Saltoun a prisoner to the Camp at Perth (see page 152).

[2] *Entry book 8, P.R.O.*

License to Return to Great Britain.

Document Preserved at Gordon Castle.

"George by the Grace of God, King of Great Britain, France and Ireland, defender of the Faith etc. To all whom these presents shall come, Greeting. Know ye that We for several reasons us hereunto moving, have given and granted, and by these presents do give and grant free leave Lycence and Liberty to ROBERT GORDON OF CLUNY, ALEXANDER IRVIN only son of Alexander IRVIN OF DRUM in the county of Aberdeen and James BISSIT OF LESSENDRUM in the same county, who have been concerned in Levying war against us, which began in this realm in the year of our Lord one thousand seven hundred and fifteen and have been since beyond the Seas, to return into and abide in our Kingdomes of Great Britain or Ireland. Given under our Privy Seal at our Palace of Westminster the nineteenth day of February in the Fourth year of our Reign."

Alexander Irvine did come back to Scotland and found his father's affairs much involved. Seven years after he succeeded he again went abroad, and on his subsequent return was found to be quite incapable of managing his own affairs; his father's brother, John, was appointed Tutor-at-law in 1731, and on Alexander's death, succeeded to the estate in 1357. (J. F. Leslie, *Irvines of Drum*, pp. 135–7.)

Kincraigie, for Drum.

Patrick Gordon of Harlaw, son of Alexander Gordon of Kincraigie and Marjorie Gordon of Terpersie. His wife was Rachel Leslie, and he had two sons, Alexander and James.[1]

He collected the Cess from Drum.

Hallhead, for Westoun.

This was Patrick Gordon of Hallhead (see Parish of Cushnie) acting for Alexander Farquharson of Westown, who had sasine on the estate of Milnbog, etc., 30th January, 1712. Alexander was grandson of the John Farquharson who was of Westown and Bellamoir in 1667 and son of the John who succeeded in 1681 and married Isobel Cumming in 1703. On 7th July, 1703, Isobel Cumming, spouse to John Farquharson of Westown, had an arent out of the Hill of Crimond, which she discharged and renounced to Alexander Cumming, her brother.[2]

Alexander Farquharson's wife, mother of his sons, was Margaret Livingstone, who, on 20th August, 1712, had a liferent on the estate.[3]

John Forbes of Inverernan.

This was the famous "Black Jock," the Earl of Mar's baillie for Kildrummy, to whom Mar wrote the letter reproaching him for sending

---

[1] J. M. Bulloch, *House of Gordon*, vol. ii, p. 187.
[2] *Aberdeen Sasines.*   [3] *Ibid.*

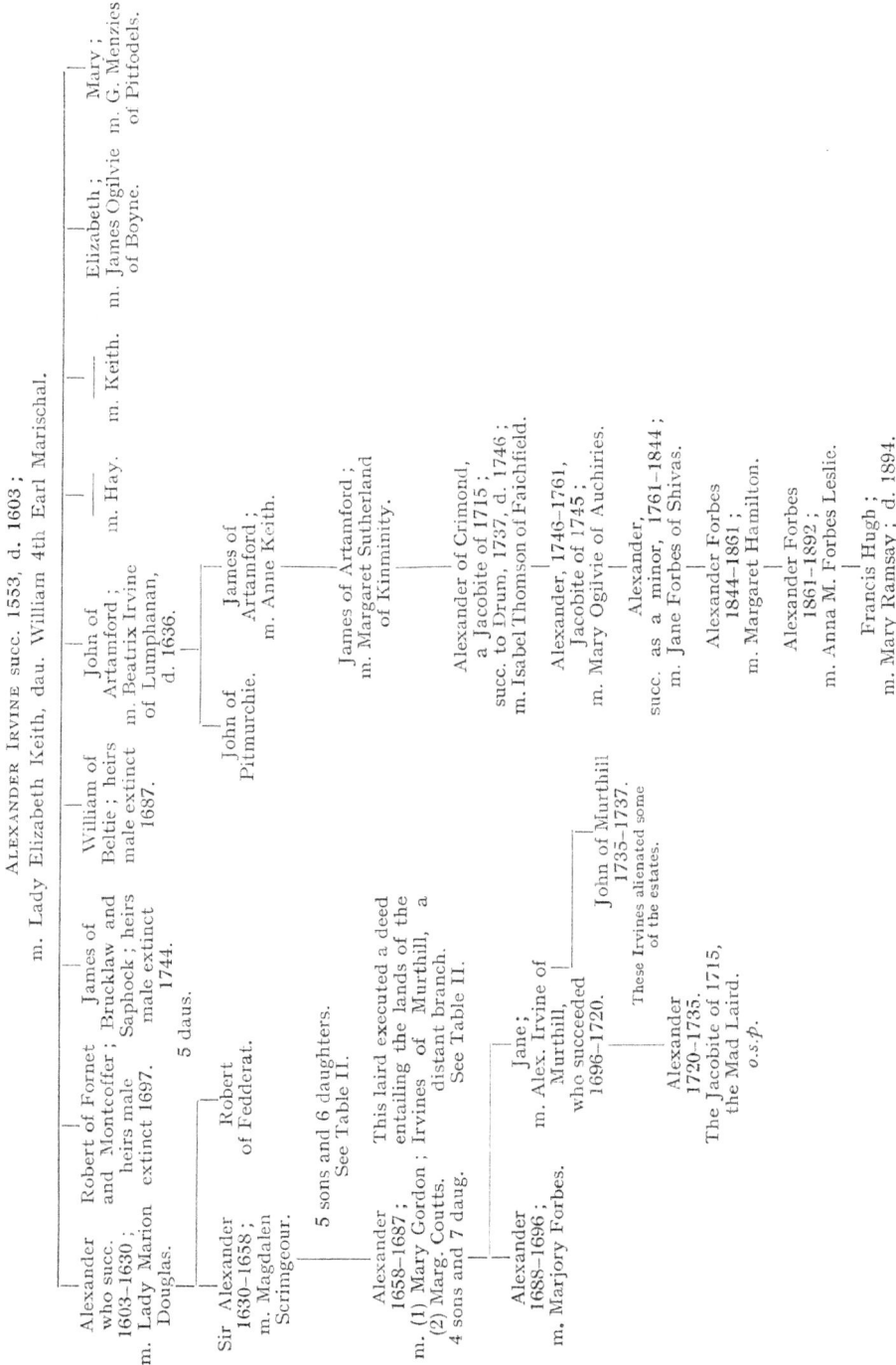

TABLE I.

ALEXANDER IRVINE succ. 1553, d. 1603;
m. Lady Elizabeth Keith, dau. William 4th Earl Marischal.

Alexander who succ. 1603–1630; m. Lady Marion Douglas.

Robert of Fornet and Montcoffer; heirs male extinct 1697.

James of Brucklaw and Saphock; heirs male extinct 1744.

William of Beltie; heirs male extinct 1687.

John of Artamford; m. Beatrix Irvine of Lumphanan, d. 1636.

— m. Hay.

— m. Keith.

Elizabeth; m. James Ogilvie of Boyne.

Mary; m. G. Menzies of Pitfodels.

Sir Alexander 1630–1658; m. Magdalen Scrimgeour.

Robert of Fedderat.

5 sons and 6 daughters. See Table II.

Alexander 1658–1687; m. (1) Mary Gordon. (2) Marg. Coutts. 4 sons and 7 daug.

This laird executed a deed entailing the lands of the Irvines of Murthill, a distant branch. See Table II.

Alexander 1688–1696; m. Marjory Forbes.

Jane; m. Alex. Irvine of Murthill, who succeeded 1696–1720.

Alexander 1720–1735. The Jacobite of 1715, the Mad Laird. o.s.p.

John of Murthill 1735–1737. These Irvines alienated some of the estates.

5 daus.

John of Pitmurchie.

James of Artamford; m. Anne Keith.

James of Artamford; m. Margaret Sutherland of Kinminity.

Alexander of Crimond, a Jacobite of 1715; succ. to Drum, 1737, d. 1746; m. Isabel Thomson of Faichfield.

Alexander, 1746–1761, Jacobite of 1745; m. Mary Ogilvie of Auchiries.

Alexander, succ. as a minor, 1761–1844; m. Jane Forbes of Shivas.

Alexander Forbes 1844–1861; m. Margaret Hamilton.

Alexander Forbes 1861–1892; m. Anna M. Forbes Leslie.

Francis Hugh; m. Mary Ramsay; d. 1894.

33

3

TABLE II.

Sir ALEXANDER IRVINE of Drum who succeeded 1630, d. 1658 ;
m. 1617 Magdalen Scrimgeour of Dudhope.

both excom. 1644.

| Alexander, who succ. ; m. Lady Mary Gordon, daug. of Huntly, in 1643. In 1681 m. Margaret Coutts. | Robert, d. prison. | James, Charles, Francis, all *o.s.p.* | Marion ; m. 1st Vis. Frendraught ; mother of 2 & 4 Viscounts. | Margaret ; m. Charles 1st E. of Aboyne. | Jane ; m. James Crichton. | Elizabeth, Isabel, & Anne, all unmarried. |

| Alexander ; m. Marjory Forbes. | Robert & Charles. *o.s.p.* | Mary, m. Patrick, Count Leslie. | Margaret ; m. G. Menzies of Pitfodels. | Jane ; m. Alex. Irvine, who succ. 1696 | Henrietta ; m. Alex. Leslie of Pitcaple. | Charles. | Catherine, Anne, Elizabeth. |

34

Alexander Irvine of Drum.

From painting in Marischal College.

up so few of Mar's own men in September, 1715. He was born, "as is said," about 1666 (or possibly 1664, as he *married* in 1684), the 5th son of William Forbes, 2nd of Skellater, and only son of his second wife, Agnes, daughter of William McIntosh of Kyllachy and widow of McGillivray of Drumnaglass. His four elder half-brothers were George, 3rd of Skellater, died in 1716 ; William of Edinglassie, died 1692 ; Lachlan and Nathaniel. It is not known whether either of the two latter took part in the Rising. They were elderly men, over 60, as their mother died in 1656.[1]

"Black Jock" married twice: (1) in 1684, Elspet Stewart, and (2) in 1709, Margaret Alexander. She married, secondly, the Rev. Donald McSwain[2] (see Invernochty, p. 136).

"Black Jock" died in prison at Carlisle, where his wife was with him. Thomas Tulloch of Tannachy wrote to his wife on 8th November, 1716 : "Poore black Jocke of Skellater dyed in prison here, to the regrate of all his acquaintances and was buried yesterday."[3] If he had not died of the wounds received a year before at Sheriffmuir, he was to have been executed next day.

According to a tree kindly supplied by Colonel James Forbes, D.S.O. (of Lockeridge, East Grinstead), he had eleven sons, nine by his first wife, of whom one, or perhaps two, may have been with him in the Rising, although there is no record of them.

In the *Poll Book* of 1696 only two are mentioned, William (afterwards of Buchaam) and Kenneth, aged respectively 11 and 6 years, but the baptisms of three others between William and Kenneth are recorded ;[4] they died young. There were two daughters, Anna and Christian, the latter married her cousin, George, 4th of Skellater.[5] These were by the first wife, Elspet Stewart. By his second wife, Margaret Alexander, he had two more sons, the elder of whom, Alexander, born 1710, succeeded to Invererman, being served heir to his father only on 28th January, 1724.[6] The younger, Charles, born 1712, was killed at Ticonderoga in 1758.

GEORGE FORBES OF SKELLATER.

George Forbes, 3rd of Skellater, was eldest son of William Forbes, 2nd of Skellater.

William, born 1615, had four wives (he died before 1696) :—

(1) Isobel, daughter of Alexander Forbes of Newe. She died 1656.
    Mother of George, above, William, Lachlan, and Nathaniel.

(2) Agnes Mackintosh of Kyllachy, who was the widow of McGillivray of Drumnaglass. Mother of John of Invererman.

---

[1] *Colonel James Forbes Papers.*   [2] *Castle Forbes Papers.*
[3] *Captain Tulloch's Papers.*   [4] *Strathdon Registers.*
[5] *Aberdeen Sasines.*   [6] *Service of Heirs.*

The Family of Forbes of Skellater.

George, 1st of Skellater, d. 1632.

Married (1) Euphame Skene ; (2) Margaret Forbes.

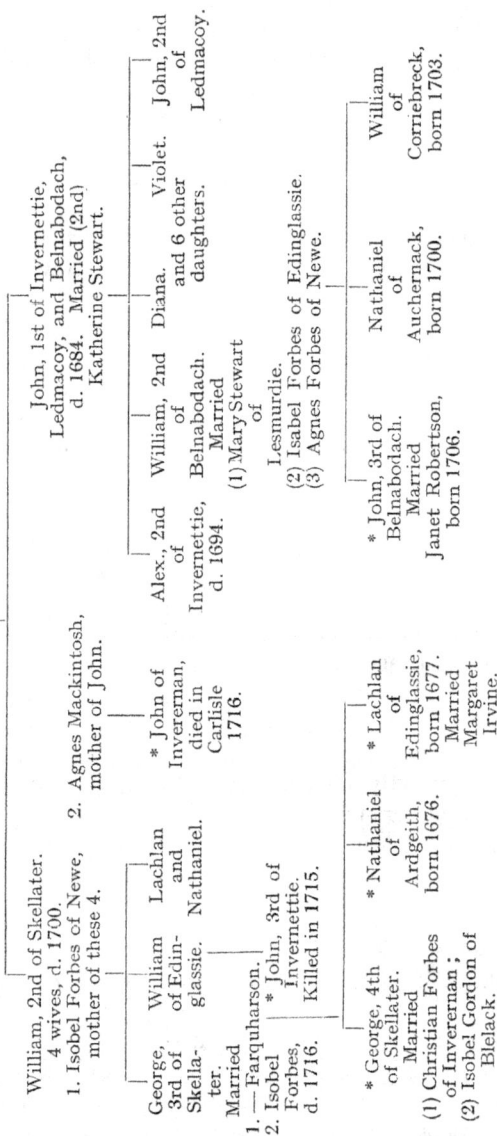

1. William, 2nd of Skellater. 4 wives, d. 1700. 1. Isobel Forbes of Newe, mother of these 4.

2. Agnes Mackintosh, mother of John.

John, 1st of Invernettie, Ledimacoy, and Belnabodach, d. 1684. Married (2nd) Katherine Stewart.

George, 3rd of Skellater. Married 1. — Farquharson. 2. Isobel Forbes, d. 1716.

William of Edinglassie. Lachlan and Nathaniel.

* John, 3rd of Invernettie. Killed in 1715.

* John of Inverernan, died in Carlisle 1716.

Alex., 2nd of Invernettie, d. 1694.

William, 2nd of Belnabodach. Married (1) Mary Stewart of Lesmurdie. (2) Isobel Forbes of Edinglassie. (3) Agnes Forbes of Newe.

Diana. Violet. and 6 other daughters.

John, 2nd of Ledimacoy.

* George, 4th of Skellater. Married (1) Christian Forbes of Inverernan ; (2) Isobel Gordon of Blelack.

* Nathaniel of Ardgeith, born 1676.

* Lachlan of Edinglassie, born 1677. Married Margaret Irvine.

* John, 3rd of Belnabodach. Married Janet Robertson, born 1706.

Nathaniel of Auchernack, born 1700.

William of Corriebreck, born 1703.

George, 5th of Skellater. "Out" in the '45. Married Christian Gordon of Glenbucket, d. 1767.

Elizabeth, daughter of George Forbes, 3rd of Skellater, b. 1685. Married John Stewart of Drumin, one of the Jacobite heritors who surrendered at Banff.

William, 6th and last of Skellater, d. 1819. Married Sophia Forbes of Newe.

Those known to be Jacobites are marked with an asterisk.

36

(3) Isobel Gordon.

(4) Janet Forbes, who survived him (she subsequently married John Smith of Drum); he had no issue by the two latter.

George, 3rd of Skellater, had two wives: (1) —— Farquharson, and (2) Isobel Forbes of Newe, whom he married 16th October, 1698.

George, 3rd of Skellater, then an old man, was not himself "out" in the Rising. He died in 1716. His youngest daughter, Agnes, married Robert Lumsden of Corrachree, 28th June, 1703.[1] His half-brother, "Black Jock" of Inverernan (above), was "out." His son, George, 4th of Skellater, who married (1) Christian, daughter of "Black Jock" (his own first cousin), and (2) Isobel Gordon of Blelack, 3rd May, 1703 (page 40), was also "out," and two younger sons, Nathaniel and Lachlan. His grandson, George, 5th of Skellater, who was about 17 in 1715, was "out" in the '45. *His* son, William, was the 6th and last laird of Skellater; he married Sophia Forbes of Newe, and died in 1819.[2]

CANDACRAIG (DUNCAN ANDERSON OF CANDACRAIG).

He had a feu charter of the lands from the Earl of Mar, 21st July, 1684.

He signed the heritors' bond of 26th April, 1700, as did the Laird of Skellater (above).[3] This was "anent the apprehending of rogues," etc. Duncan's wife was Helen Forbes of Invernochty who, in 1717, after the death of Duncan Anderson, married George Downie. Duncan was the son of Arthur Anderson of Candacraig and Marjorie Lumsden; he died in the course of the year 1715 and was succeeded by his son, another Arthur, who died in 1716.[4] The next owner was Arthur's son, Charles, born in 1711, for whom his uncle, John, second son of Duncan, acted as tutor. Charles, who died 16th March, 1776, erected in 1757 a tablet in the parish church of Strathdon (Invernochty) "to the memory of his predecessors, the Andersons of Candacraig, who have been interred here

---

[1] *Aberdeen Sasines.*   [2] *Castle Forbes Papers.*

[3] Col. J. Allardyce, *Historical Papers Relating to the Jacobite Period*, vol. i, p. 20.

[4] On 3rd July, 1704, sasine was granted by Arthur Anderson of Candacraig and Marjorie Lumsden, his spouse, to Lachlan Forbes of Edinglassie of "Lochans Reintrocin, and Meikle Glendowie."

Witnesses—John Lumsden in Auchindoir, and Harie Lumsden, his son.

The charter of 1734 gives the lands of Candacraig as including Tomantaple, Tomachon, and Feachla, together with the croft and land called Craigniach and all and sundry the lands of Belnagauld, Meikle Glencarvie, Lochans Rinstroin (above), and half the lands of Lynmore of Glencarvie, also Finnylost, Drummaline, and Tomachlewn.—*Castle Forbes Papers.*

On 26th June, 1745, Buchaam also was disponed by William Forbes, son of "Black Jock" of Inverernan, to Charles Anderson of Candacraig.—*Ibid.*

for seven generations past." Only six generations, including Charles, have been traced. His grandson, Dr. Robert Anderson, was the last direct male. The grandson of Dr. Robert's sister sold the estate in 1866 to Sir Charles Forbes of Newe.[1]

Charles, who *called himself the 8th*, died 16th March, 1776; he had a charter of the lands, 7th January, 1734 ; he was grandson of Duncan.

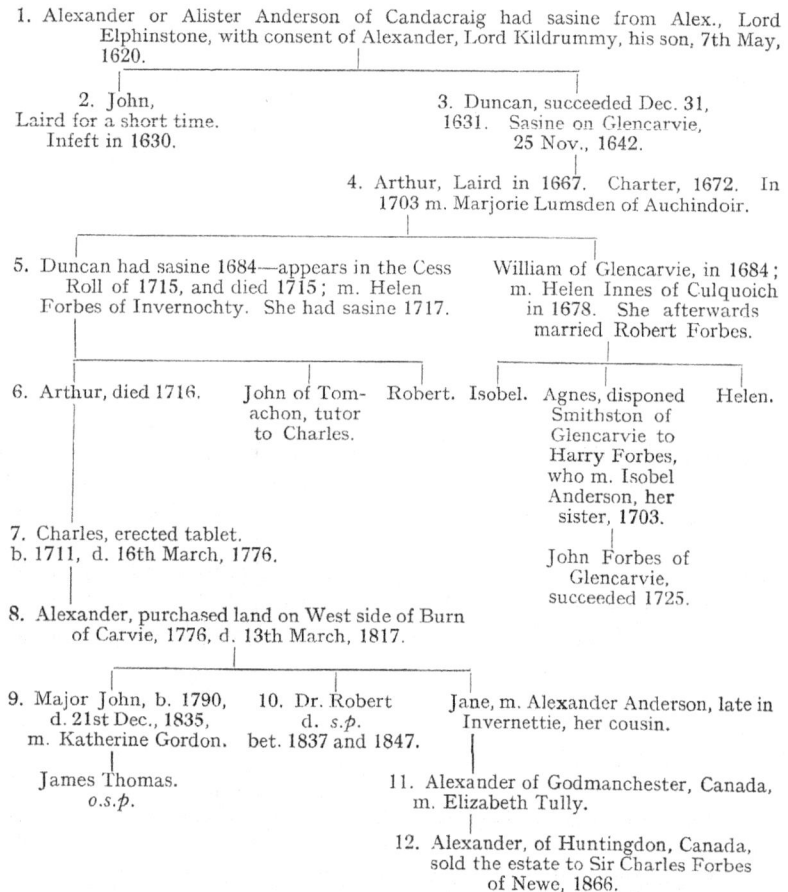

1. Alexander or Alister Anderson of Candacraig had sasine from Alex., Lord Elphinstone, with consent of Alexander, Lord Kildrummy, his son, 7th May, 1620.

2. John,
Laird for a short time.
Infeft in 1630.

3. Duncan, succeeded Dec. 31, 1631. Sasine on Glencarvie, 25 Nov., 1642.

4. Arthur, Laird in 1667. Charter, 1672. In 1703 m. Marjorie Lumsden of Auchindoir.

5. Duncan had sasine 1684—appears in the Cess Roll of 1715, and died 1715; m. Helen Forbes of Invernochty. She had sasine 1717.

William of Glencarvie, in 1684; m. Helen Innes of Culquoich in 1678. She afterwards married Robert Forbes.

6. Arthur, died 1716.

John of Tom-achon, tutor to Charles.

Robert. Isobel.

Agnes, disponed Smithston of Glencarvie to Harry Forbes, who m. Isobel Anderson, her sister, 1703.

Helen.

7. Charles, erected tablet.
b. 1711, d. 16th March, 1776.

John Forbes of Glencarvie, succeeded 1725.

8. Alexander, purchased land on West side of Burn of Carvie, 1776, d. 13th March, 1817.

9. Major John, b. 1790, d. 21st Dec., 1835, m. Katherine Gordon.

10. Dr. Robert d. *s.p.* bet. 1837 and 1847.

Jane, m. Alexander Anderson, late in Invernettie, her cousin.

James Thomas.
o.s.p.

11. Alexander of Godmanchester, Canada, m. Elizabeth Tully.

12. Alexander, of Huntingdon, Canada, sold the estate to Sir Charles Forbes of Newe, 1866.

The estate of GLENCARVIE was also, as has been seen, in the hands of Andersons. William Anderson, a brother of Arthur, owned it, and in the Poll Book of 1696 Helen Innes, relict of William Anderson of Glencarvie, and Helen, her daughter, appear.

[1] *Candacraig Papers.*

According to Forbes papers at Fettercairn, the estate of Glencarvie came into the hands of the Forbes family by the second marriage of Helen Innes, above, to "James Forbes in Kinnadie," 25th April, 1699.

Isabel Anderson, eldest daughter of William Anderson and the above Helen Innes, married 15th July, 1703, Harry Forbes, son of her step-father.

Agnes, the second daughter, disponed her third of the estate to Harry Forbes, 4th December, 1704.

And it would appear that Helen, the third daughter, who married John Grant, yr. of Blairfindy, did the same.

The instrument of resignation bears date 9th Dec., 1726.[1]

John Forbes, son of Harry and Isobel, was of Glencarvie, 26th November, 1725. But after the death of Harry Forbes, Isobel Anderson married, secondly, Robert Farquharson,[2] and appears to have conveyed the estate to him, as a "decreet arbitral" (subsequent to 1725) between Isobel and her son, John (above), gives to Robert Farquharson the title "of Glencarvie" (the decreet was passed and proclaimed by John Fullarton of Dudwick, John Innes of Tillyfour, George Leith of Overhall, and Arthur Gordon of Law).[3]

There was an earlier Forbes in Glencarvie who granted sasine to Arthur Anderson of Candacraig, 25th February, 1660.[4]

PARISH OF LOGIEMAR.

LAIRD OF DRUM (above).

JOHN LUMSDEN, FOR PART OF TILLEFOUDIE, LIFERENT.

The Gordons of Tillicphoudie or Tilphoudie were consistently Jacobites. John Gordon, 8th of Tilliephoudie, born in 1651, was still alive in 1715, with his second wife, Elizabeth Duguid of Auchinhove. His son, Francis, 9th of Tilliephoudie, was at least a sympathiser in 1715. He left a son, also Francis, who became a shoemaker, but was also an officer in Prince Charles' army in 1745.[5]

It has not been ascertained who was John Lumsden, who had a liferent on part of the estate.

MR. GEORGE GORDON OF LOGIE.

"Mr. George Gordon of Sauchen," obviously a Jacobite sympathiser, as the "Duke of Mar" freed him from 10,000 merks, as part payment

---

[1] *Castle Forbes Papers.*

[2] This Robert was a younger son of John Farquharson of Allargue, he was born in 1697, and appears as a witness in the dispute over the Marches of Glencarvie and Newe in 1767.—*Castle Forbes Papers.*

[3] *Fettercairn Papers.*   [4] *Aberdeen Sasines.*

[5] J. M. Bulloch, *House of Gordon,* vol. ii, p. 212.

for the lands of Logiemar.[1] On 14th May, 1712, Mr. George Gordon of Logiemar had sasine on Logiemar, Brownhill, etc.[2]

THE LAIRD OF BLELACK—ALEX. GORDON OF BLELACK.[3]

In the *Records of Invercauld*, by the Rev. John Grant Michie, occurs the following passage, page 283: " John Gordon was he whom the Earl of Mar compelled to join in the rising of the '15, and the father of Charles, who, with more spirit, came out in the '45." But this is an error of christian names as it is shown by the *Aberdeen Sasines* that the father of Charles was Alexander Gordon, who had an elder son, John, and that John and Charles successively owned Blelack.

On 24th September, 1708, Daniel Farquharson (the same as Donald), third son to the deceased Francis Farquharson, Finzean, granted an arent to Alexander Gordon of Blelack (father of John and Charles).[4]

On 3rd August, 1710, Barbara Stewart, spouse to Alexander Gordon of Blelack, had sasine on Blelack.[5]

John was the elder son of Alexander and Barbara, and succeeded him *after* 1718, as in that year Alexander and John, elder and younger of Blelack, had sasine.[6] (Alexander died in 1724.)

In the Valuation of 1667 it had been John Gordon of Blelack who had succeeded *his* brother, Alexander, having been previously of Bellabeg.

In 1672 it was still John, but in 1675 and in 1696 (*Poll Book*) it was John's eldest son, Charles, with two daughters. He was dead before 1703, as John, son of Alexander, was then "younger of Blelack," and also before 1700, when Alexander Gordon *of* Blelack (second son of John) signs the heritor's bond to apprehend malefactors.[7]

There was also another brother, George, at that date.

In 1718 Alexander and his elder son, John, had sasine as above.

John succeeded his father, Alexander, in 1724, and Charles succeeded his brother, John, in 1726, and married in that year Anne, daughter of John Urquhart of Meldrum.

On 12th July, 1703, George Gordon of Glastirem (a Jacobite of 1715) had a sasine on the lands of Blelack for money owing to him by John Gordon (then younger of Blelack), the cautioners being James Gordon of Letterfourie and Francis Duguid of Auchinhove.[8]

---

[1] J. M. Bulloch. [2] *Aberdeen Sasines.*

[3] Vide *Aberdeen Sasines*, 1716 and 1718.

[4] *Aberdeen Sasines.* [5] *Ibid.* [6] *Ibid.*

[7] Col. J. Allardyce, *Historical Papers Relating to the Jacobite Period*, vol. i, pp. 20, 23.

[8] *Aberdeen Sasines.*

John Gordon of Blelack
in 1667
had succeeded his elder brother, Alexander.
Dead before 1675.

Charles, Charter 1684,	Alexander,	George,
Laird in 1696; m. Agnes Gordon	Laird in 1708 and 1715;	alive in 1700.
of Craig, 2 daughters.	married Barbara Stewart.	
Died before 1700,	He died in 1724.	
when Alexander was of		
Blelack.		

John,	Charles,
younger of Blelack,	succeeded John.
in 1718.	Was " out " in the '45 ;
Succ. 1724, d. 1726.	married Anne Urquhart.

PARISH OF MIGVIE.

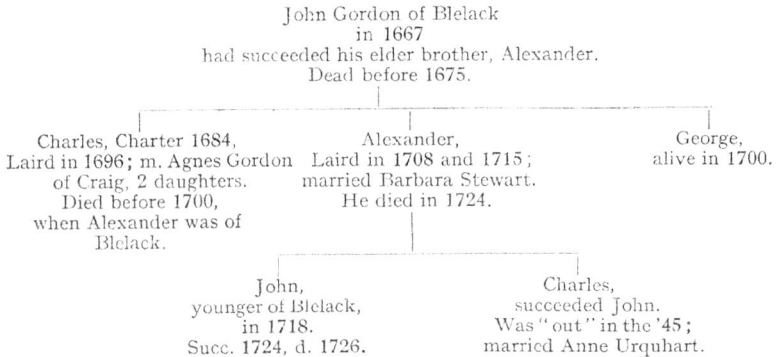

JOHN INNES OF SINNAHARD, FOR LORD ELPHINSTONE.

In the *Poll Book* of 1696 appears the Valuation of the lands "sometyme belonging to my Lord Elphinstone, now to George Forbes of Skellater, Mr. John Innes of Culquoich, and William Forbes" (i.e. of Skellater).

Alexander Innes of Towie and Sinnahard (who also bought Culquoich), a burgess of Aberdeen in 1667, had been cited, in 1668, for Sabbath-breaking.[1]   He died in 1682, aged 56, and is buried in Migvie, with his wife, Isobel Boswell. "Mr. John Innes," of the *Poll Book*, married Barbara, daughter of John Forbes of Leslie, and his son, John Leslie, 4th of Sinnahard, was the laird in 1715. He married Anna Hay of Arnbath, and she had sasine 20th September, 1715, Walter Hay of Lickleyhead, her uncle, appearing for her.   John Innes died in 1725.[2]

His son, John, 5th of Sinnahard, died without issue, and was succeeded by Patrick, his father's brother.

On 14th May, 1709, Mr. John Innes, 3rd of Sinnahard, and John Innes, younger, his son, had sasine on Sinnahard.[3]

LORD ELPHINSTONE.

John, 8th Lord Elphinstone, brother of the 7th and younger son of the 6th Baron.   Born 1649 and succeeded 1669.   The 1st Lord Elphinstone, who was killed at Flodden, had in addition to the lands in Stirling, which he inherited, received a grant of lands in Aberdeenshire from King James IV.   The 3rd Lord had a grant of the lands of Corgarff.   The 8th Lord, who was a soldier under William III,[4] sold part of his lands.   He married

---

[1] *Records of the Synod of Aberdeen.*

[2] *Innes Papers.*   [3] *Aberdeen Sasines.*

[4] He was a Captain of Dragoons and received the Freedom of Aberdeen in 1690, when his troop was stationed there.   In 1692 he was in Flanders.

Isabel Maitland, grand-daughter of the 3rd Earl of Lauderdale, when she was only 16, and she is reported to have had thirty-six children.[1] He died 24th March, 1718. His fifth son, Charles, was the 9th Lord Elphinstone.[2]

THE LAIRD OF FINZEAN, FOR BLELACK.

In the *Poll Book* of 1696 the Lands of Finzean appear without the name of their laird, Francis Farquharson. In 1715 it was Robert Farquharson, 4th of Finzean (eldest son of Francis, the 3rd Laird), who was served heir in 1707 and died 1741. He was twice married: (1) to Anna Gordon,[3] and (2) to Mary Keith. His son, Francis, succeeded as 5th Laird and, dying without issue in 1786, the succession reverted to the heirs of Donald, fourth son of the 3rd Laird.[4]

BLELACK, FOR OLD LANDS—see LOGIEMAR.

BLELACK, FOR EASTER MIGVIE—see LOGIEMAR.

PITTENTAGGART.

"Arthur Forbes of Pittentaggart to his father Robert Forbes of Pittentaggart, heir general 3rd April 1705."[5]

His mother was Anna Gordon.

On 1st May, 1707, Arthur Forbes had sasine on Pittentaggart.[6] He married Elspet Forbes of Skellater, 7th April, 1687.[7]

SMIDDYHILL, FOR BLELACK—see LOGIEMAR.

In the *Poll Book* of 1696 "John Reed" was of Smiddyhill, classing himself as a gentleman. The family had been long in possession, as Isabella Reid was served heir to Patrick Reid, her father, in the lands of Smiddyhill, in Migvy, in August, 1642.

BLELACK, FOR ISOBEL OGG'S VALUATION.

Alexander Ogg was a tenant on Finzean in 1696. This was probably his daughter.

---

[1] *Gents. Mag.* [2] *Complete Peerage*, vol. v.
[3] On 1st October, 1707, Anna Gordon, Lady Finzean, had sasine for her liferent.
[4] *Farquharson Genealogies.* [5] *Service of Heirs.*
[6] *Aberdeen Sasines.* [7] *Strathdon Reg.*

PARISH OF COLDSTONE.

Invercauld—for Pittalochie and Melgome.

These were both portions of the Invercauld estate in 1715. In the list of Freeholders of Aberdeenshire for 1690 "Elphinstone of Melgum" appears.[1]

Whitehouse.

Harry Farquharson of Whitehouse, third Farquharson laird, was the son by the second marriage of Mr. James Farquharson, 1st of Whitehouse, who married (1) Marion Hay, and had James, younger of Whitehouse, (2) Anna, daughter of Colonel Thomas Gardyne, and by her had Harry of Whitehouse, the laird of the '15, who married (1) Barbara Ross of Auchlossan, and had Francis, who gave up the wadset on Whitehouse and bought Shiels, taking sasine on the latter on 18th April, 1726. Harry was a Jacobite of the '15. Harry married, secondly, Elspet Harper, who had been his servant, and by her had Harry of Whitehouse-Mill ; killed at Culloden.

"Harry Farquharson was made prisoner in his own house for being in the army at Perth"[2] (1715). He, Henry or Harry (above), died before 22nd October, 1716, and was succeeded by his son, Captain Francis, who was taken prisoner at Preston and was carried to London but afterwards acquitted, 17th July, 1717.[3] Captain Francis married Effie Ross of Auchlossan and died 1733, leaving a son, Harry Farquharson of Shiels.

To a long letter, now in the Record Office (written from the Marshalsea prison by John Farquharson of Invercauld to Colonel Francis Farquharson at the Hague, begging for assistance in placing his case before the Government, that he may not be transported), a postscript is added— "Your cousin Francis Farquharson, younger off Whitehouse, hath the misfortune to be my fellow prisoner, taken out of my house with me, and desires your mention off him in your recommendation."[4]

Family of Whitehouse.

Donald Og, the Royalist Colonel, was killed at Aberdeen, 15th March, 1645. His son, Charles of Monaltrie, who had daughters only, was obliged by poverty to dispose of his estate in 1702 to Alexander Farquharson, youngest brother of John of Invercauld, whose son was Francis of Monaltrie of the '45.

---

[1] Kennedy's *Annals of Aberdeen*, vol. ii, p. 494. [2] Brouchdearg MS.
[3] *Warrant Book, P.R.O.* [4] *P.R.O. S.P.* 54.11.165.

James, younger brother of Donald Og, was first of Whitehouse, d. 1666.
Married (1) Marion Hay,   Married (2) Anne, daughter of
Col. Gardyne.

James, 2nd of   David.   Harry, 3rd of Whitehouse,
Whitehouse,   Married Anna   a prisoner 1715,
descendants   Farquharson.   d. 1716.
extinct.   Married (1) Barbara   (2) Elizabeth
His wife was   Ross of   Harper.
Elizabeth McGhie.   Auchlossan.
She d. 1725.

Francis, 4th of   Charles.   John,   Harry, 7th,   James.
Whitehouse, d. 1733.   a surgeon   fell at   *o.s.p.*
Married Euphemia Ross   in London.   Culloden,
of Auchlossan,   1746.
bought Shiels.   Married Barbara
Gordon of
Hallhead.

Harry, 5th   Francis.   Peter,   Harry.   William,   James.   Robert.
(and of Shiels).   *o.s.p.*   wounded at   *o.s.p.*   M.D.
Married Jane   Preston.   Married
Ross of Tilliesnaught.   Marg. Souper.

Patrick.

Harry.   Charles.   Alexander 6th.   Andrew.
o.s.p.   *o.s.p.*   *o.s.p.*   *o.s.p.*
and was succeeded by   succeeded by George
his great-uncle, Harry,   Young Leslie, a
as 7th laird.   cousin, who assumed
name of Farquharson

—*Farquharson Genealogies.*

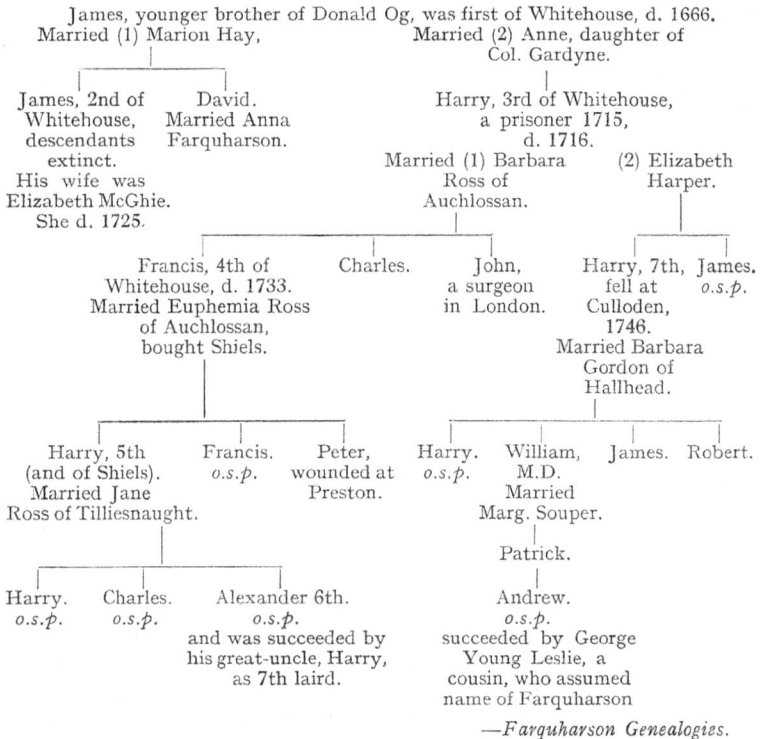

AIRS OF ROBERT DOUGLAS, FOR BLACKMILL—*D*. (This is the first case of Double Cess in the Roll.)

Mr. Robert Douglas of Blackmill died in 1725 (his father also being Robert). His will is in the Commissariot of Aberdeen. His son, a third Robert Douglas, *son* of Robert Douglas of Blackmill, was served heir to his great-grandfather, William Douglas, Minister of Aboyne, on 10th October, 1730. William was a great Royalist, deposed from his living in 1644.

The heirs of Mr. William Douglas appear in the *Poll Book*, 1696.

BLELACK, FOR SKENE—see PARISH OF SKENE.

John Skene, 15th Laird of Skene, married Jean, daughter of Alexander Burnett of Leys ; he died in 1680, leaving a son, Alexander, who succeeded him as 16th laird—see Parish of Skene.[1]

[1] *Memoirs of the Family of Skene of Skene*, p. 37.

EARL OF ABOYNE, FOR GEORGE ANDERSON'S VALUATION—For the Earl, see PARISH OF ABOYNE.

The Andersons of Tulloch had been there for generations. George Anderson, in 1650, had a son, Alexander, and he again a son, George.[1]

PARISH OF COUL.

THE EARL OF ABOYNE (see below).

THE LAIRD OF DRUM, FOR COUL.

The land in this parish was chiefly owned by Sir William Forbes of Craigievar and Alexander Irvine of Drum.

COULL, and the mill of Coull, were occupied by Irvine's tenants; AUCHTERFOULL and Auchtercoull as well.

Gellan was in the hands of Lord Aboyne, and Craigievar owned almost all the rest.

THE LAIRD OF CRAIGIEVAR—*D*—see PARISH OF FINTRAY.

He pays Double Cess.

PARISH OF ABOYNE.

THE EARL OF ABOYNE.

John, 3rd Earl of Aboyne, son of Charles, 2nd Earl, and Lady Elizabeth Lyon, succeeded in 1702 as an infant, and was still a minor in 1715. The date of his birth is not known, but he married in 1725, Grace, daughter of Lord Carnwarth, and he is surmised to have been about fourteen at the time of the Rising. The *Scots Peerage* says he was "a child." But Joseph Robertson (*Book of Bon-Accord*), quoting a contemporary MS., says that on 3rd October, 1715, when Lord Huntly and others rode into Aberdeen to proclaim King James VII, "my Lord Fraser and my Lord Aboyne" were also present, so he was able to bear arms.

He died at an early age, when probably little over 30, 7th April, 1732, leaving a son, Charles, who succeeded as 4th Earl.

The actual power at the moment of the Rising of the '15 was wielded by the boy's uncle, the Hon. John Gordon, third son of Charles, 1st Earl of Aboyne, and Lady Elizabeth Lyon, and brother of the 2nd Earl. He was born in 1677 and educated almost entirely abroad. In his own petition, now in the Public Record Office,[2] he states that he only returned from abroad about a year before the Rising, in order to look after the affairs of his "infant nephew," and lived quietly with his brother George at Dee Castle. The other guardian of the young Earl was his maternal uncle, Patrick Lyon of Auchterhouse, a declared Jacobite, and John

---

[1] *Aberdeen Sasines.*

[2] *S.P.* 35.6.86. A copy is also among the MS. in the City Chambers in Edinburgh.

Gordon's contention was that on the occasions when he was known to have been at Mar's headquarters he had only gone to consult with his fellow guardian. He certainly deliberately absented himself from Mar's famous hunting party on 26th August, 1715, though he met Mar at Inverernan,[1] and it is at least doubtful whether he was ever an *active* Jacobite. He was, however, imprisoned, and was among those conveyed to Carlisle Castle, December, 1716, but was afterwards liberated. He died in Edinburgh in 1762.[2] Lady Elizabeth Lyon, mother of the Hon. John Gordon, was aunt to the Lady Elizabeth Lyon, wife of his brother, and mother of the young Earl. The latter married, secondly, Patrick, 3rd Lord Kinnaird, and thirdly, Captain Alexander Grant.[3]

JAMES MIDLTOUN, FOR EARL OF ABOYNE.

In 1667 there was a " John Midleton of Dalquhing" in this parish, but his descendants are not known.

AUCHINHOVE.

The ninth laird, Robert Duguid, son of Francis Duguid, eighth laird of Auchinhove, and his wife, Marie Abercromby (who had sasine in 1676).[4] Francis died in 1698. He was succeeded by his eldest son, *Robert* (below), served heir in 1698, who married Teresa, third daughter of Count Patrick Leslie of Balquhain, and their son, Patrick Leslie Duguid, was a Jacobite of the '45. Although only a boy of 15, Patrick also took part in the Rising of 1715. He succeeded to Auchinhove on his father's death in 1731, and to the Leslie estates in 1775, having received a pardon for his share in the '45. Alexander Duguid, younger brother of Robert and uncle of Patrick, was also "out" in the '15, and was in Lord Huntly's squadron at Sheriffmuir.

6. William Duguid of Auchinhove, 6th Laird.
   Married Mary Forbes of Barnes.

7. Francis, succeeded about 1656.
   Married Elizabeth Seton, d. 1675.

8. Francis, took the Poll in Lumphanan.
   Married Marie Abercromby, and had sasine 1676.
   d. 1698.

9. Robert. Married (1669) Teresa Leslie   Alexander.
   of Balquhain, d. 1731.   "Out" in the '15.

10. Patrick Leslie Duguid, born 1700.
    "Out" both in 1715 and 1745.

[1] *S.P.* 54.7.96.

[2] A further curious plea advanced by the Hon. John Gordon is, that having lived so long abroad he did not know the law nor the danger of consorting with rebels, and that he " never was conversant in military affairs, but always addicted to letters."

[3] *Complete Peerage*, vol. i.   [4] *Aberdeen Sasines*.

KIRKTOWN OF ABOYNE—*D.*

John Farquharson of Kirktown of Aboyne, great-grandson of Robert, 1st of Invercauld, disponed his lands in 1671 to his son, Thomas, who had sasine on them, 30th September, 1674. John Farquharson (the son of Thomas) was "out" in the '15 and was one of those acquitted without trial.[1] John afterwards sold the lands to Robert Farquharson of Finzean in 1719 ; sasine, dated 14th February, 1722.[2]

But the man in possession of Kirkton of Aboyne at the time of the Rising was a Hanoverian, from whom Double Cess was asked, and from a sasine of date 29th June, 1715, it is known that he was John Strachan, presumably a relative of John Farquharson, whose mother was Jean Strachan, daughter to the Parson of Coldstone.

The sasine is in favour of "John Strachan of Kirktown of Aboyne, Mrs. Elizabeth Lesly, his spouse, Alexander, James, John, Anne, Elizabeth, and Mary, his children."[3] That his ownership of the estate was only temporary is proved by the fact that it was John Farquharson who sold it to Finzean four years later.

It is conjectured either that Strachan advanced money on the estate or that he took possession of it to save it from forfeiture, when his cousin went "out" with Mar, a procedure often followed both in 1715 and in 1745.

John Farquharson was twice married: (1) to Helen Muir, daughter of Dr. William Muir, Archdeacon of St. Andrews, on 20th April, 1702,[4] and (2), to a daughter of Dr. Alexander Penycuik of Newhall of Romanno.

The Brouchdearg MS. says of him, "This John was taken at Preston and kept at London till he brought himself off at his trial by drawing up such a scheme for his exculpation as procured him a pardon on first hearing of it. . . . He was bred a writer."[5]

FINZEAN—*D.*

Robert Farquharson (above).

DR. GORDON, FOR BENNACRAIG.

Balnacraig, in Aboyne, was in 1696 in the hands of William Davidson, with his lady and six children. The son of William Davidson had a wife of the name of Gordon, and both were buried in the Snow Church, Old Aberdeen, 9th July, 1726.

---

[1] *Patten's History.*　　　　[2] *Aberdeen Sasines.*
[3] *Ibid.*　　　　[4] *Canongate Marriage Register.*
[5] A. M. Mackintosh, *Farquharson Genealogies.*

BENNACRAIG, FOR WATERSYDE.

John Wight of "Watersyde of Balnacraig." As *James* Wight and his wife, Margaret Chalmers, had been in Watersyde of Balnacraig from 1659,[1] and she had a child in 1664, they were presumably both dead by 1715. Their son, John, was there in 1700.[2]

PARISH OF BIRSSE.

LAIRD OF FINZEAN—*D.*

Robert Farquharson, as before, Parish of Migvie.

TORWINLACHIE—*D.*

This, once owned by Strachans (Alexander Strachan had sasine in 1659), was in 1715 the property of Duncan Sievewright, who also owned the next estate.

MIGSTRATH—*D.*

Duncan Sievewright eventually purchased several properties in Birsse and was locally known as "Cutty Sievewright" in 1696.

He is entered in the *Poll Book* as owner of "Drumnachie" in 1696, at which time he was tenant of Migstrath, the *owner* being Francis Garden, whose son, John Garden of Migstrath, appeared personally for Anna Farquharson, daughter of Donald Farquharson of Migstrath, in 1708. Sievewright had a wife and two daughters, with James Sievewright, another tenant.[3]

KIRKTOUN—THE EARL OF ABOYNE.

BALFOUR FARQUHARSON.

Donald, son of the Donald Farquharson (second son to Alexander Farquharson of Finzean and ancestor of the present laird of Finzean), who was of Balfour in 1667. His wife was Anne Forbes, sister or daughter of William Forbes of Corsindae, and his son, Donald, above, was in possession in 1696 and 1715.[4] Anna Farquharson, his daughter, married John Garden of Migstrath (above). The younger Donald married, in 1713, Jean Gillanders, and with her had sasine on the estate on the 9th January in that year.[5]

BIRSEBEG—*D.*

JOHN TURNER.

This property was in 1667 in the hands of Alexander Ross, but on his death in 1698 it passed into those of John Turner, who was formerly

---

[1] *Records of Aboyne*, p. 323.　　[2] *Ibid.*　　[3] *Aberdeen Sasines.*
[4] *Fettercairn Papers.*　　[5] *Aberdeen Sasines.*

portioner of Kinminity, and appears in Birssebeg in the *Poll Book*, 1696. He was served heir, also in 1698, to John Turner, his great-uncle. Turner paid Double Cess, both here and for his half of Kilminaty. Margaret Ross, his wife, had sasine for her life-rent on Kilminaty in 1698.[1]

BIRSEMOIR, FOR INVEREBRY.

ADAM GORDON.

Alexander Gordon of Birsemoir had owned this estate in 1667. In 1696 it belonged to Mr. Robert Forbes, Advocate, Edinburgh, who advanced money on it, but in November, 1713, Adam Gordon, son of Alexander, had a fresh sasine on the lands.[2] Inverebry is in Methlick.

DRUMMACHIE. (Sievewright as above.)

Donald Farquharson had sasine in January, 1700.

TURNER'S HALF OF KILMINATY (as above)—*D*.

KIRK SESSION OF BIRSSE FOR ¼ OF KILMINATY.

James Turner, portioner of Birsse, had borrowed money from the Kirk Session in 1646.[3] His grandson had endeavoured to free himself from the bond granted, but the Kirk Session was not satisfied and apparently some portion of it still remained owing.

JAMES MALCOM FOR ¼ OF KILMINATY—*D*.

In 1696 " James Malcome " possessed a portion of Kilminaty of exactly the same value as in 1715, viz., £26 13s. 4d. His parents were "Andrew Malcome" of Kilminaty and Jean Sievewright.

In 1760 Kilminaty also was sold to Duncan Sievewright.

TILLIESNAUGHT—*D*. [Hew Ross.]

Alexander Ross was there in 1696. His family is not given at that date, but "John Ross, in mains of Tilliesnaught" was probably his brother.

Hew Ross (or Rose—they were of the family of Kilravock, and the name was spelt both ways) succeeded his father, Alexander, before 1711 ; he had sasine 29th December in that year ; but was only served heir in 1720,[4] and sold the estate of Tilliesnaught to the family of Forbes, who re-named it Ballogie, after their property in Midmar (see pages 65-67).

---

[1] *Aberdeen Sasines.*
[3] *Kirk Session Records of Birse.*
[2] *Ibid.*
[4] *Service of Heirs.*

Inverchatt—*D*.

George Stewart, son of Duncan Stewart and Isabella Reid, who was in possession in 1696. The *Poll Book* gives "his lady (her name was Margaret Keith) and two sons, Mr. George and Hendrie, and two daughters, Jean and Margaret." On 26th April, 1700, George Stewart of Inverchatt signed the bond to apprehend malefactors.[1]

Tilliefroskie—*D*.

By 1696 the lands of Tilliefroskie, which had belonged to the family of Gardyne, were in the hands of "James Auchterlony," with wife and four children.[2] Margaret, daughter of James Buchan, fourth of Auchmacoy, married Peter Ochterlonie of Tilliefroskie.[3]

Captain David Ochterlonie, who fell at Quebec with General Wolfe, was of this family.

John Forbes, for Easterclune—*D*.

Easter Clune, which had been in 1667 in the hands of the widow of Mr. John Ross, the minister, was owned in 1696, along with Annochie, by William Davidson of Balnacraig—*q.v.*

(John Forbes in this case is probably only the name of the collector, which has slipped into the body of the list.)

Westerclune—*D*.

Alexander Ross of Wester Clune was in possession in 1696 with Mary Ross, his daughter.

(All the family of Ross, with the majority of the other proprietors in the parish of Birse, were Hanoverians. They were just beyond the jurisdiction of the Earl of Mar and "Black Jock" of Inverernan.)

Glencatt.

In 1695 George Mortimer in Glencatt was served heir to "Captain" John Mortimer, his father.[4] His brother, William Mortimer, was of Glencatt in 1696. He was second son of John Mortimer and his wife, Elizabeth Ross, who had sasine in 1664. "The said William Mortimer will class himself no otherwayes but as ane gentleman, with his wife and son in familie." [5]

These Mortimers were of the old family of Craigievar, which, as the name shows, came from England.

---

[1] Allardyce, *Historical Papers*, vol. i, p. 20. [2] *Poll Book.*
[3] *Auchmacoy Papers.* [4] *Service of Heirs.* [5] *Poll Book.*

MARIEWELL—(MIN.).

The Minister of Birse in 1696 was Mr. David Ogilvie.

"Marywall" was part of the estate of Migstrath and the tenant was James Ross.

PARISH OF KINCAIRDEN.

MILL OF KINCAIRDEN.

George Gordon, Mill of Kincardine, son of John Gordon of the same place, had sasine on the lands 23rd December, 1710. He was one of those Jacobites captured at Dunfermline, 24th October, 1715, and was marched from Stirling to Carlisle on 3rd September.[1] He was subsequently liberated, and died in 1716. His wife was Agnes Gordon, and he appears in the *Poll Book* of 1696 as "heritor and possessor of said lands, with his wife" but no child, as his son, Francis Gordon of Kincardine-Mill (the Jacobite of 1745, Quarter-master General of the Prince's Army), was not born till after 1710. Francis was apprenticed to the law in 1731 ; was served heir to his father, George, on 5th July, 1722, and to his grandfather, John, in 1744.

AUCHLOSSEN—see also PARISH OF LUMPHANAN.

The last of the old family of Ross of Auchlossan was Francis Ross, killed at Malplaquet, 1709, when the estate was sold by his creditors. The representation of the family devolved upon the Rosses of Arnage.

KIRKTOWN OF KINCAIRDEN.

John Forbes of Kincardine, whose wife was Nicolas Forbes, only daughter to Mr. John Forbes, Parish of Kincardine. Together they had sasine, 26th September, 1709.[2]

DILHAIKIE—*D.*

The name of the owner of 1696 is not given in the *Poll Book*. The estate was valued at £470, exactly as in 1715.

DORS, FOR MIDBELTY—*D.*

"Midlettie" in the *Poll Book* (which is probably the same place) was in 1696 part of the estate of Durris (Dores or Dors) and the tenant was John Doune.

Sir Peter Fraser of Durris was the last laird of Durris of that name. The estate was bought by his father, Sir Alexander,[3] from Lord Fraser.

---

[1] *S.P.* 54.12.152.　　　　　[2] *Aberdeen Sasines.*

[3] Sir Alexander Fraser was twice married : (1) Elizabeth Dochty, and (2) Mary Carey, the mother of Sir Peter.

Sir Peter's daughter and heiress, Carey Fraser, married General Mordaunt, Earl of Peterborough, and through her daughter, Henrietta, Durris came to the second Duke of Gordon, formerly Alexander, Marquis of Huntly, Henrietta's husband.[1]

LORD FORBES, FOR LANDS AND MERCAT—see PARISH OF KEIG.

PROVOST MITCHELL, FOR EASTER BELTIE—*D*.

Easter Beltie appears in the *Poll Book* without any owner, but in 1703 Easter Beltie and Annesley were purchased from Sir Robert Forbes of Learney by Provost Thomas Mitchell, of Aberdeen, who, 13 years later, purchased from Forbes of Tolquhon the estate of Thainston in Kintore. The Provost's first wife was Janet, daughter of Provost Sir Patrick Leslie. His second was Katharine Dun, and his third Jean Mercer, who survived him. He died in 1718 and she in 1740.[2]

BALLOGIE, FOR WESTERBELTIE—*D*.

Westerbeltie, valued at £224 in 1696, has also no owner's name then attached to it. In 1667 Elizabeth Forbes had been there, and it was still in the family, the Cess being paid by Forbes of Ballogie, in the Parish of Midmar. He also paid the Cess for Forbes of "Lernie" (Learney). All these were Hanoverians.

On 25th March, 1706, Alexander Forbes of Ballogie had had sasine on the lands of Bandodle.[3]

CAMPBELL, BURNET—*D*.

William Burnett of Camphill, son of Thomas Burnett.

In the *Poll Book* William Burnett is entered as the heritor and possessor of Camphill in 1696, with his wife and two sons, William and Alexander, and five daughters, Agnes, Jean, Nicholas, Margaret, and Isobel.

The eldest son, William, as "William Burnett junior of Campfield," had sasine on 25th November, 1709. His son was a Jacobite of 1745.[4]

BALLOGIE, FOR LERNIE—*D*.

This was Alexander Forbes of Ballogie, the new laird of Learney, which he had bought from Sir Robert Forbes, Advocate, of Learney in 1704, afterwards of Cluny,[5] who had not held it long. He was third son

---

[1] *Complete Peerage.*

[2] A. M. Munro, *Memorials of the Aldermen and Provosts of Aberdeen.*

[3] *Aberdeen Sasines.*

[4] Taylers' *Jacobites of Aberdeenshire and Banffshire in the '45.*

[5] 21st February, 1704, Sir Robert Forbes, Advocate, and Dame Margaret Elphinstone, his spouse, had sasine on Learney.—*Aberdeen Sasines.*

of Sir John Forbes of Craigievar, second Baronet. On 4th August, 1696, Mr. Alexander Gordon of Learney and James Innes of Artamford had disponed Learney to Mr. Robert Forbes, who then had a charter of the estate, but disponed it very shortly afterwards to Alexander Forbes, younger of Ballogie.[1] Robert Forbes was M.P. for Inverurie, 1700 to 1707. His wife was Margaret, daughter of Sir James Elphinstone of Logie.

RELICT OF CRAIGMYLE.

Dame Nicholas Young, widow of Sir Alexander Burnett of Craigmyle, who died in 1694. She had two daughters and heiresses, Isabel, who was the first of four wives of John Farquharson of Invercauld, and Margaret, who married (1) Sir Charles Maitland of Pitrichie, and (2) Thomas Erskine of Pittodrie. Craigmyle became part of the estate of Invercauld. It was bought by Alexander Farquharson, brother of Invercauld. Dame Nicholas Young re-married, Sir Charles Maitland, second Baronet of Pitrichie (and her daughter married her step-son!). Dame Nicholas appears, however, to have continued to draw her liferent on Craigmyle.

HEIRS OF CRAIGMYLE, FOR CRAIGOUR.

The daughters as above.

PARISH OF LUMPHANAN.

AUCHLOSSEN, FOR INVEREY—AUCHLOSSAN, see KINCARDINE.

This estate, formerly belonging to the Ross family, had been sold to the Farquharsons of Inverey. Charles Farquharson, afterwards of Inverey, second son of "the Black Colonel," is designated in 1708 Farquharson of Auchlossan. He was at Marischal College in 1688–92, and afterwards apprenticed to Sir James Elphinstone.[2]

INVEREY—in CRATHIE PARISH.

Peter Farquharson of Inverey, eldest son of John Farquharson, "the Black Colonel" (who died in 1698), by his first marriage to Margaret Gordon of Leacachy (and thus half-brother to James Farquharson of Balmoral, son of the second marriage to Marjorie Leith of Overhall). Sir Walter Scott describes him as "the second man of the Farquharson Clan and not having so much to lose as Invercauld, was disposed to rise at once, but would have nothing to do with the Earl of Mar until Huntlie persuaded him." He then tried to raise the whole clan, but, as the Master of Sinclair says, he "could only raise about 100 men, for the others would

---

[1] *Learney Papers.*   [2] A. M. Mackintosh, *Farquharson Genealogies.*

take no notice of him as long as Invercauld would not engage." There is no further mention of Peter Farquharson of Inverey's services, though he is sometimes said to have "commanded a battalion." Mar offered him the command of all the Farquharsons, but the Clan would not rise until Invercauld came out, so all that Inverey commanded was his own 100 men. He fought at Sheriffmuir, later was lucky enough to reach the Continent, and returned after the Act of Indemnity, having been wrongly attainted under the name of "Alexander," whereby he escaped forfeiture. He married (1) Margaret Nairn, and (2) Elizabeth Black, and had three sons, William, died young; Joseph, and Benjamin, who survived, and both succeeded to Inverey; and six daughters—Elizabeth, who married John Forbes, son of Craigievar; Rachel, and Rebecca, all three by the first wife. By the second wife, Margaret, Emilia, and Clementina.

His younger brother was the Charles Farquharson, W.S., "of Auchlossan (above), who succeeded Peter's son Benjamin in 1739."[1]

Peter Farquharson died in 1737.

For the eleven Lairds of Inverey, see Crathie Parish, page 61.

CAPTAIN FORBES, FOR A PART OF AUCHINHOVE (*seq.*).

Probably Captain Nathaniel Forbes of Rippachy and Ardgeith, brother to George Forbes, 3rd of Skellater (see page 36), or possibly Captain William Forbes of Blackton (page 203), both distinguished Jacobite soldiers, but more likely the former as being in the same neighbourhood. It might also be Captain John Forbes of Middle Boyndlie, see next Parish.

ROBERT DUGUID, FOR AUCHINHOVE—FOR HIS PART THEREOF, see ABOYNE.

Robert Duguid of Auchinhove, who succeeded to the estate in February, 1698. He married Teresa, third daughter of Count Patrick Leslie of Balquhain.

BANNACRAIG CHALMERS—*D.*

Alexander Chalmers of Bannacraig (not to be confused with Balnacraig in Aboyne). He was the Commissioner for taking up the Poll in 1696, and was there "with his lady (Anna Leith), two sons, Alexander and Evan, and three daughters, Margaret, Anna, and Barbara." On 25th March, 1709, Alexander Chalmers of Bannacraig and Anna Leith, his spouse, had sasine.[2]

PITMURCHIE, FRAN. FRASER.

Francis Fraser, who in 1670 bought Findrack, Pitmurchie, Tolmaads, Drumlassie, Birselassie, and other lands. He was the grandson of Thomas

---

[1] A. M. Mackintosh, *Farquharson Genealogies.*   [2] *Aberdeen Sasines.*

Fraser of Durris. He died 29th April, 1718, leaving a son, Francis, who married Catherine, daughter of Sir Robert Gordon of Gordonston. On 12th October, 1709, "Francis Frasers elder and younger" of Pitmurchie had sasine on the estate.[1]

Sir Peter Fraser of Durris was a cousin.

FINLARGUE, FR. FRASER (as above).

CAMPHILL FORBES (CAMFIELD in the *Poll Book*).

Charles Forbes was son of William Forbes of Campfield or Camphill. Died 1728.

Agnes Forbes, third lawful daughter of William Forbes of Campfield, married Walter Kinnaird of Montcoffer. Marriage contract at Castle Forbes, dated 30th August, 1697.[2] Walter Kinnaird died 1714; he was the eldest son of John Kinnaird and Violet Abercromby of Birkenbog (see page 198).

CRAIGIEVAR, FOR KINTOCHER—*D*.

This in 1696 was part of the estate of Campfield.

BURNSIDE, CHARLES MCHARDIE.

Part of the estate of Auchlossan in 1696. Charles McHardie was of the family who owned Crathienard and Daldownie.

ROSS OF CLOACK—*D*. [Charles Ross.]

Son of Hew of 1667. As "C. Ross of Cloak" he signs the bond to apprehend malefactors, 26th April, 1700.[3] In 1672 Elizabeth Falconer, spouse to William Ross of Cloak, had sasine on Cloak.

On 8th September, 1703, Nicolas Ross had sasine on Cloak for her liferent. She was the daughter of Francis Ross of Auchlossan, and wife of Charles Ross, the laird of 1715.

PARISH OF KINDROCHIT.

INVEREY—PARISH OF LUMPHANAN.

DALMORE.

Kenneth Mackenzie, with his son, James Mackenzie of Dalmore (now Mar Lodge). James was the eldest son of Kenneth Mackenzie, Laird of Dalmore, who was the owner in 1696 and 1715. In 1699 "Kenneth Mackenzie of Dalmore" signed a heritor's bond, he was also

---

[1] *Aberdeen Sasines.*   [2] *Castle Forbes Papers.*
[3] Allardyce, *Historical Papers*, vol. i, p. 23.

Elder of the Parish of Kindrochit in 1701.[1] James was "younger of Dalmore" when he took part in the Rising of 1715, his activities in which ruined his father completely. He was served heir to his father in 1723. In 1728 he married "Isobel Douglas of Tilwhilly," had a daughter, Agnes, and died before 1733, when his brother Donald was served heir to him. Later in the 18th century Dalmore was added to the large estates of the Earl of Fife.

INVERCAULD—PARISH OF CRATHIE.

CAMBASNAKIST.

Donald Farquharson of "Comesnakist," in the *Poll Book*, with his lady, his four children and his mother. He was still the owner in 1715.

EARL OF MAR, FOR FEU-DUTIES AND LANDS.

AUCHINDRYNE.

This property was still in the hands of Lewis Farquharson, to whom it had been adjudged in 1678 by the Earl of Mar. He was the eldest son of James Farquharson, first of Inverey, and his second wife, Agnes Ferries. He signed the heritors' bond, 26th April, 1700, as "Lud. Farquharson, Auchendryne." His first wife was Margaret Farquharson of Allanaquoich. He is said to have declared that though he was in 1715 too old to be of much use he "could see that his lads did their duty and shoot them if they failed." The six sons were Alexander and John, William, Donald, Charles, and James ; he had also three daughters. Alexander, the eldest son, married Claudia Innes of Drumgask and died in 1727, before his father. Alexander, son of Alexander and Claudia, succeeded both to Auchindryne and Inverey.[2]

ALLANAQUOICH.

The laird in 1715 was John, son of Alexander, eldest son of Donald, 2nd of Allanaquoich, by his first wife, Violet Troup. John's uncle was Robert Farquharson, second son of Donald, 2nd of Allanaquoich, and his *second* wife, Helen Garden of Bellamoir. Robert was taken at Preston and transported to Virginia, although over 60 years of age (his petition is in the Record Office).[3] He returned and died at home, having previously married Mary Gordon, daughter to Minmore, and left a natural son. His nephew John (above) was an elder in 1701 in Kindrochit parish.[4]

---

[1] *Kirk Session Records.*
[2] A. M. Mackintosh, *Farquharson Genealogies.*
[3] *S.P.* 54.26.123.   [4] *Kirk Session Records.*

JOHN GREWER, ELDER AND YOUNGER.

By 1696 the Grewers of Auchallater had been succeeded in these lands by Grigor and Donald Erskine, the Grewers becoming tenants ; Donald Erskine had sasine on a portion of the estate as early as 15th August, 1662.[1]

JOHN ARESKINE (ERSKINE).

The son of Donald Erskine above. The father of Donald had been another John, and had held land in Wester Micras from the Earl of Mar from 1660 to 1670. John Erskine was "of Micras" in 1696.

PARISH OF GLENGAIRN.

EARL OF ABOYNE—see ABOYNE.

EARL OF MAR, FOR TAMBELLY.

These lands were part of the estate of Invercauld, and Barbara, daughter of Robert Farquharson, second laird of Invercauld, and wife of Francis Ross of Auchlossan, had sasine on them from her father as her marriage portion ; this Francis Ross died in 1690.

Presumably the Laird of Invercauld paid the Cess on them in 1715. They had been seized by Mar when in possession of Invercauld. In 1696 Arthur Farquharson was the tenant. The place is now called Balgairn.[2]

ABERGELDIE.

Charles Gordon of Abergeldie in 1715 was the tenth laird, the son of Peter Gordon of Minmore ; he married before 1690 Rachel Gordon, the heiress of Abergeldie, daughter of Alexander Gordon, 8th of Abergeldie, and Euphemia Graham of Morphie (her brother John having no children). Charles Gordon held the castle of Abergeldie in 1689–1690 for General Mackay, and by the good offices of the General, who was then very powerful in Scotland, he obtained possession of the estate in his wife's name after the death of her brother, John, which occurred in 1698.

Charles Gordon was succeeded by his son, Peter Gordon, who was at Marischal College in 1706, and subsequently married Alison Hunter.

(Abergeldie at the time of the Poll—1696—was in the hands of John, the ninth laird, with his wife, Elizabeth Rose of Kilravock, the Lady Dowager, Euphemia Graham, being still alive.)

Charles Gordon of Abergeldie had the intention of becoming a Jacobite but did not carry it out. In a letter from George Drummond,

[1] *Aberdeen Sasines.*   [2] *Records of Invercauld.*

afterwards Provost of Edinburgh, to Lord Polwarth, September, **1715**, is found—"Upon Friday last the Lairds of Invercauld and Abergeldie deserted and went off from the Earl of Mar, having refused to go along with him to the hazardy of their lives and fortunes, upon which his Lordship threatened to burn Invercauld's house."[1]

An anonymous spy wrote to Sir James Steuart of Goodtrees—"The Earl of Mar and the rest were extremely out of temper by the Lairds of Invercauld, Abergeldie and some others deserting them."[2]   As already stated, Invercauld joined the Jacobite army later on and did good service, but Gordon apparently did not.

Charles and Rachel Gordon had three sons, Peter, Alexander, and Joseph.   Peter succeeded his father as eleventh laird, and was himself succeeded by his eldest son Charles, twelfth laird, who was served heir to him, 25th October, 1737.   Joseph, the third son of Charles and Rachel, was of Birkhall.   Alexander, the second son, had an arent on Abergeldie, 5th September, 1710.[3]

CULTS, FARQUHARSON. [Patrick Farquharson.]

Findlay Farquharson had received before 1696 a grant of these lands. They afterwards came into the possession of the family of Farquharson of Monaltrie.   But on 3rd March, 1713, Patrick and Anna Farquharsons had sasine on Cults and Rynnabreck.[4]

Colonel Findlay Farquharson was the son of Alexander, third son of Robert, 1st of Invercauld.   He had a son, Arthur, who was of Cults, and Arthur's son, Harry, was taken prisoner at Preston and transported to Virginia.   He afterwards served in Spain.   He married Elizabeth Morgan, heiress of Torgalter, but left no issue.[5]

Harry was either nephew or first cousin to Patrick.

ALEX. McGRIGOR.

A scion of the family of Inverenzie (see page 4).

In 1696 Malcom McGrigor of "Delfade" held the lands for himself and representing the heirs of Duncan McGrigor of Ardochie, also the lands of Rickaharne.

John McGrigor was tenant of Ardochie and Grigor McGrigor, John McGrigor, and Archibald McGrigor were tenants in Inverenzie, in the same year.   Malcolm McGrigor had servants of the same name, who were probably relatives : Neill McGregor and Alistair McGregor, who may be the same as Alex. (above).

"Captain McGregor" of the '45 was the grandson of Malcolm (above).

[1] Marchmont MS. ; Hist. MS. Commission, *14th Report.*
[2] *Paper in P.R.O., S.P.* 54.8.   [3] *Aberdeen Sasines.*   [4] *Ibid.*
[5] A. M. Mackintosh, *Farquharson Genealogies.*

INVERCAULD—see CRATHIE.

THOMAS AND JAMES KEIRS.

In 1696 Thomas Keirs' valuation for the lands of Strulan was £80, the same amount as in 1715. He had associated with him "Alaster and Archibald Keirs" and Duncan, and the wives of all three.

PARISH OF CRATHIE.

TULLOCHOY.

James Farquharson of Tullochoy received these lands from his brother, Lewis Farquharson of Auchindryne, on 10th July, 1679, but he did not take sasine on them until eight years later. He married Agnes Ochterlonie, daughter of the minister of Fordoun, and had three sons, James, David, and Alexander. The date of his death is not known, but by 1727 his eldest son, James, was in possession, as on 20th October that year he and his wife, Marjory Farquharson, had sasine on Tullochoy and Balnalan.[1] Marjory was one of the five daughters of Charles Farquharson of Monaltrie and Elizabeth, daughter of "the Black Colonel"; she is sometimes called May.[2]

INVERCAULD.

John Farquharson, second son of Alexander Farquharson of Invercauld and his wife, Isabella Mackintosh. He was born in 1674 and married four times :—

(1) Isabella Burnett of Craigmyle,[3] (2) Christian Menzies of Weem, (3) Margaret Murray, grand-daughter of the 1st Marquis of Athole, and (4) Jean Forbes of Waterton.

He was not at all a convinced Jacobite, was not present at the Hunting Party at Aboyne, and when Mar came to his house at Invercauld he absented himself and complained that in his absence his servants were ill-treated and forced out.[4] Later, whether from compulsion or conviction, he joined himself to the Jacobite army and was with the contingent which marched into England. At the battle of Preston he greatly distinguished himself, being in command of the Guard of Foot at the Bridge, and according to Patten (an otherwise inimical witness) "was a good officer and a very bold man and would have defended that Pass to the very last drop and till the rest had advanced and drawn themselves out of the town, but he was ordered to retreat to Preston. This was another wrong step." [5]

---

[1] *Aberdeen Sasines.*   [2] A. M. Mackintosh, *Farquharson Genealogies.*
[3] On 15th May, 1712, Isabel Burnett, "Lady Invercauld," had sasine.
[4] *S.P.* 54.26.123.
[5] Patten's *History of the Rebellion*, written after he had left the Jacobite army and changed his politics.

John Farquharson was taken prisoner and confined for nine months in the Marshalsea, during which time he sent various petitions to Scottish M.P.s and others, stating, among other things, that "he was so far from contributing to the Rebellion that he was instrumental in very much restraining and in some means defeating the treasonable designes of the Earl of Mar." [1]   He was not released until 15th August, 1716, when an "order to the Keeper of the Marshalsea, to set at liberty Mr. John Farquharson of Invercauld" was signed by Lord Townshend; [2] a week later he was at Hampton Court and was presented to the Prince and Princess of Wales.   It was doubtless considered politic thus to secure his loyalty in the future.   He survived until 1750, and at the second Jacobite Rising in 1745, he remained firmly on the side of the Government. He was succeeded by his son, James.

MONALTRIE. [Alexander Farquharson, of the Second Family of Monaltrie.]

Charles Farquharson, Monaltrie, son of Donald Og, the famous Royalist Colonel, married Elizabeth, daughter of John Farquharson, the "Black Colonel," in 1694.   He was elder of Crathie in 1701.   He had five daughters who were served heirs portioners to him in 1723 (Elizabeth, Isabella, Margaret, Marjorie, and Barbara).[3]   But they did not succeed to the estate, which had passed (by 1702) into the lands of Alexander Farquharson, brother of John of Invercauld, who had sasine on Monaltrie and Daldownie, 23rd March, 1711, and again 9th August, 1715.[4]   He was the father of Francis Farquharson, the Monaltrie of the '45, whose mother was Anna Farquharson of Finzean.

BALMURRELL.

Charles Farquharson, son of William Farquharson of Inverey and his second wife, Agnes or Anna Gordon, daughter of Alexander Gordon of Abergeldie, succeeded to Balmoral on his father's death.

Charles was half-brother to John of Inverey, "the Black Colonel," and half-uncle to John's son, Peter.

He had taken part in the campaign under Dundee in 1689,[5] after which he retired to France (his estates being administered by his nephew, James), but was frequently employed as a Jacobite messenger ; his last recorded journey to Scotland being 25th April, 1708 (the date of his instructions from James).   He died at St. Germains, the date being long unknown,

[1] *S.P.* 54.11.165.   [2] *S.P. Entry book*, 8.
[3] *Service of Heirs.*   [4] *Aberdeen Sasines.*
[5] He is described as " Major Farcharson " in one of Dundee's own letters to Lord Melfort, 28th June, 1689.—Macpherson's *Original Papers.*

save that it was subsequent to 1710, when he signed a document there ; but the register of burials at St. Germains show it to have taken place in 1718.[1] James, his half-nephew, above mentioned, was the youngest son of "the Black Colonel," himself a Jacobite of 1715 and 1745, and afterwards known as "Balmurell the brave."

In 1715 he was A.D.C. to Mar, and a Major. In 1745 he commanded a battalion at Falkirk, where he was wounded. He was one of those excepted from the Act of Indemnity of 1747. His mother was Marjory Leith, daughter of George Leith of Overhall, and he married Jean Leith, his cousin, but had no children. He was injured by a fall over the cliffs at Pennan on the occasion in 1716 when Charles, Lord Fraser, lost his life, but Balmoral recovered, as he did also from wounds in the '45. He died about 1753, having succeeded in 1750 to *all* the estates of his half-brothers, Peter of Inverey and Charles of Auchlossan. He was the eighth laird. The next heir, who held the estates for a few months only, was John Farquharson, 9th of Inverey, grandson of John of Tullich. Alexander of Auchindryne then succeeded as tenth laird.

The Eleven Lairds of Inverey.[2]

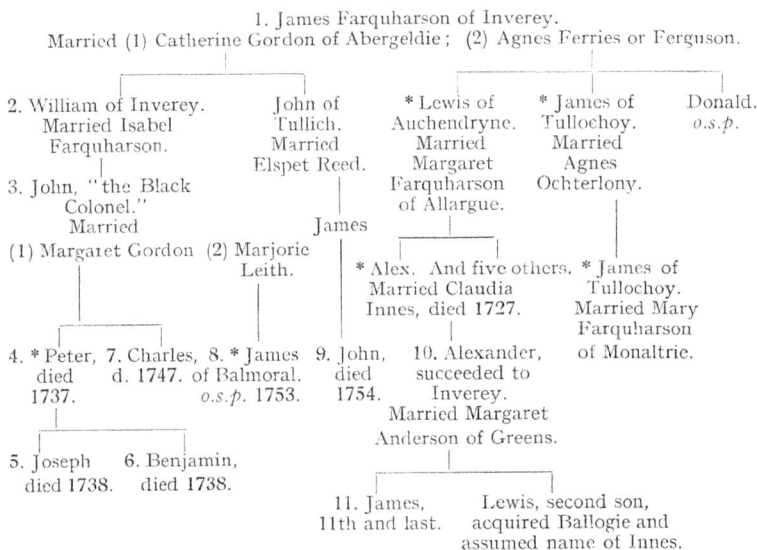

1. James Farquharson of Inverey.
Married (1) Catherine Gordon of Abergeldie ; (2) Agnes Ferries or Ferguson.

2. William of Inverey. Married Isabel Farquharson.	John of Tullich. Married Elspet Reed.	* Lewis of Auchendryne. Married Margaret Farquharson of Allargue.	* James of Tullochoy. Married Agnes Ochterlony.	Donald. *o.s.p.*
3. John, "the Black Colonel." Married (1) Margaret Gordon (2) Marjorie Leith.	James	* Alex. And five others. Married Claudia Innes, died 1727.	* James of Tullochoy. Married Mary Farquharson of Monaltrie.	

4. * Peter, died 1737.	7. Charles, d. 1747.	8. * James of Balmoral. *o.s.p.* 1753.	9. John, died 1754.	10. Alexander, succeeded to Inverey. Married Margaret Anderson of Greens.
5. Joseph died 1738.	6. Benjamin, died 1738.			11. James, 11th and last. Lewis, second son, acquired Ballogie and assumed name of Innes.

Those persons appearing in the Cess Roll are marked with an asterisk.

[1] *Jacobite Extracts from the Parochial Registers.*

[2] Inverey and Auchindryne were sold to the 2nd Lord Fife, 1786, and Balmoral in 1798. The Trustees of the 4th Earl sold the latter to Prince Albert in 1848.

—Family Papers.

ABERGELDIE—see PARISH OF GLENGAIRN.

EDWARD AND ROBERT McHARDIE.

Robert McHardie was husband of Elizabeth Erskine of Torgalter —see Kindrochit in 1667.

The McHardies of Daldownie had been long in possession. In 1696 in the *Poll Book* appears "John McHardy of Daldouny, portioner of Crathie, with wife and son; the deceast Edward McHardy, Janet McHardie his niece, Findlay McHardie, elder of Crathie in 1701, tenant in Crathinard" (of which Duncan Shaw was portioner). John McHardie's wife was Margaret Ochterlonie.[1]

David McHardie, son of John McHardie and Margaret Ochterlonie, had sasine on Crathienard, 22nd October, 1716.[2]

LAWSIE, DONALD SYMOND, "ane gentleman, with James Symond his tenant" was there in 1696. In 1701 Donald Symon in Lawsie was elder of the Kirk.[3]

On 31st August, 1703, James Symond had sasine on Lawsie.[4]

In 1673 James Shaw and Margaret McHardie, his spouse, had sasine on Crathienard and Lawsie.[5]

PARISH OF TULLICH.

ALLANAQUOICH.

John Farquharson, eldest son of Donald of Allanaquoich and his first wife, Violet Troup.

Robert, the second son of the second wife of Donald, 2nd of Allana- quoich (see Kindrochit), was a Jacobite. His brother, Donald, was another Jacobite, at least potential, of the '15; he was the eldest son of Donald Farquharson, second laird of Allanaquoich, and Helen Gairden, and had an estate of his own called Cobletown in Tullich. His son, Lawrence, "was carried out in the year 1715 to the army, though he was a man as little inclined to the wrathful principle as his father. He was transported from Liverpool to the West Indies and lives there."[6]

He had another son, George, who was also a Jacobite, and married Mary, daughter of Colonel John Farquharson of Inverey, "the Black Colonel" (see page 61).

INVEREY—see LUMPHANAN.

DONALD FARQUHARSON—see above.

---

[1] *Aberdeen Sasines.*   [2] *Ibid.*   [3] Rev. J. Stirton, *Crathie and Braemar*, p. 193.
[4] *Aberdeen Sasines.*   [5] *Ibid.*   [6] Brouchdearg MS.

EDWARD FLEMING.

Edward Fleming was in 1696 portioner of lands of Muiress (Micras). Patrick Fleming of the same parish owned the lands of Auchintoul, of which Arthur Forbes, younger son of Lord Forbes, had the superiority. The Patrick Fleming who was a Jacobite of 1745 was said to be the *fourteenth laird* of the name.

PATRICK OGG.

In the *Poll Book*, 1696, Patrick Ogg is not mentioned, but there is a cottar in "Meikle Kanders" named George Ogg, and as already seen, there was Isobel Ogg in Migvie.

WESTERMICRAS.

Donald Farquharson, a prisoner at Preston, sentenced to transportation but bought off for £50, married Murrel Gordon of Tirriesoul, and (2) Jean Grant of Knockando in 1726.[1]

ROBERT MCHARDIE (as above—CRATHIE).

JAMES MCMARQUIS. James McMarquis has not been traced.

JOHN MORGAN.

The father of John Morgan was Allaster Morgan, son of John, and he was infeft in Torgalter, 18th June, 1688, as heir to his father. John, the son, was tenant of Micras in Tullich in 1696.

EARL OF ABOYNE—see PARISH OF ABOYNE.

PATRICK GORDON, FOR EARL OF ABOYNE.

Patrick or Peter Gordon of Haugh in this parish, valued at £24 3s. 4d. in 1696.

PARISH OF GLENMUICK.

EARL OF ABOYNE (above).

ABERGELDIE (above).

BRAICHLIE, FOR LANDS AND TIENDS.

This was John Gordon, laird of Braickley, son of the John Gordon who was killed by a band of Farquharsons on 17th September, 1666,

---

[1] A. M. Mackintosh, *Farquharson Genealogies*

when the younger John was only seven years of age. His mother was Margaret Burnett of Craigmyle, and his wife was Anne Allardyce. On 16th February, 1709, "Isaac Foularton" had sasine "on the lands of Braikley, Tolden and others." [1]

27th October, 1703, Margaret Gordon of Braickley, *spouse of Alexander Ker of Menie*, had sasine for her liferent. It would appear that young John's mother married again, unless this was his sister.

BELLETRACH.

"Harie Farquharson of Belletrach with his wife and six children" (in 1696).

BELLAMORE. [Robert Farquharson.]

Robert Farquharson of Bellamore, in 1696, with his wife and six children, and his mother, Helen Garden, relict of the deceased Donald Farquharson of Allanaquoich (see parish of Kindrought). Robert was a Jacobite. In the other portion of Bellamore, in Glentanner, was William Garden.

AUCHOLZIE.

"William Stewart of Achollie in 1696, with his wife and his children, Alexander, Charles, Barbara, and Elizabeth." [2] He was a Jacobite of 1715.

He died in 1727, and his widow, Euphame Farquharson, died in 1750. His son, Alexander, married in 1714 Anna Gordon of Corse.

PARISH OF GLENTANNER.

EARL OF ABOYNE, FOR HIS OLD LANDS.

EARL OF ABOYNE, FOR THOMAS MIDDLETON'S VALUATION.

The Middletons were tenants of the Earl of Aboyne in Over Bellastrem. Alexander Middleton and John Middleton were there in 1696. Captain Alexander Middleton (page 29) was of this family; also Principal George Middleton.

BELLAMORE—WILLIAM GARDEN.

"William Garden, with his wife, his son John Garden classing himself as a gentleman, and Bethie Garden his daughter," in 1696. Helen Garden of Bellamore married as his second wife Donald Farquharson of Allanaquoich. Their son, Robert Farquharson, was a Jacobite and a prisoner in 1715 (see above).

---

[1] *Aberdeen Sasines.*   [2] *Poll Book.*

BELLASTRINE

Charles Garden of Bellastrem, son of James Garden of Bellastrem, who appears in the *Poll Book*, was one of the prisoners at Carlisle in 1716. In his petition he describes himself as "having been brought up in the Protestant religion, and for many years in defence of the religion and liberties of his country and at the outmost perrell of his life, fought against the French under the auspicious banner of the late Immortal King William of glorious memory. He was forced out by Patrick Lyon, the laird of Auchterhouse, (Curator and Manager for the Earl of Aboyne, Garden's superior), and a party of 16 armed Highlanders—escaped, but was taken again."[1] He was one of the prisoners condemned but not proceeded against.[2]

CANDYCRAIG, MIDLTOUN.

Alexander Middletoun of Candacraig was in possession in 1696 with his wife and a son, Alexander Middleton, who succeeded him.

EARL OF ABOYNE, FOR WATERNADIE AND NEWTOUN.

These were part of the estate of Bellatrich, belonging in 1696 to Henry Farquharson ; in 1715 to the Earl of Aboyne.

EARL OF ABOYNE, FOR FARQUHARSON OF TILLICAIRN.

Alexander Farquharson of Tilliecairne, who was in possession in 1696 with his wife and two children, Lewis and Mary.

PARISH OF KINERNIE.

THE LAIRD OF BALLOGIE—*D*.

Alexander Forbes, younger of Ballogie, who succeeded his father in this estate, was in 1696 one of the two Commissioners for taking the

---

[1] *S.P.* 54.6.89.

[2] " Report of the Judges acting in the Spetiall Commission of Oyer and Terminer and Goal delivery for the tryall of the Scotch prisoners at Carlisle for the late Rebellion committed in Scotland, given in to the Lord High Chancellor.

" Thirty one of the said prisoners pleaded guilty to their Indictment and in a very decent and submissive manner acknowledged their sorrow for their past guilt and promised to endeavour to atone for it. Against twenty-five of these judgment was passed in the usual form, including Charles Gardin, Sylvester Douglas [see p. 164], John Hamilton [see p. 216], etc. But execution was respited, the Judges conceiving it most prudent not to execut any who had waived all defences and thrown themselves upon his Matie's Mercy, till his Matie's pleasure should be known concerning them, and the rather because Intimation had been given that the likliest way to obtain that mercy was to rely upon it and make an ingenuous acknowledgment of their guilt."—*S.P.* 35.8.12.

Poll. His father, Alexander, was then in possession with his wife and four daughters, Alexander younger, with his lady and two sons, John and Alexander, and one daughter. A "Subscription Mr. *John* Forbes of Ballogie and his creditors," of date 23rd February, 1722, is among the papers at Fettercairn, and a disposition in consequence of decreet by Trustees of Mr. *John* Forbes of Ballogie. Showing that Alexander the younger was then dead.

CAIRNDAY.

"John Lumsden of Cairnday with his wife, three sons, Alexander, Francis, and Thomas, and a daughter, Janet," in 1696.

THE LORD FRASER.

Charles 4th and last Lord Fraser, only son of Andrew, 3rd Lord Fraser and his first wife, Katherine Fraser, daughter of the 8th Lord Lovat, widow of Viscount Arbuthnott, and before that of Sir John Sinclair of Dunbeath. He was born before September, 1662, served heir to his father, 2nd March, 1683. As early as 1692 he showed his Jacobite opinions as he went with the Laird of Inverallochy and a number of friends and tenants to Fraserburgh Cross and proclaimed King James II as King of Great Britain. They drank the royal health and fired guns and pistols. For this escapade Lord Fraser was tried a year later and fined £200, but there was great difficulty in collecting a jury to deal with the case. In 1695 he had at last taken the oath of allegiance to King William, and his seat in Parliament.[1]

He married in 1683 Lady Marjorie Erskine, daughter of the 7th Earl of Buchan, but had no issue.[2]

He does not appear to have taken any very distinguished part in the campaign of the autumn of 1715. He was in hiding at the collapse of the Rising, but in February, 1716, he surrendered, as proved by a letter from James Cockburn to Mr. Pringle, now in the Record Office, of 22nd February, 1716. "My Lord Fraser has surrendered himself and desired a guard might be sent to his house, he being so ill he cannot travel."[3] That he subsequently escaped is proved by the fact that he met his death when again in hiding, from a fall over the cliff at Pennan, near Banff, 12th October, 1716. James Farquharson of Balmoral, who was with Lord Fraser, and was likewise (it is said) attempting to descend the cliff to embark on a ship for France, was also injured.

---

[1] *Complete Peerage*, vol. v.

[2] In the *Poll Book* appears " Mrs. Marie Fraser, daughter in law to Lord Fraser." She was the daughter of Lady Marjorie Erskine by her first husband, Simon Fraser of Inverallochy, and therefore step-daughter to Lord Fraser.

[3] *S.P.* 54.11.143.

PARISH OF MIDMAR.

BALLOGIE—*D*. PARISH OF KINERNIE.

CLUNY, FOR LITTLE SAUCHEN.

James Martin was the tenant in Little Sauchen. Cluny was in the hands of Mr. Robert Gordon, Advocate, younger brother of Sir Ludovick Gordon of Gordonstown (afterwards of Cluny).

SHIELS.

In 1703 sasine was had on Shiels by George Forbes, son of Sir William Forbes of Monymusk. It was afterwards bought by Francis Farquharson of Whitehouse (see page 44), and later by Charles Gordon.

LADY BALLOGIE, LIFE RENTRIX.

The wife of Alexander Forbes (as above), in Kinernie parish. Her maiden name is not known.

In 1748 Charles Forbes, Sheriff-Substitute of Aberdeenshire, was of Ballogie.

PARISH OF ECHT.

LAIRD OF ECHT, ELDER—*D*.

Arthur Forbes of Echt, who died in 1728 ; his will is in the Commissariot of that year.

His uncle, Arthur Forbes, had been in the "Trot of Turriff," on the Covenanting side, in 1639, at which date he stated himself to have been within the age of 24 years.[1]

He married, in 1635 (when he could only have been 20, or less) (1) Anna, daughter of the 10th Lord Forbes ; (2) Margaret Blackburn, daughter of William Blackburn, burgess of Aberdeen ;[2] (3) Barbara Forbes of Asloun (who afterwards married the 12th Lord Forbes). He left a son, Thomas, who died without issue in 1687, and had a brother, Thomas of Knockquorne, afterwards of Echt, father of Arthur, the laird of 1715. (Mary, the daughter of Thomas, married the Rev. Lundie, and died 1798, aged 77.)

Arthur was born in 1671 and died in 1728. He married (1) Elizabeth, daughter of Sir Robert Innes, who died in 1695, and in the following year he married Katherine Melville, "Lady Grange."

THE LAIRD OF ECHT, YOUNGER—*D*.

He was the son of the above Arthur who married, in 1707, Mary Maitland of Pitrichie, and secondly, Margaret Forbes of Craigievar.

---

[1] *Sheriff Court Records.* [2] *Aberdeen Sasines.*

Robert Forbes of Echt,
Married a daughter of Alexander Burnett, 12th of Leys.

Arthur Forbes of Echt, born 1615. Owned Echt 1632–1680. Married in 1635 (1) Anna Forbes. (2) Margaret Blackburn. (3) Barbara Forbes of Asloun. He was at the "Trot of Turriff."	Thomas of Knockquorne, afterwards of Echt. Married daughter of Patrick Forbes of Wester Echt, died 1698.

Thomas, *o.s.p.* 1687.

Laird of Echt——Arthur, born 1671, died 1728.
"elder," In 1696 had three sons.
1715. Married (1) Elizabeth Innes, daughter of Sir Robert. (2) Katharine Melville, "Lady Grange," in 1696.

Laird of Echt,——Arthur, sold Echt to William Duff,
"younger," Lord Braco.
1715. Married (1) 1707, Mary Maitland of Pitrichie. (2) 1719, Margaret Forbes of Craigievar.

—*Castle Forbes Papers.*

LAIRD OF DRUM—see PARISH OF TARLAND.

EASTER ECHT.

David Adie was laird in 1696 and in 1715, when he was a heritor. He was afterwards denounced as a Roman Catholic. David Adie, his son, was a Jacobite, and in January, 1716, appears in the *Burgh Records* as being appointed, by the Jacobite magistrates, to be a Lieutenant of 30 horse to be raised by the town, John Bannerman being the Captain.

PARISH OF CLUNY.

LORD FRASER.

Charles, 4th Lord Fraser (see Kinernie).

LAIRD OF CLUNY.

Robert Gordon of Cluny was "out" in the '15. He was the son of Robert Gordon of Cluny, Advocate, who purchased the estate in 1680 (see page 67).

He received a licence from George I to return from abroad, 19th February, 1718 (see page 32). He had previously received another, 24th October, 1717,[1] but seems to have used neither. His son, "Robert Gordon of Cluny, Advocate, appears as served heir to his father, December, 1723," and "Kenneth Gordon, Advocate, to his nephew, Robert of Cluny, above, November 1729."[2]

[1] Sig. Roxburgh, *S.P. Entry Book,* 8.   [2] *Service of Heirs.*

Kenneth Gordon, Advocate, younger son of the first Robert of 1680, had sasine on Cluny, 17th December, 1712; and 18th March, 1715, he granted sasine to Robert Gordon of Cluny, Advocate,[1] presumably his nephew, Robert the 3rd, as Robert the 2nd does not appear to have been an Advocate. This family, like the preceding one of Cluny, was of short duration.

SHIELS—(above—MIDMAR).

SAUCHEN.

"Elizabeth Burnett, Ladie of Sauchen and present possessor of the lands of Sauchen, with Andrew Burnett her son," appears in the *Poll Book*, 1696.

"Bessie" Burnett, heiress of Sauchen, had been married in 1648, nearly 50 years before this date, to Thomas Burnett, a younger son of Sir Thomas Burnett of Leys by his second marriage. The three sons of this marriage given in the Burnett Book are Robert, William, and Alexander. Andrew must have been a younger one who did not survive.

LORD FORBES—(PARISH OF KEIG).

PRESBYTERY OF THE GARIOCH.

PARISH OF LESLIE.

THE LAIRD OF LEITH HALL—*D.*

John Leith of Leith Hall, son of James Leith of New Leslie, Peillsyde, Arnbog, etc., who built the house of Leith-Hall, which has been the residence of the family ever since. His mother was Margaret Strachan of Glenkindie, and his younger brother, Alexander, founded the families of Leith of Freefield and Leith of Glenkindie.

John Leith married Janet, daughter of George, 2nd Lord Banff, and had five sons, John, who succeeded him (married Mary Hay of Rannes), and Patrick, George, Laurence, and Antony, who were all Jacobites of the '45. John Leith died in 1727, and was succeeded by his son, John.

John Leith was not himself a declared Jacobite of 1715, although his brother, Alexander Leith of Freefield, was a Colonel under Glenbucket, but John's adherence to the house of Hanover was more than doubtful, as is shown by the following letter from Alexander Gordon of Auchlyne, now in the Public Record Office :—

[1] *Aberdeen Sasines.*

LETTER FROM ALEXANDER GORDON, J.P., TO THE LAIRD OF LEITH HALL.

ACHLYNE, Aug. 3. 1716.

SIR,

You not having appeared conspicuously in the late rebellion, for his Majesty's service, but on the contrary payed your cesse and given some assistance to his enemies, without force—I am obliged by Act of Parliament and in the King's name to call for your horses above five pounds, and arms, and likeways that of all your tenants, since all must disarm indefinitely and take the qualification, and Sir, I must also tell you that if you delay or refuse I must immediately put you in my list and transmit you to Major Williamson as ane contumacious and disaffected and refusing to obey the laws—that so impartially you and your tenants may be quartered upon by the King's forces, your cattle and horses taken according to the King's orders if not your person, until your succumb. Besides that, I must take precognition of all that you have done and send it to the Advocate or the King. If you be well-natured I may perhaps be somewhat more mild,—if not I must proceed.

You may choice what course you will take—I have told you what method I must follow.

I am yr humble servant,

ALEX. GORDON, J.P.

Leith Hall itself is, of course, actually in the Parish of Kennethmont, but the first mention of the family occurs here.

The old family of Leslie of Leslie died out in the 17th century. George Leslie, the last of the old line, married a daughter of Patrick, Lord Lindores. She, surviving him, married John Forbes, son of the Laird of Monymusk, "who for his lady's jointure, bought up the debts on the estate and became the 1st Forbes of Leslie." He died after 1645. He had, with other issue, two daughters—

(1) Lilias; who had sasine on Edinbanchory and Kirkton of Forbes-Alford, on 10th August, 1709. In 1710 she resigned to Roderick Forbes of Brux an arent out of the lands of Banchory, Bithnie and Kirkton of Forbes.[1]

(2) Barbara; made the same resignation on the same date and afterwards married John Innes of Sinnaboth.[2]

The next laird was William Forbes of Leslie, brother to the above John, to whom his second son, David, was served heir 27th November, 1708;[3] John, the elder son, having owned it for a short time.

On 9th July, 1709, David Forbes had sasine on "Browndie and Auchnagathil." The family of Forbes of Leslie thus only lasted for three generations and was succeeded by the Leiths, to whom David Forbes sold his estates.[4]

DITTO FOR HIS OLD LANDS—D.

[1] *Aberdeen Sasines.*   [2] *Castle Forbes Papers.*
[3] *Service of Heirs.*   [4] *Aberdeen Sasines.*

THE LAIRD OF WHITEHAUGH.

Whitehaugh is in Tullynessle.

John Leith succeeded his father, John, in this estate in 1672.

He married Elizabeth, daughter of William, the 12th Lord Forbes, and his daughter and heiress, Anne, married William Forbes, last laird of Tolquhon, whence the family of Forbes-Leith of Whitehaugh (see page 185).

PARISH OF PREMNAY.

LICKLEYHEAD.   [Patrick Duff—*D.*]

Formerly a property of the Leslies, who at one time owned so much of the Garioch, it was, in 1696, in the hands of Mr. Archibald Forbes, third son of the 12th Lord Forbes, with Margaret Forbes, his spouse, and his children, David and Barbara. The widow and children of the previous Forbes of Leslie were also there. In 1701 it was bought by Walter Hay, brother to the Laird of Arnbath, sasine being granted on 2nd May, 1701, by Archibald Forbes.[1] Later, it was sold to Patrick Duff of Premnay, one of the 36 children of Patrick Duff of Craigston, and husband of William Duff of Braco's daughter, Margaret.[2]

LEITH-HALL—see PARISH OF LESLIE.

ROTHNEY—see CULSAMOND.

BARNES.

James Gordon, a son of George Gordon of Shellagreen, who married Marjorie, one of the eight daughters of John Moir of Barnes and Mary Cochrane. James became "of Barnes," and was a Jacobite of 1715, and a Captain, being one of those who "came into the town and insulted the Magistrates and took possession of arms and ammunition."[3]

He had a sasine on Barnes in 1700.[4]

The date of his death is not known.[5] He had seven daughters (but apparently no son) :—

[1] *Aberdeen Sasines.*　　　　　[2] *Family Papers.*

[3] *A Short Memorandum of quhat heath occurred in Aberdeen.*

[4] *Aberdeen Sasines.*

[5] On 24th June, 1714, a caption was issued at the instance of James Gordon of Barnes, whereby Alexander Leslie of Pitcaple was denounced as a rebel and put to the horn for failing to pay a debt of 450 merks Scots (less than £25 !), "under the hand of Anne by the Grace of God, etc. The sheriffs of our Sheriffdoms, the Stuarts of our Stuartries The Baillies of our Baileries and regalities and their deputes together with the provosts and all messengers at arms and all our Judges and ordinars, are ordered to pass, take, seek and apprehend the said Alexander Leslie, rebell, and keep him in sure ward and captivity at his own proper charges until he have fulfilled the command and charge (to pay his debt) and if need be to make all his Lockfast places open and patent."—*Pitcaple Papers.*

Margaret, born 1700 ; Isobel, 1702 ; Christian, 1704 ; Margaret, 1705 ; Helen, Elizabeth, and Mary, of whom five were served heirs to him in 1748.[1]

GEORGE PETRIE, FOR NEWTON—see CULSAMOND.

OVERHALL.

Robert Leith, 8th Laird of Overhall, who had been served heir 27th February, 1678, was son of George Leith, 7th Laird, and Marjory Farquharson of Invercauld. He married Margaret, daughter of Francis Ross of Auchlossan, and was succeeded before 1696 by George Leith, 9th Laird, who had a precept in Chancery, 7th February, 1700 ; he married Cecilia Young of Auldbar, and died in 1762, being succeeded by his son, Robert, as 10th Laird.[2]

LEITH-HALL FOR ETHERLICK—*D*.

The real name of this small estate is Edenleith. It had formed part of the lands of Overhall (above), but was sold to the laird of Leith-Hall.

DITTO FOR PART OF LESLIE—*D*.

PARISH OF INSCH.

BALQUHAIN FOR MEICLE WARDHOUSE.

George, Count Leslie, 16th of Balquhain, as the superior of several properties in this parish, paid the Cess for Wardhouse, formerly owned by Leslies (Alex. Leslie of Balquhain had sasine on it in 1674), then by the Farquharsons, at present by the Gordons. (For the family of Balquhain, see Logie-Durno, pages 90 and 91.)

There were so many families of Leslie in the Garioch in the 17th and 18th centuries that it has seemed well to insert here a sketch of a family tree, showing how they all derived from the parent stock of Leslies of Balquhain.

[1] *Powis Papers.*
[2] J. Davidson, *Inverurie and the Earldom of the Garioch*, p. 461.

SKETCH TREE OF THE VARIOUS FAMILIES OF LESLIE, SHOWING THEIR
DESCENT FROM THE 4TH LAIRD OF BALQUHAIN, AND TREE OF
WARDES.

Alexander, the 3rd Laird, left only two sons, *six* having been killed at the Battle
of Harlaw, 28th July, 1411.

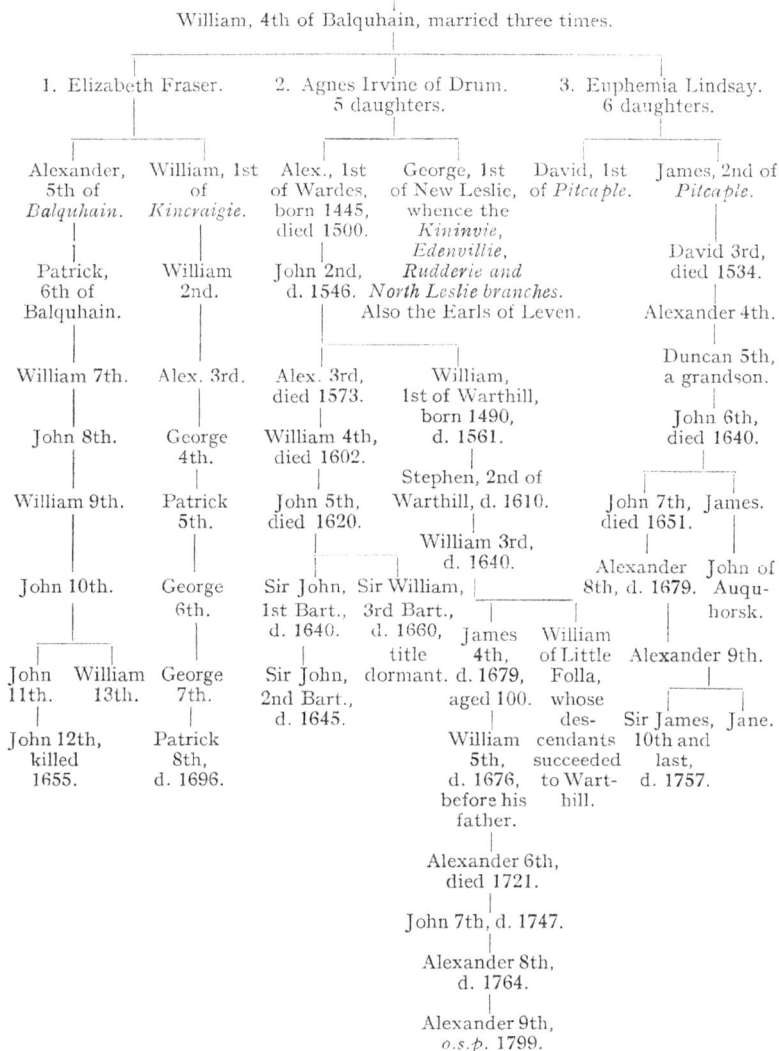

William, 4th of Balquhain, married three times.

1. Elizabeth Fraser.　　　2. Agnes Irvine of Drum.　　　3. Euphemia Lindsay.
　　　　　　　　　　　　　　5 daughters.　　　　　　　　　6 daughters.

Alexander,　William, 1st　Alex., 1st　George, 1st　David, 1st　James, 2nd of
5th of　　　of　　　　of Wardes,　of New Leslie,　of *Pitcaple*.　*Pitcaple*.
Balquhain.　*Kincraigie*.　born 1445,　whence the
　　　　　　　　　　　　died 1500.　*Kininvie*,　　　　　　　David 3rd,
Patrick,　　William　　　　　　　　*Edenvillie*,　　　　　　died 1534.
6th of　　　2nd.　　　John 2nd,　*Rudderie and*
Balquhain.　　　　　　d. 1546.　*North Leslie branches.*　　Alexander 4th.
　　　　　　　　　　　　　　Also the Earls of Leven.
　　　　　　　　　　　　　　　　　　　　　　　　　　　　Duncan 5th,
William 7th.　Alex. 3rd.　Alex. 3rd,　　William,　　　　　a grandson.
　　　　　　　　　　　died 1573.　1st of Warthill,
John 8th.　　George　　　　　　　born 1490,　　　　　　John 6th,
　　　　　　4th.　　　William 4th,　d. 1561.　　　　　　died 1640.
　　　　　　　　　　died 1602.
William 9th.　Patrick　　　　　　Stephen, 2nd of
　　　　　　5th.　　　John 5th,　Warthill, d. 1610.　John 7th,　James.
　　　　　　　　　　died 1620.　　　　　　　　　　died 1651.
John 10th.　George　　　　　　William 3rd,
　　　　　　6th.　　　　　　　　d. 1640.　　　Alexander　John of
　　　　　　　　　Sir John,　Sir William,　　　8th, d. 1679.　Auqu-
John　William　George　1st Bart.,　3rd Bart.,　　　　　　　　　horsk.
11th.　13th.　7th.　d. 1640.　d. 1660,　James　William
　　　　　　　　　　　　　　　title　4th,　of Little　Alexander 9th.
John 12th,　Patrick　Sir John,　dormant.　d. 1679,　Folla,
killed　　　8th,　2nd Bart.,　　　　aged 100.　whose
1655.　　　d. 1696.　d. 1645.　　　　　　　des-　Sir James,　Jane.
　　　　　　　　　　　　　　　　William　cendants　10th and
　　　　　　　　　　　　　　　　5th,　succeeded　last,
　　　　　　　　　　　　　　　　d. 1676,　to Wart-　d. 1757.
　　　　　　　　　　　　　　　　before his　hill.
　　　　　　　　　　　　　　　　father.

　　　　　　　　　　　　　　Alexander 6th,
　　　　　　　　　　　　　　died 1721.

　　　　　　　　　　　　　　John 7th, d. 1747.

　　　　　　　　　　　　　　Alexander 8th,
　　　　　　　　　　　　　　d. 1764.

　　　　　　　　　　　　　　Alexander 9th,
　　　　　　　　　　　　　　o.s.p. 1799.

TREE OF WARDES (Leslie).

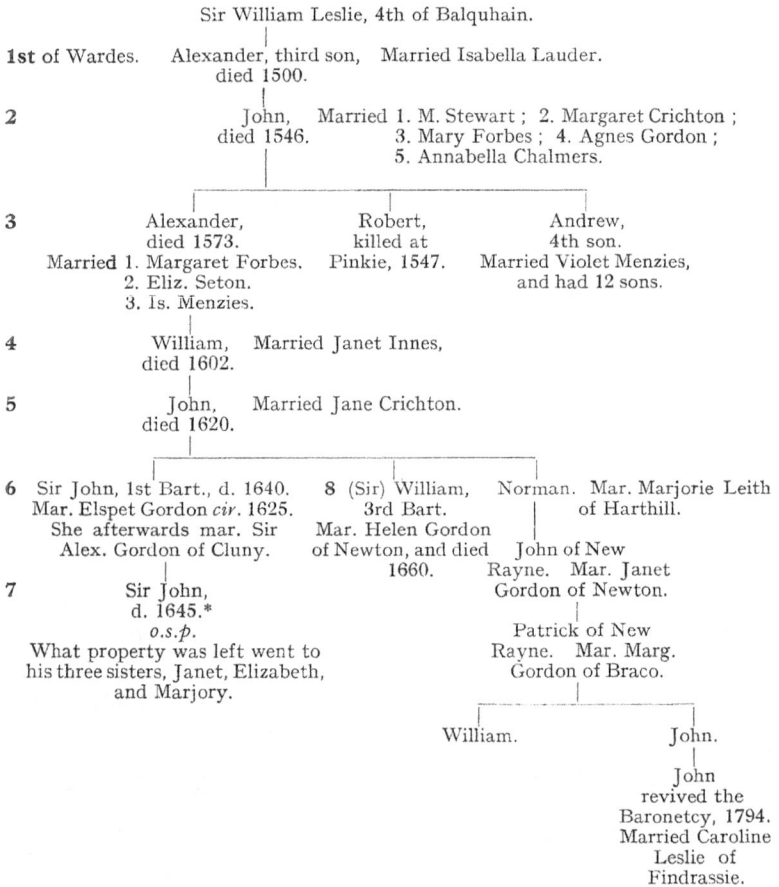

Sir William Leslie, 4th of Balquhain.

1st of Wardes. Alexander, third son, Married Isabella Lauder.
died 1500.

2 John, Married 1. M. Stewart ; 2. Margaret Crichton ;
died 1546. 3. Mary Forbes ; 4. Agnes Gordon ;
5. Annabella Chalmers.

3 Alexander, Robert, Andrew,
died 1573. killed at 4th son.
Married 1. Margaret Forbes. Pinkie, 1547. Married Violet Menzies,
2. Eliz. Seton. and had 12 sons.
3. Is. Menzies.

4 William, Married Janet Innes,
died 1602.

5 John, Married Jane Crichton.
died 1620.

6 Sir John, 1st Bart., d. 1640. **8** (Sir) William, Norman. Mar. Marjorie Leith
Mar. Elspet Gordon *cir.* 1625. 3rd Bart. of Harthill.
She afterwards mar. Sir Mar. Helen Gordon |
Alex. Gordon of Cluny. of Newton, and died John of New
1660. Rayne. Mar. Janet
7 Sir John, Gordon of Newton.
d. 1645.*
o.s.p. Patrick of New
What property was left went to Rayne. Mar. Marg.
his three sisters, Janet, Elizabeth, Gordon of Braco.
and Marjory.

William. John.

John
revived the
Baronetcy, 1794.
Married Caroline
Leslie of
Findrassie.

* Spalding says : "Vpone the thrid of Februar 1645, Sir Johne Leslie of Wardess knicht barronet, depairtit this lyf in New Abirdene, a great enemy to the Laird of Cluny, who had mellit with his estait. Cluny wairdit in the tolbuith of Edinbrugh."
—Memorials of the Trubles, vol. ii, p. **441**.

Sir Alexander Gordon had married the widow of the 1st Sir John Wardes, and having fled from his creditors in 1642 had endeavoured after her death, which occurred in the same year, to mend his fortunes, with the help of her jointure, having been given four months' grace in which to pay his debts, and came to blows with Thos. Nicolson, one of his creditors, hence his imprisonment.—*Ibid., passim.*

James Gordon, son of Alexander Gordon "of Candell," and himself 9th of Beldorney, married Mary, eldest daughter and eventually heiress of John Gordon, 3rd of Law and 1st of Wardhouse. They had sasine on 8th June, 1730. James Gordon died in June, 1740; from him descends the present family of Gordons of Wardhouse.

TREE OF WARDHOUSE.

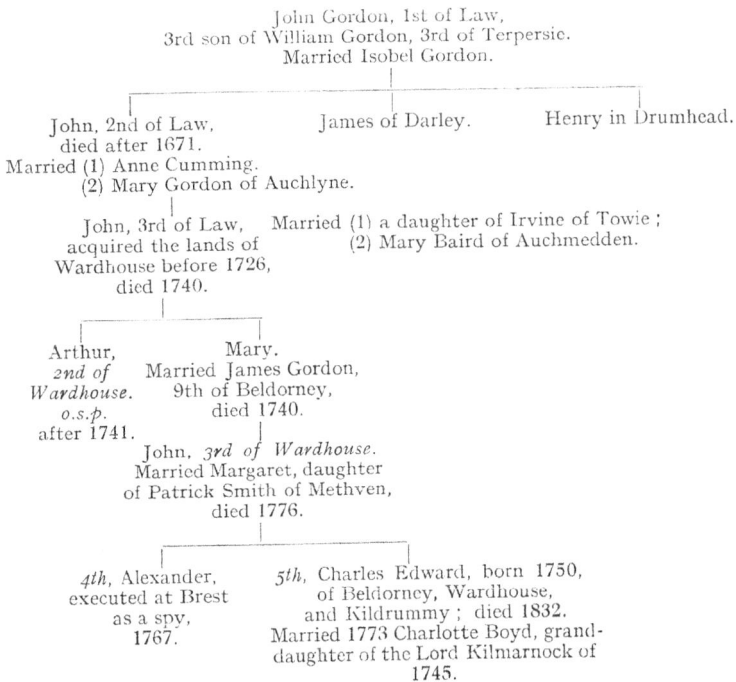

John Gordon, 1st of Law,
3rd son of William Gordon, 3rd of Terpersie.
Married Isobel Gordon.

| John, 2nd of Law, died after 1671. Married (1) Anne Cumming. (2) Mary Gordon of Auchlyne. | James of Darley. | Henry in Drumhead. |

John, 3rd of Law, acquired the lands of Wardhouse before 1726, died 1740.
Married (1) a daughter of Irvine of Towie; (2) Mary Baird of Auchmedden.

| Arthur, *2nd of Wardhouse*. *o.s.p.* after 1741. | Mary. Married James Gordon, 9th of Beldorney, died 1740. |

John. *3rd of Wardhouse*.
Married Margaret, daughter of Patrick Smith of Methven, died 1776.

| *4th*, Alexander, executed at Brest as a spy, 1767. | *5th*, Charles Edward, born 1750, of Beldorney, Wardhouse, and Kildrummy; died 1832. Married 1773 Charlotte Boyd, grand-daughter of the Lord Kilmarnock of 1745. |

DITTO FOR EARL OF MAR—see KILDRUMMY.

THREEFIELDS VALUATION—see RAYNE.

DUNNYDEER.

David Tyrie, "a gryte Jacobite," eldest son of John Tyrie and his wife, Mary Tulloh of Tanachie (whose brother was one of the Jacobite prisoners in Carlisle). "John Tyrie and Mary Tulloh, with their three sons, John,[1] David, and James[2] Tyries and four daughters, were denounced

---

[1] John appears in the Rome register for the year 1711, where he was said to be 15 years of age. In 1719 he was sent out as Mission Priest and died at Shenval, 19th May, 1755.

[2] James appears in the Rome register for 1717 at the age of 17. On the 24th February, 1725, he is reported to have "abandoned his studies and become apostate."

as Papists before the Presbytery of Garioch in 1704." David was factor to the Duke of Gordon.

David married (1) Elizabeth Gordon of Rothiemay (who had sasine for liferent in 1672), and (2) Anna Menzies of Pitfoddels. One of his sons by the latter, David, was a zealous Jacobite of the '45, the elder David being still alive, as he did not die until 1750. On 22nd February, 1712, Mr. Archibald Ogilvie of Rothiemay had a bond over Dunnydeer.[1] He was another Jacobite.

WARDHOUSE.

John Gordon of Wardhouse and Law had a registered entail of the lands of Law and others, 6th July, 1726—see above.

He was succeeded first by his son, Arthur, and then by his daughter, Mary, and her husband, James Gordon of Beldorney.

BALQUHAIN, FOR KIRKTOWN OF INCH.

This had been the property of Mr. Alexander Ross (or Rose), minister of Monymusk and Laird of Insch. His son, John Ross, minister of Foveran, succeeded. He married, in 1669, Isobel Udny of Udny, and had a son, Alexander, who succeeded him in 1680 and was the laird in 1715. He married Anne Forbes, daughter of Alexander Forbes of Ballogie, and had three sons and four daughters. He sold Insch and bought Lethenty in Daviot.[2]

OVERBODDAM.

It was John Logie of Overboddam in 1696.[3]

In 1700 William Logie, his son, married Maria Rait.

CAIRNSTOWN (CARNIESTON).

Part of Boddam—owned by Gordon of Rothney and Wrangham.

NETHER BODDAM. [Alexander Gordon.]

"Thomas Gordon of Netherboddome" in 1696. Two years later his son, Alexander, was served heir.[4]

DRUMROSSIE—D.

Alexander Ross, the son of the minister of Foveran, and grandson of the minister of Monymusk (as above).

LESMOIR FOR JONESLEYES.

Glens of Johnsleys belonged to Sir James Gordon of Lesmoir, eighth Laird and 4th Baronet. He married Jane, only child of Sir John Gordon

---

[1] *Aberdeen Sasines.* [2] *Ibid.* [3] *Poll Book.* [4] *Service of Heirs.*

of Haddo, and had five sons, two of whom, John and Robert, were Jacobites of 1715, and entered Aberdeen with the Earl Marischal on the 20th of September.[1]

On 25th August, 1662, Mr. Andrew Massie, minister of Drumblade, had had a charter on the lands of Johnsleyes.[2]

PARISH OF CULSAMOND.

NEWTOUN, DAVIDSON.

The Davidson family followed the first Gordon family who owned the estate of Newton.

Alexander Davidson bought Newton from the Gordons, and died 2nd April, 1685. He married, first, Jean Burnett, and secondly, Isobel Leslie. His eldest son, Alexander Davidson, was a Jacobite and a member of the Jacobite Committee in Aberdeen in 1715. He married Marie or Mary Gordon, heiress of Gight, and his son was the Alexander Gordon who married Margaret Duff, and died in 1760. There were also four daughters, Elizabeth, who married James Gordon of Techmurie, son of the minister of Rothiemay ; Isobel, Jean, and Christian, the youngest, who married Alexander Leith of Freefield.

Alexander Davidson himself had not apparently as yet assumed his wife's name of Gordon in 1715.

At the date of the *Poll Book*, Alexander Davidson, that is, the second of the name, who became laird of Gight, was resident in Aberdeen, where he owned some property and some fishing rights, though he was also described as "the greatest heritor in the parish of Culsamond."

(George Petrie, who paid Cess for Newton, in the Parish of Premnay, has not been identified though he was a " messenger-at-arms.")

ROTHNEY, FOR WRANGHAM—*D.* (See also PARISH OF INSCH.)

George Gordon of Rothney and Wrangham, who also had sasine on Carnieston, 20th December, 1703. He was son of John Gordon, third son of Gordon of Rothney, which John was in possession in 1696 with his wife (Elizabeth Udny)[3] and three sons—George (above), Alexander,

---

[1] On 2nd August, 1683, James Gordon, then younger of Lesmoir, and Patrick Leslie, 15th of Balquhain, made a contract settling the Marches of the hill of Foudland between the lands of Johnsleys and those of Largie and Meikle Wardis.
—*Historical Records of the Family of Leslie*, vol. iii, p. 123.

[2] *Register of Great Seal*, 1660-8, No. 309.

[3] And on 11th February, 1713, there was a discharge and renunciation by William Gordon, second son of George Gordon and Marjory Moir, to the said George Gordon, elder, and George Gordon, younger, of an arent on Rothney.—*Aberdeen Sasines.*

and William, and four daughters—Anne, Jean, Janet, and Margaret Gordon.

Elizabeth Udny, "Lady Shellagreen," had sasine on Little Wrangham, 6th February, 1713.[1]

TILLIEMORGAN—*D.*

This estate has changed hands many times. In 1657 it belonged to Robert Forbes of Tilliemorgan. In 1668 and 1676 it was Seton property.[2] In 1696 James Davidson, brother to Newton, owned it,[3] and in 1715 it appears to have been in the hands of a Hanoverian. James Davidson may have handed it over to some relative for safe keeping.

He himself was a prominent Jacobite, being, like his brother, a member of the Committee appointed 26th October, 1715, for stenting and proportioning £500 sterling among the inhabitants of Aberdeen, as a contribution to Mar's funds.[4]

James Davidson was second son of Alexander Davidson (who bought Newton) and his first wife, Jean Burnett. He died in 1720.

PARISH OF RAIN.

THREEFIELD AND NEW RAIN—*D.*

Alexander Leith (second son of James Leith, 1st of Leith Hall, and Margaret Strachan) bought the lands of Treefield and Bonnytown in 1702, with the consent of his son, Peter, and had them erected into a Barony with a crown charter under the name of Freefield.

He married Christian, daughter of Alexander Davidson of Newton, and had four sons—Alexander, Walter, Patrick (Peter), and George. He afterwards bought Glenkindie from his cousin, Patrick Strachan. He was born in 1664 and lived to be 90. During the Rising of 1715 he was a Colonel under Gordon of Glenbucket. (In 1696 he was residing in Aberdeen with his two children, George and Isobel.[5]) New Rayne was an old Leith property which had been at one time in the hands of the Leslies, who sold it in 1700.

LONEHEAD (*Seq.*).

Andrew Logie, of Loanhead, Rayne, on which he had had sasine in 1700. He was an Advocate in Aberdeen, son of George Logie and Anna

---

[1] *Aberdeen Sasines.*   [2] *Ibid.*   [3] *Poll Book.*

[4] *Short Memorandum of quhat heath occurred, etc.*

[5] Alex. Leith of Freefield bought, after the Rising of 1715, the superiority of Fettercairn which was part of the estate of the attainted Earl Marischal. This was bought from his son, Alexander, by Sir John Belshes Stuart, Bart. of Fettercairn.

—*Lord Clinton's Papers at Fettercairn.*

Paton of Kinaldie, and grandson of the famous Mr. Andrew Logie, so long minister at Rayne. He was proprietor of Loanhead, Muirhillock, and one-third part of the lands of Bonnytown.[1]

Mr. John Elphinstone of Logie—*D*.

Son of James Elphinstone, W.S., who bought the lands of Craighouse, Midlothian, hence known as James Elphinstone of Craigs, and between 1670 and 1680 bought also the lands of Logie-Durno, afterward called Logie-Elphinstone. James was M.P. for Aberdeenshire from 1673 to 1701.[2] In 1701 he was made a baronet. He married "Cecil" or Cecilia Denholme of Muirhouse and left two sons—John (above), who became Sheriff-Depute of Aberdeenshire in 1707, and Robert, and two daughters —Margaret (who married Sir Robert Forbes of Learney) and Anna. John was afterwards the 2nd Baronet, succeeding his father in 1722. He married Mary Elliot of Hearnshaw, and his two sons, James and John,[3] were the 3rd and 4th Baronets, after which the title became extinct. His daughter, Mary, married Colonel Dalrymple-Horn,[4] son of Hew Dalrymple and Anne Horn, heiress of Westhall, who assumed name of Elphinstone.

Blackford—see Parish of Fyvie.

Rotmais (Rothmaise).

There were Gordons of Rothmaise in the 17th century, and the names of various "wadsetters" have been preserved—notably George Leslie, in 1634. By 1696 Alexander Ross was "of Rothmaithe but lives for the time at Loanhead," according to the *Poll Book*.

Little Wartle—*D*.

The Leslies of Warthill descend from the Leslies of Wardes (see family tree, page 73).

Alexander Leslie, 6th of Wartle, in 1696. He succeeded his father, William, and his grandfather, James, in 1679. He was born in 1656 and died 1721. He married Elizabeth Gordon of Badenscoth. On 14th October, 1709, his son, John Leslie, had sasine, but he was still "younger of Wartle," and in the following year, on 20th May, 1710, John had a contract of marriage with Margaret Dun, only daughter of Patrick Dun of Tarty, with the consent of Alexander Leslie, his father. She was his 2nd wife.[5] John succeeded in 1721 as 7th of Wartle.

---

[1] *Aberdeen Sasines.*   [2] *Foster's M.P.s.*

[3] *Complete Baronetage*, vol. iv, p. 399.

[4] Colonel Dalrymple-Horn was a friend and protector of Lord Pitsligo when the latter was in hiding after the '45.

[5] *Aberdeen Sasines.*

FAMILY OF WARDHOUSE AND WARTHILL.

Sir William Leslie, 4th of Balquhain,
had a younger son, Alexander, born about 1445,
1st of Wardes. Married Isabella Lauder.

2. John, his son, d. 1546.
Married 1. The daughter of Alexander Stewart, Bishop of Moray.
2. Margaret Crichton, daughter of Lord Frendraught.
3. Margaret Forbes of Echt.
4. Agnes Gordon of Haddo.
5. Annabella Chalmers of Balbithan.

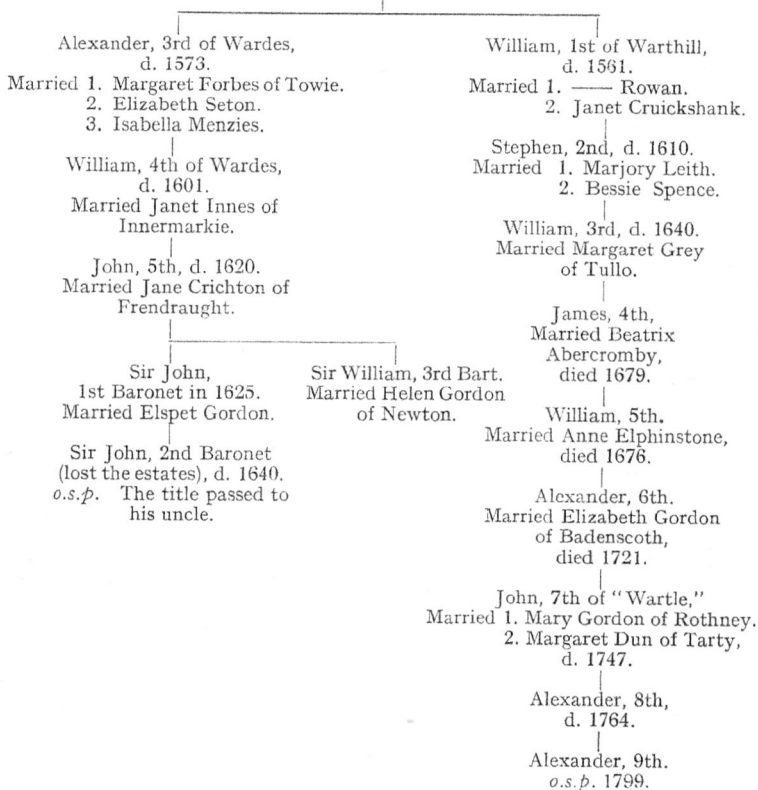

Alexander, 3rd of Wardes, d. 1573. Married 1. Margaret Forbes of Towie. 2. Elizabeth Seton. 3. Isabella Menzies.	William, 1st of Warthill, d. 1561. Married 1. ——— Rowan. 2. Janet Cruickshank.

William, 4th of Wardes,
d. 1601.
Married Janet Innes of
Innermarkie.

Stephen, 2nd, d. 1610.
Married 1. Marjory Leith.
2. Bessie Spence.

John, 5th, d. 1620.
Married Jane Crichton of
Frendraught.

William, 3rd, d. 1640.
Married Margaret Grey
of Tullo.

Sir John, 1st Baronet in 1625. Married Elspet Gordon.	Sir William, 3rd Bart. Married Helen Gordon of Newton.

James, 4th,
Married Beatrix
Abercromby,
died 1679.

Sir John, 2nd Baronet
(lost the estates), d. 1640.
o.s.p. The title passed to
his uncle.

William, 5th.
Married Anne Elphinstone,
died 1676.

Alexander, 6th.
Married Elizabeth Gordon
of Badenscoth,
died 1721.

John, 7th of "Wartle,"
Married 1. Mary Gordon of Rothney.
2. Margaret Dun of Tarty,
d. 1747.

Alexander, 8th,
d. 1764.

Alexander, 9th.
o.s.p. 1799.

OLD RAIN (see page 7).

Another property of the Leith family, William Leith being there
in 1661. In 1674, Janet and Isabel Bisset had sasine on these lands.[1]

By 1696 the possession of these lands had passed to Erskine of
Pittodrie, "not living within the paroch." [2]

---

[1] *Aberdeen Sasines.*   [2] *Poll Book.*

On 2nd May, 1702, William Leith and Barbara Forbes had sasine on "ane pleugh of land in Old Rain."[1]

27th February, 1713, William Leith in Ryhill had a sasine on an arent for his daughter, Jean Leith, "out of Old Rain."

PARISH OF MELDRUM (formerly BETHELNIE).

EARLE OF ABERDEEN—*D*.

The 1st Earl of Aberdeen, formerly Sir George Gordon of Haddo, 3rd Baronet, was made Lord High Chancellor of Scotland in 1681, he married Anne Lockhart of Torbrecks and was father of William, the 2nd Earl; he died in 1720.

LAIRD OF MELDRUM, FOR LIFERENT LANDS.

John Urquhart of Meldrum, eldest son to Adam Urquhart and Lady Mary Gordon (sister to the 1st Duke of Gordon). He was born in 1668 and served heir to his father on 17th June, 1691 (Adam having died 10th November, 1684), in the lands and barony of Meldrum, the town and lands of Ardfork, Kilblean, Old Meldrum, Forester Hill, Cathie, etc. In the reign of Queen Anne he was joint Master of the Office of Works for Scotland (his colleague being the Hon. John Campbell of Mamore). He also was M.P. in the last Scottish Parliament.

He married Jean, daughter of Sir Hugh Campbell of Cawdor, and had two sons and four daughters. He died in 1726 and was succeeded by his second son, William, who was thrice married, and was great-great-grandfather to Garden Alexander Duff of Hatton.

PROVOST ROSS, FOR A PART OF MELDRUM —see PARISH OF TURRIFF.

TOWN OF ABERDEEN—A PART OF MELDRUM.

DITTO FOR ARDFORSK AND CULBLEN (KILBLAIN).

These lands, originally part of the Meldrum estate, were mortgaged by Patrick Urquhart of Meldrum to Dr. William Guild, whose widow, Mrs. Catherine Rolland or Guild, mortified them with other lands "for the support of bursars, burghers, widows, maidens and poor of Aberdeen." By the terms of John Urquhart's succession to his father, above, these lands would seem to have been redeemed by the Urquhart family before this date; though the "ditto" may refer either to the town of Aberdeen or to "Meldrum."

THE LAIRD OF MELDRUM, FOR LANDS UNLIFERENTED—*D*.

[1] *Aberdeen Sasines.*

PARISH OF OYNE.

TILLEFOUR.

The lands of Tilliefour were in the hands of the Earl of Mar as superior at this period. On 20th February, 1711, James Gordon of Tilliefour and Anna Sandilands, his spouse, had sasine on the lands.[1]

After the Rising of 1715 they were bought by George Keith, son of Sir William Keith of Ludquharn, who was assessor for the County in 1714, and Treasurer for the Society of Advocates. He was already a laird, for on 3rd August, 1709, he had had sasine on Mill of Arneidle [2]. He died on 24th September, 1738, and was succeeded by his brother, John Keith, who married Annas Grub.

PITODRY ELDER.

William Erskine of Pittodrie, the laird in 1667, survived until 1724. He married Mary, daughter of Patrick Grant of Ballindalloch. Three years before his death, 1721, he was served "heir of conquest" [3] to his elder brother, John, who had died in 1702, he himself being then an old man.

The Jacobite "Pittodrie" of the 1715, though not a very active one, was Thomas, eldest son of the above William, who died in 1761 at a very advanced age. He was twice married, first, to Margaret Burnett of Craigmyle, and secondly, 20th November, 1746, to Anne, daughter of the 16th Lord Forbes. She died in November, 1750, aged 27.

His first wife had a son, William, who was of weak intellect and died unmarried, and the second had an only daughter, Mary, who became the heiress. She married Colonel Henry Knight (hence the Knight-Erskines of Pittodrie).

William, brother of Thomas, was also a Jacobite in the '15. He was born 1688 and died 1774.

Thomas Erskine's sister married James Moir, third of Stoneywood, and was mother of the famous Jacobite, James Moir of the '45. Thomas Erskine himself, who had been cautious in the '15, was still more so in the '45, and refused to "come out" or to take any real part in the Rising, urging "a broken constitution," though he offered to "scrimp himself" to give money to raise men.

In 1696 the Laird of Pittodrie (William) is polled with two sons and four daughters. Also the Lady Dowager of Pittodrie (Mary Grant) with John and James Erskine, her sons. James was also a Jacobite of 1715, with his nephews, Thomas, the laird, and William, above. He died at Dorlethen, Logie Durno, 1st July, 1718.

---

[1] *Aberdeen Sasines.*   [2] *Ibid.*
[3] That is to a relative either older or of an older line.

WESTHALL AND PITMEDDAN.

"Mr. John Horn of Westhall, son of James Horn, Minister of the Gospel, who had sasine in 1674." [1]

In the *Poll Book* of 1696 "James Horn of Westhall" appears with his wife, who was Isobel Leslie, and Agnes Horn, their daughter. Also "Mr. John Horn, younger of Westhall, with Anna Arbuthnot, his wife, and Anna Horn, his daughter." The latter must have been a mere infant. Her father married Anna, sometimes called Agnes, daughter of Robert, 2nd Viscount Arbuthnot, on 20th November, 1693, and Anna, the daughter, married, in 1721, Hew Dalrymple of North Berwick, and died ten years later.[2] John Horn had a second wife, for on 14th November, 1711, John Horn of Westhall and Anna Simson, his spouse, had sasine on Buchanstone[3] (formerly the property of Captain James Leslie—see next page).

James Horn (above), the minister, was the third son of Mr. John Horn of "Balgounie" in Forgue, and his second wife, Agnes Touches. He was born about 1645, became schoolmaster at Grange and afterwards minister at Bellie and then at Elgin, which charge he resigned in 1682 rather than subscribe to the Test Act.[4]

In 1674 he had bought from John Campbell of Moye the estate of Westhall, in Oyne,[5] and in 1683, after his retirement, he also bought Pitmedden. He married Isobella, daughter of John Leslie, 7th Laird of Pitcaple, and had two sons, John,[6] who succeeded him, and James, and two daughters, one named Isabel, who married, in 1688, Robert Douglas of Bridgford, whose father, Gavin Douglas, was son of William, Earl of Angus.

Robert Douglas and Isabel Horn had sasine on those lands in 1702, and the other daughter, Agnes, married, after 1696, John Douglas of Tilquhillie. The date of James Horn's death is not known, but he was alive in 1707 and probably also in 1711. In 1712 his son, John, was "of Westhall." (The statement that he died in 1743 is certainly erroneous, as he would have been about 100, and may refer to his grandfather, James Horn, who died in 1643, or to his younger son, James.)

---

[1] *Aberdeen Sasines.*

[2] Long afterwards, viz., in 1760, David Dalrymple appears in the entail of Pitcaple in right of his great grandmother, Isobel Leslie (page 96).

—*Pitcaple Papers.*

[3] *Aberdeen Sasines.*　　　　　[4] Scott's *Fasti*, vol. v, pp. 299, 303.

[5] In 1654 this estate had been the property of John Abercromby.

—*Aberdeen Sasines.*

[6] John Horn, younger of Westhall, signed a deed at Pitcaple, 24th March, 1695, witnessed by "Mr. Robert Chein, William and Robert Cheins, his sons," and William Cassie.—*Pitcaple Papers.*

John Horn, who was laird in 1715,[1] was certainly a Jacobite at that date, and was still alive and active in 1745 (though he must have been then at least 65, as he was admitted Advocate in 1691). In 1711 he, with Dundas of Arniston, was deputed to thank the Duchess of Gordon for her gift of the Jacobite medal (see page 217).

In 1745 he had ranged himself definitely on the side of the Hanoverian Government, and suffered at the hands of Lord Lewis Gordon and his men at the time of the Skirmish of Inverurie, "When they (the Prince's men) were informed of Mr. Horn's design of joining the Macleods they were exceedingly keen in their resentment against him, and immediately sent a party to seize him, but he had gone out of the way. The party lived a good while at his house at Westhall at free quarters and made very free with everything, demanding the arms and the Cess levy money."[2]

In the Record Office (*S.P.* 54.9.43) is an order from Mar, which runs as follows :—

> The necessity of the King's affairs and the safety of the country att this juncture requyring that every good Scots man be assisting to the public according to his ability, I desyre therefore that you forthwith send hither the sum of one hundred pounds sterling money for the use of the King's army for which you shall have the public credit to be repayed with interest from the time of the advance. Your speedy complyance herewith will prevent ffurther trouble.
>
> I am, Sir,
>
> Your most humble servant,
>
> MAR.
>
> ffrom the Camp att
> Perth, 13th October 1715.

At the foot is written "Horne of Westhall"; the letter being obviously a duplicate of one sent out to many lairds, but this one alone survives in the P.R.O. Besides being a Jacobite sympathiser (for he is among those marked S who paid six months' cess instead of twelve), John Horn also appears to have busied himself in collecting and handing over to John Forbes the Cess from his neighbours, for we have—

rec. from Westhall and Pitmedden
     ,,   ,,   for part of Overhall (George Leith)
     ,,   ,,   for Buchanstone (Capt. James Leslie[3] in 1696. He afterwards sold these lands to Mr. John Horn).

---

[1] He and his wife, called "Lady Anne Arbuthnott," had sasine on Westhall, 8th April, 1712.—*Aberdeen Sasines.*

[2] *Origins of the Forty-five*—Scottish History Society (page 146).

[3] The *Historical Records of the Family of Leslie* give the origin of the Buchanston family thus :—William, 4th of Balquhain had a natural son, Patrick Leslie of Logie-

for Newlands (John and William Leiths)

,,　　　,,　　　for Mr. Pat. Coupland (the Minister of Cushnie who owned Raithie's plough in the Parish of Oyne. He had a wife, Jean Gordon, three sons and four daughters, and seems to have been a man of means. He was long Professor of Natural Philosophy in Marischal College. He died in 1710).

Possibly John Horn [1] was advancing money on some of these estates, for, some years after the Rising, he obtained a crown charter of the Barony

durno, whose second son was Walter Leslie of Steenbridge, and Walter's son was the James Leslie of Buchanston above (see also page 83).

The following document still exists at Pitcaple re a debt by James Leslie :—

" And because the above named and designed Captain James Leslie of Bouchhanstonne has most contemptiously disobeyed the command and charge given to him formerly by James Sandie Messr. in manner above written. Therefore I the said James Sandie Messr past upon the thirty day of Sept. 1699 years at the Mercat Crose of the head burgh of the sheriffdome thereof and thereat. In his Matres name and authre I duely lawfully and orderly denunced the sd Capt. James Leslie his Maties rebell and putt him to the Horn by three blasts of ane horne as use is and ordained all his moveable goods and gear to be escheat and in brought to his Maties use for his Contemptione and disobedience. This I did before these witnesses Robert Brysone and John Butler, notars, in Edn.—James Sandie Mess."

[1] Since the above was written a new light has been thrown upon the family of Horn by the discovery in an old pamphlet at Castle Forbes of the following :—

" Of the Sirnaime of Horn and several branches John Horn of that Ilk and Westhall bears the paternal coat armorial and hath in some measure retrieved the Breaches made by his predecessors. For in the late civil wars John and Andrew Horns, his two uncles, raised all they could for the service of King Charles II, their royal Master whom they attended to Worcester, leaving nothing to James their younger brother, his (i.e. John's) father—then a child, save some small reversions. John, who commanded a Troop of Horse, was killed, and Andrew obliged to flee to Sweden, where he was kindly received and advanced by Count Henry Horn the then Swedish General."

Another curious note about Mr. John Horn of Westhall is also at Castle Forbes, in MS. It is in the form of a letter by the Duke of Gordon to John Hamilton, his chamberlain, of date 6th June, 1726 :—

" You are to procure a receipt from Mr. John Horn of Westhall for a Silver cup taken by Hutcheon Calder of Aswanley at the Battle of Brichen containing ye weight of said cup and obliging the sd Mr. John Horn to preserve the same saiff and intire in his own custody untill the same be called for from him by us, our heirs and successors."

The paper does not explain why Mr. John Horn should have been in possession of this interesting relic of the battle of Brechin, fought on 18th May, 1452, when the Earl of Huntly defeated the Earl of Crawford, and Hugh or Hutcheon Calder distinguished himself.

John Hamilton, the chamberlain of the Duke of Gordon, was the Jacobite of 1715 and 1745 (see page 216).

of Horn, including Pitmedden, Ardoyne, Buchanston, and Old Rayne (1728), and in 1725 matriculated arms. His daughter, Anna, above mentioned, who married Hew Dalrymple of North Berwick, had a third son, Robert, who succeeded to the estate and took the name of Horn.

In the same way "Pitodry younger," i.e. Thomas Erskine, above, seems to have either collected or paid the Cess on behalf of

Kirktown of Oyne (William Leith) in 1696,

Torries (George Gordon, gentleman) in 1696,

and Old Harthill (George Robertsone) in 1696, both Leith properties.

GORDONSTOWN FOR RYHILL.

Sir Robert Gordon, 3rd Baronet of Gordonstown, eldest son of Sir Ludovick, who married Elizabeth Farquhar of Mounie, and had four sons and three daughters. Robert was born in 1645 and educated abroad, where he became a skilled chemist (and friend and correspondent of Robert Boyle). Such an accomplishment being rare in those days, he acquired the reputation of a wizard, and many fantastic stories of his dealings with the Evil One were current in his lifetime and since. He seems to have had Jacobite sympathies. His wife, who was Elizabeth, heiress of Sir William Dunbar of Hempriggs, married after his death the Hon. James Sutherland, second son of Lord Duffus, who assumed name and arms of Dunbar.[1] Sir Robert Gordon's son and successor, the 4th Baronet, also Sir Robert, was the owner of Gordonstown in the '45 who made so many complaints as to the exactions levied upon him by the Jacobite army in the days of their ascendancy before Culloden. He died in 1772, leaving two sons, Robert and William, who successively succeeded to the Baronetcy ; Sir William died in 1796.

AUCHORSK—D (AUQUHORSK).

The only payer of Double Cess in this parish was John Leslie, grandson to Alexander Leslie, the Laird of Pitcaple, who owned Auquhorsk and Auchquhorthies,though various other persons appear as owners or occupiers of these estates.

On 12th March, 1712, John Leslie, great-grandson to Alexander Leslie, eighth Laird of Pitcaple, had sasine on Auquhorsk and Drummies.[2]

An earlier sasine on 23rd March, 1683, was in favour of John Leslie of Auquhorsk, heir of John Leslie, his father, on Auquhorsk, Auquhorthies, Blairdaff, and other lands.[3] John had been served heir to John in the same year (1683). They were the son and grandson of James, killed at Worcester.

There was also John Abercromby "of Afforsk" in this parish, second

---

son of Alexander Abercromby of Fetternear and Jean Seton, but as he was a Jacobite and one of those taken prisoner at Dunfermline, the entry cannot refer to *him*. The property had been sold to the Leslies— only the superiority retained.

In 1700, Alexander Forbes of Auchquhorthies, Merchant and Burgess of Aberdeen, had had sasine on the estate.[1]

On 3rd August, 1703, there was an assignment by John Leslie of the Mansion House of Auquhorsk to Mrs. Elizabeth Douglas, second daughter of Robert Douglas of Blackford or Bridgford.[2] Elizabeth's mother was Isabella, daughter of James Horn of Westhall.

In 1717 John Leslie of Aquhorsk granted discharge of all his claims to the Miln and Milnlands of Pitcaple "for the love and favor I carie to Alexander Leslie off Pitcaple off whose family I am descended." [3]

CAIRDEN LIFERENT.

(John Leith of Cairden in 1696.)

PITODRY, YR. FOR OLD HARTHILL.

The last of the Leiths of Harthill, who sold the estate to Pittodrie, was Patrick, son of Patrick Leith and Joanna Ogilvie. He was born in 1688, and in the year 1712 appears in the Register of the Scots College in Rome.

"April 1. Patricius Leith, filius etc. Suspectus de Jansenismus Obiit London 5 May 1760."

His brother, Walter, was also at College in Rome in 1653.

In 1691 William Leith of Torries was cautioner for a bond granted by William and Patrick Leith, older and younger of Harthill, to Alex. Lumsden of Auchinleck.[4]

WESTHALL FOR MR. PAT. COUPLAND'S VALUATION (see above).

---

[1] *Aberdeen Sasines.* [2] *Ibid.* [3] *Pitcaple Papers.*

[4] Alexander Lumsden was father of Professor John Lumsden, who was Professor of Divinity in King's College, and married Jean Lumsden, eventual owner of Pitcaple. The Professor was served heir to his brother Alexander Lumsden in 1745, which Alexander Lumsden was son of Alexander Lumsden of "Auchinlett."

—Service of Heirs

The relationship to the family of Cushnie has not been established, but it certainly existed (see page 113).—*Pitcaple Papers.*

PARISH OF DAVIOT.

LUMPHARD LETHENTY—*D.*

Lumphard was the property of Robert Burnett. He was a Quaker, whose relationship to the family of Leys has never been established.

Lethenty was owned at this period by Alexander Rose, eldest son of the Rev. John Rose or Ross, of Insch, minister of Foveran. Alexander had sold Insch and bought Lethenty. He appears to have been a Hanoverian—while his grandfather of the same name was one of those who signed the address to Charles II praying for the restoration of Episcopacy.

GLACK AND FOR DAVIOT.

John Elphinstone of Glack, eldest son of James Elphinstone of Glack, M.P. for Inverurie, who was eldest son of the first James Elphinstone of Glack (who married (1) Elizabeth Wood, and (2) Jean Leslie of Balquhain).

James Elphinstone, M.P., had sasine on Glack in 1700 (his father having died more than thirty years before), and he apparently died *in* that year, his son, John (above), also having sasine on the same date.

The Sir James Elphinstone of 1715 was M.P. for Aberdeenshire ; he was first cousin to John—see family tree (also under Logie-Durno).

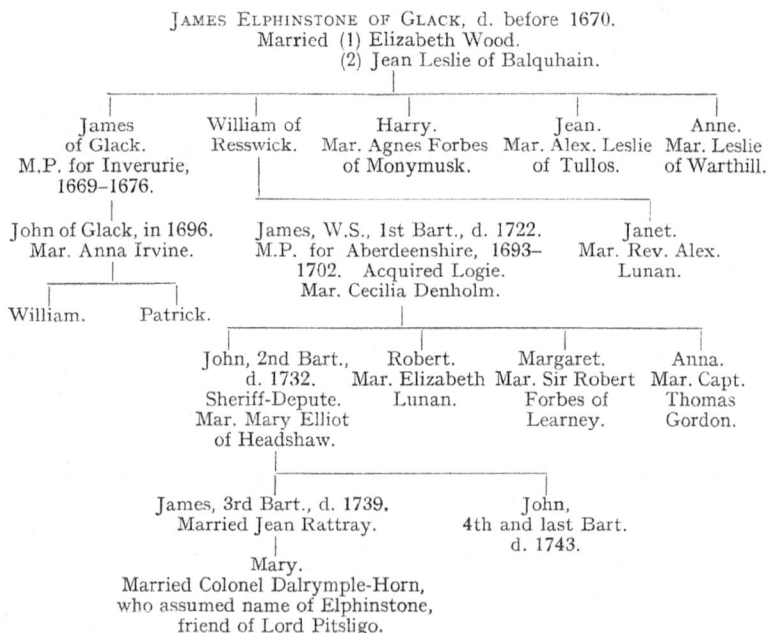

JAMES ELPHINSTONE OF GLACK, d. before 1670.
Married (1) Elizabeth Wood.
(2) Jean Leslie of Balquhain.

James of Glack. M.P. for Inverurie, 1669–1676.	William of Resswick.	Harry. Mar. Agnes Forbes of Monymusk.	Jean. Mar. Alex. Leslie of Tullos.	Anne. Mar. Leslie of Warthill.

John of Glack, in 1696. Mar. Anna Irvine.	James, W.S., 1st Bart., d. 1722. M.P. for Aberdeenshire, 1693–1702. Acquired Logie. Mar. Cecilia Denholm.	Janet. Mar. Rev. Alex. Lunan.

William.	Patrick.

John, 2nd Bart., d. 1732. Sheriff-Depute. Mar. Mary Elliot of Headshaw.	Robert. Mar. Elizabeth Lunan.	Margaret. Mar. Sir Robert Forbes of Learney.	Anna. Mar. Capt. Thomas Gordon.

James, 3rd Bart., d. 1739. Married Jean Rattray.	John, 4th and last Bart. d. 1743.

Mary.
Married Colonel Dalrymple-Horn,
who assumed name of Elphinstone,
friend of Lord Pitsligo.

John of Glack married Anna Irvine and had two sons, William and Patrick.

Daviot was, in 1696, the property of William Robertson, late Baillie of Aberdeen. Elphinstone may have acquired the estate or merely have paid or handed over his neighbour's Cess.

SIR JOHN REID OF BARRA—see PARISH OF BOURTIE.

BARRA, YOUNGER—*D*—see PARISH OF BOURTIE.

MUNIE—*D*. [William Seton.]

Sir Robert Farquhar of Mounie left the lands to his representative, Patrick Farquhar, who was followed by Alexander, formerly of Tonley. The latter lost the estate through bankruptcy in 1702. Walter Hay of Arnbath bought it, but sold it in 1714 to George Seton, who represented the old family of Seton which had disponed these lands in 1623 to John Urquhart of Craigfintray, from whom they passed to Sir Robert Farquhar. George Seton, the purchaser, was second son of Lord Pitmedden. He married twice: (1) a daughter of Sir Alexander Gibson of Pentland, and (2) Anna Leslie, grand-daughter of James Leslie, 4th of Warthill; by the latter he had a son, William Seton, who succeeded to Mounie. He died unmarried, and his estates passed to his sister, Margaret, the wife of James Anderson, LL.D., who took the name of Seton.

PARISH OF LOGIE-DURNO.

PITODRY, ELDER—see PARISH OF OYNE.

EARL OF MAR, FOR FEU DUTIES.

PITODRY, YOUNGER.

BALQUHANE, FOR OLD LANDS.

This was Count George Leslie, 16th Baron, son of Patrick, Count Leslie (who succeeded his father, Alexander Leslie of Tullos, in 1677). Alexander had been created a Count of the Holy Roman Empire by the Emperor Leopold, 31st March, 1672, and this honour descended to his son and grandson, George (above). Alexander's wife was Jean Elphinstone of Glack. Patrick married (1) Elizabeth, daughter of Gavin Douglas of Bridgford, and (2), in 1679, Mary, daughter of Alexander Irvine of Drum. By his second marriage contract he bound himself to leave the estate of Balquhain to the son of Mary Irvine, and at his death, in 1710, George, their only son, succeeded, and was the Balquhain of the 1715.

THE FAMILY OF BALQUHAIN.

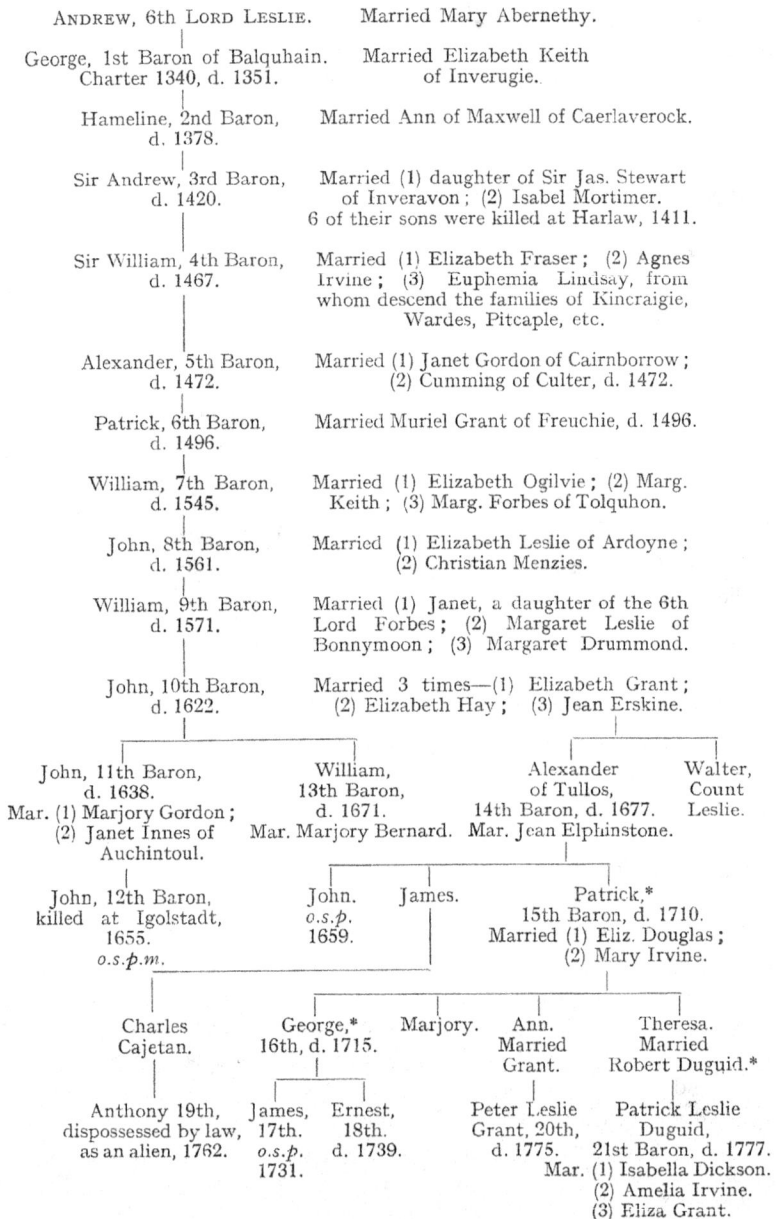

ANDREW, 6th LORD LESLIE.   Married Mary Abernethy.

George, 1st Baron of Balquhain.   Married Elizabeth Keith
     Charter 1340, d. 1351.   of Inverugie.

Hameline, 2nd Baron,   Married Ann of Maxwell of Caerlaverock.
     d. 1378.

Sir Andrew, 3rd Baron,   Married (1) daughter of Sir Jas. Stewart
     d. 1420.   of Inveravon ; (2) Isabel Mortimer.
             6 of their sons were killed at Harlaw, 1411.

Sir William, 4th Baron,   Married (1) Elizabeth Fraser ; (2) Agnes
     d. 1467.   Irvine ; (3) Euphemia Lindsay, from
             whom descend the families of Kincraigie,
             Wardes, Pitcaple, etc.

Alexander, 5th Baron,   Married (1) Janet Gordon of Cairnborrow ;
     d. 1472.   (2) Cumming of Culter, d. 1472.

Patrick, 6th Baron,   Married Muriel Grant of Freuchie, d. 1496.
     d. 1496.

William, 7th Baron,   Married (1) Elizabeth Ogilvie ; (2) Marg.
     d. 1545.   Keith ; (3) Marg. Forbes of Tolquhon.

John, 8th Baron,   Married (1) Elizabeth Leslie of Ardoyne ;
     d. 1561.   (2) Christian Menzies.

William, 9th Baron,   Married (1) Janet, a daughter of the 6th
     d. 1571.   Lord Forbes ; (2) Margaret Leslie of
             Bonnymoon ; (3) Margaret Drummond.

John, 10th Baron,   Married 3 times—(1) Elizabeth Grant ;
     d. 1622.   (2) Elizabeth Hay ; (3) Jean Erskine.

John, 11th Baron, d. 1638. Mar. (1) Marjory Gordon ; (2) Janet Innes of Auchintoul.	William, 13th Baron, d. 1671. Mar. Marjory Bernard.	Alexander of Tullos, 14th Baron, d. 1677. Mar. Jean Elphinstone.	Walter, Count Leslie.

John, 12th Baron, killed at Igolstadt, 1655. *o.s.p.m.*	John. *o.s.p.* 1659.	James.	Patrick,* 15th Baron, d. 1710. Married (1) Eliz. Douglas ; (2) Mary Irvine.

Charles Cajetan.	George,* 16th, d. 1715.	Marjory.	Ann. Married Grant.	Theresa. Married Robert Duguid.*

Anthony 19th, dispossessed by law, as an alien, 1762.	James, 17th. *o.s.p.* 1731.	Ernest, 18th. d. 1739.	Peter Leslie Grant, 20th, d. 1775.	Patrick Leslie Duguid, 21st Baron, d. 1777. Mar. (1) Isabella Dickson. (2) Amelia Irvine. (3) Eliza Grant.

Those appearing in the Cess Roll are marked by an asterisk.

SECOND TREE.

William Leslie, 9th Baron of Balquhain, and his descendants in fuller detail.

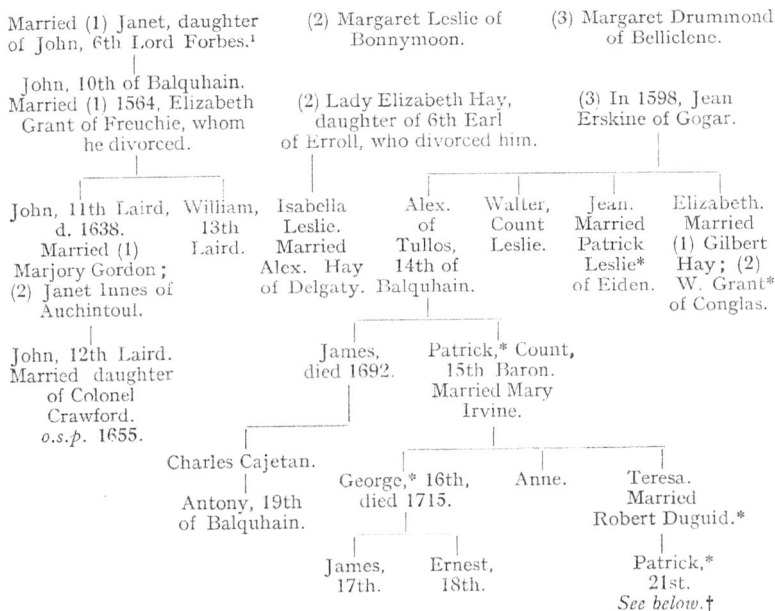

Married (1) Janet, daughter   (2) Margaret Leslie of   (3) Margaret Drummond
of John, 6th Lord Forbes.[1]   Bonnymoon.   of Belliclene.

John, 10th of Balquhain.
Married (1) 1564, Elizabeth   (2) Lady Elizabeth Hay,   (3) In 1598, Jean
Grant of Freuchie, whom   daughter of 6th Earl   Erskine of Gogar.
     he divorced.   of Erroll, who divorced him.

John, 11th Laird,   William,   Isabella   Alex.   Walter,   Jean.   Elizabeth.
   d. 1638.   13th   Leslie.   of   Count   Married   Married
  Married (1)   Laird.   Married   Tullos,   Leslie.   Patrick   (1) Gilbert
Marjory Gordon ;   Alex. Hay   14th of   Leslie*   Hay; (2)
(2) Janet Innes of   of Delgaty.   Balquhain.   of Eiden.   W. Grant*
  Auchintoul.   of Conglas.

John, 12th Laird.   James,   Patrick,* Count,
Married daughter   died 1692.   15th Baron.
of Colonel   Married Mary
Crawford.   Irvine.
o.s.p. 1655.

             Charles Cajetan.   George,* 16th,   Anne.   Teresa.
                 Antony, 19th   died 1715.   Married
            of Balquhain.   Robert Duguid.*

                        James,   Ernest,   Patrick,*
                        17th.   18th.   21st.
                                          See below.†

The 20th Baron of Balquhain was Peter Leslie Grant, grandson of Anne, elder sister
to Teresa (above). After him succeeded Teresa's son, (above).

† Patrick Leslie Duguid, 21st of Balquhain.
Married (1) Isabella Dickson (all children died young).
        (2) Amelia Irvine, and had James, Charles and Elizabeth.
        (3) Eliza Grant.

The 4th son, John, became 22nd of Balquhain.
Married Violet Dalzell, and had 15 children.

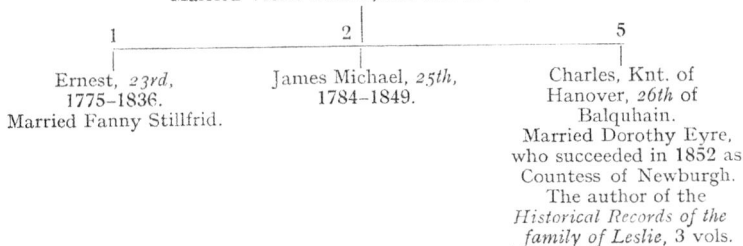

    1   2   5

Ernest, *23rd,*   James Michael, *25th,*   Charles, Knt. of
1775–1836.   1784–1849.   Hanover, *26th* of
Married Fanny Stillfrid.   Balquhain.
                                  Married Dorothy Eyre,
                            who succeeded in 1852 as
                           Countess of Newburgh.
                            The author of the
                           Historical Records of the
                           family of Leslie, 3 vols.

Those appearing in the Cess Rôll are marked by an asterisk.

[1] Janet Forbes was already twice a widow, having married first, John, 3rd
Earl of Atholl, and secondly, Alexander Hay of Delgaty.

Patrick was the third but second surviving son of Alexander of Tullos. The prosperity of his uncle and cousins [1] in Germany enabled him to re-assemble some of the family estates. Fetternear, having been bought from the Abercrombies in 1690, became his principal residence.

George, as already seen, succeeded at his father's death, in 1710; his half-brother, James, son of Count Patrick's first wife, Elizabeth Douglas, grand-daughter of the Earl of Angus, had ceded all rights and become a German subject.

George married Margaret (daughter of John, 8th Lord Elphinstone and Isabel Lauder), and died on 17th June, 1715, being succeeded by an infant son. Margaret Elphinstone subsequently married (2) Sir James Gordon of Park, and (3) John Fullarton of Dudwick.

The Castle of Balquhain was never inhabited after his day, and was burnt by Cumberland's soldiers thirty years later.

SIR JAMES ELPHINSTONE (*Sup.*).

Sir James Elphinstone was second son of James Elphinstone of Glack. About 1670 he acquired the lands of Logie-Durno, on which he had a Crown Charter, 28th February, 1677.

It was for the use of the tenants on Logie that Alexander Leslie, 9th of Pitcaple, bound himself to keep a boat on the water of Urie, 1736. The Agreement is at Pitcaple.[2]

James Elphinstone was a W.S. in 1671 and Judge 1679. From 1693 to 1702 he was Member of Parliament for Inverurie, and in 1701 was made a baronet. He married Cecilia Denholme of Muirhouse in 1673, and had two sons and two daughters :—

1. John, the 2nd Baronet, Sheriff-Depute of Aberdeenshire. He married Mary, daughter of Sir Gilbert Elliot of Headshaw.

2. Robert, who married Elizabeth Lunan, his cousin, daughter of Alexander Lunan, minister of Daviot, and Janet Elphinstone, sister of Sir James. (Janet had sasine on Daviot for her liferent in 1708.) Alexander Lunan was deposed in 1716 for refusing to join in the thanksgiving for the accession of George I.

3. Margaret, married Robert Forbes, Advocate, son of Sir John Forbes of Craigievar, afterwards Sir Robert Forbes of Learney.

4. Anna, married Captain Thomas Gordon, R.N.

BALQUHAIN, FOR FETTERNEIR.

The estate of Fetternear had been bought by Count George Leslie's father from Francis Abercromby, Lord Glasford. It still remains in the Leslie family, though the mansion house was burnt down in 1920.

---

[1] See tree, page 91.   [2] *Pitcaple Papers.*

Patrick Abercromby (brother of Francis), third son of Alexander Abercromby and Jean Seton, was born 1656 and educated at Douai. He became an M.D. of St. Andrews and physician to King James VII. He was an ardent Jacobite, and was used as a messenger by the Earl of Mar to King James. He died some time after the Rising in poor circumstances. He wrote *The Martial Achievements of the Scottish Nation.*

LETHENTY—*D*—see PARISH OF DAVIOT.

INVERAMSAY. [Patrick Smith.]

Admitted to the Society of Advocates, 16th November, 1705, he was the son of John Smith of Inveramsay and was also proprietor of Drimmies.

He married, 8th November, 1705 (sasine of that date), Elizabeth Ker of Menie, born 1686 and died 1761,and had three sons and six daughters (vide *Poll Book*). David, the eldest, was a Jacobite in '45 with his younger brothers, Alexander (who succeeded to Menie) and Andrew. Andrew was transported but Alexander left the Prince's army, while David was tried and acquitted. Their sister, Helen, married Charles Hacket, another Jacobite of '45.

PITCAPLE.

Alexander Leslie, 9th of Pitcaple, who died between 1736 and 1738, was father of the so-called last Leslie, Laird of Pitcaple, Sir James Leslie, Knight of St. Louis. Sir James died 1757—he left no children (see page 73). Two half-brothers, Charles and John, nominally succeeded, but the estate ultimately came to James' half-sister, Jane, who married Professor John Lumsden, and their two daughters sold Pitcaple to Henry Lumsden, Advocate in Aberdeen.

Alexander Leslie, father of Sir James and Jane, with the eight others, was infeft in Pitcaple on 18th April, 1704, though his father, Alexander, had died before 1679.

Alexander Leslie was twice married: (1) to Marjory Leslie, (2) to Henrietta Irvine.

By his first wife he had one son only :—

Sir James, 10th Laird of Pitcaple, died 1757.

By the second wife—four sons, who are thus given by Colonel Charles Leslie (see page 91) :—

George, R.N. (died without issue).

John, in holy orders.

Alexander, a Jesuit.

Charles, a goldsmith in Dublin ;

and five daughters—Jane, married Professor John Lumsden and succeeded to Pitcaple ; Isabella, Teresa, Agnes, and Anne, who married Robert Cumming of Allathen (Colonel Leslie gives his name wrongly as Alexander).

Sir James died abroad, at Lille, and a curious account exists of "the intromissions" at the time of his death.

Among the assets are :—

> For partnership in a Privateer of Dunkirk, during all the war.
> For interest in a partnership in Gottenburg.
> An order for his pension as Major for the years 1755 and 1756.

And on the debit side :—

> To hors hire to announce Sir James's death.
> To acolytes at the Mass.
> To beat the mattress on which Sir James died.
> To Madame Leslie's hair curler till Sir James' death.
> To the Milliner for her memoire of things sold to Sir James's lady before his death.
> To the Harpsicord master for a year. [1]

The net result was a balance due to the Executors !

The name of the wife was "Deniset," *her surname.* She signs her letters, of which a good many exist, as "Deniset, Baronne de Leslie." Her mother's letters are signed Blattier Deniset. A great deal of trouble was occasioned by Teresa Leslie's inability to read French, and the business consequent on Sir James' death dragged on for several years.

Colonel Charles Leslie, in the *Historical Records of the Family of Leslie,* is curiously incorrect concerning the last Leslie Lairds of Pitcaple, who died a hundred years before he wrote his book. Alexander, the 9th Laird, got into hopeless financial embarrassment, as is shown by letters from London and elsewhere from his eldest son, Sir James, who expresses the pious intention of paying his father's debts. This he was apparently unable to do, for service in the Royal Swedish Regiment of France, though it was worth a knighthood of St. Louis to him, brought very little money. He married a Frenchwoman of the name of Deniset, as the accounts of the executry give "sa veuve et Madame Deniset sa belle mere." The widow claims thirty thousand livres "de son port et amandement," which she probably did not get, and another three thousand for mourning according to the laws and customs of the country, which included ceremonial draperies for the mourning chamber, etc. Sir James does not seem to have left a will, and it appears that Professor John Lumsden, husband of Jane Leslie, paid some of the debts for the estate of Pitcaple before 1766 and settled it on his daughters, Agnes and Teresa, with the consent of Henrietta, who was the wife of Dr. Patrick Duff, minister of Old Aberdeen. In regard to the half-brothers of James, Colonel Charles Leslie would appear to have got them in the wrong *order*, as Charles is called the third in the codicil to his father's will. The fact that he was a Goldsmith in Dublin is correct ; probably George, R.N., was dead, as well as Alexander, "a Jesuit," of whom a good deal is known. In any case Charles called himself "of Pitcaple" for the two years during which he survived Sir James, and his sister, Teresa, was his factrix in Scotland. His end is described in the following letter to Teresa Leslie from her nephew, Alexander Leslie, dated Dublin, 19th June, 1759 :—

Dear Madam,

The publick papers have probably ere this brought you the melancholy news of my uncle Charles' death, and it was not for want of the proper respect and a fixed resolution to do it as soon as I could give you any reasonable information about the circumstances, that I did not, much sooner, take this very disagreeable opportunity of introducing myself to a Lady for whom I have long, unacquainted had the highest esteem and respect. Yr. brother, Madam, from the way you last saw him and the advice he thought it necessary to take in Edinburgh, you may easily conceive had ever since been losing ground and visibly to himself and his friends in a bad state of health and yet this did not prevent Irregularity. On Thursday now three weeks past he went about seven miles off to a fair to buy a saddle horse, came home about three in the afternoon in a most violent heat, shifted, dined and wt only his slippers on late in the evening went out to one of his Alderman friends, sat up late and was the next day seized with a fever of which he dyed the 12th day without being capable in all that time to make a will or give any directions about his affairs. . . . My sister who lives in this town came immediately to him and assisted his poor wife in taking all proper care of him but alas fruitlessly, no quiet no ease could he gett till a very short time before his Death, when he was too weak and far gone to mind worldly affairs. On a letter wrote by my sister the day he was first blistered I came in 32 hours to Dublin, a journey of about 70 miles [*he must have walked !*] . . . he knew me for a short Interval and seemed greatly raised, obliged me four times after one another to come and kiss him and repeatedly and with great earnestness blessed me my wife and child.

. . . All the care I could I have taken to search for a will but none has been found. His wife was therefore entitled to administration and has administered, but I have, you may rely upon it taken and am taking proper care of his effects. . . . I have enquired closely and looked myself into the stock in the shop and find it would answer his debts. I called in the assistance of a man of skill and credit in the same way of business, and sett him and my uncle's shopkeeper to weigh measure and value every ounce of goods. . . . I cannot help observing to you for all mankind are more or less vainglorious, that had I not been here when he dyed matters would in the opinion of my aunt and everyone else have been quite otherwise. . . . I have just room at the bottom to give a sketch of what I have discovered about his circumstances, and must beg leave to stop here and subscribe myself, dear Madam,

Yr. truly afft. and most obedt. humble servant,

A. LESLIE.

The portion of letter below, beginning "Debts on record," has been torn off.

The letter is addressed :—

To Mrs. TERESA LESLIE AT PITCAPLE
NEAR ABERDEEN,
NORTH BRITAIN.

From Donaghadee. postage paid 2/-

and endorsed—

ALEX. LESLIE, DUBLIN.

A Will was afterwards found (in a secret drawer !) by which he left something to his nephew, the Rev. Alexander Leslie, and *his* son Henry.

In a registered "Destination," date 1731, or codicil to his Will in favour of the children of the second marriage, Alexander Leslie, 9th of Pitcaple, left the whole sum to the five daughters, expressly cutting out "Charles Leslie, my third son by the above marriage for good and onerous causes to myself well knowen," and bequeathing him nothing. The other sons are not mentioned. Possibly Alexander Leslie believed them to be dead ; though, as proved by other documents, Charles lived until 1759, John was alive in 1760, while George apparently left a son, Alexander, and a daughter.

In another Will, of date 1736, Alexander Leslie makes further mention of his goldsmith son :—

I Alex. Leslie of Pitcaple by this doe testifie and declare that the disson of silver tea spoons marked at the end A.L.H.I. [*that is with his own and his wife's initials*], doth belong to Charles Leslie, goldsmith in the city of Dublin, and that they were made by him and given the use of them to me during my Lifetyme and att my death to be returned to him or his order.

After the death of Charles, John, presumably the 4th son of the second marriage, took out a "birth brieve" to prove himself heir of Pitcaple, and called himself "now of Pitcaple." His Will, written and signed at Erfurt, "in Thuringia," on 15th July, 1760, duly witnessed by two Professors(!), still exists at Pitcaple. In it he states that he never intends to marry or return to Scotland (he was, therefore, *not* a priest, as stated by Colonel Charles Leslie), and leaves everything to his four sisters—Jane, wife of Professor John Lumsden ; Teresa, Isabella, and Agnes.

Anne, wife of Robert Cumming of Allathen, was apparently dead, but her children are mentioned.

John expressly states that, in 1760, he is the *only* son now in life of the deceased Alexander Leslie of Pitcaple, so the Jesuit must also have been dead. Failing all the heirs of his two married sisters, Jane Lumsden and Anne Cumming, John appoints as ultimate heir "David Dalrymple,

2nd son of Hew Dalrymple of Drummore and Ann Horn his spouse, who was grand-daughter to Mr. James Horn of Westhall and —— Leslie, his spouse" (she was Isobel, daughter of John Leslie, 7th Laird, who was great-aunt to John—David Dalrymple, therefore, was second cousin once removed). Jane Lumsden was to have during her life the exclusive use of "the House and croft of Pitcaple which she has possessed and enjoyed for many years bygone, since our father's decease." (The ultimate heir of Pitcaple was to be liable to pay the debts!)

After the death of Jane Leslie (Mrs. Lumsden), her daughters, Teresa and Agnes, became owners—then Agnes became sole proprietrix, and there is a good deal of correspondence as to whether under the somewhat grandiloquent settlements she was obliged to take the name of Leslie. This she did not do, but sold the estate (with its debts) to her cousin, Henry Lumsden, Advocate, Aberdeen, whose great grandson, Rear Admiral Walter Lumsden, C.I.E., C.V.O., still possesses it, and by his kindness the above particulars are now printed for the first time.[1]

PITODRIE, FOR KNOCKOLLACHY.

This was part of the estate of Auquhorsk, having been sold by Balquhain to Pitcaple in 1624 and thereafter joined with Pitbee to Auquhorsk. The tenant of 1715 seems to have shared the political opinions of Erskine of Pitodrie and not of his own laird, who paid double—see below.

AUCHORSK—*D*—see PARISH OF OYNE.

EARL OF ABERDEEN—*D*. PARISH OF METHLICK.

BLAIRDAFF.

This estate, which was until nearly the end of the 17th century in the hands of Leslie of Balquhain, had passed to the Smiths, an ardent Jacobite family according to Davidson's *Inverurie*. In 1696 it was Alexander Smith.[2]

PITODRY ELDER, FOR ALEX. ANDERSON—see PARISH OF BOURTIE.

HARLAW.

Patrick Gordon of Harlaw, who was alive in 1705 was the son of Alexander Gordon of Kincraigie. He married Rachel Leslie and had two sons, Alexander and James, both merchants in Poland in 1707, and a daughter, Jane, who married Charles Lumsden, second son of John Lumsden of Auchindoir, younger brother of Harry who succeeded to Harlaw.

---

[1] From the *Pitcaple Papers.*   [2] *Aberdeen Sasines.*

In the *Poll Book* Patrick Gordon appears in 1696 as "residenter in Aberdeen, with his wife Rachel, and William and Jean, his children, being said to be pollable for his lands in Logiedurno and Tullich."

Patrick Gordon appears in Tullich in this Valuation.

William *Leslie*, younger of Harlaw, is mentioned in the *Pitcaple Papers* in 1690.

GLACK—see PARISH OF DAVIOT.

PARISH OF KEITHALL (formerly MONTKEGIE).

THE EARL OF KINTOIR.

John Keith (fifth and youngest, but third surviving son of William, 6th Earl Marischal), who was created Earl of Kintore and Baron Inverurie in 1667, left one son, William, the 2nd Earl, who married Catherine, daughter of David, 4th Viscount Stormont. He and his son, John, Lord Inverurie, afterwards 3rd Earl, born 1699, were both Jacobites of the '15 and were present at Sheriffmuir, but curiously enough seem to have managed to conceal their very active participation, though Lord Kintore is said to have mourned for the loss of the Jacobite cause all the rest of his life by not shaving his beard. He gave himself up to the authorities, along with Lord Rollo. That his activities were surmised appears from a letter from the Lord Justice Clerk to the Secretary of State in London, 7th August, 1716, in which he says, "Our Advocate depute is att a loss to know how and before whom he can cite a peer, i.e. the Earl of Kintore. You have not taught him that point of forme all the tyme you have had him among you in London." [1]

He was, however, not cited, and neither he nor his eldest son, Lord Inverurie, seem to have suffered in any way for their share in the Rising, save by being deprived of the office of Knight Marischal. It is said that the Duke of Argyll used his influence on Kintore's behalf, and the office was restored to John, Lord Inverurie, when 3rd Earl. William, 2nd Earl, died 5th December, 1718. The 3rd Earl married Mary, daughter of James Erskine, son of the Earl of Mar, and died without issue, being succeeded by his brother William, who died unmarried, in 1761, when the estates devolved upon his cousin, George, the attainted 10th Earl Marischal.

ELRICK, FOR NEW PLACE—D.

In 1707 Sir John Johnston, 4th Baronet of Caskieben, who succeeded in 1690, disponed New Place to his son-in-law, Andrew Burnett of Elrick, whose son, John, sold it in 1739 to the Synod of Aberdeen.

[1] *Public Record Office, S.P.* 54.12.97.

Sir John Johnston was an active Jacobite of the '15 and was present at the battle of Sheriffmuir, where his only son, John, was killed by his side. He left two daughters—Marjory, married Andrew Burnett of Elrick, and Janet, who married Charles Forbes of Shiels.

Sir John did not return home after the failure of the Rising but lived in Edinburgh, where he died in 1724, and was succeeded by his distant cousin.

PARISH OF BOURTIE.

SIR JOHN REID, FOR BARA.

Sir John Reid of Barra, the 3rd Baronet, who succeeded in 1709.

John Reid, 1st Baronet, was the son of James Reid, Advocate in Aberdeen, who had bought the estates of Bourtie and Barra from the family of Seton. John was created a baronet of Nova Scotia in 1702. He married Marion Abercromby. At the time of the taking of the poll in 1696 John Reid was in possession, with his wife, his eldest son, Alexander, 2nd Baronet, and three daughters. On 15th September, 1709, Sir John Reid of Barra, 3rd Baronet, and Alexander Reid, his son, had sasine. It is curious that while the father appears in 1715 to have been a Jacobite, the son was on the opposite side; he became Alexander, 4th Baronet, and was M.P. for Aberdeenshire.

The Baronetcy became extinct with the death of the 8th Baronet, Sir Alexander, in 1885.[1]

BARRA, YOUNGER—*D.*

BOURTIE ANDERSON, FOR HALF OF BOURTY.

CAPTAIN ANDERSON, FOR THE OTHER HALF.

According to Spalding, during the troubles of 1688–89, John Anderson, son of John Anderson of Bourtie (who had bought that estate from John Reid when the latter bought Barra), was known to both sides as "Skipper Anderson." He died in 1673, and in 1696 the estate was owned by his sons, "Alexander and John Andersons, heirs proportionally of the said lands, who live in Aberdeen."[2] John was called "a Skipper

[1] Sasine 2nd March, 1702. "Mr. John Reid of the town and lands of Easter Balbrydie. Ditto 19th Dec. 1716, John and Alexander Reids of the town and lands of Fingask."—*Aberdeen Sasines.*

[2] He had another son, William, who in 1672 had sasine of "ane tenement in Torrie," but he must have predeceased his father. Alexander and John had sasine in 1697 only.—*Ibid.*

in Aberdeen." Alexander Anderson died before 1728, as his Will is in the Commissariot Record for that year.

The next owner was Patrick Anderson, second son of Alexander.

In 1696 Alexander, living in Aberdeen, had five children—John, Peter, Margaret, Isobel, and Rachel.

AUCHORTIS, FOR COLLIEHILL.

This was Alexander Abercromby of Cothall (a Jacobite of 1715), son of Thomas Abercromby of Cothall or Colliehill, who was a brother of Alexander Abercromby, late of Fetternear. The wife of Thomas was Isabel Bisset. Alexander of Cothall was born in 1662 and was, therefore, 53 at the time of the Rising. John Forbes of Auchquhorthies apparently paid for him, and subsequently owned Colliehill.

THORNTOWN—*D.* [Robert Sympson.]

A double Cess. The lands of "Thorntoune, Lawelsyde and Pitgavenie" belonged in 1696 to Robert Sympson, son of Alexander Symson of Thornton. He had a son, Robert Sympson, younger of Thorntoun, who was then possessor and tenant of Lawelsyde, as well as a younger son, John, and a daughter, Elizabeth.

HEIRS OF BLAIR (DR. STEWART).

The lands of Blair in Bourtie were in the hands of Margaret and Elizabeth Seton. Dr. Stewart apparently acted for them.

BLACKHOUSE was owned in 1696 by John Panton and his mother, Margaret Strachan.

PARISH OF KINKELL.

THE EARL OF KINTOIR. (PARISH OF KEITH HALL.)

BALBITHAN—*D.* [James Balfour.]

James Chalmers, of the old family of Balbithan, had before 1696 disponed of his estate to James Balfour, merchant in Edinburgh.

THE LADY BALBITHAN, who pays single, was probably the widow of James Chalmers.

THAINSTON

Was at this period still in the possession of the Laird of Tolquhon.

It was not till 1717 that it was purchased by Provost Thomas Mitchell, son of Baillie Thomas Mitchell and Marjory Moir.

He married first a daughter of Provost Sir Patrick Leslie, secondly Isabella, sister of Alexander Paton, Provost, and thirdly, Jane Mercer, who survived him. The famous Sir Andrew Mitchell of Thainston, British Minister to the Prussian Court, was his son-in-law and nephew.

PARISH OF KEMNAY.

The Earl of Kintore (above).

The Laird of Kemnay.

Thomas Burnett of Kemnay, son of Thomas Burnett (second son of James of Craigmyle, who bought the estate in 1688, and his wife, Margaret Pearson), was born in 1656. He was a member of the Scottish Bar but did not practise, as he preferred residing abroad, where he formed one of the Court circle round that remarkable woman, Sophia, Electress of Hanover, youngest of the eleven children of Elizabeth of Bohemia ("Queen of Hearts," the favourite sister of Charles I). Sophia was sister of Prince Rupert and mother of George I, and only missed by six weeks her great ambition of reigning in England. She died at the age of 80, in June, 1714, and her first cousin once removed of the younger generation (Queen Anne) died 4th August in the same year. When Thomas Burnett was not in residence in Hanover, Sophia wrote him frequent and friendly letters in French. He also corresponded with Leibnitz, Locke, and other personalities of his day. In September, 1696, he wrote from London to his cousin, Sir Thomas Burnet, complaining that his state of health does not permit him "to ramble backwards and forwards to Scotland."

He felt himself very much aggrieved by arrangements for the succession to Craigmyle, which had been in 1686 entailed by his nephew, Alexander, or heirs male of his body (of which he had none), and failing any to "Thomas Burnet of Kemnay his uncle" and *his* heirs male, and successively to James and Robert, his other uncles. Two years later Alexander (of Craigmyle) had signed a declaration in Edinburgh to the effect that he revoked this entail and intended to revert to a former entail on his daughters, Isabel, Anna, and Margaret. He omitted to destroy the original entail, which was found at his death, in 1694, with the declaration cancelling it. Litigation ensured, and after five years a decision was given in favour of the daughters, of whom one was already dead. Isabel had become the first of the four wives of John Farquharson of Invercauld. Margaret, the youngest, subsequently became the wife of Sir Charles Maitland of Pitrichie, and secondly of Thomas Erskine of Pittodrie. Craigmyle remained in the family of Farquharson (Alexander, the brother of John, having purchased it).

In 1701 Thomas Burnett was again at the Court of Hanover and in the following year he was in Paris, when the War of the Spanish Succession broke out, followed by the declaration of war against France by Queen Anne's Government. This was made a pretext for arresting Thomas Burnett while copying an inscription, and was followed by eighteen months in the Bastille. The Electress Sophia and the Duchess of Orleans, procured his release and he then went to Geneva. He returned to England before 1713, in which year, when nearly 60, he married an English girl, Elizabeth, daughter of Richard Brickendon of Inkpen, Berks,[1] and resided at Kemnay towards the end of his life. He died 26th February, 1729, leaving one son, George, born 1714, who married in 1733 his cousin, Helen Burnett of Leys, daughter of Alexander, the 4th Baronet, and had a daughter, Anna, born 1717.

His widow married Dr. Lamont, who had been tutor to her son, George.[2]

PARISH OF MONYMUSK.

The Lord Cullen—D.

Sir Francis Grant, eldest son of Alexander Grant of Ballintomb, Morayshire, and his wife, Christian Nairne of Cromdale, was born in 1658 and became an Advocate in 1691. In 1705 he was made a baronet of Nova Scotia, with remainder to his heirs whatsoever, and four years later he was raised to the Bench with the title of Lord Cullen, which he took from his estate in Gamrie. In 1711 he bought the estate of Monymusk from Sir William Forbes, 4th Baronet, whose son, John, "younger of Monymusk,"[3] married Mary, only sister of the 4th Lord Forbes of Pitsligo.

He was a prominent Whig, a supporter of William of Orange, of the Union, and of the Hanoverian dynasty. He was also a noted philanthropist. He married three times, first, in 1694, Jean, daughter of the Rev. William Meldrum ; secondly, in 1708, Sarah Fordyce ; and thirdly, in 1718, Agnes Hay, by whom he left a son, Sir Archibald. He had another son, William, who became Lord Advocate by the title of Lord Prestongrange, and three daughters :—

Jean, married Alexander Garden of Troup ; Christian, married George Buchan ; and Helen, married Andrew McDouall.

Lord Cullen died in 1726.

(Sir William Forbes of Monymusk, 4th Baronet, was served heir to his father, Sir John Forbes, 3rd Baronet, who died in January, 1702.

---

[1] In a sasine of date 29th June, 1714, she appears as "Elizabeth *Brebner*, spouse to Mr. Thomas Burnett of Kemnay."—*Aberdeen Sasines*.

[2] All this is taken from the *Family of Burnett of Leys*, edited by Col. J. Allardyce (Spalding Club).

[3] He never succeeded, as he predeceased his father.

The title of Baronet of Monymusk was long retained although the estate had been sold.)

On 17th November, 1707, before the sale, there was a sasine, granting money to Agnes Forbes and John Forbes, sister and brother of Sir William, and to John Forbes, younger son of Sir John (who was the collector of this Cess) and Susanna Morison, spouse of the said John Forbes (afterwards of Upper Boyndlie). John and Susanna married in 1704. In 1707 they had three children.

The first Forbes of Monymusk was Duncan, second son to William Forbes of Corsindae, who "seized" the priory lands of Monymusk at the Reformation, having previously advanced money to the Priory on the security of the lands and foreclosed the mortgage.

Duncan was prosecuted in 1564 for coining false money. He married Agnes, daughter to Baillie Wm. Gray of Aberdeen, and died in 1584.

William, 2nd Laird, had a Crown Charter in 1589. He married Margaret, daughter of Sir Wm. Douglas of Kemnay.

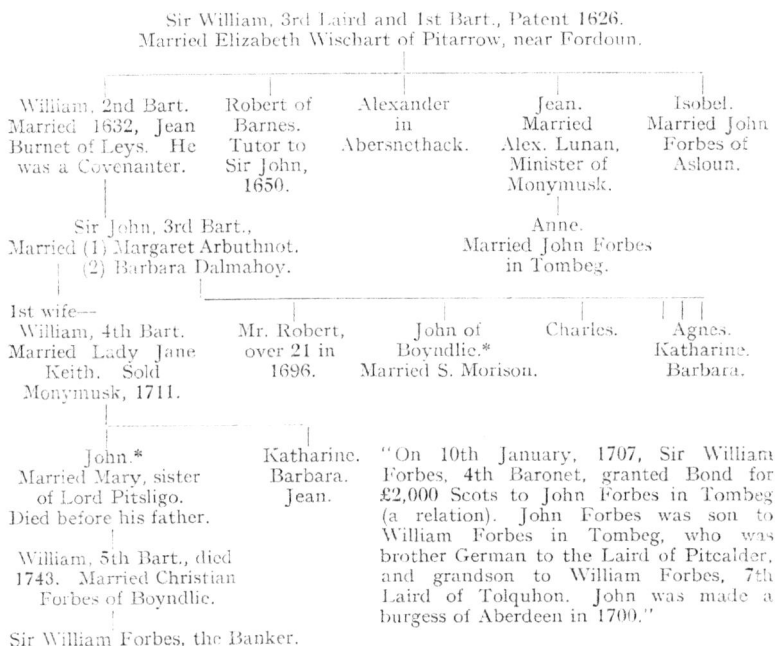

Sir William, 3rd Laird and 1st Bart., Patent 1626.
Married Elizabeth Wischart of Pitarrow, near Fordoun.

William, 2nd Bart. Married 1632, Jean Burnet of Leys. He was a Covenanter.	Robert of Barnes. Tutor to Sir John, 1650.	Alexander in Abersnethack.	Jean. Married Alex. Lunan, Minister of Monymusk.	Isobel. Married John Forbes of Asloun.

Sir John, 3rd Bart.,
Married (1) Margaret Arbuthnot.
(2) Barbara Dalmahoy.

Anne.
Married John Forbes
in Tombeg.

1st wife— William, 4th Bart. Married Lady Jane Keith. Sold Monymusk, 1711.	Mr. Robert, over 21 in 1696.	John of Boyndlie.* Married S. Morison.	Charles.	Agnes. Katharine. Barbara.

John.* Married Mary, sister of Lord Pitsligo. Died before his father.	Katharine. Barbara. Jean.	"On 10th January, 1707, Sir William Forbes, 4th Baronet, granted Bond for £2,000 Scots to John Forbes in Tombeg (a relation). John Forbes was son to William Forbes in Tombeg, who was brother German to the Laird of Pitcalder, and grandson to William Forbes, 7th Laird of Tolquhon. John was made a burgess of Aberdeen in 1700."

William, 5th Bart., died
1743. Married Christian
Forbes of Boyndlie.

Sir William Forbes, the Banker.

The names appearing in the Cess Roll are marked by an asterisk.

PARISH OF KINTOIR.

THE EARLE OF KINTOIR—see PARISH OF KEITH HALL.

PARISH OF INVERURIE.

EARL OF KINTORE—see PARISH OF KEITH HALL.

BALQUHAIN, FOR HIS OLD LANDS—see PARISH OF LOGIE-DURNO.

DITTO, FOR A PART OF FETTERNIER (FETTERNEAR).

PITODRY ELDER, FOR CONGLASS.

This estate had passed by 1696 into the hands of Erskine of Pittodrie (see Parish of Oyne). For Grants of Conglas, see page 196.

EARL OF ABERDEEN, FOR BRACO—*D.*

Braco of Knockinlews, formerly in the possession of Leslie of Balquhain, wadset by him in 1610 to William Blackhall of that ilk.

It had been bought by Lord Aberdeen shortly before 1696 (*Poll Book*).

AUCHORSK, JOHN LESLIE (*Ser.*).

John Leslie, grandson of James Leslie of Auquhorsk, killed at Worcester (see Parish of Logie-Durno). In Inverurie he owned Drummies.

BLACKHALL.

William Thain, for the Lands of Blackhall in 1696—a very small estate at that date. Blackhall of that ilk had formerly been one of the Barons of the Garioch. The warrandice of these lands was granted to Abercromby of Fetternear in 1657.

ARDTANNIES (*Sup.*).

Andrew Jaffray, son of Provost Jaffray, owned this estate in 1696, with a wife and ten children—Andrew, John, James, Samuel, Margaret, Christian, Sarah, Patience, Anna, and Mary, names all rather reminiscent of the eminent divine, Andrew Cant, his grandfather. He resided in Aberdeen, and in 1724 he sold his estate to Lord Kintore.

Andrew Jaffray, merchant, was one of the Jacobites "who met at Mistress Hepburn's," 1715.[1]

He was also one of those entrusted with the spending of a small amount of the Cess collected by John Forbes (see page 30).

---

[1] *A Short Memorandum, etc.*

BADEFURROW, LIFERENT.

The family of William Forbes of Tolquhon owned Badefurrow in 1715, having bought it from James Ferguson.[1] In the *Poll Book* of 1696 the "heritor of Badefurrow" is said to be "out of the Kingdom." He was William Forbes of Tombeg, son of John Forbes and Anna Lunan, daughter of the minister of Monymusk.

He was born in 1687 and married Anna, daughter of Alexander Forbes, minister of Fintray. He was apparently a Jacobite sympathiser.

Badefurrow is now Manar.

J. A. Henderson says[2] the purchaser in 1699 was Mrs. Jean Forbes, widow of Alexander Forbes, minister of Fintray, 1693.

There is a resignation of Badefurrow by Jean Forbes, with consent of William, John, and James Forbes of Badefurrow, in June, 1700, but the same Jean Forbes was still there, 7th December, 1708.[3] It was probably she who had the liferent.

PRESBYTERY OF ALFORD.

PARISH OF ALFORD.

SIR JOHN GUTHRIE, FOR BREDA.

Sir John Guthrie was the eldest son of Sir Henry Guthrie, 1st Baronet of King Edward. No date of creation of this Baronetcy is given in the *Complete Baronetage*. It only lasted for three generations, Sir John's son, Sir Alexander, being the third and last Baronet, and died unmarried, 1761. Sir John's wife was Barbara Urquhart of Dunlugas.

Sir John appears to have been a Jacobite sympathiser since he only paid single Cess. His daughters all married into prominent Jacobite families.

Anna married William Burnet of Campfield, before 1715.

---

[1] James Ferguson, who sold Badefurrow and bought Pitfour, in Buchan, was an Advocate, son of William of Badefurrow and his first wife, Jean, sister of Sir James Elphinstone of Logie.

He married Anna, sister of Captain Stewart of Dens and Crichie (see page 157), Parish of Deer.

Their son was James Ferguson of Pitfour, M.P. for Aberdeenshire for 31 years, during which period it is said that he only spoke once, and that was to ask that the window behind his seat in the House might be mended. He was, however, a most "useful" member, as he voted consistently with the Government, having left it on record that only twice during the whole of his Parliamentary career—1789-1820— did he ever disagree with Pitt and Dundas, and he erected a monument to their memory in his grounds.

[2] *Aberdeenshire Epitaphs and Inscriptions*, p. 84.　　[3] *Aberdeen Sasines*.

Christian married George Cumine of Pitullie in 1728—her cousin (see page 168).

Mary married John Fullarton of Dudwick. She was the youngest, and was not born till 1718. She died 1805, aged 87.

There was a fourth daughter, Jean, who is believed to have married Alexander Thomson of Faichfield, at whose house Sir Alexander Guthrie died, 26th November, 1761, aged 41.

Before this date Sir John Guthrie owned other properties besides King Edward. He had purchased the bankrupt estate of Ludquharn in the Parishes of Peterhead and Longside (*q.v.*), for which, however, it will be seen, he paid *double Cess*.

In 1696 Ludquharn had still been in the hands of Sir William Keith.[1]

Master Arthur Forbes, for Asloun and Dorsell.

Arthur Forbes, third son of the 12th Lord Forbes, elsewhere called of Auchintoul. On 27th August, 1703, Arthur Forbes of Auchintoul gave "letters of Obligation" to Sir John Forbes of Craigievar.[2]

Many of the smaller properties on Donside were constantly changing hands among members of the Forbes' family, and money was advanced by one to the other on landed security, so that they frequently appear in the book of Sasines.

On 4th November, 1704, an obligation was signed by Isobel Forbes, daughter to William Forbes of Asloun (and wife to George Forbes, son of William Forbes of Newe) and Margaret Forbes, his sister, of monies due to "Arthur Forbes of Breda, formerly of Auchintoul." Mrs. Elizabeth Forbes, "Lady Breda," widow of "the Hon Master Arthur Forbes of Breda," died in 1758, aged 96.[3]

Dorsaill is frequently mentioned in connection with various members of the Forbes family. In the *Poll Book* of 1696 it is part of the estate of Arthur Forbes of Asloun and Auchintoul, but on 28th May, 1703, Arthur Forbes, Laird of Brux, had a sasine on "Dorsaill" as "pror. and attorney for his children, Sophia and Mary."[4]

The Laird of Balfluig.

John Forbes, who appears in the *Poll Book* of 1696 as "living in familie with his father" (also a John Forbes). He married Mary Ogilvie and succeeded to the estate before 1715. In 1696 he had "2 sons George and Alexander, both children." His second wife was Margaret Garioch.[5] In 1692 he had witnessed a deed, now at Castle Forbes, as John Forbes, younger of Balfluig.

---

[1] *Poll Book.* [2] *Aberdeen Sasines.* [3] *Castle Forbes Papers.*
[4] *Aberdeen Sasines.* [5] *Ibid.*

Agnes Forbes, sister to John Forbes of Balfluig, was "Lady Finzeauch" (see page 109).

The family of Balfluig derived from that of Corsindae in the 16th century.

In 1715 young Alexander Forbes of Balfluig had the misfortune to be one of the Jacobite officers taken at Dunfermline by Colonel Cathcart on 24th October. He was also one of those marched from Edinburgh to Carlisle, Monday, 3rd of September, 1716. His petition is in the Record Office.[1]

In it he states that he is "now a prisoner in Carlisle, that he was baptized by Mr. Andrew Jaffray, minister of Alford, upon the 8 day of May 1699, as witness the hands of 4 of the elders of Alford on November 20. 1716." The *date* of the baptism is presumably correct, but according to the entry in the *Poll Book* (above), Alexander must have been three or four years old at the time, unless, of course, he is a subsequent Alexander, the first having died ! He pleads for mercy on the ground of his extreme youth, "not being yet 16 years of age." On the petition this figure 16 is clumsily erased and *19* substituted, which was probably nearer the truth ! It may have been because of trouble over verifying the age of Alexander Forbes, that when the young William Sharpe presented a similar petition in 1746, he adduced as evidence, not only his baptismal certificate but the signed testimony of the midwife and doctor who attended his birth ![2]

Alexander Forbes added that he "was indeed induced to go out by the threats and importunities of several persons of distinction and deeply sensible of the sin thereof, pleaded guilty upon his arraignment and now implores the Royal mercy." He was among those discharged, on account of his youth, with young Hay of Arnbath, Charles Garden of Bellastrem, and others.

In the official English accounts of prisoners, he is always described confusingly as "son to Buffley," or "son to Bustley."

KINSTAIR (*Min.*). [George Garioch of Kinstair.]

In the *Poll Book* of 1696 it is "Alexander Garioch of Kinstair and George Garioch yr., with Elizabeth Burnett his wife and 5 children, George, Alexander and William, Elizabeth and Margaret."

George Garioch, the "younger" of 1696, had succeeded by 1700, in which year he signed the "heritors bond re keeping the peace,"[3] and Alexander Garioch of Tilliechetly (see below) did the same.

George was dead before 1708, as on 2nd July in that year Elizabeth Garioch, "spouse to umquhile George Garioch, and wife of Patrick Walker of Torrieleith" had sasine for her liferent on Torrieleith.[4]

---

[1] *S.P.* 54.17.253. [2] *Jacobites of Aberdeenshire and Banffshire in the '45*, p. 393.
[3] Allardyce, *Jacobite Papers*, vol. i, p. 21. [4] *Aberdeen Sasines*.

In 1715 George's son, George, had a fresh sasine on the lands of Kinstair. The Cess paid was on the minister's stipend.

PATRICK DUGUID, FOR ONE-THIRD OF KINSTAIR.

This refers to Duguid of Auchinhove. Patrick Duguid, eldest son of Robert Duguid, 9th of Auchinhove, and Teresa, third daughter of Count Patrick Leslie of Balquhain, was only 15 years old at this time, but is said to have been "out."

HAUGHTON.

William Reid, with his wife, Barbara Farquharson.

In the *Poll Book*, 1696, it had been his father, "Patrick Reid, with his wife, Elizabeth Lindsay, and William, John, Archibald and Peter Reids, their children."

After the Rising, Haughton passed to a branch of the Farquharson family ; William Reid, the son of Patrick Reid and Elizabeth Lindsay, having sold the estate in 1721 to John Farquharson "in Breda."

CARNEVERAN.

No owner for this small estate is given in the *Poll Book*.

TILLIECHETLY—D.

Alexander Garioch, who was the owner in 1696 and appears as Commissioner for taking the Poll in the Parish of Leochel, was also tenant in the mains of Craigievar. His wife was Barbara Forbes and he had four sons, William, Alexander, Patrick, and Ludovick, and one daughter, Elizabeth.

In 1699 he had had sasine over Little Endovie.[1]

On 15th May, 1719, William Garioch, eldest son of the above Alexander, had sasine.[2]

BRAINLY—D.

Bordley, which *may* be the same place, was part of Balfluig, but if so, it must at that time have been in other hands, as the Laird of Balfluig was a Jacobite, and the owner or tenant of this estate paid double Cess.

PARISH OF TOUGH.

KINCRAIGIE. [George Leslie.]

"Patrick Leslie of Kincraigie, with Jean Forbes (of Corsindae), his spouse, and Christian Leslie, his daughter, in 1696."

Patrick Leslie, the 8th Laird, had a son, George, who was the 9th and

---

[1] *Aberdeen Sasines.*   [2] *Ibid.*

last laird of Kincraigie. He was served heir in 1705, 2nd November. He became an Advocate in Edinburgh and was married twice—first to a daughter of Dr. Hay, and secondly, to a daughter of Baillie Brand. His son by his first marriage, John Leslie, became an Episcopal clergyman in Ireland. Returning to Scotland on his father's death he found the estates left to his stepmother, but obtained £5,000, with which he bought an estate in Ireland and named it Kincraigie.

The original Kincraigie was afterwards bought by Alexander Auchinachy and later became part of the estate of Tonley.

ARRINBATH (ARNBATH).

Alexander Hay of Arnbath bought in 1702 the estates of Alexander Farquhar of Tonley, Laird of Mounie, who had got into debt and was forced to sell. (In 1696 Peter Garioch was in occupation of Tonley, though Alexander Farquhar was still the heritor.) Hay sold it in 1720 to Patrick Byres.

Alexander Hay of Arnbath was an active Jacobite of 1715 and one of those who carried the unwilling Lord Saltoun to Mar's camp at Perth.[1] The son (also Alexander) was among those taken prisoner by Colonel Cathcart at Dunfermline and imprisoned at Stirling with his servant, George Steill, 24th October, 1715. In a petition among the State Papers in the Record Office,[2] Alexander Hay states that "being not yet 18 years of age he was forced out by Stewart of Bogs." He was among those carried to Carlisle and was tried but "no judgment passed upon him" because of his youth. His mother was Christian, daughter of Alexander Abernethy of Mayen.

THE LADY FINZEACH.

Wife of George Wilson, born 1659 (son of George Wilson, who died 1675), he became an Advocate and a burgess of Aberdeen. His second wife, Elizabeth Collinson, was buried with him in St. Nicholas Churchyard, but the Lady Finzeauch referred to was probably Agnes Forbes, his first wife, a daughter of Balfluig, who had sasine 1706. He was one of those who came into Aberdeen with the Earl Marischal, 20th September, 1715,[3] to proclaim King James VIII, but is not afterwards heard of in the Rising. He died 4th June, 1725.

TILLIECHETLY, FOR A PART OF CAMPFIELD—*D.*

The Laird of Foulis and Campbell in Touch in 1696 was William Forbes, with his wife, Margaret Forbes, his sons, James and William, and his daughter, Mary. Garioch of Tilliechetly pays double on a part.

---

[1] *S.P. 54.11.159.*   [2] *P.R.O., S.P. 54.6.82.*   [3] *A Short Memorandum, etc.*

TILLIERIACH, MR. ROBERT STRACHAN FOR DITTO—*D.*

Presumably the other part of Campfield. The Will of Robert Strachan is in the Commissariot of Aberdeen, date 7th September, 1725. He was married 24th January, 1710, to Marjorie Garioch of Kinstair; her father, George Garioch, appearing for her in the settlements. On 18th October, 1739, Marjorie Garioch, relict of Mr. Robert Strachan of Tillieriach, and Alexander, her son, had sasine on the lands.[1]

Like nearly all of the name, Mr. Robert Strachan was a Hanoverian. In 1696 Tillieriach was part of the estate of Forbes of Tilliefour. On 12th July, 1709, John Innes had had sasine on Tilliefour. He was son of Patrick Innes, who was in 1696 the principal tenant of William Forbes, younger of Monymusk, the owner of the estate.

TILLIEFOUR, JOHN COUPLAND—*D.*

Mr. Patrick Coupland had been minister of Cushnie in 1696, at which date he appears in the *Poll Book* with his wife, Jean Gordon, and three sons—John (above), Charles, and William, and four daughters—Agnes, Margaret, Elizabeth, and Mary.

Patrick Coupland had property in the Parish of Oyne as well as in Cushnie; he died 1710. His eldest son, John, bought part of the estate of Tilliefour before 1715. In 1749 his daughter, Helen, married the Rev. Patrick Thomas, minister of Tough.

ARDGOUS (ARDGOWSE).

John Gordon of Hallhead had a sasine on the property, 25th January, 1709. On 1st December, 1712, Patrick Gordon, son of John, and 11th Laird, had sasine on Ardgowse, Woodside, and Conquonderland (see Parish of Cushnie).

PARISH OF LEOCHEL.

CRAIGYVAR—*D.*

Sir William Forbes, 3rd Baronet, eldest son of " Red Sir John " and Margaret Young of Auldbar. He was born in 1660, and married in 1684 Margaret, daughter of Hugh Rose of Kilravock. He had seven sons, of whom the five elder died before their father. Arthur, the sixth, became the 4th Baronet, and married Christian Ross of Arnage. In 1696 William Forbes, then "younger of Craigievar," was the Commissioner for the Poll in the Parish of Coull. His daughter, Elizabeth, became "Lady Monboddo," and had sasine for her liferent, 30th May, 1710.[2]

---

[1] *Aberdeen Sasines.*   [2] *Ibid.*

LENTURK (*seq.*).

Alexander Irvine of Lenturk. This branch of the family was descended from the Irvines of Beltie.

Alexander Irvine of Lenturk had a sasine from Alexander Irvine of Drum on Lenturk, Drumdargue, Bridgend, etc., 6th July, 1711.[1]

LADY LENTURK.

" Jean Gordon, relict of Alexander Irvine of Lenturk and now spouse of John Gordon of Edentore," had sasine, 18th October, 1710.[2]

PARISH OF CUSHNY.

HALHEAD.

Patrick Gordon, 11th Laird and son of John Gordon, who had sasine on part of the estate on 1st December, 1712. The date of John's death is not known, but he had various sasines in 1708 and 1709 (see parish of TOUGH). He was the son of Patrick, the 9th Laird, and was himself served heir to his father in 1683.

John Gordon, the 10th Laird, was the owner in 1696 and appears in the *Poll Book* with his wife, Mary Ross of Auchlossan, his sons—Patrick, Robert, and William ; his brothers, Patrick and Charles ; his mother, Margaret ; and his sisters, Margaret and Marie.

He signed a heritors' bond, 26th April, 1700,[3] and was succeeded, between 1709 and 1712, by his eldest son, Patrick (above). Besides John's two brothers, Patrick and Charles, mentioned in the *Poll Book*, he had another brother, Robert, who had left Scotland before the date of the *Poll Book*, and was a successful wine merchant in Bordeaux.

Patrick Gordon, the 11th Laird, was obliged to sell his estate in 1717 to his uncle, Charles, who became the 12th Laird, and he again sold it in 1726 to Robert, the wine merchant, who thus became the 13th Laird. Robert Gordon was a good friend to many exiled Jacobites who had a meeting ground in Bordeaux. He wrote to the Earl of Mar, January, 1717—" I am willing to die an honourable death for my King or to starve for him." The portraits of James and Clementina belonging to him are now at Esslemont, which he bought in 1728. He was known as "Mr. Lyburn." He died in 1738.[4]

His wife was Isabel Byres of Tonley, and his son was George Gordon of the '45, 14th of Hallhead and 2nd of Esslemont, whose wife was so badly treated by General Hawley when he lodged in her house in Aberdeen and appropriated all her household effects.[5]

The family of Hallhead is now represented by that of Esslemont.

[1] *Aberdeen Sasines.* [2] *Ibid.*
[3] Allardyce, *Jacobite Papers*, vol. i, p. 21. [4] *Esslemont Papers.*
[5] See *Jacobites of Aberdeenshire and Banffshire in the '45*, p. 225.

LAIRDS OF HALLHEAD.

George Gordon—son of Thos. Gordon of Daach of Ruthven,
acquired the lands of Hallhead.
|
John Gordon of Hallhead, 2nd Laird, died 1553.
|
John, killed at Pinkie, 1547.
|
Robert, married Janet Innes.
|
Patrick, 5th, died 1617.
|

Patrick, 6th, died 1617.	Robert, 7th, died 1622.	George, 8th.
		Patrick, 9th, died 1683.

John, 10th. Married Mary Ross, died before 1712.	Robert, 13th. Married Isabella Byres. Bought it in 1726, died 1738.	Charles, 12th. Sold it in 1726.
Patrick, 11th. Sold Hallhead, 1717, to his uncle, Charles.	George, 14th. Married Amy Bowdler.	
	Robert, died 1792. Married (1) Madeline de Rabutin. (2) Lady Harriet Gordon, daughter of 2nd Earl of Aberdeen.	

THE LAIRD OF CUSHNY.

David Lumsden, son of Alexander Lumsden, 13th Laird of Cushnie,
who was son of Robert Lumsden, 1st of Clova and then of Cushnie also;
he succeeded to the latter on the death of his cousin of the same
name.

Alexander Lumsden appears in the *Poll Book*, 1696, with "his lady,
two sons, David and Ludovick, and a daughter, Elizabeth."

David was either the eldest surviving or the eldest at home of the
sons of Alexander Lumsden. He was actually the third son, and his
mother, Elizabeth Leith of Whitehaugh, was the second wife. She had
sasine on Cushnie with her husband in 1709.

David, who was born in 1682 and succeeded in *1714*, married Margaret,
sister of Sir William Forbes of Craigievar. He wrote a document, signed
at Cushnie, 26th September, 1715, stating that "being obliged to go
abroad on necessary affairs, relating to the King his service, wherein I
am highly concerned," he gives over the management of the estates to
his wife. This seems to indicate that he took an active part in the
Jacobite Rising, but he was at home again in 1717.[1] He died on 23rd
December, 1718. His wife afterwards married Thomas Forbes of Echt,

[1] *Cushnie Papers.*

and his only daughter, Margaret, married Dr. Andrew Skene. He was succeeded by Harry Lumsden, eldest son of John Lumsden of Auchindoir, who had succeeded to Auchindoir in 1716 (also a Jacobite). Harry's sister, Marjorie, was the wife of Arthur Anderson of Candacraig—Marriage Contract, 1703.[1]

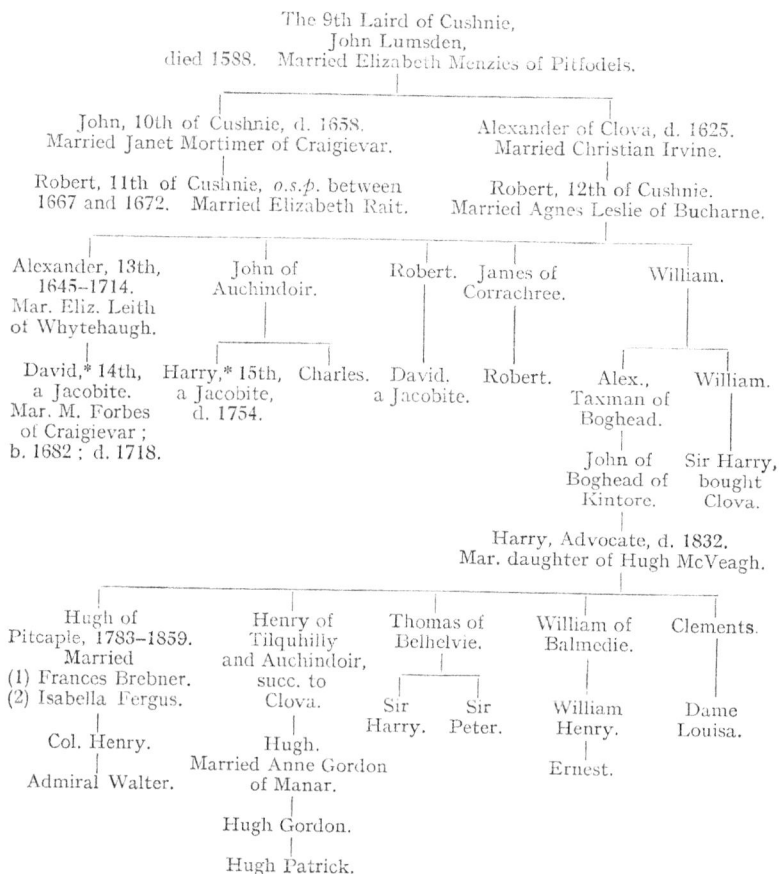

The 9th Laird of Cushnie,
John Lumsden,
died 1588. Married Elizabeth Menzies of Pitfodels.

John, 10th of Cushnie, d. 1658.
Married Janet Mortimer of Craigievar.

Alexander of Clova, d. 1625.
Married Christian Irvine.

Robert, 11th of Cushnie, *o.s.p.* between 1667 and 1672. Married Elizabeth Rait.

Robert, 12th of Cushnie.
Married Agnes Leslie of Bucharne.

Alexander, 13th, 1645–1714. Mar. Eliz. Leith of Whytehaugh.

John of Auchindoir.

Robert. James of Corrachree.

William.

David,* 14th, a Jacobite. Mar. M. Forbes of Craigievar ; b. 1682 ; d. 1718.

Harry,* 15th, a Jacobite, d. 1754.

Charles.

David, a Jacobite.

Robert.

Alex., Taxman of Boghead.

William.

John of Boghead of Kintore.

Sir Harry, bought Clova.

Harry, Advocate, d. 1832.
Mar. daughter of Hugh McVeagh.

Hugh of Pitcaple, 1783–1859. Married (1) Frances Brebner. (2) Isabella Fergus.

Henry of Tilquhilly and Auchindoir, succ. to Clova.

Thomas of Belhelvie.

William of Balmedie.

Clements.

Col. Henry.

Admiral Walter.

Hugh. Married Anne Gordon of Manar.

Sir Harry. Sir Peter.

William Henry.

Ernest.

Dame Louisa.

Hugh Gordon.

Hugh Patrick.

Those appearing in the Cess Roll are shown by an asterisk.

CRAIGIEVAR—*D*—see PARISH OF LEOCHEL.

BRUX—see PARISH OF KILDRUMMY.

[1] *Pitcaple Papers.*

PAROCH OF KEARN, AND PAROCH OF FORBES.

The only payer of Cess in these two parishes was the LORD FORBES. As some of his family appeared on the Jacobite side, he only pays single Cess.

William, 13th Lord Forbes, who succeeded in 1697, was a Privy Councillor under William III and Queen Anne. He supported the Union in 1707 and the Government in 1715, being made Lord Lieutenant of Aberdeen and Mearns on the outbreak of the Rising.[1] He married Anna, daughter of James Brodie of Brodie, and died July, 1716, leaving three sons—William, the 14th Lord Forbes (whose son, Francis, was the 15th), James, subsequently the 16th, and Archibald. James Forbes, the second son (16th Lord Forbes), was a Jacobite, as is proved by a letter in the *Stuart Papers* relative to "A licence lately procured for my Lord Forbes' brother" to return to Scotland, 17th October, 1717 ; also by several letters in the *Stuart Papers* relative to raising troops, etc. He married Mary, daughter of Alexander, 3rd Lord Pitsligo, widow of John Forbes, younger of Monymusk, and was father of the 17th Lord Forbes. His three daughters married Jacobites of the '45, viz. :—(1) Sophia, married Charles Cumming of Kininmonth ; (2) Mary, married James Gordon of

---

[1] Lieutenant of the Shire of Aberdeen & Mairns.

WHITEHALL, Aug. 27th. 1715.

MY LORD.

His Majesty having appointed your Lordship Lord Lieutenant of the Shires of Aberdeen and Mairns, I herewith transmit to your Lordship His Majesty's Instructions for regulating yourself by which I doubt not but your Lordship will pursue with that zeal which His Majesty's service in this juncture requires.

I am with great respect

MY LORD,

your Lordship's

most humble and most obedient servant,

JAMES STANHOPE.

Lord Forbes.

WHITEHALL, 30th Aug. 1715.

MY LORD

His Majesty's service requiring your Lordship's presence in the shires of Aberdeen and Mairns, where your Lordship is appointed Lord Lieutenant I am commanded to signify to your Lordship His Majesty's pleasure that you do with all possible expedition repair thither and pursue the Instructions you have received from His Majesty.

I am, MY LORD,

Your Lordship's

most humble and most obedient servant,

JAMES STANHOPE.

Lord Forbes, Lord Lieut. of Aberdeen. etc.

—Castle Forbes Papers.

Cobairdy; (3) Anne, married Thomas Erskine of Pittodrie. The second wife of James, 16th Lord Forbes, was Elizabeth Gordon of Park.

"James Forbes died at his seat of Putachy on 20th February, 1761, in the 73rd year of his age. Possessed of all the virtues that adorn human life." [1]

In the *Poll Book*, 1696, it is noted that the Master of Forbes and family are "out of the Kingdom." That is William, 13th Lord Forbes (above).

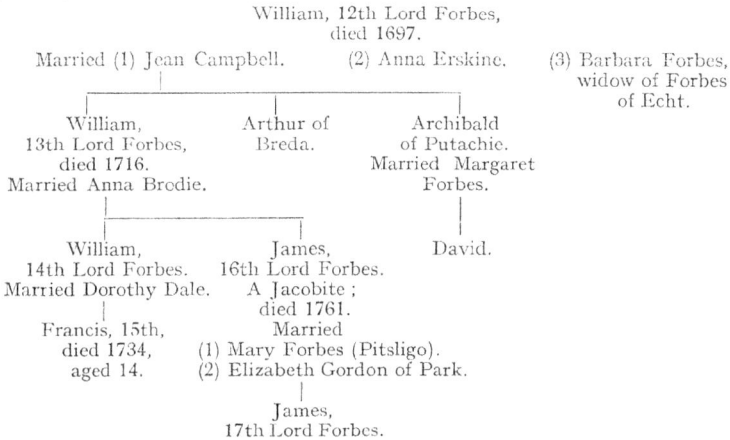

```
                        William, 12th Lord Forbes,
                                died 1697.
Married (1) Jean Campbell.      (2) Anna Erskine.    (3) Barbara Forbes,
         |                               |                 widow of Forbes
         |                               |                    of Echt.
    William,             Arthur of          Archibald
  13th Lord Forbes,        Breda.          of Putachie.
    died 1716.                           Married  Margaret
  Married Anna Brodie.                        Forbes.
         |                                        |
    William,            James,            David.
  14th Lord Forbes.   16th Lord Forbes.
  Married Dorothy Dale.   A Jacobite ;
         |                 died 1761.
    Francis, 15th,         Married
     died 1734,    (1) Mary Forbes (Pitsligo).
      aged 14.     (2) Elizabeth Gordon of Park.
                                |
                             James,
                         17th Lord Forbes.
```

PARISH OF KEIG.

PUTACHIE.

On 4th August, 1707, "Arthur Forbes of Breda and Archibald Forbes of Puttachie" had an arent on the latter lands.

They were the second and third sons of William, 12th Lord Forbes, who died 1697, and his first wife, Jean Campbell.

The 12th Lord Forbes was three times married—(1) Jean Campbell of Calder, as above; (2) Anna Erskine, daughter of Lord Kelly; (3) Barbara, daughter of Forbes of Asloun, and widow of Forbes of Echt.

Archibald Forbes of Putachie had formerly been of Lickleyhead, parish of Premnay, where he was in residence at the date of the *Poll Book*, with Margaret (sometimes called Marjorie) Forbes, his wife, David, his son, and Barbara, his daughter.

LESLIE.

David Forbes, Laird of Leslie, Parish of Leslie (*q.v.*).

FINZEAUCH—see PARISH OF TOUGH.

[1] *Aberdeen Journal* of that date.

BALGOWAN.

Adam Gordon of Balgowan, second son of William Gordon, and his wife, Isobel Leith, who had sasine 16th September, 1659. He appears in the *Poll Book*, 1696, having succeeded before that date.

He was a Jacobite of 1715 and was one of those who surrendered at Banff, 8th September, 1716. The Lord Justice Clerk erroneously included him among the heritors of Banffshire.[1]

"Young Balgowan" is said to have escaped from Banff with Carnegie of Boysack, Fullarton of Dudwick, and Charles Forbes of Brux, *vide* letter in *Stuart Papers*.[2] "Young Balgowan" must have been Adam's son, John, who was there in 1749, and to whom Jean and Henrietta, daughters of Peter Gordon, Mill of Smithston, were served heirs, 15th December, 1785.[3]

The lands of Balgowan were held under the condition of the annual delivery of a nest of merlin Hawks.[4] It does not state to whom the hawks were to be delivered, presumably to the Crown. The estate is now the property of Blairs College.

TERPERSIE—see PARISH OF TULLYNESSLE.

TULLOCH, FOR HALF LIFERENTER—*D*. (Double in spite of its being a liferent.)

In 1696 it was William Forbes of Tulloch with Jean Ross, his spouse; William and John, his sons; Margaret, Anna, Jean, Elizabeth, and Marie, his daughters.

On 8th September, 1709, Alexander Gordon of Old Machar had sasine on the lands of Tulloch.[5]

PARISH OF CLATT.

KNOCKESPOCK—*D*.

George Gordon, younger son of Henry Gordon of Auchlyne, bought Knockespock in 1705, and had sasine on the 14th June in that year. (*Aberdeen Sasines.*)

[1] *S.P.* 54.12.165.

[2] John Carnegie of Boysack, writing to Mar from Rouen, 15th July, 1716, says: "Having by messages agreed upon signals and a place of embarkment with the master of a ship at Inverness, I embarked at a little bay near to Banff. My two brothers-in-law, Fullerton and young Balgowan, Charles Forbes and Dudwick were with me."—*Stuart Papers.*

[3] *Service of Heirs.*

[4] J. A. Henderson, *Aberdeenshire Epitaphs and Inscriptions*, p. 270.

[5] *Aberdeen Sasines.*

His son was James Gordon, who died 1768; *he* also owned Auchlyne.[1]
The John Gordon who appears in the *Poll Book* as of Knockespock
in 1696 was a cousin of the above, to whom he sold that estate and bought
Glenbucket in 1701.

THE LORD FORBES—see KEIG.

TILLYANGUS.

William Forbes of Tillieangus in 1696.

AUCHLYNE (*Sup.*).

The family of Auchlyne played a curious role in the '15. Harry
Gordon, 1st of Auchlyne, fifth son of William Gordon, 3rd of Terpersie,
was a convinced Royalist and adherent of the Stuarts. He was one of
the heritors of the County who met "in the Laigh Tolbooth of Aber-
deen on 2nd December 1659" in response to a letter from General
Monk at Berwick, and appointed Charles, Lord Aboyne, to go to
Berwick and confer with Monk; this conference contributing to the
Restoration of Charles II.[2]

He married Marion or Marjory Innes "of Tilbourie," and with her
had sasine on Auchlyne, 14th July, 1663 (*Aberdeen Sasines*), and, with
his son, James, he had sasine on Seggieden in 1661 (*Ibid.*).

James, 2nd of Auchlyne, married Rachel Burnett, and secondly,
Anne Reid.

His family consisted of :—

Alexander, the eldest, who did not succeed.

James, 3rd of Auchlyne, to whom his father left the estate.

George of Knockespock (*q.v.*).

John, Burgess of Aberdeen,

and three daughters—Katherine, Barbara, and Mary, the last-named
married John Gordon, 2nd of Law, her first cousin, as his second wife.

Henry Gordon died May, 1707, and is buried in the church of Clatt.
In the *Poll Book* he appears as "Auchlyne, elder with his lady and
his daughter. The Principal heretor in the Parish being Auchlyne
younger"—that is James, to whom his father made over the estates of
"Cleatt, Newbigging, and Auchmenzie."

James Gordon, younger of Auchlyne, had sasine on the lands of
Whiteley and Bogheads in 1700, and as "Jas. Gordon of Auchlyne" had
sasine on Bogshead and Whyteley, 23rd September, 1709.[3]

For the superiority of Auchlyne James Gordon paid in 1715 single
Cess on £640—exactly the value of the estate held by himself and his

---

[1] See below.　　　[2] *Records of Aboyne*, p. 323.　　　[3] *Aberdeen Sasines*.

father jointly in 1696. In 1667 £200 was paid—presumably the estate of Auchlyne only.

Henry's eldest son, Alexander, was a convinced adherent of the House of Hanover. A petition by him, now at Castle Forbes, has been already printed *in extenso* in Colonel Allardyce's *Jacobite Papers*, Vol. I, p. 59, and summarised in J. M. Bulloch's *House of Gordon*, Vol. I, p. 218. The date is given in both places as 1715, but this is not written *on* nor *in* the body of the letter, which, from internal evidence, could only have been written in *1716*, since the writer refers to events in the course of the Rising : notably to the surrender of the Marquis of Huntly, which took place on the 27th February of 1716, and also says he has been "reduced to straits this long whyle, from the Rebellion." Alexander Gordon claims to have contributed by his advice to the surrender of Huntly, also to the establishing of bad blood between Mar and Huntly—To have given warning of the attempt on Edinburgh Castle and to have been " the only Gentleman of the name of Gordon of all the County of Aberdeen who remained firm to his Majesty" (i.e. George I). He states that, in consequence he suffered great losses in his estate to the value of £3,000 and that "his unnatural father has disinherited him and left the estate to a younger brother who was very active in the rebellion" (i.e. James, who, other accounts say, was killed in the Rebellion). Alexander, therefore, begs for relief. No answer to this letter has been found, but another, written later, from Auchlyne, 3rd August, 1716 (now in the Public Record Office and never printed), shows that he had achieved his ambition to become a J.P., had recovered possession of his ancestral estate, and was busy harrying his neighbours.[1]

Alexander Gordon, younger of Auchlyne, was known as "Laird Tertius" during the lifetime of his father and grandfather. He was said to have been "next to being an absolute fool, committing every day ridiculous extravagancies." He died between 1727 and 1728.

The son of James, 3rd of Auchlyne, who became James, 4th Laird, was a cadet in the North British Fusiliers and was served heir to his grandfather, James, 1st of Auchlyne, 10th August, 1734 ; in applying for a Commission in the Regiment he said that his "family was very antient and his small estate had suffered much" in the late Rebellion. Also that "his father had been killed in the Rebellion." He must have hoped that the authorities would not enquire upon which side ! His mother was Anne Sandilands ; he himself died without issue, when the estate of Auchlyne was united (in the hands of his first cousin) with that of Knockespock.

---

[1] For letter from Alexander Gordon, J.P., to the Laird of Leith Hall, desiring him to give up his arms and horses and take the qualification, from Auchlyne, August, 1716, see page 70, under Leith Hall—Parish of Leslie.

Henry or Harry Gordon of Auchlyne,
fifth son of William Gordon, 3rd of Terpersie,
died 1707.
Married Marjorie Innes of Tilbourie.

James II of Auchlyne.
Married (1) Rachel Burnett.
(2) Anne Reid.
He died before 1715.

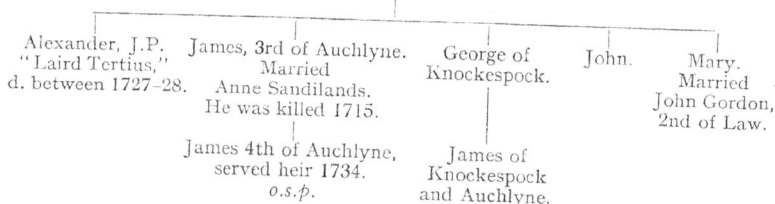

Alexander, J.P. "Laird Tertius," d. between 1727–28.	James, 3rd of Auchlyne. Married Anne Sandilands. He was killed 1715.	George of Knockespock.	John.	Mary. Married John Gordon, 2nd of Law.
	James 4th of Auchlyne, served heir 1734. *o.s.p.*	James of Knockespock and Auchlyne.		

PARISH OF TULLYNESSELL.

WHITEHAUGH.

"John Leith of Whitehaugh was served heir to his father, John Leith, in 1672." He appears in the *Poll Book* with his daughters, Anna and Margaret Leith. His wife was Elizabeth, daughter of William, 12th Lord Forbes, and the eldest daughter and heiress married William Forbes, last of Tolquhon. William and his wife were evicted from Tolquhon in 1718 (see page 185). He died in 1728. He was therefore laird both of Whitehaugh and Tolquhon in 1715. His second son, John Forbes Leith, succeeded to Whitehaugh, Montgarrie, etc.[1]

TERPERSIE. [Charles Gordon, hanged at Carlisle, 1746.]

James Gordon, 4th Laird of Terpersie, who married Anna, daughter of John Gordon of Craig, had an only son, *George Gordon*, 5th of Terpersie. He was in possession at the date of the *Poll Book*, 1696, with his wife, four daughters, and two sons, but no names given (one was Charles ——), and was there up till *1712*. Charles Gordon, the Laird of Terpersie in 1745, and one of the most pathetic victims of that Rising, was probably already in possession in 1715, as he was over 60 when made prisoner in his own home at Terpersie under romantic circumstances,[2] and was executed at Carlisle, 15th November, 1746. His wife was Margaret, daughter of Adam Gordon of Artlach, and she survived until 1777. His second son, James, was also, as a boy of 16, a Jacobite, and made prisoner but was reprieved and banished, and survived until after 1764. The estate was confiscated. In 1746 it appears to have been quite small, but in 1667 it extended into five parishes—Keith, Clatt, Tullynessle, Auchindoir,

---

[1] *Service of Heirs.*

[2] See *Jacobites of Aberdeenshire and Banffshire in the '45*, p. 214.

and Cabrach. The Gordons were a Roman Catholic family for many generations and appeared several times before the Presbytery of Tullynessle. "Anna Gordon, sometime Lady Terpersie," grandmother of the Jacobite Charles Gordon, is buried in the churchyard of Tullynessle. She died 3rd December, 1672.

The family of Gordon of Terpersie was prominent and powerful in Aberdeenshire in the 17th century. From it descended the Gordons of Law and of Auchlyne.

The estate now forms part of Knockespock and the Castle is a ruin.

On 1st January, 1712, George Gordon of Terpersie and Charles his son granted an arent to Anna Gordon, daughter of George, and spouse of Mr. William Leslie, minister at Chapel of Garioch on the lands of Micklehaugh, which is part of the estate of Terpersie in the Parish of Keig.[1]

Five years earlier George Gordon and his sons had been concerned in a cruel outrage, the account of which is preserved in a manuscript at Castle Forbes :—

THE INDYTEMENT OF GEORGE GORDON OF TARPERSIE, CHARLES AND THOMAS GORDONS HIS SONS, ANENT THE MURDER OF ALEXANDER CLERIHEW SOMETIME IN DUBSTON. 1707.

You, the saids, George Gordon, Charles and Thomas Gordons your Sons are Indyted and accused of murder in so far as you, an ilk of you and more especially you George Gordon of Tarpersie, being of cruel and implacable temper used to threaten, and what lay in your power, to execute your threat, as can be proven in the severall instances of your carriage to William Reid of Pittendreigh in the year 1684 : To Mr. Andrew Livingston, Minister of Keigg[2] in the year 1688 : And to one of the Elders of the paroch of Tillinessle many years ago, And your carriage to ——— Leith of Whythaugh in September or October or one or other of the moneths of the year 1693, and being of this cruel and outragious temper you and ilk an of you did conceive a causles malice against the deceast Alexander Clerihew in Dubston and did utter threatening expressions before severell witness long before the barbarous murder of the said Alexander Clerihew intimating a design to destroy the said Alexander Clerihew or that you would kick or shoot him and five, or six moneths before the murder aftermentioned, the said Alexander Clerihew having gone up to a hill or mount above his own house in company with Alexander Ker, you the said George Gordon and Charles Gordon father and son, ran after the said Alexander Clerihew to the said hill or mount with a design to murder him and which ye hade effected at that time if it hade not been discovered by giving him notice of your being in pursuit of him, But your malice and cruel purpose nothing abating you the said Charles Gordon younger of Tarpersie did some dayes before the horrid murder of the said Alexander Clerihew being at a fishing of the water of Esseck (Esset) with company and seeing there John Mitchell sister's son to the said Alexander Clerihew ye did thrust at him with a fishing spear and endeavoured to kill him and being hindred by the

---

[1] *Aberdeen Sasines.*

[2] Andrew Livingstone had been chaplain to the Earl of Kintore ; he was appointed to Keig in 1683 but deposed in 1716 "for supporting the cause of the Pretender."

company ye did vowe that er long ye would pistol one or other of the Clerihews. And sick like you the said George Gordon of Tarpersie being to hold a court for a blood-week between two of your tenants and being informed that the said Alexander Clerihew had settled the difference, you and everyone of you did publickly on the very day the murder happened or the day preceding it solemnly vowe that ye should never sleep til ye were avenged of the said Alexander Clerihew for that agreement (although a most charitable and honest undertaking) and for other offences and you the said pannells and ilk one of you came from the said court to the Change House of James Donald at the Kirk of Tillinessle about three quarters of a mile distant from the house of the said Alexander Clerihew in Dubston and the said Alexander having met with you, the said Charles there, having passed by without offence you the said George Gordon afterwards coming to the knowledge of it did openly curse the said Charles for not running the said Alexander through with his sword, thereby inhumanly and against the duty of a father to a son inciting him to the most barbarous and cruell wickedness, and this happened a few hours before the murder. You did all three openly and with execrable oaths and implications vowe that ye should never go to bed till ye had killed the said Alexander Clerihew and for accomplishing this your wicked and premedit malice ye went to the house of the said Alexander Clerihew under silence and cloud of night that same night the twentyninth of October or one or other of the days of the said moneth of October or the moneth of November in the year 1707 and there coming to the window of the room where the said Alexander Clerihew and his wife were lying in bed, about ten eleven or twelve oclock at night you the said Thomas Gordon did call upon the said Alexander by his name and with great importunity desired him to come out for heaven's sake to speak to a person about some thing that concerned him assuring him that there was no ill meaned and the said Alexander being unfortunately prevailed with to believe came in a manner naked to the door of his house where you the said Thomas took him by the hand and led him down to the foot of the closs after which a gun was heard to be shot and that the defunct's wife having come out and called upon the servants the body of the said Alex was found inhumanely butchered and wounded in twentytwo places and the bowels bruised with all the marks of mercyless and savage cruelty. Like as you three were seen by the help of the moonlight to go quickly towards the house of Tarpersie where being come ye called for linnens to weep the blood off your swords and hands and you the said George Gordon of Tarpersie was overheard telling your wife that the said Alexander Clerihew was now sleeping in his shoes for all the offences he had done upon which she your said wife was heard to weep bitterly. And all be it by the common respects of good neighbourhood upon such occasions the neighbours used to inquire concerning the state of the family and accidents yet ye did not only neglect that common humanity but retired yourselves armed till the body was buried fearing the ordinary observation that if ye should either come where the body was or be brought to touch it the murdered body might bleed afresh in presence of you the murderers. And the Minister of the Paroch having very seasonably preached against the crying sin of murder you the said George Gordon of Tarpersie were so impious and bold as to reprove him for it, And calling to your mind how much that also would give light to the truth, ye did desire the minister to conceal it, And to this unparalleled barbarity and murder you the said George Gordon did add insolent boasting, And having employed a certain person to go to a fair and buy some pouder for you, declaring that it was to kill more Clerihews, By all which circumstances before, in the act and after, you and ilk an of you are guilty art and part of the forsaid execrable murder and being so found you and each of you ought to be punished with the pains of Death and confiscation of Moveables.

The unfortunate Clerihew was a tenant of Lord Forbes, and the family is said to have been brought by him from the South, but at the date of the *Poll Book*, 1696, there were over 20 persons of that name residing in the presbytery of Alford.

The victim of the outrage appears as :—

> " Alexander Clerihew, tennent, Dubstone, Forbes, with Janet Mitchell his spouse
> 3 menservants and 3 maidservants
> paying altogether £3.8.2. poll."

In the same parish were John Mitchell and Jean Clerihew, his wife ; and William Chrystie with Agnes Clerihew his wife, probably both sisters of Alexander ; also, in 1680, Patrick Clerihew was an elder of Tullynessie.

No account of the murder appears in the Privy Council or other records and the Gordon family continued to reside at Terpersie. It would seem, therefore, that the matter was hushed up.

Charles Gordon peacefully possessed the estate until 1745, and Thomas Gordon witnessed a deed at Pitcaple many years after the outrage.[1]

PARISH OF KENNETHMONT.

LEITH HALL—*D.*

John Leith of Leith Hall was the owner in 1696 with "Mrs. Jannet Ogilvie, his lady, and one son." Janet Ogilvie was the daughter of George, second Lord Banff. John Leith, who acquired the whole estate of Leslie in the Garioch, was a nominal supporter of the Hanoverian Government, and in consequence pays double, but see under PARISH OF LESLIE for his *real* opinions. He died in 1727. Of his five sons, John, the eldest, who succeeded, died in 1736, leaving a young son, but the four others—Patrick, George, Laurence, and Anthony, were all active Jacobites of 1745.

There was one daughter, who married Richard Gordon of Craigmyle.

LAW.

" John Gordon, 3rd of Law in 1696 (John Gordon, his father, 2nd of Law, having died that year), with Anna Irvine his lady and Arthur Gordon his son." John Gordon was also, later, first of Wardhouse. He died in 1740. His daughter and heiress, Mary (Arthur having died), married James Gordon, son of Alexander Gordon of Candell and Beldorney, and the estates of Law and Wardhouse both came to their son, John, at his father's death in 1748.

[1] *Pitcaple Papers.*

KIRKHILL—*D*.

The Laird in 1715 was William Gordon, merchant in Aberdeen, who had sasine, 22nd July, 1709, from his brother, John Gordon, second son of Hew Gordon and Elizabeth Hay. (Elizabeth, as Hew's relict, married Thomas Abercromby.) William Gordon married Isobel Davidson and had four sons, of whom Robert was the last Roman Catholic Chaplain at Gordon Castle. He made a translation of the Scriptures, was imprisoned on suspicion of being a Jacobite in 1745 and was deported to Holland. He died in Paris, 1764.[1]

The other sons were Patrick, who succeeded to Kirkhill, Francis and the Rev. George.

CULTS—*D*. [George Gordon of Cults.]

In 1696 "Patrick Gordon of Cults, with his lady, his sons, Patrick and William, and his daughters, Jean and Elizabeth."

In 1715 it was George Gordon of Cults, who succeeded in 1707 and was alive in 1727. His wife was Grisell Hog, who died in that year.

CRAIGHALL. [Alexander Gordon.]

Patrick Leith of Craighall in 1696. He was son of George Leith and Helen Leith, his spouse, who were there in 1667 and 1672.

On 5th August, 1708, Alexander Gordon, son to John Gordon of Craighall, had sasine on the estate.[2] It belonged later to the family of Wemyss.

WARDHOUSE—see PARISH OF INSCH.

LEITH HALL FOR LESLIE (above)—*D*.

PARISH OF KILDRUMMY.

THE EARLE OF MAR. (INVERNOCHTY.)

BRUX.

This is young Arthur Forbes, 12th Laird, the eldest of the three sons of Roderick Forbes, whose father, another Arthur Forbes, 10th Laird, was Commissioner for taking the Poll (1696) in the Parish of Kildrummy, in which Brux is situated, but in this valuation he appears also in Cushnie, where much of his land lay.

[1] See J. M. Bulloch, "The Gordons of Kirkhill," in *Huntly Express*, 16th June, 1905.

[2] *Aberdeen Sasines.*

Tree of the Family of Forbes of Brux.

1st Laird, Alistair Cam Forbes.
Married daughter of Sir Hugh Cameron of Brux.

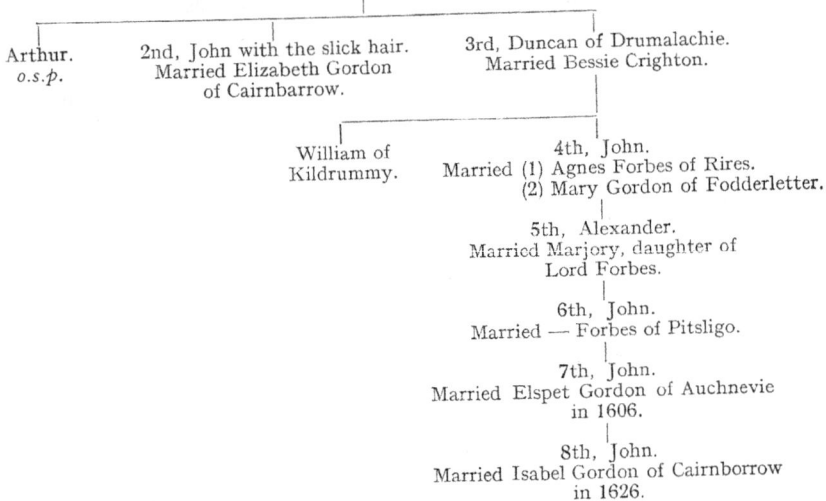

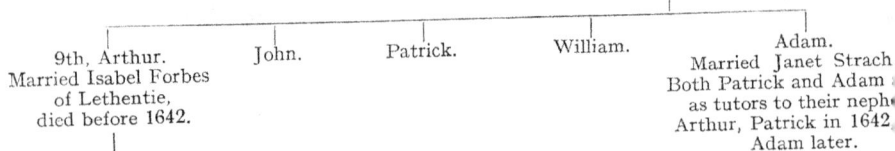

Arthur.
o.s.p.

2nd, John with the slick hair.
Married Elizabeth Gordon
of Cairnbarrow.

3rd, Duncan of Drumalachie.
Married Bessie Crighton.

William of
Kildrummy.

4th, John.
Married (1) Agnes Forbes of Rires.
(2) Mary Gordon of Fodderletter.

5th, Alexander.
Married Marjory, daughter of
Lord Forbes.

6th, John.
Married — Forbes of Pitsligo.

7th, John.
Married Elspet Gordon of Auchnevie
in 1606.

8th, John.
Married Isabel Gordon of Cairnborrow
in 1626.

9th, Arthur.
Married Isabel Forbes
of Lethentie,
died before 1642.

John.

Patrick.

William.

Adam.
Married Janet Strach
Both Patrick and Adam a
as tutors to their nephe
Arthur, Patrick in 1642,
Adam later.

Arthur Forbes, 10th Laird of Brux.
Married in 1696 Elizabeth Murray.
He was fiar of Brux in 1622; died 1707.
6 sons and 3 daughters.

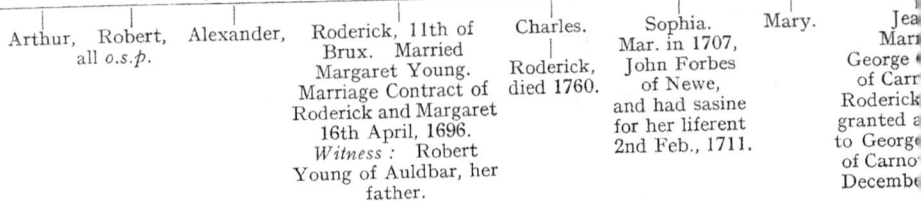

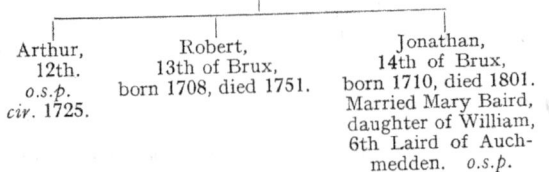

Arthur, Robert, Alexander,
all *o.s.p.*

Roderick, 11th of
Brux. Married
Margaret Young.
Marriage Contract of
Roderick and Margaret
16th April, 1696.
Witness: Robert
Young of Auldbar, her
father.

Charles.

Roderick,
died 1760.

Sophia.
Mar. in 1707,
John Forbes
of Newe,
and had sasine
for her liferent
2nd Feb., 1711.

Mary.

Jea
Marr
George (
of Carr
Roderick
granted a
to George
of Carno
Decembe

Arthur,
12th.
o.s.p.
cir. 1725.

Robert,
13th of Brux,
born 1708, died 1751.

Jonathan,
14th of Brux,
born 1710, died 1801.
Married Mary Baird,
daughter of William,
6th Laird of Auch-
medden. *o.s.p.*

—Aberdeen Sasines and *Castle Forbes Po*

124

The wife of Arthur, 10th Laird, was Elizabeth Murray, and he had six sons—John, Arthur, Robert, Alexander, Roderick, and Charles. Roderick succeeded in 1707 (and had three sons—Arthur, Robert, and Jonathan, the last being a Jacobite of 1745). Charles, the younger brother of Roderick and uncle of Arthur, was a Jacobite agent before 1715 and was concerned in the abortive attempt to seize Edinburgh Castle. The Master of Sinclair in his *Memoirs of 1715* mentions "Charles Forbes, whom we sent to France"; and the Lord Justice Clerk, in a letter dated 12th September, 1715 (now in the Public Record Office), says "the Gentleman in the Red coat" (who was concerned in tampering with the sentinels of the Castle) "is one Charles fforbes of Bruicks in Aberdeenshire, he was laitly come from Bar-le-Duck before Earl Mar came hither and was not with his Lordship in Braemar." [1] There is no other record of his doings in 1715 save that he was appointed A.D.C. to the Chevalier, 18th September in that year,[2] and a letter in the *Stuart Papers* of date 1st November, 1716, says he had "a Colonel's Commission promised him and would be glad to be ranked as such." He afterwards had an allowance from the Old Chevalier. He married and had a son, Captain Roderick, who died in Persia in 1760.

The Marriage Contract between John Forbes of Newe and Sophia Forbes of Brux, 2nd July, 1707, is at Castle Forbes.

In May, 1703, Arthur Forbes, senior of Brux, signed a deed as procurator and attorney for his daughters, Sophia and Mary Forbes, granting them liferents on Dorsaill—he also had a daughter, Jean, who married George Gordon of Carnousie. Charles of Brux in letters to Mar speaks of his nephew, "Carnousie's son."

In the Indices of heirs, 1751, Jonathan is described as second son to Roderick Forbes of Brux, being served heir to Robert Forbes, eldest son of Roderick, but Arthur, the eldest of the three, had then been dead some time. He succeeded in 1714, but is not mentioned after 1724; he died without heirs and presumably unmarried. On 30th July, 1717, at Edinburgh, there was an adjudication against the above Arthur Forbes as heir of his deceased father, Roderick Forbes of Brux, and deceased grandfather, Arthur.

Charles Forbes of Brux was alive October, 1719, as he is mentioned in some papers of that date in Lord Pitsligo's handwriting (justifying the latter's own conduct), now at Fettercairn.

He had several younger children, since Lord Pitsligo, in his account of the intrigues and unfortunate quarrels between the followers of the Old Chevalier in Rome in 1719 and 1720 instances him as one with a wife and young family, to whom it would be very serious if he were to lose the small pension allowed him by his royal master.[3]

---

[1] *S.P.* 54.7.53. [2] *S.P.* 54.9.34. [3] *Fettercairn Papers.*

Charles' nephew, Arthur Forbes, seems to have taken no active part in the Rising. He must have been very young at his father's death, which occurred before 11th January, 1714. His parents were only married in 1696, and his next brother, Robert, was not born till 1708.

Roderick, elder brother of Charles, the Laird of Brux (in 1715), married Margaret Young, and had three sons, Arthur, Robert, and Jonathan, who all succeeded to Brux.

CUSHNY—see PARISH OF CUSHNIE.

MIDCLOVA.

Alexander Reid was of Midclova in 1696. His son, Robert, was a Jacobite of 1715 and was transported, but returned, as is shown by letters of Harry Lumsden, 1st of Auchindoir, and afterwards the Laird of Cushnie, of date 1723, after Lumsden's marriage.[1]

GLENKINDY—see PARISH OF INVERNOCHTY.

Patrick Strachan, a violent anti-Jacobite and Government Agent.

PARISH OF AUCHINDORE.

AUCHMILLEN (AUCHMULLEN).

In 1696 these lands were in the hands of the Earl of Mar. He had upon them six tenants each described as "no gentleman" (i.e. did not wish to pay the three pound Poll). In 1699 William Reid of Haughton had sasine on a third of Auchmullen.

NEWMILL.

The Laird was the same Alexander Reid "of Newmill and Midclova," [2] whose father was Robert, and he was a younger brother of Mr. James Reid of Bourtie (*q.v.*). Alexander's son, another Robert, was the Jacobite tenant of Cushnie who was transported. There is a sasine between Robert Lumsden of Cushnie and Robert Reid (brother to Mr. James Reid) on the town and lands of Newmill, 25th July, 1659.[3]

There was a John Gordon of Mill of Auchindoir in 1708.

LORD FORBES. (PARISH OF KEIG.)

---

[1] These letters are printed in the *Memoirs of the Family of Lumsden*, by Lt.-Col. H. W. Lumsden, 1889.

[2] *Aberdeen Sasines.*   [3] *Ibid.*

CRAIG.

Francis Gordon, 7th Laird of Craig, son of Francis Gordon, 6th Laird, and his first wife, Elizabeth, daughter of Sir Gilbert Menzies of Pitfodels. The 7th Laird was "out" in the '15 ; was wounded and taken prisoner, 24th October, 1715, at Dunfermline, and died of his wounds in Stirling in September, 1716, having been certified a few days previously, by three surgeons, as "unfit to march" with the other prisoners to Carlisle.[1] He married Agnes Ogilvie, eldest daughter of George, 2nd Lord Banff, and left a son, Francis, 8th of Craig, who was born in 1680, succeeded in 1716, and died in England in 1727.[2]

In the *Poll Book* of 1696 Francis Gordon, 7th Laird, appears in possession with his wife, his eldest son, Francis, 16 years of age, two younger sons, William and Alexander, and five daughters—Agnes, Mary, Elizabeth, Jane, and Barbara. Agnes afterwards married Charles Gordon of Blelack. Mary married George Skene, parson of Kinkell. Elizabeth married Alexander Stewart of Lesmurdie (factor to Lord Fife).

The second wife of the 7th Laird, and mother of some of the younger children, was Anna, daughter of William Gordon of Corrachree.

Francis, 8th of Craig, was probably out with his father in 1715. He married three times—

(1) Elizabeth Barclay of Towie, widow of John Gordon of Rothiemay.
(2) Agnes Forbes of Balfluig, sister of the Jacobite, mother of the 9th Laird of Craig.
(3) Catherine Campbell of Lundie, widow of Patrick Russell of Moncoffer.

On 18th January, 1711, Mr. Charles Bisset, brother of the Laird of Lessendrum and other creditors of Francis Gordon of Craig, had sasine on the lands of Craig.[3] This was probably only temporary. On 3rd September, 1719, Francis Gordon of Craig had sasine on Auchindoir.[4]

LESMOIR—see RHYNIE.

BOGSHEADS—Jo. LUMSDEN.

"John Lumsden of Bogheids, formerly George Randell or Ronald, and now for him John Lumsden of Corrachrie, 1696." [5]

John Lumsden of Bogheid was father of Henry Lumsden, advocate, who bought Pitcaple. For his descent, see Tree of Lumsden of Cushnie, page 113.

---

[1] *S.P.* 54.12.152.

[2] See J. M. Bulloch, "The Gordons of Craig," in *Proc. Soc. Ant. Scot.*, vol. lxiv, p. 96.

[3] *Aberdeen Sasines.*   [4] *Ibid.*   [5] *Poll Book.*

TERPERSIE—PARISH OF TULLYNESSLE.

BIRKENBREUL (*Ser.*).

In 1696 it was "Alexander Smith, sometime of Birkenbrewell, now for him John Lumsden of Corrachrie as being the next heritor of greatest valuation in the parish of Auchindoir." [1]

(Alexander Smith had been there in 1667.)

On 17th September, 1703, John Lumsden of Auchindoir had sasine on Birkenbrewell.[2]

PARISH OF GLENBUCKET.

GLENBUICKET.

The famous John Gordon of Glenbucket, who was served heir to his father, John Gordon, formerly of Knockespock, who died October, 1704, "Heir general to Over and Nether Knockespock in Clatt." On 7th April, 1708, John Gordon had sasine on the town and lands of Kirktown of Glenbucket.[3]

He married in 1702 Jean, elder daughter of Harry Forbes, 4th of (Middle) Boyndlie, who died in 1704, when his brother, John Forbes, was served heir to him.

On 13th December, 1703, Jean Forbes, Lady Glenbucket, yr., had sasine—"Appeared a discreet young man, Alexander Gordon, second lawful son to John Gordon of Knockespock, now of Glenbucket, elder, as pror on behalf of Jean Forbes, lawful spouse to John Gordon of Glenbucket, and with consent of John Forbes of (Middle) Boyndlie, her uncle."

She had been infeft in March, 1702, " in her pure virginity" in the lands of Belnaboth [4] in parish of Glenbucket." [5]

Of this marriage there were eleven children :—

(1) John, (2) David, and (3) George, who all accompanied their father when he took part, as an old man of over 70, in the second Jacobite Rising of 1745.

Alexander, the fourth son, was killed in the Black Sea while serving with the Russian Navy in 1740.

Helen, married to John Macdonnell of Glengarry.

Isobel, to Donald Macdonnell of Lochgarry.

Christian, to George Forbes of Skellater ;

and Henrietta, Clementina, and Cecila unmarried, besides another, Jean, who died young, as proved by one of his own letters.

---

[1] *Poll Book.* [2] *Aberdeen Sasines.* [3] *Ibid.*

[4] There is another estate of the same name belonging to Charles Innes, in parish of Kinbethack.

[5] *Aberdeen Sasines.*

The career of John Gordon, "Old Glenbucket," is too well known to be repeated here. His brother, Alexander, was also a Jacobite of 1715, and was mate of a vessel, "the Hope packet," which cruised about among the Western Islands after the collapse of the Rising, and was instrumental in bringing off some refugees and landing them in Bordeaux, vide *Stuart Papers*. They came from Barra, Uist, Stornoway, and Skye. Alexander Gordon was afterwards commander of a small ship.

In Bordeaux all exiled Jacobites found a friend in Robert Gordon of Hallhead (see page 111).

PARISH OF CABRACH.

DUKE OF GORDON—see DUNBENNAN.

PARISH OF KINBETACK.

EARLE OF MAR—see PARISH OF INVERNOCHTY.

BALNABOTH, FOR LORD ELPHINSTONE AND ONE HALF TO SKELLATER.

In the *Poll Book* Charles Innes was of Balnaboth, with Margaret Forbes, his wife, and Isobel Innes, his daughter. In 1700 Charles Innes signed the heritors' bond to apprehend malefactors.[1]

LORD ELPHINSTONE—see PARISH OF MIGVIE.

SKELLATER—see PARISH OF TARLAND.

SINNAHARD AND SINNABOTH.[2] JOHN INNES—see MIGVY.

"J. Innes of Sinnahard" signed the bond of Heritors sworn to keep the peace, 1700. Lachlan Forbes of Edinglassie had sasine on Sinnahard, 3rd February, 1719.

GLENKINDY—*D*—see PARISH OF INVERNOCHTY.

BRUX—see PARISH OF KILDRUMMY.

In 1726 Arthur Forbes of Brux and his son, Roderick, granted moss

---

[1] Allardyce, *Jacobite Papers*, vol. i, p. 21.

[2] In 1753 the Lands of Sinnahard and Sinnaboth were purchased by Alexander Leith of Glenkindie and Jonathan Forbes of Brux from William Grant of Glenbeg.

9

tolerance to George Forbes, yr. of Skellater, for his tenants in Kinbethack and Rippachy to cut peat.[1]

KINCLUNE.

ROBERT MCHARDY—see PARISH OF CRATHIE.

PARISH OF INVERNOCHTY.

THE EARL OF MAR.

John, 6th Earl of Mar—"Bobbing John" of the '15—was the eldest son of Charles, 5th Earl of Mar, and his wife, Mary Maule, only daughter of George, Earl of Panmure.

During the reigns of William and Mary, and of Queen Anne he remained on the side of the established Government. He was Secretary of State for Scotland from 1705 and a Knight of the Thistle, 1706. He did much to aid the passing of the measure for the Act of Union between the two Kingdoms, 1707, and was appointed one of the sixteen representative Peers to go to London to the British Parliament. Having had in a very great degree the management of Scots affairs during the reign of Queen Anne, he hoped to continue this under the new foreign monarch, and even sent to King George before his arrival a congratulatory address to which he obtained a good many signatures. But George from the first refused to see him and deprived him of his offices of Secretary of State and Governor of Stirling Castle. Mar, therefore, threw in his lot with the Jacobite party, departed in disguise for Scotland, and having landed at Elie in Fife made his way to his own country of Aberdeenshire, where he raised the standard at Braemar, 6th September, 1715. The old Chevalier, who had much of his grandfather's (Charles I) unfortunate inability to trust the right men, sent him a commission as Commander in Chief, and a patent as Duke of Mar, which commission Mar forestalled by taking upon himself the management of affairs, and thus alienating Huntly, the Master of Sinclair, and others, who should have been the most ardent supporters.

Cockburn, the Lord Justice Clerk, who no doubt had good spies in the Jacobite camp, writes that Huntly was "surprised" at the appointment, and later, that "there is great deserting from Mar's camp."[2]

A history of the Rising cannot be given here, but it is common knowledge that its failure was chiefly owing to Mar's incompetent generalship. After the failure, when the Jacobite army was in retreat to the North, Mar embarked with his master at Montrose on 4th February (six weeks after the Chevalier's landing at Peterhead) and arrived with him at St. Malo. His exact movements after this are not known, but he was one of

---

[1] *Castle Forbes Papers.*　　　　[2] *S.P.* 54.10.96.

those who arrived at Avignon on 2nd August, 1716 (according to an unpublished MS. in the library there).[1]

He was made prisoner at Voghera in 1719 ; later he was in Switzerland, and then in Rome, with his master, and in 1721 acted as Jacobite minister in Paris till 1724, when he was relieved of this office. He appears to have changed sides again, and accepted a pension from the British Government, though there is no proof that this was ever paid. When James Murray, afterwards Earl of Dunbar, became the chief confidant of James, Mar was set aside, and this had chagrined him.[2]

He died at Aix-la-Chapelle, May, 1732.

He was twice married. First to Margaret, eldest daughter of the Earl of Kinnoull, and had two sons—Thomas (Lord Erskine) and John. Secondly, July, 1714, to Frances, daughter of the 1st Duke of Kingston, and sister of Lady Mary Wortley Montagu, and by her (who became a lunatic and was looked after by her famous sister) had a daughter, Frances, who married her first cousin, James Erskine, son of James Erskine of Grange. Part of the estates forfeited by the attainder of John, Earl of Mar, were purchased by James Erskine, and settled on the issue of Lady Frances, whose son became 7th Earl. In 1735 a great part of the estates of Mar was bought by William Duff (Lord Braco), afterwards 1st Lord Fife.

The following account of Mar's progress in the North is taken from the *State Papers* [3] :—

My Lord Marr had his passage from South to North Britain in John Spence of Leith his boat, having only in Company with him General Hamilton and his own meniall Servants ; the boat was sailed by two Seamen. His design was to have landed at or near by St. Andrews, but was forced into the South East part of ffyfe where he went on shoar near to Ely and in the hurry he landed with one of his principal servants dropt over a Plank which was laid from the boat on a Rock and was drowned in the sea.

And being put on shoar he travelled over land to his father in Law's my Lord Kinoul his house and being supplied of Horses by him for his Journey he took his way towards the country of Marr and the first night thereafter came to Thomas Rathay of Craighall near to Blair of Gowrie his house and having intimated his design to him of taking up arms and declaring for the Pretender and consorting measures with him for the accomplishment thereof he passed from Craighall towards Strathairdlie where the informer had occasion to see him by ye Way being accompanied by eighteen horsemen and some of his vassals in Mar having intelligence of his approach came and awaited of him to Spalden of Ashentullie his house, knowing him to be firm for the interest he was to sett up for he talked very freely in public of his designs, and knowing he could raise some 2 or 3 hundred men promised him a Colonel's commission in ye Pretender's service and withall told him that whether the Pretender landed or not, General Hamilton and he were to lead an army South for the dissolution

---

[1] *Bibliothèque Calvet MS.* 2827.   [2] *Pitsligo's MS. at Fettercairn.*
[3] *S.P.* 59.   Bundle 8.   124.

of Ye Union and to have ye Grievance of ye Nation redressed for he was at pains all the way as he passed to spread a false report of ye Parliament being designed to lay unsurportable Taxes upon the Nation on lands, corn, cattle, meal, malt, horse, sheep, and not only so, but even on Cockes and Hens, and that this was no mean reason for him to take up arms since otherwise in a very short time the nation should sink under such burdens. This took extreamly with the common people and animated them to take up arms. He passed two days with that gentleman in great Jollity and as they were merry together told him that at every house he had touched by the way he had borrowed something and he must needs borrow somewhat of him also and being demanded what that might bee, he told him that it was his fiddler which the Gentleman readily granted. From thence he went to the Spittal of Glenshee where he lodged at a public house and from thence to Marr and having no house of his own in that country under repair he lodged in ffarquharson of Envercauld a vassal of his own, and having assured him of an Invasion to be made of the three Kingdoms at once and that he was to head the Pretender's forces till the Duke of Berwick's arrival. (Invercauld refused to join unless he saw Mar's commission,* and stole away in the night, taking with him what arms he had. Mar then ill-treated and threatened his servants—see page 59.)

GLENKINDIE—*D.*

Sir Patrick Strachan of Glenkindie, whose father was Alexander, grandson of Alexander, 6th of Glenkindie. Alexander, 7th of Glenkindie, the elder brother, succeeded in 1675, in which year both his father and grandfather died.[1]

On 21st November, 1705, Patrick Strachan "now of Glenkindy," had sasine on Auchnagatt.[2]

In 1726 the estate of Glenkindie was taken possession of by the creditors of Sir PATRICK STRACHAN, and twelve years later was purchased from these creditors by Alexander Leith of Freefield (whose mother had been Margaret Strachan, aunt of Sir Patrick), and his father, James Leith of New Leslie.

Like all his family, Patrick was a Hanoverian and particularly obnoxious to the Jacobites of his own county.

In a letter from a spy, in the Record Office, headed :—

INTELLIGENCE FROM THE NORTH.

Sept. 7. 1715.

It is informed that several of Mar's own vassals such as Glenkindy, ffinzean etc. have refused to join the said Earl against King George and the Government and have gone off from their houses, notwithstanding of his many great and repeated promises and threatenings and that the said Earl is in hopes to gain some of them if not all, by reason of the slackness of the Government.—*S.P.* 54.8.30.

* Or "to stir until the King's landing."—Master of Sinclair.
[1] *Aberdeen Sasines.* [2] *Ibid.*

He married twice—(1) Isobel Forbes, daughter of Sir Samuel Forbes of Foveran,[1] and (2) Elizabeth Allgood, an English woman.

Sir Patrick Strachan was imprisoned in Dundee by the Jacobites during the Rising. After his release he was very active in disarming the country, and was knighted by King George in 1717.

At his death, which occurred at Aberdeen, 2nd January, 1726, it was said he was "not regretted by any person, and if he had lived longer, the gentry of the county were to pursue him for taking of sums of money from them for protection"[2] (which he had not given them).

BUQUHAM—INVERNAN FOR.

The Forbeses in this Parish are numerous and can only be understood by reference to the Genealogical Tables.

A charter was granted, 18th April, 1592, by Alexander, Master of Elphinstone, to John Forbes of Buchaam in Liferent, and James Forbes, his eldest son, in fee.[3]

John Forbes of Buchaam had sasine on 4th May, 1664, and his son, John, was in possession in 1696, with James Forbes, who was his uncle, "a gentleman and tenant," and the wife of James.[4] (*Poll Book.*) John Forbes of Buchaam, with the consent of his uncle, James, sold it to Inverernan, 12th February, 1696.

On 25th June, 1714, William Forbes, eldest son to John Forbes of Inverernan, had sasine on Buchaam, his father having had one on 12th February, 1696, and another 15th October, 1700.[5]

Inverernan, who paid (or at any rate handed over) the Cess for Buchaam, was "Black Jock," born 1664, brother to Skellater, and father of William (see Parish of Tarland). William sold these lands to Candacraig in 1745.

Probably John of Buchaam of 1592 was of the Skellater family, but the exact relationship has not been found; in 1610 his son, James, was dead, as Patrick Forbes was then described as his eldest son, and was confirmed in the estate in 1626—John succeeded in 1633. His son, John, sold the estate to "Black Jock" in 1696, as seen above.

---

[1] "On 29th June 1703, William Strachan of Coltown appeared for ane honourable woman, Isobel Forbes, wife of Patrick Strachan of Glenkindy. The witnesses being William Forbes, junior of Craigievar, John Forbes of Inverernan, Charles Innes of Belnabo (Belnaboth) and John Smith, Notary Public."—*Aberdeen Sasines.*

[2] *Francis Steuart's News Letters, 1715, 1716.*

[3] *Castle Forbes Papers.*

[4] One John Forbes of Buchaam died before 1676, as his widow, Isobel Ross, married in that year Alexander Forbes of Invernochty.—*Strathdon Registers.*

[5] *Aberdeen Sasines.*

CULQUHUNNY—JO. FORBES.

John Forbes, son of Arthur Forbes, who was the laird in 1667, and was a cadet of Newe. The estate of Culquhonny is on the North side of the Don, below Newe: a small fragment of the old castle remains.

" John Forbes of Culonnie," eldest son of Arthur, appears in the decret of Lawboroughs, 1683.[1] He had five brothers—Patrick, who succeeded and had already signed the heritors' bond of 26th April, 1700 ; Adam, George,[2] born 1678, married 1708 Elizabeth Gordon of Auchindoir ; Alexander, and Roderick.

CONDRYSIDE, DITTO.

It has not been found possible to identify this place, nor to find the owner in 1715, but " Jo. Forbes" paid the Cess, so apparently it was part of Culquhonny.

TOLDAWHILL, DITTO—PART OF INVERERNAN.

Cess also paid by Jo. Forbes. On 2nd October, 1679, Duncan Catanach in Toldaquhill and Jean Forbes, daughter to John Forbes of Invernettie, were married.[3]

It was formerly Farquharson property and spelt Tolaquhill and Tolduchall.

DITTO, FOR ROBERT MOIR'S VALUATION.

That is for another part of Toldaquhill. Cess still paid by " Jo. Forbes," as the three dittos in succession must refer to him. Robert Moir was presumably his factor.

NEW.

John Forbes, 7th Laird of Newe. He had sasine on 31st January, 1711. William Forbes, 5th of Newe, son of Alexander Forbes and Janet Robertson, was the owner in 1696, with his wife, Helen Forbes of Culquhanny, two sons and a daughter, Jean. William died 19th January, 1698, aged 76, and is buried in Strathdon. His eldest son, William, succeeded him as 6th Laird, being served heir in 1701, and John (above) was the 7th. (William, the 6th, was "younger of Newe" in 1696.) The 7th Laird of Newe was born in 1686, and his brother, William, 1689 ; George of Bellabeg and John of Deskrie were younger brothers of William,

---

[1] *Records of Invercauld.*

[2] George Forbes was the ancestor of Col. James Forbes, D.S.O., of Lockeridge, East Grinstead, who believes him to have been a Jacobite of 1715 and to have "disappeared in the Rising."

[3] *Strathdon Registers.*

6th Laird. From George descends the modern family of Newe, and from John, the Forbes in America.

FAMILY OF NEWE.

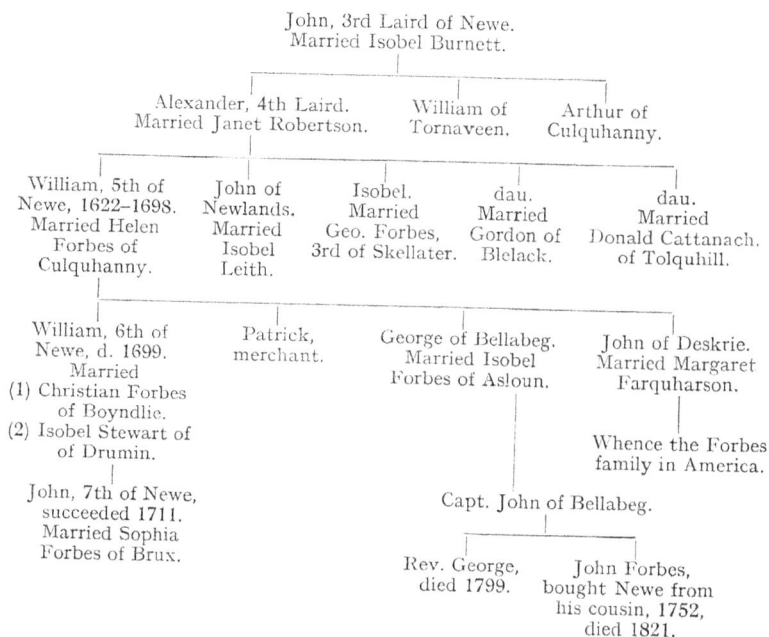

John, 3rd Laird of Newe.
Married Isobel Burnett.

Alexander, 4th Laird.   William of   Arthur of
Married Janet Robertson.   Tornaveen.   Culquhanny.

William, 5th of   John of   Isobel.   dau.   dau.
Newe, 1622–1698.   Newlands.   Married   Married   Married
Married Helen   Married   Geo. Forbes,   Gordon of   Donald Cattanach.
Forbes of   Isobel   3rd of Skellater. Blelack.   of Tolquhill.
Culquhanny.   Leith.

William, 6th of   Patrick,   George of Bellabeg.   John of Deskrie.
Newe, d. 1699.   merchant.   Married Isobel   Married Margaret
Married   Forbes of Asloun.   Farquharson.
(1) Christian Forbes
   of Boyndlie.   Whence the Forbes
(2) Isobel Stewart of   family in America.
   of Drumin.

John, 7th of Newe,   Capt. John of Bellabeg.
succeeded 1711.
Married Sophia
Forbes of Brux.   Rev. George,   John Forbes,
                                  died 1799.   bought Newe from
                                                    his cousin, 1752,
                                                    died 1821.

In connection with the purchase of Newe serious disputes occurred. From an Inventory of writs produced in the process Newe *versus* Candacraig, 1767, the following interesting details are extracted. (A copy of this Inventory is among the papers at Castle Forbes) :—

The matter in question was the line of the marches of that portion of the estate of Glencarvie, sold by John Forbes of Glencarvie to Capt. John Forbes of New, and further the disposition of the lands of Lesmoir, Forest of Bunzeach and others by John Gordon of Wardhouse and his son. The Lands of Glencarvie had belonged in 1684 to William Anderson, brother of the Laird of Candacraig, and on 26th June, 1745, Buchaam also had disponed to Charles Anderson of Candacraig certain lands.

One important witness for Candacraig was Alexander Forbes of Inverernan. He was the eldest son by the second marriage of "Black Jock" of Inverernan, and was born in 1712 so that he was only a child of between three and four at his father's death.

His mother, Margaret Alexander, who had devotedly attended her husband's death-bed in prison in Carlisle, subsequently married "Mr. Macswean," Minister of Strathdon, and Alexander Forbes depones that about 40 years ago, i.e. in 1727, when he was a boy of 15, he remembered "his tenants of Inverernan being called to carry home to the Manse, Mr. Macswean, Minister of Strathdon's Turf. (Deponent's mother being then the Minister's wife.)"

On which occasion John Anderson of Candacraig, John Forbes of Glencarvie and John Wathie then in Stroin, went to the ground and stopped the Defendant's tenants from carrying the Turf. On which Mrs. Macswean, the deponent's mother, carried the Deponent, then a scholar in the school house of Strathdon, and Roderick Farquharson in Brughs, along with her to the spot and ordered the Tenants to carry off the Turf and as the tenants proceeded in their loading of the Turf, Candacraig's Tutor stopped the Tenants and threw the Turfs off their horses, whereupon a scuffle ensued between the Tutor and the said Roderick Farquharson who pulled the Tutor to the ground, upon which the Deponent's Mother ordered the Tenants to return home without any Turf; and farther depones that the Deponent made a push with a Fox-click at one of the Tenants for being so dilatory in obeying his Mother's orders; and depones that the Turfs were let alone for a day or two, until Mr. Lumsden of Cushny, Uncle to Candacraig, was applied to by Mr. Macswean and gave liberty to carry them away.

Mr. Macswean, then a tenant of part of the lands of Culquharry, depones that Lauchlan Forbes of Edinglassie, being a man of influence in the country, and having a prejudice against the said Mr. Macsween, hindered or stopped him from carrying peats from other mosses through his grounds, and that through Lachlan Forbes' influence, Invernetty did the same, and he does not know whether the same influence was used with the Tutor of Candacraig to stop the Minister from carrying said Turfs or not.

Black Jock's widow would appear to have married for the second time a man younger than herself, or at least 30 years younger than her first husband, and one whose Highland second-sight was looked on as dangerous by the practical inhabitants of Aberdeenshire.[1]

CULQUHARRIE.

Alexander Forbes of Culquharrie, with wife and three daughters, was there in 1696, also Arthur Forbes of Culquharrie, with wife and four children ; Arthur was son of Alexander.

Elspet Forbes, one of the daughters of Alexander, above-mentioned, had married, in 1680, John Farquharson, son of Robert Farquharson of Old Largue (Allargue).

There is a charter of resignation of the lands of Buchaam and Culquharry, by John, Earl of Mar, in favour of John Forbes of Invernernan, 15th October, 1712. (*Castle Forbes Papers.*)

---

[1] From Scott's *Fasti* the following account of "Mr. McSween" is taken :—

"1718. Invernochty or Strathdon—Donald McSwain a native of Skye had his degree from the University and King's College, Aberdeen, 1711, became tutor to the family of Capt. afterwards Major Hugh McKay of Scourie, licensed by the Presbytery of Aberdeen 25th June 1718, died 8th June 1730, aged 38. It is said that walking in the fields one day with a brother who had come to visit him, he was lost in thought and assured of his Mother's death, which actually took place at the time. Some people attempted to smother him with a wet canvas one evening when at family prayers. Being a man of considerable bodily strength however he extricated himself from his assailants. He married Margaret Alexander, who survived him."

INVERNOCHTIE.

This was William Forbes, son to Alexander Forbes of Invernochty, who was first cousin to William Forbes of Newe, Alexander being son of Arthur Forbes of Invernochty, who was brother of Alexander Forbes of Newe. William was served heir to his father on 12th November, 1702. (*Commissariot of Aberdeen.*)

He had three sons—William, Adam, and Arthur (born 1684), and a daughter, Helen, who had sasine for herself, 4th July, 1704, of an arent out of the lands of Finnelost and Drummellan. (*Aberdeen Sasines.*)

William Forbes of Invernochty married Margaret Robertson, daughter of John Robertson, Minister of the Gospel at Invernochty, on 7th December, 1711. (*Ibid.*)

CORRIEBRECH. [William Forbes.]

"*7th October, 1703.* Sasine in favour of

"John Forbes of Invernettie and Diana Forbes, his lawful daughter, procreate betwixt John Forbes and the deceased Katherine Stewart of the lands of Corriebreach and Blairnamuck, heiress to unquhile Violet Forbes her sister."

Corriebreck afterwards came to William, nephew of Violet and Diana, fifth son of William, 1st of Belnabodach, who was son of John Forbes of Invernettie.

Diana afterwards married Roderick, third son of John Farquharson of Allargue.

James Grant was of Corriebreck in the *Poll Book*, with his wife, John and George, his sons, and Anna and Elizabeth, his daughters. William Forbes of Corriebreck in 1715 (fifth son of William Forbes of Belnabodach), was ancestor of Forbes of Seaton, Forbes of Callendar, and Forbes of Rothiemay—Corriebreck having previously been the property of Diana and Violet Forbeses, the aunts of William—daughters of John Forbes, 1st of Invernettie, 1st of Ledmacoy, and 1st of Belnabodach.

BELNABODACH.

John, 3rd and last of Belnabodach, son of William Forbes, 2nd of Belnabodach, appears in the *Poll Book* in 1696 with his wife, Mary Stewart of Lesmurdie, and two children, John and Isabel. John, 3rd of Belnabodach, married 7th November, 1706, Janet, daughter of John Robertson, minister of Invernochty. On 1st December, 1711, John Forbes and Janet Robertson had sasine on Belnabodach. (*Aberdeen Sasines.*)

John afterwards sold the lands.

William Forbes, his father, was the second son of John Forbes, who was the second son of George Forbes, 1st of Skellater, and John owned

Invernettie, which he left to Alexander, his eldest son; Belnabodach to William, his second; and Ledmacoy to John, his third (see Tree on page 141).

BELLABEG.

George Forbes, son to 5th Laird of Newe, and brother to the 6th, held these lands in 1715. He is the ancestor of the modern Forbes family of Newe, which was bought by his son, John. George Forbes of Milne of New (the same man), sold Bellabeg to Lachlan Forbes of Newbigging and Edinglassie, and on July, 1716, William Forbes, eldest son of Lachlan Forbes of Edinglassie, had sasine on Bellabeg. Lachlan was fourth son of George, 3rd of Skellater, and his wife was Margaret, daughter of Robert Irvine, minister of Towie.

Lachlan Forbes himself had sasine on Bellabeg, 14th July, 1719, and on Sinnahard, 3rd February, 1719. He was a younger brother of George, 3rd of Skellater, and an active Jacobite of 1715,[1] and had a son Benjamin who was "out" in the '45. John Forbes of Bellabeg, son of Benjamin, born 1725, appears in the Glencarvie March dispute, 1767. (*Castle Forbes Papers*.)

SKELLATER, ELDER.

George, 3rd of Skellater, who married (1) —— Farquharson, (2) Isobel Forbes of Newe, and died 1716 (see Parish of Tarland).

OLDERGUE.

John Farquharson, son of Robert of Allargue, *or* his son, Andrew.

In the *Poll Book* John appears with his second wife, Elspeth Forbes, and five children—Andrew, Gustavus, Roderick, George, and Jean Farquharson. He signed the heritors' bond in 1700. The date of John's death is not known. Andrew was the son of his first wife, who was Farquharson of Bellamore. There was a younger son than George—Robert, whose son Robert succeeded.[2]

Andrew married Barbara Stewart of Aucholzie and was the father of John Farquharson of Allargue of the '45, who figures so largely in "the Lyon in Mourning." To him succeeded his cousin, Robert.

---

[1] Captain Nathaniel Forbes of Rippachy and Ardgeith, second son of George Forbes, 3rd of Skellater, writing to the Earl (Jacobite Duke) of Mar from Paris in 1717, says: "No doubt your Grace has heard of Black Jock's death at Carlisle" (his uncle, John Forbes of Inverernan), and adds—"both my brothers are skulking in the hills" that is George, 4th of Skellater, and Lachlan of Edinglassie. Lachlan had, in 1719, sasine on Sinnahard. Nathaniel was born in 1676, and married Jean Forbes of Newe. He was a Captain in Mar's army.

[2] *Records of Aboyne*, p. 278.

(William Stewart of Aucholzie, brother of Barbara, married as his second wife, Euphemia Farquharson, and died 1750. His first wife had been Barbara Farquhar. He was a Jacobite of the '15.)

Roderick, the third son of John Farquharson of Allargue, married Diana Forbes of Invernettie.

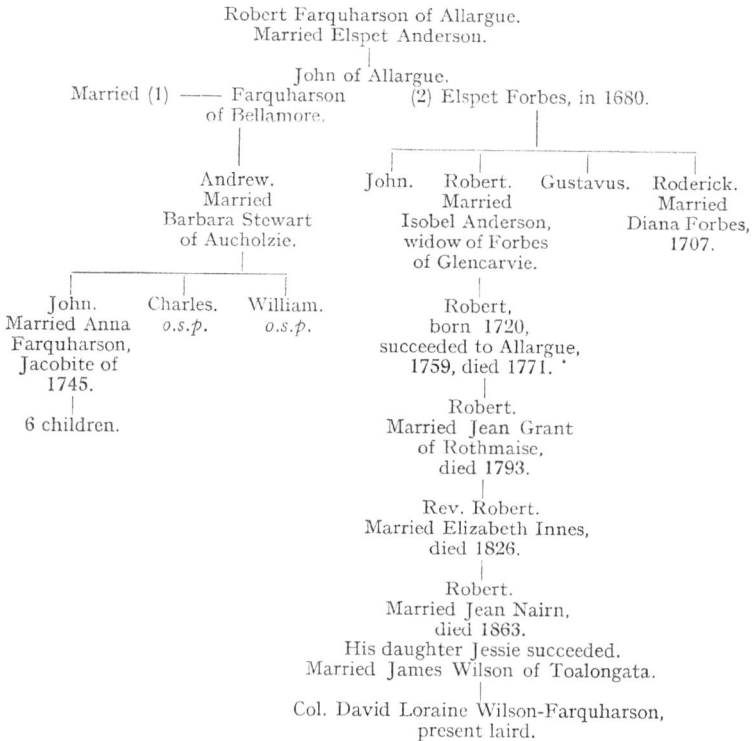

```
              Robert Farquharson of Allargue.
                 Married Elspet Anderson.
                             |
                    John of Allargue.
Married (1) ——— Farquharson      (2) Elspet Forbes, in 1680.
         of Bellamore.                         |
              |               ┌────────┬──────────┬─────────┐
          Andrew.           John.   Robert.   Gustavus.  Roderick.
          Married                   Married               Married
       Barbara Stewart          Isobel Anderson,      Diana Forbes,
        of Aucholzie.            widow of Forbes          1707.
              |                  of Glencarvie.
   ┌──────┬────────┬────────┐            |
  John.   Charles.  William.         Robert,
Married Anna  o.s.p.  o.s.p.      born 1720,
Farquharson,                   succeeded to Allargue,
 Jacobite of                    1759, died 1771.
   1745.                                |
     |                              Robert.
 6 children.                  Married Jean Grant
                                of Rothmaise,
                                 died 1793.
                                       |
                                 Rev. Robert.
                            Married Elizabeth Innes,
                                  died 1826.
                                       |
                                   Robert.
                            Married Jean Nairn,
                                 died 1863.
                          His daughter Jessie succeeded.
                        Married James Wilson of Toalongata.
                                       |
                       Col. David Loraine Wilson-Farquharson,
                                 present laird.
```

—Farquharson Genealogies.

SKELLATER FOR TOLLOSKINK—see PARISH OF AUCHINDOIR.

Charles Bisset and others had sasine on Tolloskink for debt in 1711.[1]

Tolloskink is also mentioned in the marriage contract between "Christian Forbes, second daughter of the now deceased John Forbes of Inverernan ('Black Jock') and George Forbes (then) 'younger of Skellater'" (afterwards George, 4th of Skellater, first cousin to Christian). The marriage contract was dated 7th April, 1714, at which date both John of Inverernan and George, 3rd of Skellater, were alive. It was "implemented" 7th December, 1718, with sasine on Tolloskink and other lands.[2]

[1] *Aberdeen Sasines.*　　　　　[2] *Ibid.*

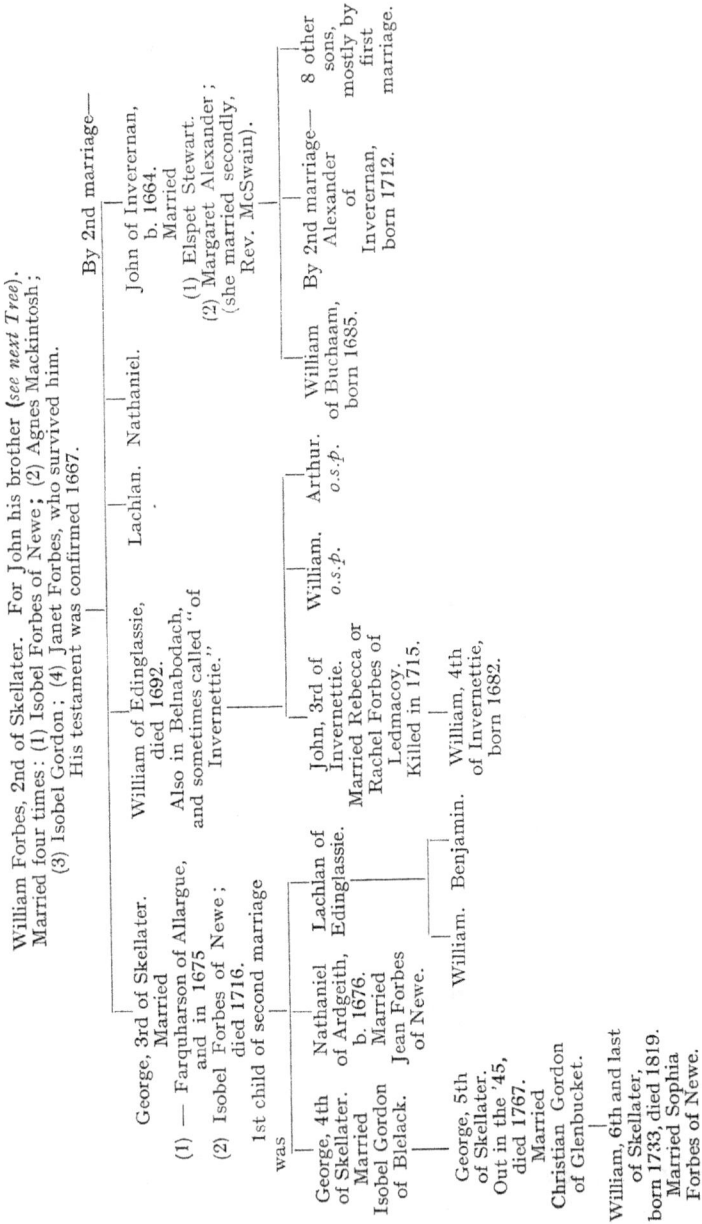

William Forbes, 2nd of Skellater. For John his brother (*see next Tree*).
Married four times: (1) Isobel Forbes of Newe; (2) Agnes Mackintosh;
(3) Isobel Gordon; (4) Janet Forbes, who survived him.
His testament was confirmed 1667.

By 2nd marriage—

George, 3rd of Skellater.
Married
(1) — Farquharson of Allargue,
and in 1675
(2) Isobel Forbes of Newe;
died 1716.
1st child of second marriage
was

William of Edinglassie,
died 1692.
Also in Belnabodach,
and sometimes called " of
Invernettie."

Lachlan. Nathaniel.

John of Invernernan,
b. 1664.
Married
(1) Elspet Stewart.
(2) Margaret Alexander;
(she married secondly,
Rev. McSwain).

Nathaniel
of Ardgeith,
b. 1676.
Married
Jean Forbes
of Newe.

Lachlan of
Edinglassie.

John, 3rd of
Invernettie.
Married Rebecca or
Rachel Forbes of
Ledmacoy.
Killed in 1715.

William.
o.s.p.

Arthur.
o.s.p.

William
of Buchaam,
born 1685.

By 2nd marriage
Alexander
of
Invernernan,
born 1712.

8 other
sons,
mostly by
first
marriage.

George, 4th
of Skellater.
Married
Isobel Gordon
of Blelack.

William. Benjamin.

William, 4th
of Invernettie,
born 1682.

George, 5th
of Skellater.
Out in the '45,
died 1767.
Married
Christian Gordon
of Glenbucket.

William, 6th and last
of Skellater,
born 1733, died 1819.
Married Sophia
Forbes of Newe.

140

John Forbes {1st of Invernettie, 1st of Ledmacoy, 1st of Belnabodach} Brother of William, 2nd of Skellater.

Married (1) —— Brown; (2) in 1675, Katherine Stewart of Lesmurdie. He died 1684.

Alexander, 2nd of Invernettie, also called of Ledmacoy, died 1694. Married 1682. (1) Isabel Catanach. 1689. (2) Elspet Anderson of Tomaclen. *o.s.p.*	William, 2nd of Belnabodach. Married (1) Mary Stewart, Lesmurdie. (2) Isabel Forbes of Edinglassie, in 1693. (3) Agnes Forbes of Newe.	John, 2nd of Ledmacoy. Married (1) Jean Anderson of Candacraig in 1685. (2) Marie Grant.	Nine daughters—
	Nathaniel of Auchernack.	William and others.	1. Violet, *o.s.p.* 1698.
	William of Corriebreech, Patrick, Hugh and others.		2. "Nans," Married Duncan Anderson of Candacraig in 1674.
			3. Elspet. Married William Elphinstone of Bellabeg.
	John, 3rd of Belnabodach. Married Janet Robertson.		4. Jean. Married Duncan Catanach of Toldaquhill.
			5. Helen. Married, 1676, Grant.
			6. Agnes. Married Anderson.
			7. Diana. Married Roderick Farquharson.
			8. Isobel. Married "Alexander Thomson in the Culsh. 1686."
			9. Rebecca or Rachel, youngest daughter. Married John Forbes, 3rd of Invernettie, her 1st cousin once removed.

All from *Strathdon Registers.*

LEDMACOY.

John Forbes, 2nd of Ledmacoy, who was there in 1696, with his wife, his son, William, and daughter, Elizabeth.

He was third son of John, 1st of Ledmacoy, and his second wife, Katherine Stewart of Lesmurdie. This John Forbes was second son of George, 1st of Skellater. John, the second, succeeded in 1684, married in 1685 Jean Anderson of Candacraig, and secondly Marie Grant, and had three sons—John, William, and Nathaniel. John died young, and Nathaniel was born in 1697. The estate of Ledmacoy was valued at £330. John of Ledmacoy paid in 1696, £130 of this, while John of Invernettie, his first cousin, once removed, paid £200.

John, 1st of Ledmacoy, had sasine on Invernettie, 1st September, 1673.[1]

He died in 1684, while Invernettie passed to his eldest son, Alexander, who died in 1694. It *then* passed to John Forbes, below.

INVERNETTIE.

JOHN FORBES, 3rd of Invernettie, owned Invernettie in Invernochty in 1696, when his son, William Forbes, is also mentioned (he was 14 years old). John was first cousin to George, 4th of Skellater, and is the "Invernettie" who brought his men to join Mar.[2] His father was William of Edinglassie, brother of George, 3rd of Skellater. John is believed to have been killed in 1715 "by Lord Forbes' men."[3]

John Forbes of Invernettie signed the heritors' bond, 26th April, 1700, with George Forbes of Skellater, his cousin. On 7th October, 1703, there is a sasine already mentioned in favour of John Forbes of Invernettie (above) and "Diana Forbes, lawful daughter procreate between John Forbes, 1st of Ledmacoy (previous entry in Roll), and the deceased Katherine Stewart," of the "lands of Corriebreech and Blairnamuck and heiress to umquhile Violet Forbes, her sister ;

before witnesses, William Forbes of Invernochty.

George Forbes and Adam Forbes, sons to umquhile Arthur Forbes of Culquhanny.

The said Diana Forbes cannot write, but touching the pen with her hand." (*Aberdeen Sasines.*)

[1] *Aberdeen Sasines.*

[2] A paper in the Record Office of date 1st October, 1715, says : "Invernettie had a body of men which marched into Perth in 24 ranks, 9 men in each rank." —*S.P.* 54.9.2.

[3] On the south bank of the Don is a small eminence of natural wood intermixed with plantation, called Daln Handy, i.e. Alexander's Haugh. Here is a tumulus, said to point out the spot where the above John Forbes was shot in 1715 or 1716 by some of the dragoons commanded by Lord Forbes.

Diana and Violet were cousins to the John of Invernettie in question, and their sister, Rebecca, ninth and youngest daughter of John Forbes, 1st of Ledmacoy and formerly of Invernettie, was his wife (she is sometimes called Rachel!). Diana afterwards married, 26th June, 1707, Roderick Farquharson, son of Allargue.

CANDYCRAIG—see PARISH OF TARLAND.

PRESBYTERY OF DEER.

PARISH OF PETERHEAD.

THE EARLE MARISCHAL.

George, 10th and last Earl Marischal, eldest son of William, 9th Earl Marischal (a strong opponent of the Union), and Mary Drummond, eldest daughter of James, Earl of Perth. There was one other son, James, the famous Field-Marshal Keith, and two sisters, Lady Mary Keith, who married the 6th Earl of Wigton, and Lady Anne, married the Earl of Galloway.

The 9th Earl Marischal died in 1712, when George Keith was only 18. He had been in the English army, having received a commission from Queen Anne in Hyndford's Dragoons in 1711, when 17. Three years later he became Lieut.-Colonel of the 2nd Troop of Horse Guards, but being deprived of his commission at the instigation of the Duke of Argyll, he set out for Scotland, where he and his younger brother, whom he met and turned back at York, were among the most prominent and valuable supporters of the Jacobite rising. The Earl Marischal attended Mar's hunting party, 26th August, 1715. He proclaimed King James VIII at Aberdeen, commanded the right wing at Sheriffmuir, entertained James at Fetteresso, though not personally, and attended him at Perth and until he left the country.

When the King escaped from Montrose to France in February, 1716, he wished to take the Earl Marischal with him, the latter, however, remained with the army till it was disbanded, and later followed James to France, arriving at Avignon on 2nd August, 1716 (according to an unpublished MS. in the library there, which gives a list of nearly 200 of James' followers—English, Scots, and Irish).[1]

The Earl Marischal commanded the forces engaged in the abortive Jacobite attempt at Glenshiel on 18th June, 1719, and was badly wounded but escaped, after which he retired to Spain and lived the greater part

[1] *Bibliothèque du Musée Calvet MS.* 2827.

of his life abroad. He took no part in the Rising of 1745, the intrigues of Lovat, Balhaldie, and others having convinced him that the whole affair was being mismanaged.

On 29th May, 1759, he received a free pardon from George II, and the right to inherit any estates or title which might come to him, though not a re-grant of his own estates. In the following year he did inherit the estates and title of his cousin, the 4th Earl of Kintore, grandson of Sir John Keith, but refused to take the title. He came to Scotland in 1763, and having been granted over £4,000 out of the proceeds of the sale of his attainted estates to the York Buildings Society, he bought back part of the estate, which he re-sold to James Ferguson of Pitfour, and the Castle of Dunnottar, which he sold to Alex. Keith of Ravelston, a distant cousin. Fetteresso itself was bought by Admiral Robert Duff of Logie from the York Buildings Society after the death of the Earl Marischal, which occurred at Potsdam (where he was the honoured friend of Frederick the Great) on 28th May, 1778. He was unmarried.

The family of the Earls Marischal is so often given incorrectly that it seems important here to set down the complete family tree. Sir William Keith, "Great Marischal of Scotland," married the niece of King Robert Bruce and acquired the Castle of Dunnottar. Eleventh in descent from him was another Sir William Keith, who was created Earl Marischal of Scotland in 1455.

WILLIAM MOIR OF INVERNETTY.

The third son of John Moir, 1st of Stoneywood, and Jean Sandilands. He was youngest brother of James Moir, second Laird of Stoneywood, and of Alex. Moir, regent of Marischal College. Born in 1669, he was a merchant in Aberdeen, and bought Invernettie in 1708 from Keith of Ludquharn, having a charter in the same year.[1]

He married (1) Christian Guthrie, who had a liferent on Invernettie, in October, 1710, and (2) Jean, daughter of Colonel Lewis Hay.

He was certainly a Jacobite sympathiser; there is no record of his activities, but according to a paper at Castle Grant he "left Banff by ship, 8th April, 1716," along with some other Jacobites.[2]

His Will is in the Commissariot of Aberdeen for 22nd December, 1744.

He had two sons by his second wife—James, who succeeded his father in 1744, and married Katharine Arbuthnot, and William, who succeeded James. The latter was a Jacobite of 1745 and married Jean Hay.

SIR WILLIAM KEITH.

The 3rd Baronet of Ludquharn, who succeeded about 1680 on the death of his father, Sir Alexander, 2nd Baronet, and married the daughter

---

[1] *Aberdeen Sasines.*   [2] *Seafield Papers.*

George, 10th Earl Marischal.

From painting in Marischal College.

WILLIAM, 1ST EARL Marischal,
In 1455 married Mary Hamilton of Cadzow, and died before 1476.

WILLIAM, 2ND EARL.
Married Muriella Erskine, daughter of 1st Lord Erskine.

| WILLIAM, 3RD EARL. Married Lady Elizabeth Gordon, daughter of 2nd Earl of Huntly; died 1527. | Robert. | Alexander of Auquhorsk. | John of Craig. |

| Robert (Lord Keith), killed at Flodden, 1513. | William. | Alexander. | 4 daughters. |

| WILLIAM, 4TH EARL. Married Margaret Keith of Inverugie. | Robert, Abbott of Deer; d. 1551. | 3 daughters. |

| William (Lord Keith). Married Elizabeth Hay of Erroll, made prisoner at Pinkie, 1547. | Robert (Lord Altrie), Commendator of Deer. | Alex. | 7 daughters. |

| GEORGE, 5TH EARL, founded Marischal College, 1593. Married Lady Margaret, daughter of Lord Home; d. 1623. | 3 sons. | 4 daughters. |

| WILLIAM, 6TH EARL. Married Lady Marie Erskine in 1609 (she mar. secondly, Lord Panmure). Died 1635. | James. | John of Kirktown of Deer. |

| WILLIAM, 7TH EARL. Mar. (1) Lady Eliz. Seton; (2) Lady Anne Douglas; d. 1671. | GEORGE, 8TH EARL. Mar. Lady Mary Hay; d. 1694. | Robert, Capt., d. after 1659. | Alexander, d. 1645, at Fyvie. | John (Lord Kintore). | 3 daughters. (1) Mary. Married Lord Kilpont. (2) Jean. Mar. 1st Lord Pitsligo. (3) Anne. |

| William (Lord Keith). *v.s.p.* | 4 daughters. | WILLIAM, 9TH EARL. Married Lady Mary Drummond; died 1712. |

| GEORGE, 10TH EARL, 1692–1778. *o.s.p.* | James, Field-Marshal, 1695–1758. *o.s.p.* | Mary. Married 6th Earl of Wigton. | Anne. Married Earl of Galloway. |

Clementina.
Married Chas., 10th Lord Elphinstone.

4th son, George,
created Viscount Keith, 1814.
Married Jane Mercer.

Margaret, Baroness Keith, died 11th Nov., 1867,
leaving only daughters by her husband,
Ct. de Flahault de la Billarderie.

and co-heiress of George Smith of Rapness in the Orkneys. (She married, secondly, Sir Robert Murray of Abercairney.) Sir William was forced to part with the estate of Ludquharn, and was succeeded (in the title only) by his son, Sir William, the 4th Baronet, who married a daughter of J. Newberry. The 4th Baronet was from 1716 to 1726 Governor of Pennsylvania, and died 18th November, 1749, aged 80, being succeeded as 5th Baronet by his son, Robert, who served in the foreign wars under his cousin, Field-Marshal James Keith, and after the death of the latter entered the Danish service. He married, in 1751, Margaret Albertine Conradina, daughter of Frederick von Suchin, Ambassador from Poland to Russia, and on his death, without issue, the baronetcy became dormant.[1]

On 26th September, 1710, William Keith, "younger of Ludquharn," had sasine on the lands of Concraig.[2]

His father, the 3rd Baronet, was therefore still alive, and lived to take part in the Jacobite Rising of 1715. A letter in the *Stuart Papers* from William Gordon to John Paterson, of 13th July, 1716, from Paris, says— "Sir William Keith (the 3rd Baronet) and his son, George, came here yesterday" (this was a younger brother of William, the 4th Baronet), they were among "a party of Jacobites who had embarked at Buchan Ness, and had had a tedious and fatiguing journey via Copenhagen and Dantzig and thence by land." Two years later, Sir William himself wrote to Mar from Rouen, 17th July, 1718: "I must beg you to tell his Majesty there is none followed him on this last occasion, *in my circumstances* but General Buchan and Robertson of Strowan. There was never any appearance in Scotland for his father or himself but I was there, which will undoubtedly make my cause much more unfavourable should I be forced home." [3]

He is known to have been one of those who elected the Jacobite magistrates in the New Church, Aberdeen, 29th September, 1715, and by his own account must also have taken part in the campaign which ter- minated at Killiecrankie (on behalf of the old Chevalier's father). The date of his death is not known, but it was before 1741 (as his Will is in the Commissariot of Aberdeen). It must, of course, have taken place *many* years before that date, when he would have been nearly 100 years old! His son, the 4th Baronet, died 1749, aged 80 (born 1669), so that Sir William, the 3rd Baronet, was presumably born at least in 1649, and must have been a very old man, nearing 70, when he wrote to Mar, as above, in 1718.

In 1718 Thomas Hay, Sheriff Clerk of Aberdeen, was appointed Trustee for the creditors of Alexander Forbes of Ludquharn, and in that capacity granted a discharge to Alexander Leslie of Pitcaple, so the next Laird was no more fortunate financially than Sir William Keith had been. Various other persons had sasine on the estate, including Mr. Robert

[1] G.E.C., *Complete Baronetage.*   [2] *Aberdeen Sasines.*   [3] *Stuart Letters.*

Forbes of Learney, a certain James Grant, and others. It eventually passed into the hands of Sir John Guthrie of King Edward.[1]

BALMUIR—*D*.

In 1696 the heritor of Balmuir was John Jamiesone, with Janet and Elizabeth, his sisters.

BLACKHOUSE.

This part of the estate of Ludquharn, was occupied in 1696 by Alexander Ogston and his wife, Christian Davidson. The purchaser before 1715 was a Hanoverian sympathiser, as was the case with the greater part of the Ludquharn lands.

COLONEL OGILVIE, FOR LITTLE COCKLAW.

In 1696 Little Cocklaw was occupied by William Prott, Chamberlain to the Laird of Ludquharn, to whom it belonged. In 1715 it was in the hands of Colonel Patrick Ogilvie of Lonmay, brother to the Chancellor, Earl of Seafield, who was naturally a Hanoverian, formerly known as "Patrick Ogilvie of Pattenbringan."

He was third son of James, 3rd Earl of Findlater, and Anne, daughter of Hugh, 7th Earl of Eglinton. He was Lieut.-Colonel in 1704, but left the army and settled down as a cattle breeder after the Union. He married (1) Elizabeth Baird of Auchmedden (the widow of Sir Alexander Abercromby of Birkenbog), who was greatly older than himself, and (2), Elizabeth Montgomerie of Giffen. He was Member for the Elgin Burghs, 1708–1710, and owned first Lonmay and then Inchmartine. He died in 1737.

FAICHFIELD, FOR MEIKLE COCKLAW.

Meikle Cocklaw had belonged to William Seton of Mounie in 1696, and in 1704 to Thomas Thomson, who died there on 25th October in that year.

CLERKHILL—*D*.

Formerly in the possession of the family of Martin. Henry Middleton of Clerkhill, who was there in 1680 and "erected the harbour of Peterhead," had before 1696 parted with the estate to Alexander Tulloch (vide *Poll Book*).

ALEX. GORDON OF KINMUNDIE.

This was Alexander Gordon, one of the younger sons of James Gordon, the parson of Rothiemay. He bought the estate from the Frasers. His

[1] *Pitcaple Papers.*

Will was proved on 8th February, 1737, when his heirs succeeded, but he died in 1722. James Gordon, his father, who wrote *The History of Scots Affairs*, published by the Spalding Club in 1870, was also the producer of two views of Aberdeen, and "a map of the town which he delivered to the Council well drawn upon ane mickle sheet of paper," for which he was rewarded, on 16th October, 1661, with a silver cup of 20 ounces and silk hat for himself and "ane silk gown to his bedfellow."

DOUNYHILLS.

Thomas Robertson, son of Thomas Robertson, had sasine on Downie-hills as far back as 1630, and the family long retained it.

In the *Poll Book* of 1696 it is entered as belonging "to Mr. Thomas Robertson, minister at Longside." In the account (in the same volume) of the parish of Longside his name is given as *Alexander* (which is correct), with his wife, Christian Mercer (daughter of John Mercer, minister of Kinellar), four sons—John, Thomas, Alexander, and Arthur, and a daughter, Lilias. In Scott's *Fasti*, Alexander Robertson is shown as having taken his degree, 13th July, 1675, and having been chaplain to the Lord Pitsligo till presented to Longside by the Earl Marischal. He took the oath of allegiance in 1689, but was "deposed on 3rd July, 1716, for complying with the rebellion. He was proprietor of Duniehills, and is mentioned as having seen a mermaid."

"William Robertson, brother of Downiehills," was one of the Jacobite officers captured at Dunfermline, 24th October, 1715, and sent to Carlisle.[1]

COLLIELAW, FOR EARL MARISCHAL.

George Gavin, who appears in the Valuation of 1667, was also in 1696 owner of Collielaw. Before 1715 this small estate had been sold to the Earl Marischal.

PARISH OF LONGSIDE.

THE EARL MARISCHAL—see PETERHEAD.

INVERQUHUMRIE.

The descendants of Roger Pattone and Marjorie Smith, who were in Inverquhomery 60 years before this date.

Alex. Forbes of Ludquharn had sasine on lands of Inverquhomery, 5th January, 1711. He was one of the creditors of Ludquharn who became possessed of a portion of the estate of Sir William Keith, 3rd Baronet.

[1] *S.P.* 54.8.95.

AUCHMEDDEN—see ABERDOUR PARISH.

FORTRIE, LIFERENTED.

Arthur Dalgarno of Fortrie, with his wife, Grisell Dalgarno, in 1696. The widow was still alive in 1715.

ANDREW ARBUTHNOT—*D*.

The Arbuthnots of Cairngall, in Longside, cadets of Arbuthnot in the Mearns, were mostly ardent Jacobites. One was at Killiecrankie, and Thomas Arbuthnot, eldest son of Nathaniel Arbuthnot in Auchlee, Longside, was one of those who assisted the Chevalier on his landing at Peterhead, 25th December, 1715, and was also a supporter of Prince Charles in 1745. It is not known who was this Andrew Arbuthnot who took the other side in 1715.

The Laird of Cairngall in 1696 was Alexander Arbuthnot, but Nathaniel Arbuthnot, father of Thomas, had a second son, Andrew, who may be the man mentioned—he was a shipowner in Peterhead.

HEIRS OF MR. JOHN PATON, INVERQUHUMMERY—see above.

HEIRS OF WM. SMITH.

Unknown.

AUCHTYDONALD.

Thomas Cargill "with Anna Abercromby his lady, Alexander Cargill his brother, Jean and Janet his sisters," were in Auchtydonald in 1696. Thomas Cargill was a Jacobite of 1715. The daughter of Thomas Cargill of Auchtydonald married, 7th March, 1739, Robert Pringle, merchant in Edinburgh.

In 1657 it was William Dalgarno of Auchtydonald.

LUDQUHARN—*D*.

This was sold by the old family of Keith to Alexander Forbes, and by his creditors (to whom Thomas Hay was appointed Trustee in 1718) to Sir John Guthrie, 2nd Baronet of King-Edward, son of Sir Henry. Sir John Guthrie's sister, Christian, married William Cumine of Pitullie, and had sasine on the lands of Balmad, 5th June, 1704. His four daughters all married Jacobites, though he himself was a Whig.[1]

ALEX. GORDON OF KINMUNDY—see PETERHEAD.

[1] A. and H. Tayler, *Jacobites of Aberdeenshire and Banffshire in the '45*, p. 405.

FAICHFIELD.

Thomas Thomson was of Faichfield in 1696 (*Poll Book*), with his wife, Janet Gregory, and three daughters. She was his second wife. The first was Anna Gordon, who was mother of his son, Alexander Gordon, afterwards of Faichfield—a Jacobite of 1745. Thomas was born in 1655 and died 1722.

THUNDERTOUN—*D*

"The lands of Thundertoune (in 1696), pertaine to Robert Dunbar, who is living in Murray with Marjorie Tate his spouse." (*Poll Book*.)

Archibald Dunbar of Thunderton, his son, was well known at a later date, and gave the name of his estate to his house in Elgin, which sheltered Prince Charles Edward in 1746.

CAIRNGALL—see above.

BUTHLAW.

Charles Gordon, 5th of Buthlaw, in 1715.

In 1696 William and James Gordons were factors for the lands of Buthlaw. William had a wife, "Elizabeth Martine, and 4 children, Charles, Anna, Elizabeth and David Gordons." The eldest son, Charles (above), owned it and sold it to another Charles Gordon, his first cousin, who was an advocate in Aberdeen and a Jacobite ; he married in 1720 Jean, daughter of John Udny, M.P. of Cultercullen and proprietor of a portion of New Tyll, the greater portion of which had already been purchased by William Gordon of Buthlaw in 1680 from Alexander Skene of New Tyll.

Charles Gordon, Advocate, was the son of Thomas Gordon of Buthlaw, "Commissioner to the Signet." The father of Thomas, W.S., and of William and James, the factors, was James Gordon, the purchaser of Buthlaw in 1664.

Charles Gordon died in 1752 and is buried in Foveran ; he left a son, John.

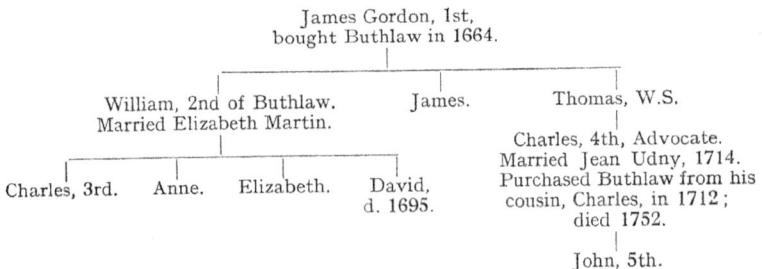

James Gordon, 1st,
bought Buthlaw in 1664.

William, 2nd of Buthlaw. Married Elizabeth Martin.	James.	Thomas, W.S.

Charles, 3rd.	Anne.	Elizabeth.	David, d. 1695.

Charles, 4th, Advocate.
Married Jean Udny, 1714.
Purchased Buthlaw from his cousin, Charles, in 1712 ;
died 1752.

John, 5th.

PARISH OF STRICHEN.

ADIELL, FOR PITFOUR.

This was part of the original estate of the Earl Marischal (which he bought back from his forfeited estates in 1764 and sold to James Ferguson of Pitfour).

STRIECHEN.

The Laird of Strichen in 1696 was Alexander Fraser, 4th Laird, with Marjorie Fraser, his daughter. He died in 1702, and was succeeded by his son, James.

Alexander (Lord Strichen) was the Laird in 1715. He was second son of Alexander, the 4th Laird.

1. Thomas Fraser of Knockie
    (second son of Alex., 4th Lord Lovat, and Jean Campbell).
    Married the widow of Chalmers of Strichen, also widow of
    Fraser of Philorth.

2. Thomas, succeeded 1628.
    Married Christian Forbes of Tolquhon.

    Thomas.   Married Christian Forbes of Pitsligo.
    Died 1656 in the lifetime of his father.

3. Thomas, succeeded his grandfather in 1657.
    Married Marion Irvine.

4. Alexander.

5. James.   6. Alexander, Lord Strichen.

HEIRS OF WM. KNOX, FOR PITFOUR.

In 1696 "the Airs of William Knocks" are said to be "out of the kingdom." His holding appears to have been the Miln of Adiell, of which the sole tenant was Alexander Brown.

William Knocks of Crichie in 1670 was "brother German to the Laird of Knocks." He married Janet Keith, daughter of John Keith of Duffus, who was son of John Keith of Northfield.[1]

PARISH OF REATHEN.

AUCHIRIES.

James Ogilvie of Auchiries in 1715.

Patrick Ogilvie of Hallyards, a cadet of the house of Findlater, bought Auchiries and Cortes from William, 9th Earl Marischal, in 1701, and this estate remained in possession of the family for exactly 100 years. On

[1] *Aberdeen Sasines.*

6th July, 1703, there was a decreet and renunciation by Patrick Ogilvie of Auchiries of a wadset granted by the Earl Marischal to James Gordon of Techmurie (son of the parson of Rothiemay).

Patrick's wife was Helen Garioch, and together they had sasine on 8th November, 1709.[1] Patrick died in 1710 and was succeeded by his son, James, who had sasine on 2nd November, 1710. He married Margaret Strachan, daughter of Alexander Strachan, Writer in Edinburgh, and built the house of Auchiries in 1715. She had sasine 25th April, 1716.[2] He died in 1741 and was succeeded by his son, Alexander. One daughter, Mary, married Alexander Irvine of Drum, and another, Rebecca, married John, the Master of Pitsligo, who died at the house of Auchiries in 1762. Alexander, who was not of age at the time of his father's death, joined the Jacobite Rising of 1745, under Lord Pitsligo, who was his guardian, and so did the younger twin brothers, John and William. In the *Poll Book* of 1696, Auchiries was still the property of the Earl Marischal and the tenant was William Keith. In 1801 it was sold to the executors of George, 3rd Earl of Aberdeen. The Ogilvies of Auchiries continued to hold their Baron's Courts for dispensing of justice even after heritable jurisdictions were abolished in 1747.[3]

THE LORD SALTOUN, AND HIS VASSALS—*D*.

Alexander, 12th Lord Saltoun, born 1684, succeeded his father, William, the 11th Earl, only in 1715, shortly before the Rising. In 1696 Alexander, when Master of Saltoun at the age of 22, had been destined by his father to marry Adela, the heiress of Hugh, 11th Lord Lovat, who was only 9 years old. But *force majeure*, engineered by "Lord Simon Fraser," induced Lord Saltoun to abandon this project,[4] and Alexander married in 1707 Mary Gordon, daughter of the 1st Lord Aberdeen. He seems to have been a genuine adherent of the House of Hanover and the Protestant succession, but living in the remotest corner of the Jacobite county of Aberdeen he not only suffered under great pressure from Mar's adherents, but also fell under the suspicion of the Government, though he claimed that he "prevented the Jacobite proclamation from taking place in Fraserburgh, the only town of importance in the county where it was not done." (After he had left the neighbourhood, the proclamation was, in fact, made.)

He was forcibly carried to Perth by a party of Jacobites under Hay of Arnbath and Irvine of Crimond, and remained some time with the Jacobite army, but certainly unwillingly. He escaped and went home, but when, after the collapse of the Rising he attempted to "wait upon" Argyll in Aberdeen, he was imprisoned by order of the Government,

[1] *Aberdeen Sasines.* [2] *Ibid.*
[3] *Papers of J. C. M. Ogilvie-Forbes.* [4] See Major Fraser's Manuscript.

and wrote several peevish letters to Argyll and to the Lord Justice Clerk complaining of the treatment he received, the earliest being dated 18th February, and the last 16th August, in which he states that he had "rude Sentinels in his bedchamber." [1] On 1st September Lord Townshend wrote to Lord Cockburn that if there was "really no evidence against him," he might be set at liberty. This was done and he survived till 1748, managing to keep out of all connection with the Rising of 1745.

His descent from the old family of Abernethy of Saltoun was as follows :—

Alexander, 9th Lord Saltoun, last of the Abernethys, died in 1669 without issue. He had sold his estate of Saltoun to Andrew Fletcher in 1643; but his title went to his "heir of line," grandson of the 7th Lord Saltoun by his daughter, Margaret Abernethy, who married Sir Alexander Fraser, and *their* son, Sir Alexander Fraser of Philorth, succeeded in 1669.

The first FRASER Lord Saltoun, Alexander, the 10th (above), was a zealous Royalist, and, like so many Aberdeenshire Lairds, fought at the battle of Worcester.

He married (1) a daughter of Sir William Forbes of Tolquhon, by whom he had one daughter, married Alexander Fraser of Techmurie; (2) Elizabeth Seton of Meldrum, whose son, Alexander, Master of Saltoun, was father of William, the 11th Lord.

He married Margaret, second daughter of Archbishop Sharp, and was father of Alexander, 12th Lord.

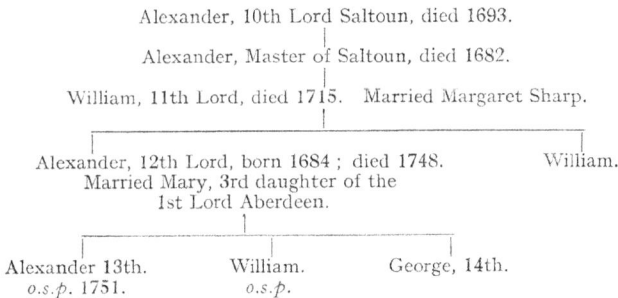

Alexander, 10th Lord Saltoun, died 1693.

Alexander, Master of Saltoun, died 1682.

William, 11th Lord, died 1715.   Married Margaret Sharp.

Alexander, 12th Lord, born 1684 ; died 1748.   William.
Married Mary, 3rd daughter of the
1st Lord Aberdeen.

Alexander 13th.   William.   George, 14th.
o.s.p. 1751.   *o.s.p.*

The 11th, 12th and 13th Lords Saltoun were all Hanoverian in sympathy.

The youngest brother of the 12th Lord, the Hon. James Fraser, was "out" in 1715 but seems to have suffered no inconvenience.

He married Lady Eleanor Lindsay, daughter of Colin, Lord Balcarres, and in 1718 bought the estate of Lonmay, by which title he was afterwards known. He had one son, William, who died unmarried. Lady

[1] *P.R.O., S.P.* 54.11 *passim.*

Eleanor survived her husband, and disponed Lonmay to William Moir of Whitehills. (William Moir of Lonmay of the '45.)

The eldest sister of Alexander (Lord Saltoun) and James Fraser was Helen, who married the Jacobite Sir James Gordon of Park as his first wife ; his second being Margaret, daughter of the 8th Lord Elphinstone, and she subsequently married John Fullerton of Dudwick.

TECHMURIE. [James Fraser (formerly Gordon).]

Jane, only daughter and ultimate heiress of Alexander Fraser of Techmurie, married James Gordon, son of Rev. James Gordon, parson of Rothiemay, who, after the death of Jane Fraser's brother, Alexander (before 1696), became the owner. His grandson, Lewis Gordon, sold the estate in 1785 to Garden of Troup.

COLONEL BUCHAN.

Colonel John Buchan (fourth son of James Buchan, 1st of Auchmacoy, who died 1728) bought the estate of Cairnbulg from Charles, 4th Lord Fraser, in 1703. He was the younger brother of Major-General Thomas Buchan who commanded the Jacobite troops after the death of Dundee at Killiecrankie in 1689. In March, 1715, Colonel John Buchan granted a discharge and renunciation to his brother, Thomas, who died 1721.[1]

(James Buchan, 1st of Auchmacoy, and his wife, Margaret Seton, had four sons—Alexander, 2nd Laird ; James, formerly of Oykhorne, 3rd Laird ; Major-General Thomas, and Colonel John, above.) Colonel John's son, Thomas, was served heir to him, 20th February, 1739.[2]

On 4th December, 1709, Colonel John Buchan had also sasine on a house and garden in Old Aberdeen.[3] He died before 1724. (He was *said* to have been "a Whig" but only single Cess was asked from him.)

CRAIGELIE *D*—see PARISH OF LONMAY.

In 1696 Craigellie was in the possession of Doctor Thomas Gordon, but James Shand, Provost of Banff, who married in 1709 Janet, daughter of Alexander Leslie of Kininvie, owned the estate in 1715 and left it to his son, "James Shand of Craigellie" in 1736.

COLLONELL OGILVIE.

Patrick Lonmay—brother of Lord Seafield (see Peterhead).

INVERALLOCHIE. [William Fraser.]

Alexander Fraser of Inverallochy was one of the Commissioners for taking up the Poll in the Parish of Rathen in 1696. He was the eldest

---

[1] *Aberdeen Sasines* and *Auchmacoy Papers.*   [2] *Ibid.*   [3] *Aberdeen Sasines.*

son of Simon Fraser, 2nd of Inverallochy, who married Lady Marjorie Erskine, daughter of the Earl of Buchan. She subsequently married Charles, Lord Fraser of the '15, having had one daughter, Marie, by Simon Fraser.

Alexander Fraser's wife was Elizabeth Erskine, daughter of Lord Kelly. He was served heir to his father in 1696, but himself died in 1698, and William, the second son, who appears in 1696 as "William Fraser, gentleman," was served heir to his elder brother-german, Alexander, 23rd November, 1698, and had sasine on Inverallochie in 1699.[1] William Fraser was killed at Sheriffmuir, and was succeeded by his brother, Charles, whose son, also Charles, was killed at Culloden. Captain Simon Fraser, who served under Lord Kenmure and was wounded at Preston on the same day, was a cousin-german. He was made prisoner and taken to London, but escaped.

CORTHIS, FOR AUCHIRIES—above (CORTES).

In 1696 it was in the possession of Alexander Jaffray, but in 1701, as has been seen, it was bought by Patrick Ogilvie, whose son held it in 1715.

MR. ALEX. MUIR, FOR REATHEN, LIFERENTED.

A deed in the Register House of 1663 gives Dorothea Muir, daughter of Alexander Muir, Baron of Calvaly, and wife of William Pringle ; no nearer clue has been found.

PARISH OF DEER.

EARL MARISCHAL—see PETERHEAD.

EARL MARISCHALL'S VICARAGE.

TROUP, FOR ELRICK—D.

Alexander Garden of Troup, Advocate, afterwards agent for the forfeited lands of the Earl Marischal.

Robert Burnett of Cowtoun, Tutor of Leys, who died in 1687, was "possessed of the estate of Elrick," but according to Colonel Allardyce [2] this estate afterwards fell into the hands of a different line of Burnetts, relationship not stated. They seem, however, to have been, like the parent-line, Whigs and supporters of the new Government. Alexander Garden of Troup afterwards purchased the lands, as on 2nd July, 1731, Alexander Garden, 3rd of Troup, was served heir to

---

[1] *Aberdeen Sasines.*   [2] *Family of Burnett of Leys,* p. 87.

his grandfather, Alexander Garden, "in the Lands of Elrick including Blackpotts, Windiewalls, Craigiehill, and Burngrange Croft."[1]

AUCHMEDDEN—PARISH OF ABERDOUR.

DUDWICK, FOR PARCOCK.

Dudwick is in the Parish of Ellon.

Parcock, in Old Deer, also belonged to Fullarton of Dudwick in 1696. At the same date, Skelmuir belonged to Katherine Gordon, whose tenant was Alexander Gordon. On 3rd February, 1708, James Gordon had sasine on Parcock and Skelmuir. Katherine was the widow and James the son of James Gordon, parson of Rothiemay. He was Laird of Techmurie.

Katherine and her son James appear in the *Poll Book* as residents in Aberdeen, where James, minister of Rothiemay, is described *in error* as "Merchant of Rothiemay."

TECHMURIE—see above. PARISH OF RATHEN.

PITLURG, FOR KINMUNDY, LIFERENTED. [Alexander Gordon.]

The eldest son of Robert Gordon, the great Straloch, was Robert Gordon of Pitlurg, born 1609, who married Katherine Burnett of Leys, and died 1681. His eldest son, William, died young. His second son, Robert, married Jean Maitland of Pitrichie and had a large family, but died after a short possession, and was succeeded by his only surviving son, Alexander, who was served heir to his father, Robert, in 1692.

Alex. Gordon of Pitlurg, great grandson of the great Straloch, married Mary Gordon, daughter of James Gordon of Ellon, and he and she had sasine on the lands of Pitlurg, 5th December, 1718.[2]

His affairs becoming embarrassed, Alexander was obliged to sell the estates of Pitlurg and Kinmundy in 1724 to Charles Gordon, merchant, Elgin, a cousin, who died 1731, retaining only Straloch.

Alexander Gordon had been Member of Parliament for Aberdeenshire in the last Scottish Parliament, 1702–1707, and in the first Union Parliament, 1708.

On 27th June, 1708, Alex. Gordon, then of Pitlurg, had sasine on the lands of Ardgouse.

On 26th August, 1703, Alexander Gordon, "lawful son to the Umquhile James Gordon, parson of Rothiemay," had sasine of the lands of Kinmundy granted by "ane honourable lady Mistress Elizabeth Fraser[3] (Lady Kinmundy), lawful daughter of umquhile Francis Fraser of Kin-

---

[1] *Service of Heirs.* [2] *Aberdeen Sasines.*
[3] The lands pertained to her in 1696.—*Poll Book.*

mundy, with special consent of Charles, Lord Fraser." These lands were disponed to Katherine Gordon, relict of James Gordon in liferent, and to Alexander, second son of James, and his heirs male, whom failing to Lewis Gordon, third son, whom failing to Alexander's heirs whatsoever.

The "heir of Alexander" would seem to have been his cousin, Alexander of Pitlurg.

PITFOUR.

James Ferguson (see Parish of Inverurie) who sold his estate of Badifurrow in 1699 and bought Pitfour from George Morrison, nephew and heir of William Morrison, Burgess of Aberdeen (died 1658), who held the lands of Pitfour in 1667. In 1696 it is his son, William, with "Charles Morrison his brother, possessor of the Maynes."

KININMONTH, FOR KNOCK—*D.*

John Cumming, son of Gavin Cumming of Kininmonth. (In the *Poll Book* spelt "Cumeing.") He obtained Kininmonth from the Hays of Delgaty, 7th July, 1682, and married Katherine, daughter of John Hay of Seafield, appearing in the *Poll Book* with Katherine Hay, his lady, and his sons, John and Charles Cumming. John succeeded, and married Mary Keith, of the Earl Marischal family. John and Mary had sasine, 15th March, 1711. John's son, Charles, who married Sophia, the daughter of James, 16th Lord Forbes, on 29th January, 1732, succeeded on the death of John in 1736, and he and his brother, Alexander, were Jacobites of 1745. Charles executed a disposition in favour of his eldest son, James, 21st April, 1760.[1] (John, the father, was apparently a Hanoverian in 1715.)

The estate of Knock was purchased by Charles Cumming and his wife Sophia from the heirs of Major George Keith of Whiteriggs (after 1732), but apparently John Cumming was already paying the Cess in 1715.)

CAPT. STEWART, FOR LITTLE CRICHIE.

Captain Stewart of Dens and Little Crichie, progenitor of the family of Burnett-Stewart. (In 1696, according to the *Poll Book*, these lands belonged to "George Dalgarno heretor, and Arthur Dalgarno his son.")

Captain John Stewart (usually so spelt) was the son of Col. James Stewart, a Jacobite of 1689. Captain John was born in 1659 and died 1729. He bought Crichie in 1709 from the Earl Marischal. He had served in the foreign wars and lost a hand at the siege of Namur in 1693, his wooden hand being still preserved at Crichie, but there is not much

---

[1] *Aberdeen Sasines* and *Aden Papers.*

record of his activities in the 1715 Rising. He married Agnes Gray, who lived at Schivas House, near Ellon, and their only son, James, died unmarried in 1749 ; the daughter, Theodosia, married John Burnett of Daleladyes,[1] a cadet of Leys, who, under the deed of entail of Crichie, had to add the name of Stewart to his own.

Anna, sister of Captain Stewart, married James Ferguson of Pitfour, Sheriff-Substitute of Aberdeenshire, father of the M.P.

The Will of Captain John Stewart of Dens and Crichie is in Commissariot, dated 11th December, 1729.

COYNACH—*D.* [John Gordon.]

In 1696 the Lands of Coynach belonged to John Gordon of Myrestone, son of Thomas Gordon of Myrestone and Anne Hamilton. Thomas died before 1687. John, who acquired both Auchmill and Coynach, died about 1723. His wife was Jean, daughter of William Lumsden of Culsh, and he left a son, Thomas, who succeeded to Coynach, and had a daughter, Anna, who married Alexander Gordon, younger of Badenscoth, who predeceased his father. She was "relict" in 1710.[2]

CUTHILL AND SAPLENBRAE. [George Forbes.]

On 4th December, 1668, Thomas Forbes, younger in Saplinbrae, was served heir to his father, Walter, in the lands of Cuthill in Deer, and two years later "Mary, Anna and Margaret Forbeses" were also served heirs portioners in Cuthill. In 1696 "George Forbes, gentleman," was tenant of Saplinbrae.

HEIRS OF GEORGE RANKINE.

"In 1696 the Milne of Aden and other lands of Quithell belonged to the heirs of George Rankine. Alexander Gordoune being the *tenant* with George Rankine his son-in-law." The explanation of this is found in the special service of heirs under date 16th August, 1678, when "Helen Strachan, relict of George Rankine of Mill of Aden,[3] now spouse of Alexander Gordon," was served heir "to a just and reasonable third of the Mill of Aden and other lands." George Rankine, Yr., was her son, and *stepson* to Alexander Gordon. The remainder of the lands of Quithill belonged to Arthur Dalgarno of Fortrie.

CLACKRIACH. [George Keith, Advocate.]

On 25th September, 1706, there was a contract of Moss Tolerance between George Keith of Clackriach and James Keith of Bruxie.[4]

---

[1] Dalladies, in *Burnett Book.*   [2] *Aberdeen Sasines.*
[3] George Rankine himself had sasine on Mill of Aden in 1672.—*Ibid.*
[4] *Ibid.*

In 1696 John Keith late of Clackriach was "out of the kingdom."

George Keith was of Clackriach in 1699 ; was Sheriff-Depute. He had sasine on Clackriach, 27th February, 1703.[1]

(In 1718 Jean Leslie, second wife and relict of George Keith, had sasine on Artamford in New Deer.)

On 1st March, 1712, Isobel, daughter of George Keith of Clackriach and spouse of William Irvine of Artamford, had sasine.[2] George also left two sons, James and Alexander, the former of whom succeeded.

CRICHIE (MEIKLE CREICHIE).

This belonged to George Keith, Advocate in Aberdeen (above).

On 5th April, 1704, it was James Keith of Crichie who was the tenant, also in 1696.

1st August, 1705, Margaret Gordon, spouse of James Keith of Crichie, had sasine.[3]

KIDSHILL.

This very small property, which appears to be the same as Reidshill, was part of the estate of Clackriach. On 4th January, 1703, George Keith "of Kidshill" granted sasine to Alexander Keith.[4] This Alexander (of Reidshill) was served heir to his father, Alexander Keith of Reidshill, who died in June, 1708, in "Reidshill, Burntbrae, etc., in the Parish of Old Deer." Alex. Leslie of Pitcaple owed 300 merks to Alexander Keith of Kidshill in 1736.[5]

BRUNTBRAE.[6] [Alexander Keith.]

Robert Martin of Bruntbrae in 1696. The name is now Burnbrae.

Robert Martin was a relation of Captain Martin and of Mr. Nathaniel Martin of Peterhead, and a grandson of Robert Martin of Clerkhills of 1667. He resided in Aberdeen in 1696 with his wife and his children, Nathaniel, Elizabeth, Jean, and Isobel. His daughter, Isobel, married the Rev. John Mercer, minister of Tyrie, and died in 1765.[7]

In 1715 it appeared to belong to Alexander Keith, above.

HEIRS OF PROVOST ROSS.

John Ross of Clochan and Arnage was Provost of Aberdeen, 1710–11. He was the second son of John Ross of Clochan and Christian Howieson,

---

[1] *Aberdeen Sasines.*   [2] *Ibid.*   [3] *Ibid.*
[4] *Ibid.*   [5] *Pitcaple Papers.*
[6] Bruntbray was originally part of the estate of the Irvines of Drum.
[7] In 1703 William Dunbar, parson of Cruden, had sasine on the lands of Brunthill.
—*Aberdeen Sasines.*

daughter of Andrew Howieson, merchant of Aberdeen. The Provost represented, after 1709, the male line of the Rosses of Auchlossan in Lumphanan ; Francis Ross of Auchlossan being killed at Malplaquet in that year.

John Ross bought the property of Arnage in Ellon on 14th February, 1702, from David Rickart, and in the same year it was erected into a free barony. He obtained the property of Clochan in Old Deer in 1711, after the death of his elder brother, George (whose "airs" owned it in 1696). He married, in 1704, Jean, only daughter of Arthur Forbes of Echt, and had two sons and four daughters, of whom Christian, the second, married Sir Arthur Forbes, 4th Baronet of Craigievar, and Jean, the youngest, married Alexander Aberdeen, younger of Cairnbulg, and Provost of Aberdeen, 1742.

Provost Ross died in 1714 at Amsterdam, and his heirs in 1715 were his eldest son, John, deaf and dumb, and only 8 years of age, a younger son, Arthur, aged 4, and three daughters, all young children.

TROUP FOR ANACHIE. LIFERENTED BY SHIVAS.

Andrew Strachan of Annachie, nephew and heir of Patrick Strachan, who was son of Alexander, 7th Laird of Glenkindie. Why it should be liferented by Shivas (Andrew Gray) is not known.

BITHIE, FOR MINISTER.

The lands of Biffie belonged to Alexander Elphinstone of Wartle.

CAPTAIN STEWART, FOR DENNS AND PART OF MARISCHAL.

Denns was part of the estate of the Earl Marischal, and was bought in 1709, with the estate of Little Crichie, by Captain John Stewart.

PARISH OF LONEMAY.

LAW, FOR THE HEIRS OF CUMMIN.

Alexander Cumming of Crimond was the owner in 1696 with his lady, his mother, and his sister.[1] His father was for long factor to Lord Erroll, and purchased from him the lands of Crimond. Alexander, the elder, died in 1690, and the son was served heir to him as "Alexander Cumming, sometime of Brunthill, afterwards of Birness." The second Alexander Cumming was dead before 1715. He had sasine of Crimond and Mill of Crimond on 17th February, 1703.[2] John Gordon of Law and Wardhouse seems to have been acting as sub-collector.

---

[1] Alexander Cumming of Crimond and Elizabeth Hay, his spouse, had sasine in 1697.—*Aberdeen Sasines.*

[2] *Ibid.*

COLONEL OGILVIE FOR CAIRNESS—*D.*

Colonel Ogilvie, the brother of Lord Seafield, had purchased part of Cairness ; the remainder being still the property of Inverallochy.

DITTO, FOR LONEMAY—*D.*

Colonel Ogilvie bought Lonmay from Tolquhon and afterwards sold it to the Hon. James Fraser (see page 169).

DITTO, FOR MILLBOG—*D.*

Thomas Forbes in 1696. Colonel Ogilvie paid double on all his estates.

KININMONT.—*D*

Among the family papers of Mr. Sidney Russell of Aden are preserved the following :—

Disposition, John Earl of Erroll, with the consent of George Hay, sometime of Kininmont and —— Lumsden his spouse, in favour of Gavin Cuming of Midmiln and John Cuming, his eldest son, 7th and 20th July 1682.

A sasine following on the above, 8th May, 1684, and charter of confirmation.

The above Gavin Cumming married on 20th October, 1662, Katharine Hay, lawful daughter to John Hay of Seafield. Gavin is there described as son to James Cumming of Brunthill. From 1682 he was "of Kininmonth," and appears as such in the *Poll Book* of 1696 with " Katharine Hay his lady, and their sons, John and Charles Cumings." [1]

John Cumming, who succeeded to Kininmonth, married Mary Keith. Both here and for his holding in the Parish of Deer he pays double.

John died in 1736 and was succeeded by his son, Charles.

James, a younger brother of Charles, went abroad in 1738, with the consent of Mary Keith, his mother, and "the now deceased George Keith," Advocate, presumably her father. The exact relationship of these Keiths to the family of the Earls Marischal is not stated.

Charles Cumming of Kininmonth married, 29th June, 1732, the Hon. Sophia, daughter of James, 16th Lord Forbes, and niece of Lord Pitsligo. Charles and his brother, Alexander, were Jacobites of the '45.

James Cumming, son of Charles and Sophia Forbes, succeeded in 1764. He married Mary Ferguson of Kinmundy, and their eldest daughter and heiress married in 1792 Alexander Russell of Montcoffer.[2]

---

[1] "Charles Cuming, son of Gavin Cuming," had sasine on part of the estate in 1703.—*Aberdeen Sasines.*

[2] *Aden Papers.*

CRIMONMOGAT, *sequestrate*.

Mr. William Hay, parson of Crimonmogate, and William Hay, his son, in 1696. A son, John, of the younger William (according to J. A. Henderson), succeeded and built the mansion house, but by 1721 the estate was in the hands of creditors and was sold to William Abernethy, then to Alexander Miln, merchant, Aberdeen, who married the daughter of Patrick Bannerman, Provost of Aberdeen, whose descendants still possess it.

INVERLOCHY, FOR PART OF CAIRNESS—see above (PARISH OF RATHEN).

Inverlochy is a slip for Inverallochie.

CRAIGELLIE—*D*.

In the *Poll Book* Dr. Thomas Gordon was of Craigellie, and on 3rd June, 1704, James and Elizabeth Gordons, lawful children to the deceased Thomas Gordon of Craigellie and Mrs. Elizabeth Fraser, his lady, had sasine.[1] Sophia Gordon, another daughter of Thomas Gordon, had had sasine during his lifetime, in 1699.

Thomas Gordon of Craigellie had sasine on Hillhead, 28th February, 1713.[2]

Later, James Shand, son of James Shand, Provost of Banff, and Janet Leslie of Kininvie, became possessed of Craigellie. He also became Provost of Banff, as did his son, William (see also Parish of Rathen).

Lonmay is another of the rare Aberdeenshire parishes in which the majority of the heritors were Hanoverians.

PARISH OF TYRIE.

LORD PITSLIGO—PARISH OF PITSLIGO.

BOYNLIE—*D*.

This was Captain John Forbes of Middle Boyndlie (not the estate which had been purchased by John Forbes, the Collector of Cess, in 1711 from Lord Pitsligo; that consisted of Upper Boyndlie, Nether Boyndlie, Ladysford, etc.).

Middle Boyndlie remained in the possession of another family of Forbes, cadets of Pitsligo, represented by Captain John Forbes, as 6th Laird. He was the younger son of Alex. Forbes, "Tutor of Pitsligo," who had been guardian of his cousin, the 2nd Lord Pitsligo. John succeeded his brother, Henry, the 5th Laird, who died in 1699, but John was only served heir in 1702.

---

[1] *Aberdeen Sasines.*   [2] *Ibid.*

Captain John Forbes married on 6th April, 1714, "Agnes Foularton," and together they had sasine.[1] She had been previously married to James Fraser of Tyrie.

Captain John Forbes did not share the Jacobite opinions of his namesake and remote cousin, the Collector of Cess.

TYRIE.[2]

John Fraser of Tyrie, son of James Fraser of Tyrie, and grandson of Alexander, who began to build the house of Tyrie, but died (before it was finished) in 1696.

James married (1) Christian Abercromby of Birkenbog, daughter of Sir Alexander, the first Baronet, and (2) "Agnes Foularton." John Fraser succeeded and sold the estate, before 1728, to George Leslie of Eden. After passing through the hands of several owners it was re-united to the estate of Philorth (from which it had been detached in 1570 as a portion for James Fraser, third son of the Sir Alexander Fraser of the day).

STRIECHEN—see PARISH OF STRICHEN.

FEDDRAT—see NEW DEER (AUCHREDDIE).

BONNYKELLY—(BOMAKELLIE), belonging to the Laird of Fedderat.

PARISH OF ABERDOUR.

FOVERAN, FOR LORD PITSLIGO—*D*.

Sir Samuel Forbes (see Parish of Foveran).

Lord Pitsligo was the greatest heretor in this parish, owning nearly half of the whole sum of the Valuation.

AUCHMEDDEN—ALSO IN LONGSIDE PARISH.

William Baird of Auchmedden, 6th Laird, was born 1676 and succeeded his grandfather, Sir James Baird, in 1691. He married (1) Mary, only daughter to Robert Gordon of Pitlurg, grandson of the Great Straloch, and had two sons, William, who succeeded his father, and James, who died young, and three daughters, Katherine, Mary, and Jean.

Mary married (1) William Gordon of Badenscoth, (2) John Gordon of Wardhouse, and (3) Jonathan Forbes of Brux (the Jacobite of 1745).

---

[1] *Aberdeen Sasines.*

[2] " John Fraser of Tyrie to his father, James Fraser of Tyrie, heir male in Mains of Tyrie, Ardley, etc., 15th June, 1705."—*Commissariot of Aberdeen.*

William, 6th Laird, married (2) Elizabeth Abercromby of Glassaugh and had a son, Alexander, and three daughters.

William Baird died in London, 1720, and was succeeded by his eldest son, William, 7th and last Laird, who married Anne, eldest daughter of William Duff of Dipple by his second marriage, and was the Jacobite of 1745. He died 1775.

The sisters of William, 6th Laird, were Margaret, who married in 1716 John Gordon of Fechil ; Katherine, married John Douglas of Whiteriggs, brother of Sylvester ; and Mary, married James Irvine of Kingcausie.[1]

PITTENCALDER—*D.*

John Forbes, 1st of Pitnacalder, was one of the five sons of William Forbes of Tolquhon, who built the Castle and died in 1631. His grandson, James Forbes, 3rd of Pitnacalder, son of another John, who died in 1687, was one of the Commissioners of the Poll of 1696. He had a wife, two sons and five daughters. His mother was Christian Johnston of Caskieben.

COWBURTY.

In 1690 Fraser of Coburty was the heritor, as appears from a heritors' roll in Kennedy's *Annals of Aberdeen.* This was Andrew Fraser of Kinmundy, and in the *Poll Book* it is Lady Kinmundy.

In 1715 it was in the hands of James Baird.

PARISH OF PITSLIGO.

PITSLIGO.

Alexander Forbes, 4th and last Lord Pitsligo, is one of the well-known figures of Aberdeenshire in the 18th century, in both Jacobite Risings, and his history has often been written.

Some extracts from his own personal papers, now at Fettercairn, bearing upon 1715 and later years, may appropriately be given here.

He was born in 1678 and survived until 1762.

He was twice married, (1) to Rebecca Norton, and (2) to Elizabeth Allen. By his first wife he had one son, John, the Master of Pitsligo, who died without issue. Letters as to his birth and baptism, October, 1713, still exist at Fettercairn.

Pitsligo. Oct. 8. 1713. To the Laird of Boyndley.

It has pleased God to give me a son and I design to have him christened tomorrow and his name John. I need not tell you that your company would be very agreeable for I hope it is an article you have no doubts of, but I must use so much plain dealing to shew you that the manner of the Church of England is to be observed, so in case

---

[1] W. N. Fraser, *Account of the Surname of Baird.*

Alexander Lord Forbes of Pitsligo
from the picture by Alexis Belle at Fettercairn House

you have any scruple to witness any thing of that Liturgy you may let us see you about twelve oclock that we may at least eate a little together, which I am persuaded will be in great friendship, not withstanding our differing in other points, which difference may even stand the world in good stead when improved to exercises of forbearance and charity. Let me tell you again that if you allow us your company any way you shall be heartily wellcome to

Dear Sir,

Your most affectionate humble servant,

PITSLIGO.

Lord Pitsligo was a man of deep religious feeling, a member of the Episcopal Church, though in his early days in France he is said to have been much attracted by the tenets of Madame Guyon and the Quietists. He took an active part in the Rising of 1715 and was one of those attainted, so that he had, after the dispersal of the Jacobite army in 1716, to go into hiding, and eventually escaped abroad.

Both the wives of Lord Pitsligo were English women. Rebecca Norton is described as the daughter of John Norton, "Virginia merchant" of the city of London, and brought to her husband a tocher of £3,000 sterling. After the troubles of the '15 her brothers and sisters, "Daniel Norton, James Norton, Anne and Mary Nortons," doubtless pitying her forlorn state, with her husband a hunted exile, "granted each of them £100 out of the portion to be left them by their father, to the Lady Pitsligo and her son John Forbes."

Elizabeth Allen, 2nd Lady Pitsligo, whom he married in September, 1731, is said to have been companion to the first wife, who died early in the same year.

The attainted estates were bought in 1788 by Sir William Forbes the banker, grandson of Lord Pitsligo's sister, Mary, who had married John Forbes, younger of Monymusk, and are now in the possession of his descendant, Lord Clinton. After the death of John Forbes, younger of Monymusk, his widow married James Forbes, afterwards 16th Lord Forbes, and renounced her liferent on Pitsligo in consideration of a bond of £100 per annum granted by her future husband—then James Forbes of Putachie, 19th November, 1728.

Long after the '15, when in Italy, Lord Pitsligo wrote a narrative, apparently designed for posterity, which has never been printed. In it he gives an interesting account of the little court which surrounded the unfortunate Chevalier ; of the preparations for the abortive attempt at another Jacobite rising, which ended at Glenshiel, and of James' marriage to the Princess Clementina Sobieski, both in the year 1719.

The account begins :—

"I had the confusion to see our army disperse in the beginning of the year 1716 and to sculk myself with many others in the country where 'tis true we had occasion to discover the humanity of the poor country people, but being weary of that way of life and still in danger, chose to go abroad and I was some moneths privately in London. From there I went to Holland and Flanders. I had a letter from my Lord M—r while I was at Brussells to come and talk with him at Paris. I came back to Brussells, found myself excluded from the Indemnity. A desire awakened now and then of seeing the K——, I resolved to go to some places in Germany and pass'd some moneths pretty easily at Vienna, from whence I went to Italy. From Venice in October 1718 I went to Ferrara, where the King was to come to meet the Princess. We heard the bad news of the arrestment at Innspruck and I came that night to Bologna, where I found the King in good health."—*Fettercairn MS.*

Clementina had been arrested on her way to meet her bridegroom, and had to be rescued by Charles Wogan and others.

There follows a long account of the intrigues and quarrels of the Jacobites at Bologna (when Clementina did get there, 8th May, 1719, while the King was in Spain), and misunderstandings about presentations to her, those who should attend on her as Queen, etc.

The King's chief favourite at the time was James Murray, brother of Lord Mansfield—himself afterwards Earl of Dunbar.[1] He seems to have upset many of the faithful followers, including Lord Nithsdale and Lord Pitsligo.

Lord Pitsligo also writes, on 2nd November, 1719, to Sir David Nairne that after leaving Italy he had some intentions of visiting Lord Mar at Geneva

" but was dissuaded from so doing by some persons who thought it was but a needless exposing myself to be confined with him. In a letter I had from Lord Mar to Paris he said he was very glad I had let Geneva alone.

"Ld. Mar also told me after his coming to Rome from Milan he would medle no more as Secretary. . . . He told me withall he believed his own days would not be many, that he found the trouble in his stomach still worse and would try the waters of Bourbon. But some days after, the report came of the D. of Ormond's being landed in England wh. put him into an extasie of joy and made him leave Rome again upon some other view than drinking waters in France." [2]

Writing from Paris in December Pitsligo says: " I could have wished Charles Forbes [3] here, since Mr. Law may yet be useful to him. I believe J. Edgar and he only stay for want of money, but the loss of Charles's time is more to be pitied because he has a wife and children."

Mar had been seized at Voghera, 1719, and imprisoned at Geneva.

[1] His sister, Marcelle Murray, was Mrs. Hay, afterwards Lady Inverness, who was made Governess to Prince Charles, and caused Clementina to be jealous, and at one time to leave her husband and retire to a convent.

The Will of the Earl of Dunbar, who became a Roman Catholic during his residence in Italy, is preserved at Avignon. He did not die until 1771, and besides a few legacies all his effects went to the Cardinal York as "héritier universel."
—*Bibliothèque du Musée Calvet MS.* 1614, 61.

[2] This refers, of course, to the disastrous Jacobite attempt at Glenshiel, June, 1719.

[3] Forbes of Brux.

Pitsligo writes :—

A day or two before I left Paris I spoke privately with Mr. Law and begged of him to use his best endeavours to get my Lord Mar out of Geneva. He said he would certainly do his best to serve my Ld. both with the Regent and in his own particular (so he exprest it) and desired I might bid Will. Gordon call at him for a letter he was to write to him. I reckoned also by some words he dropt that he was not averse to the King's interest, of which I had some information afterwards and it was conjectured that the Abbe du Bois' hatred and Argenson of him was increased upon that account.—*Fettercairn MS.*

Owing chiefly to the misrepresentations of James Murray, Pitsligo had left Italy without seeing James again, and never completely regained his King's favour, but his loyalty remained unabated, and when Prince Charles landed in Scotland in 1745, Pitsligo, in spite of his advanced years, was one of the first to join him, and by his example to "bring out" many of the lesser lairds of Aberdeenshire.

A letter at Fettercairn, written to John Home when he was engaged on his history of the '45, throws fresh light on Lord Pitsligo's actions in that Rising. It was communicated to Home by a friend of Rebecca Ogilvie, widow of the Master of Pitsligo, and states :—

Mrs. Forbes informs me that so far from Lord Pitsligo having brought to the Highland Army such a body of men as you had been told, he was merely attended by from 20 to 30 gentlemen of his neighbourhood on horseback, many of whom did not even bring servants along with them and neither his Lordship nor any of the gentlemen who accompanied him attempted to raise their tenants or country neighbours finding the general disposition of the lower ranks in Buchan to be averse to the Party. Lord Pitsligo was withheld by conscientious motives from drawing his dependants into a contest, which how much soever he thought it his own duty to engage in, he could not but conclude to be of too doubtful an issue to allow him to persuade others to embark in.

This letter, of course, was written and the information was supplied long after the glamour of the '45 had faded, and after all the trials and executions of Jacobites, which had caused even ardent spirits like James Farquharson of Balmoral, or Charles Gordon of Terpersie (at the point of death), to belittle what they had done or tried to do for the cause.

Lord Pitsligo's attainder, first pronounced in 1715, was somewhat naturally maintained after the later Rising.

At Castle Forbes is to be found a paper headed :—

Information for Alexander Lord Forbes of Pitsligo against his Majesty's Advocate Respondent. Nov. 3. 1749.

Stating his case why his attainder should not hold. He having been attainted as Alexr. Lord Pitsligo whereas his correct designation should be

Alexander, 4th Lord Forbes of Pitsligo.

The paper quotes various cases in England and two Scottish cases : Major-General Gordon of Auchintoul and Peter Farquharson of Inverey.

The General was attainted in 1716 as Thomas, whereas his name was Alexander. He escaped forfeiture in 1719, as did Peter Farquharson, who was attainted as Alexander, also for his share in the Rising of 1715. As is well known, the Edinburgh Court of Session gave judgment in 1749 in favour of Lord Pitsligo, but the decision was reversed by the House of Lords in 1750, who held that the description was substantially correct and that the attainder held good.[1]

PITULIE.

George Cumine of Pitullie was the only son by the third marriage of Provost William Cumine of Auchry, who sold Lochtervandich to William Duff of Braco and bought Auchry and Pitullie.

Provost William Cumming or Cumine was married three times—

(1) Isabella Gordon, daughter of the Provost of Banff, by whom he had a son, John, who succeeded to Auchry;

(2) Jane, daughter of James Sandilands of Cotton, and widow of John Moir of Stoneywood; and

(3) Christian, daughter of Sir Henry Guthrie of King Edward, who was the mother of his second son, George (above), who was born 1695—during his minority Lord Pitsligo was his guardian.

William Cumine and George, his son, together had sasine on Pitullie, 16th March, 1705.[2]

In the '15 George Cumine was one of those who came into Aberdeen with the Earl Marischal and was afterwards appointed his aide-de-camp. He married twice: (1) Jean Urquhart of Burdsyards, and (2) Christian Guthrie of King Edward and Ludquharn, daughter of Sir John, and his own first cousin. He had in all twenty-four children, his eldest son, William, being a Jacobite of 1745, but he himself did not go "out" again. He died in 1767, and is buried inside the church at Pitsligo with his first wife and some of his children.

LORD SALTOUN, FOR BOGHEAD—*D*—see PARISH OF RATHEN.

WESTER TYRIE. FRASER—see PARISH OF TYRIE.

PARISH OF FRASERBURGH.

THE LORD SALTOUN—*D*—see PARISH OF RATHEN.

MY LADY DOWAGER SALTOUN.

Margaret, daughter of Archbishop Sharp, who was widow of the 11th Lord, having married 11th October, 1683, four years after the murder of her father, of which she is said to have been a spectator, 3rd May, 1679.

---

[1] *Castle Forbes Papers.*　　[2] *Aberdeen Sasines.*

TYRIE—see above.

BOYNLY, FOR HIS LADY'S JOINTURE—*D*.

Captain John Forbes of Middle Boyndlie for his wife, "Agnes Foularton," married 1697 (see Parish of Tyrie).

(Middle Boyndlie was only joined to Upper and Nether Boyndlie in 1812.) [1]

TECHMURIE. PARISH OF RATHEN.

LORD SALTOUN—PARISH OF RATHEN—including LADY DOWAGER OF SALTOUN (above).

She survived until 1724. She had besides the 12th Lord Saltoun, two sons—William Fraser of Fraserfield, and James Fraser of Lonmay (a Jacobite), and four daughters, of whom Helen, the eldest, married Sir James Gordon of Park.

PARISH OF CRIMOND.

LAW, FOR MILL OF CRIMOND.

John Gordon of Law, afterwards of Wardhouse, was acting apparently as a sub-collector.

LAIRD OF CRIMOND—see PARISH OF LONMAY.

BRODLAND—*D*.

In 1696 William Fraser was Laird of Broadland. He was son of the Patrick Fraser who purchased the estate from the Gordons of Broadland in 1664.

THE HEIRS OF MR. JOHN BARKLAY.

Anne Gordon, relict of Mr. John Barclay, Episcopal minister at Peterhead. Her Will is in the Aberdeen Commissariot, 23rd February, 1766.

LOGIE GORDON—*D*. [Alexander Gordon, son of Ardmeallie.]

The lands of Logie, in Crimond, were divided in 1674 between three Meldrum nieces of the late John Hay—Isabella, married James Gordon of Ardmeallie ; Marie, married David Stewart ; and Elspeth, David Cumming. In 1696 the lands belonged jointly to David Stewart and James Gordon, but afterwards Gordon became the sole owner. He died before 1708, leaving two sons, Peter of Ardmeallie and Alexander of

[1] *Papers of Mr. J. C. M. Ogilvie-Forbes.*

Logie. Peter Gordon of Ardmeallie was a noted Whig in the Rising of 1745. His younger brother, Alexander, already in possession of Logie in 1715, seems to have shared his views. On 15th July, 1708, Alexander Gordon, son of James Gordon of Ardmeallie, and in the name of Isobel Meldrum, spouse of the said James Gordon, and of Elizabeth Meldrum, spouse of David Cumming, had sasine on the lands of Logie-Crimond for himself. His only child, Mary, married John Gordon of Avochie of the '45, a noted Jacobite. Her estate helped him to pay his fines.

Ratray, Auchmacoy.

Rattray and Broadland are the same estate.[1] In a paper in the Record Office (*S.P.* 54.8) an anonymous letter from an informer in Dundee to the Lord Justice Clerk says, "there is another parcel of Rebels at Craighall's home in Rattray."—9th September, 1715. On 7th July, 1711, Mary, Jean, Christian, and Isabella Bissets were portioners in Rattray.[2]

John Scott—*D.*

Was, in 1696, a tenant in Rattray.

Haddo. [Patrick Black of Haddo.]

David Watson of Haddo who was in possession in 1696, sold his estate to William Black, Sub-Principal of King's College, Aberdeen. Principal Black died in 1714 and was succeeded by his son, Patrick.

Alex. Dalgairdno, Milhill—*D.* (This name is spelt in a variety of ways.)

In 1696 Alexander was in possession with his wife and his son, James. In 1701, James Dalgarno of Millhill had sasine.[3]

On 29th January, 1705, "Isabel Keith, spouse to James Dalgardno of Millhill," had sasine.[4] Alexander was son of James and Isabel.

Jean Bisset—*D.*

Christian and Beatrix Bissets were in Bilbo in this Parish in 1696, and Mary, *Jean,* Christian, and Isabella Bissets, as above, in Rattray in 1711.

---

[1] In 1672 Andrew Hay was of Rattray, with Isabel Dalgarno, his spouse.

—*Aberdeen Sasines.*

[2] *Ibid.*   [3] *Ibid.*   [4] *Ibid.*

PARISH OF AUCHRYDIE.

EARL OF ABERDEEN—*D*—see TARVES.

NETHERMUIR, ELDER AND YOUNGER.

John Gordon, 5th of Nethermuir, and Elizabeth Gordon, his spouse, daughter of James Gordon, Laird of Rothiemay, had sasine, 6th June, 1712.[1] John Gordon was already in possession in 1696, having been served heir to his brother Patrick, 24th March, 1683, and did not die until 1732.

Nethermuir, younger, was his son, George. John had four daughters, of whom Anne, the eldest, married William Dingwall of Brucklay in 1711, and Elizabeth married James Brodie of Muiresk.[2]

FEDDRET. [Patrick Chalmers.]

The lands of Fedderat have had various owners. The Irvines of Drum were there for many years, but in 1683 Mr. Robert Keith, who married Marjory, daughter of John Irvine of Brucklay, bought it. Shortly after the date of the *Poll Book*, 1696, Dr. Patrick Chalmers, son of William Chalmers, minister of Skene, and Janet Fergus, acquired it. He was Professor of Medicine, Marischal College, 1701 ; he married Rachel, daughter of Alexander Forbes of Foveran, and had ten children. He was a Jacobite. The Chalmers' family were still in Fedderat in 1715, but in the following year it was again sold, to Mr. Forbes of Ballogie.

SHIVES FOR AUCHNAGATT—*D*.

The owner in 1696 and in 1715 of Auchnagatt was Patrick Strachan, son of Alexander, 7th of Glenkindie.

"Shives," who collected the money, was Gray of Schivas (*q.v.*).

The whole of the Strachan family, formerly strong Covenanters, were now Hanoverians. In 1703 Mr. Arthur Forbes, W.S., had advanced money on Auchnagatt.[3]

WHITEHILL, STONEYWOOD (*Sequestrate*).

The lands of Whitehill in New Deer belonged in 1696 to James Elphinstone of Logie in the Garioch, who resided in Edinburgh. On 5th February, 1722, sasine was granted by Alexander Irvine of Drum to James Moir of Stoneywood on "Whytehill, Whytingshill, Aucheoch, Aughath," etc.[4]

---

[1] *Aberdeen Sasines.*   [2] *Muiresk Papers.*
[3] *Aberdeen Sasines.*   [4] *Ibid.*

LUDQUHARN, FOR AUCHRYDIE (*Sequestrate*).

In 1696 it was Sir William Keith of Ludquharn.

Sir Henry Guthrie had purchased this estate before 1715 and had apparently also purchased the bankrupt estate of Auchrydie (Alexander Forbes), who in 1701 had an arent on Pittenor, Pitblair, and Newcraig.[1]

BARRACK.

Alexander Gordon of Barrack, who was there in 1696 with Christian Grant, his mother, and his five sisters—Jean, Catherine, Janet, Mary, and Elizabeth Gordon. He had a fresh sasine on Barrack, 10th July, 1713.[2]

Before 1736 Isobel Udny, "in Barrack," was wife of Alexander Gordon (above). Her Will is in the Commissariot, 27th February, 1736.

AUCHMUNZELL—*D*. [Alexander Gordon.]

Alexander Gordon of Auchmunzell, who appears in the *Poll Book*, was son of Gilbert Gordon of Auchmunzell and had sasine in 1662. His wife was Elizabeth Keith, and he had a son, William, and a daughter, Jean.

Thomas Irvine, fourth son of James Irvine of Artamford, and Margaret Sutherland, daughter of James Sutherland of Kinminity, born 1685, was of Auchmunzell shortly after this date.

CAIRNBANNO—LIFERENTED.

The relict of the deceased Alexander Dalgarno of Milnhill, in 1696, with Andrew, Isobel, and Mary, his children. She was still enjoying her liferent in 1715.

MR. ADAM HAY, FOR CHEINS AND KEITHS VALUATIONS.

The minister of Monquhitter, the neighbouring parish (see page 207). He died in 1729. His Will is in Commissariot of Aberdeen.

AUCHINLECK (AFFLECK)—THREE-QUARTERS UNLIFERENTED—*D*.

DITTO—ONE-QUARTER LIFERENTED.

Alexander Lumsden in 1650 and 1667, father of Professor John Lumsden who married Jane Leslie of Pitcaple.[3]

In 1696 the lands of Afleet (as Auchinleck was pronounced and often written) are said to be held jointly by Pitcaple and Artamford.[4]

Three-quarters of this estate pays double, one-quarter single Cess, as do all lands liferented, according to Mar's original instructions.

---

[1] *Aberdeen Sasines.*   [2] *Ibid.*   [3] *Pitcaple Papers.*   [4] *Poll Book.*

BRUCKLAW AND IRONSYDE—*D.* Probably WILLIAM DINGWALL.

These two estates were originally properties of the Irvines, which, in 1696, were administered by the "Factor of Drum." "Adam Irvine of Brucklaw" was one of those who rode into Aberdeen with the Earl Marischal, 20th September, 1715. He was son of the Rev. Robert Irvine, minister of Towie, and his wife, Agnes, daughter of Patrick Murray of Blairfindy. The Rev. Robert belonged to the family of the Irvines of Kingcausie.

Adam married secretly in 1710 Margaret, daughter of Sir John Reid, 1st Baronet of Barra, the marriage being afterwards recognized. Adam was not prosecuted for his share in the Rising of 1715, but lived to take part also in that of 1745, and again to escape scot-free. In 1728 he had been Collector of Supply for Kincardineshire.

As early as 1709, Alexander Irvine granted a bond on Brucklaw and Ironsyde to Mr. William Dingwall, whose father, Arthur Dingwall, had married Lucrece Irvine, daughter of John Irvine of Brucklay. William Dingwall married Anne Gordon of Nethermuir on 25th October, 1711, and on 15th July, 1712, together they had sasine on Whitecairns. He had been clerk to Sir Samuel Forbes of Foveran, but sometime before his death, which occurred in 1723, he had become Laird of Brucklaw or Brucklay. Arthur's grandson, Baillie John Dingwall of Rannieston, was the first stocking manufacturer.[1]

ARTAMFORD.

William Irvine, in 1715, brother of the Laird of Drum. In 1696 James Irvine of Artamford, with Margaret Sutherland, his spouse, and five sons—Alexander, William, Robert, Thomas, and Charles Irvines, appear in the *Poll Book,* and Marjorie Irvine, a daughter. James was the son of James Irvine of Artamford, and had an uncle, Alexander, who was taken prisoner, when fighting with Montrose in 1644.[2]

He married in 1674, as he and his wife had sasine on Artamford in that year. Besides the children mentioned in the *Poll Book,* he had two other sons, Richard and Francis, and a daughter, Anna ; the baptisms of all three being recorded in the Parish of New Deer.[3]

James Irvine was served heir to his father in 1675.

He was succeeded in Artamford by his son, Alexander (formerly of Crimond, and a Jacobite), served heir 13th August, 1702. Later, William, the second son, became of Artamford when Alexander succeeded to Drum. William married Isobel Keith, who, in 1705, gave birth to *triplets !*— George, James, and William—these were baptized at New Deer on 8th

[1] *Family Record of Dingwall-Fordyce*, by Alex. D. Dingwall-Fordyce.
[2] *Spalding's Trubles*, vol. ii, p. 380.   [3] *Parish Records.*

January, two of the godfathers being George Keith of Clackriach and James Keith of Crichie. In 1707 William and Isobel had a son named Alexander, and in 1710 a son named Hugh.

The eldest son, George, succeeded to Artamford, which had been disponed by Alexander to William in 1703, though he himself did not succeed to Drum till 1737 (see Family Tree, page 33).

William Irvine of Artamford was an active Jacobite, and on 17th October, 1715, is noted as "having come from the Camp at Perth with Stoniewood elder, with letters from the Earl Marischal requiring a loan of £12,000" (i.e. from the town of Aberdeen).

CULSH—*D*.

In 1696 William Lindsay of Culsh, Writer in Edinburgh, was there with his mother, Barbara Guthrie, and Barbara Lindsay, a child.

He was twice married: (1) to Agnes Mercer, and (2) Elizabeth Leslie.

Culsh at one time formed part of the estate of the Irvines of Drum. It was sold to John Fordyce (of Gask and Culsh), whose daughter, Jean (heiress, after the death of her brother, William), married, in 1744, William Dingwall, Writer in Edinburgh, and owner of Brucklay—hence the family of Dingwall-Fordyce of Brucklay and Culsh.

OLD WHAT (ABROAD).

In 1696 it was Mr. George Forbes, with his wife, Isobel Chalmer, and his mother-in-law, Isobel Forbes. She had had sasine on Old What in 1668, whereas in 1672 George Chalmers was entered as owner.

Formerly this estate belonged to a branch of Irvines, descended from Gilbert Irvine, brother to the Laird of Drum in 1586.

ALLATHEN—*D*. [Robert Cumming.]

In 1696 it was Robert Cumming of Allathen, Elizabeth Irving, his spouse, Margaret and Jane Irvings (*sic*), his daughters. (*Poll Book.*)

Down to the middle of the 17th century there were Irvines of Allathen, John Irvine of Allathen and Isobel, his spouse, being the last mentioned (in the *Irvines of Drum*, by Col. J. G. Leslie) in 1650.

By 1672 the above Robert Cumming was already in possession. His son, Robert Cumming of Allathen, married Anne, youngest daughter of Alexander Leslie, 9th Laird of Pitcaple, about 1710, and in the Will of Sir James Leslie, last Leslie Laird of Pitcaple, the three sons of the deceased Anne are mentioned—Joseph, James, and Charles Cumming. The Will was dated 1760. Joseph became a merchant in the West Indies.[1]

---

[1] *Pitcaple Papers.*

PRESBYTERY OF ELLON.

PARISH OF CRUDEN.

THE EARL OF ERROLL.

Charles, 13th Earl of Erroll, eldest son of the 12th Earl and Lady Anne Drummond, only daughter of James, 3rd Earl of Perth, succeeded 30th December, 1704, and died unmarried 16th October, 1717.

He took the oath in the Scots Parliament in 1705 but was a firm opponent of the Act of Union, and was known to be so strongly in favour of the exiled dynasty that on the alarm of the Invasion of 1708, although in bad health, he was imprisoned in Edinburgh Castle. He had provided the pilot who should have guided Admiral Forbin and the French Fleet, but they were driven away from the Firth of Forth by Admiral Byng and the English ships.

Lord Erroll was known, in the years that followed, among the Jacobite councillors as "deservedly and much trusted and as having sent Mr. George a skipper and Mr. Malcolm to pilot the king up the Firth." Mr. George, the skipper, it is to be noted, would have been of no use to the French commander, even had the latter approached near enough to the coast to require one, since he (Mr. George) "got drinking with his friends."

In Patten's *History of the Rebellion of 1715*, Lord Erroll is described as "himself neutral, but has 500 men most of them against the Government." He was one of those summoned by the Government to Edinburgh who disregarded the summons. He attended Mar's "Hunting Party" but did not actively join the Rising. In the *Poll Book* of 1696 he had appeared as "my Lord Hay, with 2 younger brothers, James and Thomas," but they died without issue.

He had two sisters—*Mary*, who became (at her brother's death) Countess of Erroll in her own right, being the 14th holder of the title. She married Alexander Falconer and bestowed upon him the name and dignity of Hay of Delgaty. She had no children, but was succeeded, in 1758, by the grandson of her sister, who thus became James, 15th Earl. Lady Erroll was a prominent figure in the Rising of 1745.

The younger sister, *Margaret*, married James, 5th Earl of Linlithgow and 4th Earl of Callendar, who was attainted as a Jacobite of the '15.

Their only daughter, Lady Anne Livingstone, married the 4th Earl of Kilmarnock, he who was beheaded for his share in the Rising of 1745. The eldest son, James Boyd, succeeded as 15th Earl of Erroll, and but for the attainders of his grandfather and father would have also held the titles of Earl of Linlithgow, Callendar, and Kilmarnock. He, as is well known, attended the coronation of George III in his capacity as Constable of Scotland, and excited the admiration of Dr. Johnson by his splendid figure, which reminded the lexicographer of "Homer's description of Sarpedon." James Boyd had fought under Cumberland at Culloden and witnessed the capture of his father. Charles Boyd, his younger brother, fought *with* his father, but escaped to France. Charles's daughter, Charlotte, married Charles Gordon of Wardhouse (see page 75).

AUCHLEUCHRIES.

Patrick Gordon in 1715.

In 1696 it was "John Gordon of Auchleuchries, Elizabeth Grant, his lady, and Patrick Gordon, his son." Elizabeth was the daughter of William Grant of Crichie (see page 195), and had sasine on the lands and manor of Auchleuchries in 1702, with Gilbert, John, *Patrick*, Margaret, Anne, and Mary, her children.

John, husband of Elizabeth, was the son of General Patrick Gordon, and great grandson of Patrick Gordon of Nethermuir, whose third son, John, married, in 1633, Marie, only child and heiress of James Ogilvie of Auchleuchries. In October, 1663, "Marie Ogilvie, spouse to John Gordon of Auchleuchries, granted sasine to herself in liferent and to Alexander her youngest son, in fee of Westertoun of Auchleuchries" [1] (see Family Tree below)

Patrick Gordon, the famous General in the Russian Army, was second son to John Gordon and Marie Ogilvie, but became the owner in 1660. He died in 1699, aged 64. His wife was Katherine von Bockhoven.

Patrick, the third son of the John Gordon of the *Poll Book*, and grandson to the General, succeeded to Auchleuchries on his father's death in 1712, being then twenty—Gilbert and John (above) being dead. He was a Roman Catholic and, therefore, obnoxious to the Presbytery of Ellon. He sold Auchleuchries in 1722 to his brother-in-law, Alexander

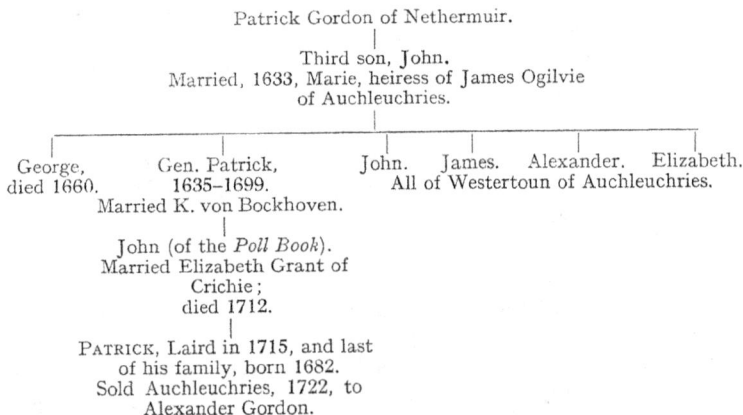

Patrick Gordon of Nethermuir.
|
Third son, John.
Married, 1633, Marie, heiress of James Ogilvie
of Auchleuchries.

| George, died 1660. | Gen. Patrick, 1635–1699. Married K. von Bockhoven. | John. | James. | Alexander. | Elizabeth. |

All of Westertoun of Auchleuchries.

John (of the *Poll Book*).
Married Elizabeth Grant of
Crichie;
died 1712.
|
PATRICK, Laird in 1715, and last
of his family, born 1682.
Sold Auchleuchries, 1722, to
Alexander Gordon.

[1] *Aberdeen Sasines.*

Gordon of Sandend. He was a Jacobite of 1715, and on 6th March, 1718, sent a petition to James III, stating that "after lurking for some time he had been forced to leave Scotland and had received 35 livres a month for ten months from December 1716, at Paris and had then gone to Vienna with recommendation to Count Hamilton, privy counsellor to the Emperor, to procure employment against the Turks, but on his arrival found the Count was dead and so came to Italy," where he had already been in 1717, begging from the Earl of Mar.

The date of his death is not known.

LAIRD OF ELLON, FOR MUIRTACK—see PARISH OF ELLON, FOR LAIRD OF ELLON.

Muirtack is a small property, close to the hill of Dudwick, on which James Gordon of Ellon had sasine in 1712.

LUDQUHARN, FOR AUQUHARNIE [1]—*D*.

Either the creditors of Alexander Forbes of Ludquharn or the purchaser of Ludquharn, Sir John Guthrie, would appear to have paid in 1715 double Cess for these lands which had belonged, in 1696, to Dr. Hay, heritor, Edinburgh. They were part of the Erroll property till sold early in the 18th century. John Hay, burgess of Aberdeen, had been served heir on 5th October, 1653, as "heir of conquest (as an elder, see page 82, footnote) to George Hay of Aucharnie, his immediate younger brother, in Earlseat and Aquharnie, with the pendicles thereof."

On 7th May, 1706, Elizabeth and Helen, daughters of David Hay, M.D., of Aucharnie (the Dr. Hay above) had sasine.

SANDEND—LIFERENT.

George Hay, son of Thomas Hay of Sandend and Agnes Gavin,[2] was heritor in 1696, with Isobel Leask, his spouse. The widow still had her liferent in 1715, but Alexander Gordon was the owner (the brother-in-law of Patrick Gordon of Auchleuchries and purchaser of that estate in 1722).

THE EARL OF PANMUIR—see PARISH OF BELHELVIE.

THE EARL OF ERROLL.

For the Cess he should pay in four other parishes in which he owned land, viz. :—Turriff, Monquhitter, Slains, and Ellon, and for the Parsonage of Turriff, and a portion of that owed in Cruden, but some was obviously still owing, i.e. *rests* (see page)18.

---

[1] In 1703 George Forbes, formerly of Auchquharnie, had sasine on the Mill of Cruden.—*Aberdeen Sasines*.

[2] *Ibid., 1659*.

PARISH OF SLAINES.

THE EARL OF ERROLL—see above.

SEAFIELD—JOHN HAY.

Gilbert Hay was of Seafield in 1672.

In 1696 it was reckoned as part of the Erroll estate of Slains, and Robert Forbes was the *tenant*. On 13th October, 1709, John Hay, Merchant in Edinburgh, had an arent on the lands of Seafield, and the daughter of John Hay of Seafield, as has been already seen, married Gavin Cumming of Kininmonth in 1662.

BIRNESS, FOR LEASK—*D.*

ROBERT CUMMING.

In 1696 it was Mr. Alexander Leask, son of William Leask, with his son, Gilbert, and two brothers. This was the son of the minister of Maryculter and his wife, Margaret Cumming, of the Cummings of Birness.

In 1704 it was Robert Cumming of Birness, probably nephew of Alexander Leask. He married Mary Skene of Dyce, and their daughter, Barbara, married, in 1730, James Gordon of Hilton ; their grandson was the well-known John Gordon-Cumming-Skene.

EARNHILL.

These lands had been acquired before 1699 by Mr. William Hay, minister of Crimond, who died in February of that year. He was the son of Mr. William Hay, minister of Crimond, and himself left a son, also William, and probably the owner in 1715.[1]

PARISH OF FOVERAN.

LAIRD OF FOVERAN—*D.*

The Laird of Foveran was Sir Samuel Forbes, eldest son of Mr. Alexander Forbes of Ardo and his first wife, Margaret, daughter of Samuel Hunter, of Edinburgh. He was born 1653, and made a baronet of Nova Scotia in 1700. In 1673, as Samuel Forbes, eldest son to Mr. Alex. Forbes of Ardo, he was made a burgess. He was one of the M.P.s for Aberdeenshire in two Scottish Parliaments, 1693 and 1700. He married Anne, daughter of John Udny of Udny, and had three sons—Alexander, John, and Patrick, and a daughter, Anna ; he died January, 1717.

[1] *Aberdeen Sasines.*

Sir Alexander Forbes was served heir to Sir Samuel, 13th March, 1718.

Isobel Forbes, sister to Sir Samuel Forbes, married, in 1701, Patrick Strachan of Auchnagatt, afterwards of Glenkindie.[1]

UDNY—see PARISH OF UDNY.

NEWTYLE.

AUCHTERELLON AND CULTERCULLEN—all belonging to Udny (*q.v.*).

Mary Cheyne, spouse to John Udny of Newtyle, had sasine, 6th April, 1713.[2]

RICKARTON, FOR AUCHNACANT—*D.*

This was David Rickart, second son of David Rickart of Auchnacant, who was served heir to his eldest brother, George, and nephew, George, on 15th December, 1692, in Auchnacant.[3] He afterwards purchased another estate (which he re-named Rickarton) in Kincardine, and died 29th July, 1718. His wife was the Hon. Katharine Arbuthnot, and he had three daughters—Catherine, Janet, and Margaret, who were served heirs in 1721.[4] John Rickart, who eventually succeeded to Auchnacant, was born in 1671 and died 1749, aged 78.

He married Marjorie, daughter of John Gordon of Fechil. Rickarton is now part of the estate of Urie.

PARISH OF UDNY.

LORD PITMEDDAN.

Alexander Seton of Pitmedden succeeded his brother, James, in 1667 (James having been killed in the naval action against the Dutch in the Medway, 12th June, 1667). Alexander was an advocate, knighted in 1664, and made a baronet of Nova Scotia in 1684. In 1677 he became a Lord of Session under the title of Lord Pitmedden. He died in 1719 at a very advanced age. His wife was Margaret Lauder. In 1696 he had two sons at home, Alexander and James, and three daughters.[5] He was removed from being a Lord of Session in 1688 for opposing King James *re* the Test Act.

LAIRD OF PITMEDDAN.

Already, on 17th November, 1703, " Mr. William Seton, Sir Alexander's eldest son," was granted a sasine on Pitmedden. This was William,

---

[1] *Aberdeen Sasines.* [2] *Ibid.* [3] *Service of Heirs.*
[4] *Ibid.* [5] *Poll Book.*

afterwards 2nd Baronet, whom Sir Alexander had put in possession of the estate in his own life-time. He was M.P. for Aberdeenshire 1700–1702, and appointed one of the Commissioners to treat for the Union of the Kingdoms in 1706. His wife was Catherine, eldest daughter of Sir Thomas Burnett, 3rd Baronet of Leys ; she died 1749 ; he in 1744.

BARON MAITLAND OF PITRICHIE—*D*. [Alex. Arbuthnot, husband of Jean Maitland.]

Richard Maitland of Pitrichie was created a baronet in 1672, and as a Lord of Session assumed the title of Lord Pitrichie. He died in 1677 and was succeeded by his eldest son, Richard, who died in 1679, and was succeeded by his brother, Charles, and he again, in 1700, by his only son, Charles, who died in 1703 without issue, when his sister, Jean, and her husband, the Hon. Alexander Arbuthnot, assumed the name and arms of Maitland.

LIFERENTED LANDS OF PITRICHIE.

The liferented lands of Pitrichie, according to Mar's instructions, only paid single. Jean Maitland, who succeeded, had four younger sisters who appear in the *Poll Book*—"Mary, Margaret, Kathren and Elizabeth Maitland, and an aunt, Sophia Maitland." But subsequent to the date of the *Poll Book*, Sir Charles Maitland, brother of Jean, had married Margaret Burnett of Craigmyle, daughter of his step-mother, and it was she who enjoyed the liferent.

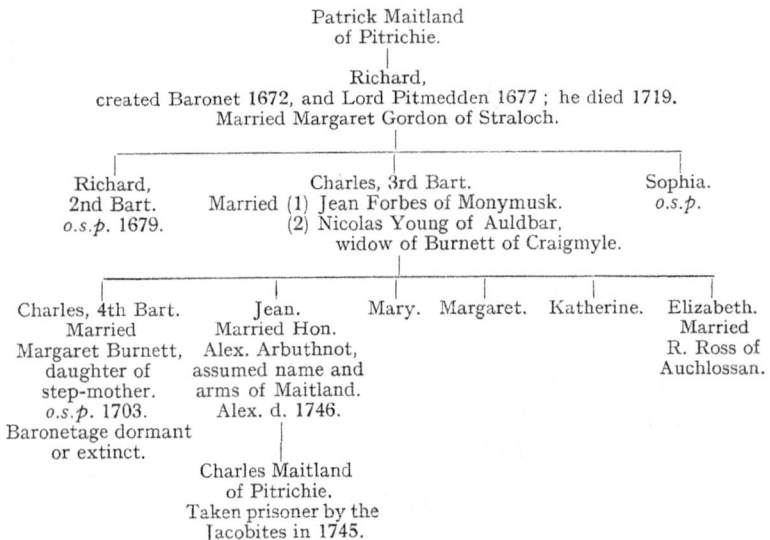

Patrick Maitland
of Pitrichie.
|
Richard,
created Baronet 1672, and Lord Pitmedden 1677 ; he died 1719.
Married Margaret Gordon of Straloch.
|

| Richard, 2nd Bart. *o.s.p.* 1679. | Charles, 3rd Bart. Married (1) Jean Forbes of Monymusk. (2) Nicolas Young of Auldbar, widow of Burnett of Craigmyle. | Sophia. *o.s.p.* |

| Charles, 4th Bart. Married Margaret Burnett, daughter of step-mother. *o.s.p.* 1703. Baronetage dormant or extinct. | Jean. Married Hon. Alex. Arbuthnot, assumed name and arms of Maitland. Alex. d. 1746. | Mary. | Margaret. | Katherine. | Elizabeth. Married R. Ross of Auchlossan. |

Charles Maitland
of Pitrichie.
Taken prisoner by the
Jacobites in 1745.

UDNY.

John Udny of Udny, eldest son of Alexander Udny and Anna Renton. Alexander was the laird in 1696, though not served heir till 1699.

John Udny (then younger of Udny) was one of those who collected the Poll, 1696. He had a younger brother, Alexander, and three sisters—Elizabeth, Anna, and Christian.

John Udny married, in 1701, Lady Martha Gordon, second daughter of George, 1st Earl of Aberdeen.

The eldest son of John Udny and Lady Martha was Alexander, who married, in 1758, Margaret, only child of William Duff of Braco, and widow of Patrick Duff of Premnay ; when Alexander Udny died without issue, in 1789, the widow claimed the estates from her husband's brother, William Udny, but the claim was compounded for £10,000, which she left at her death, in 1793, to her cousin, James, 2nd Lord Fife.[1] She was then 83, having been married for 42 years to her first husband, who made her his wife when she was only 11 years of age, and after five years of widowhood she married Alex. Udny, with whom she had 21 years of matrimony, and then four years of second widowhood.

WATTERTON, FOR BONAKETTLE.

Thomas Forbes of Waterton, grandson of the 1st Thomas Forbes of Waterton, who was fourth son of William Forbes, Laird of Tolquhon, received Waterton from his father in 1616. He had married Jean Ramsay of Balmain and had four sons and six daughters.

The second son, Sir John Forbes of Waterton, who married Jane Gordon of Haddo, and died 1675, was father of Thomas, the Laird of 1715, who was born in 1664, and married in 1689 Elizabeth Nicholson of Balcaskie, daughter of Sir George Nicholson, afterwards Lord Glenbervie. The son of this marriage, John Forbes, was killed at Sheriffmuir. He was made a burgess of Aberdeen in 1707, and had been much abroad.

His half-brother, Thomas (by his father's second wife, Katherine Galloway), succeeded to Waterton, and *his* grandson, John, wrote a brief account of the family, published 1857.

Bonnakettle was a part of the estate of Waterton, occupied (in 1696) by William Wischart.[2]

---

[1] In one of Lord Fife's letters to his factor, William Rose, he mentions a report which had reached him on 7th April, 1792, "that Mrs. Udny Duff had married her footman." She was then 82, and the report was of course untrue.

—A. and H. Tayler, *Lord Fife and his Factor*, p. 234.

[2] *Poll Book.*

William Forbes, 8th of Tolquhon.
Married Jean Ogilvie of Banff, 1580.

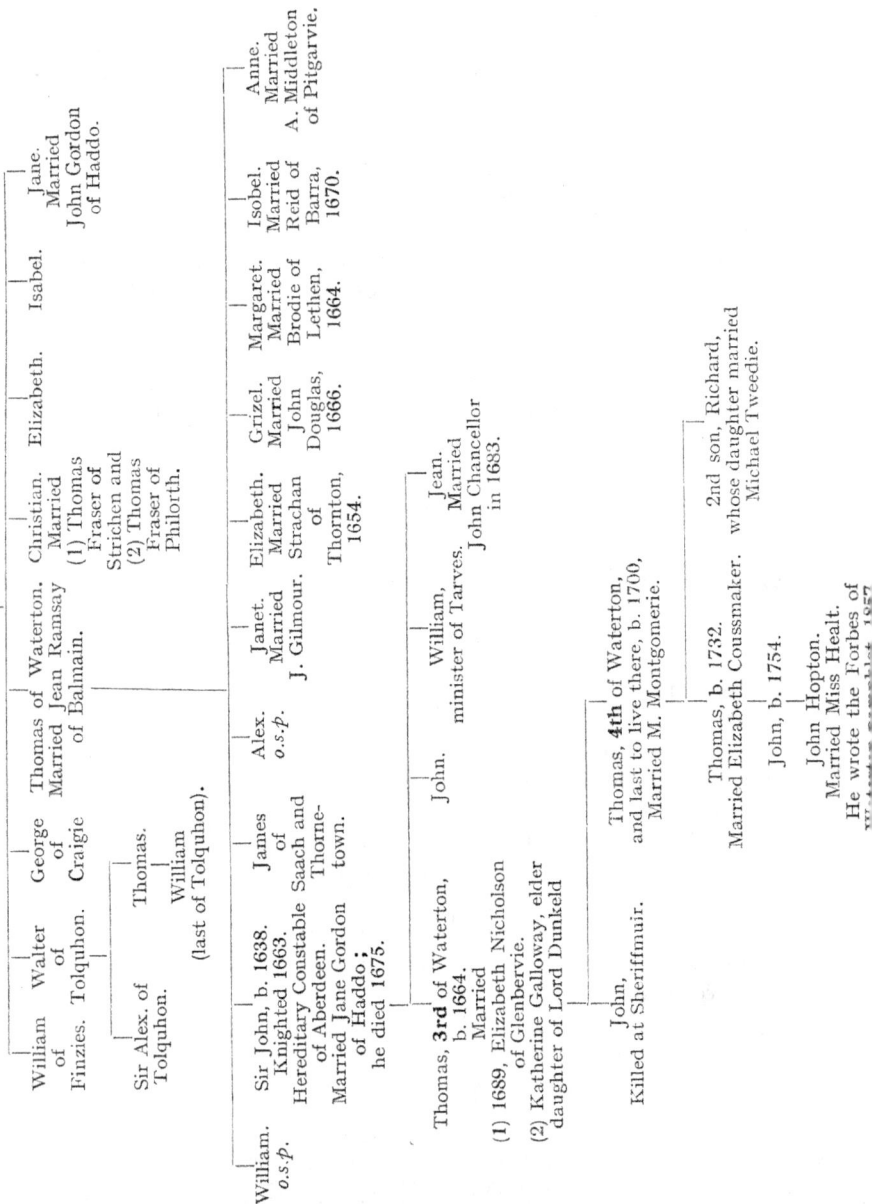

William
of
Finzies.

Walter
of
Tolquhon.

George
of
Craigie

Thomas of Waterton.
Married Jean Ramsay
of Balmain.

Christian.
Married
(1) Thomas
Fraser of
Strichen and
(2) Thomas
Fraser of
Philorth.

Elizabeth.

Isabel.

Jane.
Married
John Gordon
of Haddo.

Thomas.

William
(last of Tolquhon).

Sir Alex. of
Tolquhon.

Alex.
o.s.p.

James
of
Saach and
Thorne-
town.

Janet.
Married
J. Gilmour.

Elizabeth.
Married
Strachan
of
Thornton,
1654.

Grizel.
Married
John
Douglas,
1666.

Margaret.
Married
Brodie of
Lethen,
1664.

Isobel.
Married
Reid of
Barra,
1670.

Anne.
Married
A. Middleton
of Pitgarvie.

William.
o.s.p.

Sir John, b. **1638**.
Knighted 1663.
Hereditary Constable
of Aberdeen.
Married Jane Gordon
of Haddo **;**
he died 1675.

John.

William,
minister of Tarves.

Jean.
Married
John Chancellor
in 1683.

Thomas, **3rd** of Waterton,
b. 1664.
Married
(1) 1689, Elizabeth Nicholson
of Glenbervie.
(2) Katherine Galloway, elder
daughter of Lord Dunkeld

John,
Killed at Sheriffmuir.

Thomas, **4th** of Waterton,
and last to live there, b. 1700,
Married M. Montgomerie.

2nd son, Richard,
whose daughter married
Michael Tweedie.

Thomas, **b.** 1732.
Married Elizabeth Coussmaker.

John, b. 1754.

John Hopton.
Married Miss Healt.
He wrote the Forbes of
Waterton pamphlet, 1857.

TILLIECORTHY.

Part of the estate of Udny, which was sold by Robert Udny in 1615 to his brother, the Rev. Alexander Udny, the latter disponing what remained in his hands to Robert Clark, son of James Clark of Tilliecorthie,[1] the husband of his daughter, Jane.   In 1696 William Clark, son of James and Jane, was heritor thereof with Jean Strachan, his wife, and James Clark, his son.   James Clark, who died in 1741, is buried in Old Aberdeen, with his wife, Margaret Thomson.   Tilliecorthie was afterwards sold to Burnett of Kirkhill.

TORRELEITH—*D.*

"Mr. Patrick Walker of Torrieleith living in Old Aberdeen in 1696" was still the owner in 1715.

There was a charter, dated 23rd March, 1672, by John Irvine of Murthill and Alexander Irvine, his son, whereby the lands and teinds of Torrieleith were disponed to Andrew Walker, Writer in Edinburgh.

Patrick was his son, and on 2nd July, 1708, Patrick Walker of Torrieleith granted a liferent on the lands of Torrieleith to Elizabeth Garioch, his spouse, daughter to "umquhile George Garioch of Kinstair."   The Gariochs were prominent Whigs.   Rachel Walker, who married Thomas Cassie, Old Aberdeen, was sister to Patrick Walker of Torrieleith.

On 29th August, 1712, John (Lord Gray) had sasine over some portion of Torrieleith.[2]

KNAPERNAY.   (*I want receipt from Knappernay for Cesse, Lamas 1715, which I've allowed.*)

John Forbes of Knaperna, younger brother of Sir Samuel Forbes of Foveran, purchased these lands from William Moir of Knaperna.   It was a very large estate, valued at £1,000.   In the *Poll Book* of 1696 the "mains and Miln of Knapernay" are included in the estate of Waterton, but the whole of that estate is only valued at £900.   John Forbes, the collector, appears to have excused John of Knaperna from payment.

FOVERAN—*D*—see above.

SLAGMAGULLY.

Formerly part of Torrieleith in 1715, but paid single.   George Gordon was of Ranieston and Slugmally.

In 1669 these lands had been in the possession of Mr. Alexander Hervie of Mamewlay.   He had sasine thereon on 14th July, with the consent of James Forbes of Tilliegrig and Margaret Hervie, his spouse ; James Hervie, father ; and Mr. Robert Hervie, elder brother of Alexander.

---

[1] His grandfather had been there in 1613.   [2] *Aberdeen Sasines.*

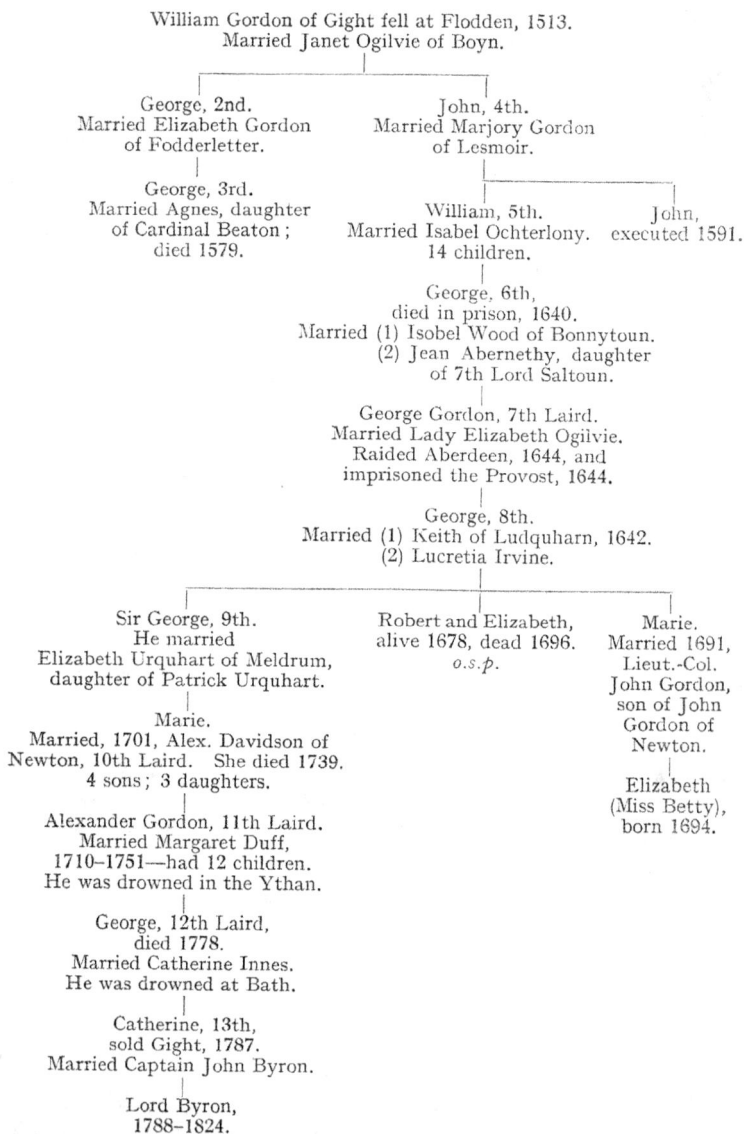

TREE OF GIGHT.

William Gordon of Gight fell at Flodden, 1513.
Married Janet Ogilvie of Boyn.

George, 2nd.
Married Elizabeth Gordon
of Fodderletter.

John, 4th.
Married Marjory Gordon
of Lesmoir.

George, 3rd.
Married Agnes, daughter
of Cardinal Beaton ;
died 1579.

William, 5th.
Married Isabel Ochterlony.
14 children.

John,
executed 1591.

George, 6th,
died in prison, 1640.
Married (1) Isobel Wood of Bonnytoun.
(2) Jean Abernethy, daughter
of 7th Lord Saltoun.

George Gordon, 7th Laird.
Married Lady Elizabeth Ogilvie.
Raided Aberdeen, 1644, and
imprisoned the Provost, 1644.

George, 8th.
Married (1) Keith of Ludquharn, 1642.
(2) Lucretia Irvine.

Sir George, 9th.
He married
Elizabeth Urquhart of Meldrum,
daughter of Patrick Urquhart.

Robert and Elizabeth,
alive 1678, dead 1696.
o.s.p.

Marie.
Married 1691,
Lieut.-Col.
John Gordon,
son of John
Gordon of
Newton.

Marie.
Married, 1701, Alex. Davidson of
Newton, 10th Laird. She died 1739.
4 sons ; 3 daughters.

Elizabeth
(Miss Betty),
born 1694.

Alexander Gordon, 11th Laird.
Married Margaret Duff,
1710–1751—had 12 children.
He was drowned in the Ythan.

George, 12th Laird,
died 1778.
Married Catherine Innes.
He was drowned at Bath.

Catherine, 13th,
sold Gight, 1787.
Married Captain John Byron.

Lord Byron,
1788–1824.

PARISH OF METHLICK.

EARL OF ABERDEEN—*D*—see PARISH OF MELDRUM.

PITRICHIE—*D*—see PARISH OF UDNY.

GIGHT.

The owner of Gight in 1715 was Marie Gordon, only child of George Gordon, 9th Laird of Gight. She married in 1701 Alexander Davidson of Newton, who took the name of Gordon and became the 10th Laird. Her great-grand-daughter, the 13th and last Gordon to own Gight, was Catherine, who married Captain the Hon. John Byron, by whom the whole of her estate was dissipated. Her son was the poet.

While Marie Gordon was a child, her estate seems to have been in the hands of her aunt of the same name, who married Colonel John Gordon of the *old* family of Newton, and he is confusingly described in the *Poll Book* as "Laird of Gight," since he no doubt acted as factor, until the heiress was of age to take a husband and give to him the name of Gordon.

A complete tree of the family of Gordons of Gight is here given (see opposite page).

PARISH OF TARVES.

EARL OF ABERDEEN—*D*—see above. PARISH OF MELDRUM.

TOLQUHON (*Seq.*). WILLIAM FORBES.

Sir Alexander Forbes of Tolquhon was in possession at the date of the *Poll Book*, 1696, with his wife, Elizabeth Forbes. He died on 31st July, 1701, and his brother, Thomas, a few weeks afterwards. The son of Thomas, William 11th and last Laird of Tolquhon, married Anna Leith of Whitehaugh, and owing to the embarrassed circumstances in which he found himself at the deaths of his father and uncle (who had been speculators in Darien), his creditors took possession of his estate in 1716, which already, in 1715, was bankrupt. Their title not being clear, William Forbes was unwilling to leave, until forcibly ejected from the Castle of Tolquhon in 1718 at the instance of his creditors by soldiers, who wounded him and took him prisoner. His circumstances afterwards improved, and at his death in 1728, aged 42, he was buried in Westminster Abbey.

Thomas, William's younger brother, born 1689, was an active Jacobite of the '15, and afterwards escaped to France. James Menzies, writing to the Earl of Mar on 3rd September, 1716, mentions that "one Forbes, a son, Tochon" was among those who were stopped while going aboard a ship at Greenwich, but afterwards got away.[1]

SHIVES—*D.* ARTHUR FORBES.

It was George Gray of Schivas in 1696. He had an only daughter and heiress, married to Arthur Forbes, a younger son of Sir John Forbes of Craigievar, who thus acquired Schivas. Arthur Forbes died before 1744.

CAIRNBROGIE.

George Johnston in 1696 was tenant *in* Cairnbrogie, which was part of the estate of Lord Aberdeen, having been sold to him by the old family of Davidson of Cairnbrogie.

KEITHFIELD—*D.*

This was the estate formerly called Tilliegonie, which already, in 1696, was in the possession of John Keith, with his wife and seven children, and re-named by him. He was brother to George Keith, Advocate. The owner in 1715 was his son.

DITTO, LIFERENTED.

AUCHORTIS. JOHN FORBES.

John Forbes of Auchquhorthies—called in the *Poll Book* "Achorthes" —was in possession, in 1696, with his wife and seven children.

Colliehill in Bourtie (Presbytery of Garioch) also then belonged to "John Forbes of Auchortis in Tarves."

In 1672 Sir Alexander Forbes of Tolquhon, who had not then lost all his money, had a sasine on "that part of the moss of Craigie next the lands of Auchquhorthies."[2]

On 3rd July, 1714, "John Forbes of Auquhortis" had sasine, as "Pror" for George Forbes, his second son, on a portion of these lands.

PARISH OF LOGIE-BUCHAN.

TARTIE—*D.*

Patrick Dunn of Tarty, Little Tipperty, and Logie-Buchan, succeeded his father, Dr. Robert Dunn, in 1666, when a child. He was one of the Commissioners for taking up the Poll in 1696.

[1] *Stuart Papers.*   [2] *Aberdeen Sasines.*

TURNERHALL, FOR LANDS UNMORTIFIED.

Robert Turner was fourth son of Andrew Turner of Kinminity, in Birse, who died before 1688. In 1693 the lands and barony of Rosehill, formerly Hilton, were bought from John Rose of Rosehill, erected into the barony of Turnerhall, and the estates entailed upon Robert Turner, 18th May, 1694. Robert married the eldest daughter of John Rose, by whom he had 14 children. On 30th June, 1710, Margaret Rose, spouse to Robert Turner of Turnerhall, had liferent on "Mieckle Tipperty, Waterichmoor, and mains of Turnerhall." [1]

Robert, and his eldest son, John, both joined the Rising of 1715 and were with the Earl Marischal at Aberdeen on 20th September, 1715.[2] John was only 21 at the time, and lived on until 1755, his own son, John, taking an active part in the Rising of 1745. In the 1667 Valuation, the estate of Hilton appeared in the Parish of Ellon.

MOSTOUN.

No owner is given for this small estate in the *Poll Book*, but in the special service of heirs, under date 21st February, 1677, Thomas Forbes appears as nearest heir to his father, Mr. John Forbes of Waterton, in the lands of Ardgrew, Broomfield, Borrowley, Mosstoun, and others.

AUCHMACOY. [James Buchan, 4th Laird.]

James Buchan of Auchmacoy, formerly of Oykhorne, succeeded in 1669. He married Jean Fraser of Tyrie and had a son, James, who

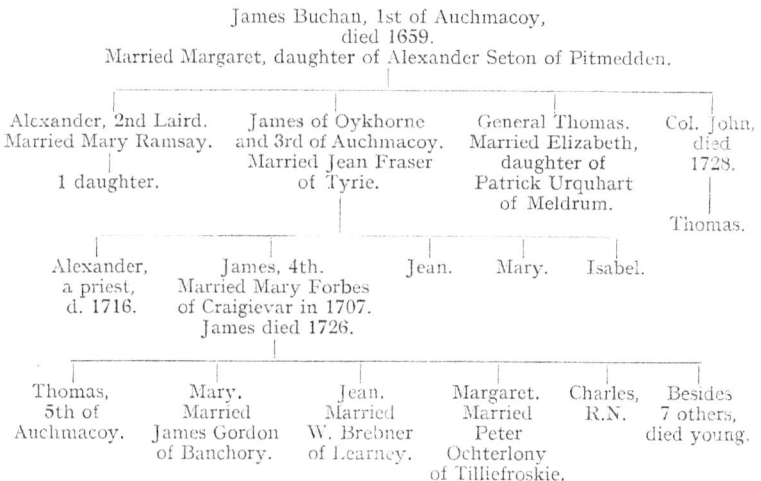

James Buchan, 1st of Auchmacoy,
died 1659.
Married Margaret, daughter of Alexander Seton of Pitmedden.

| Alexander, 2nd Laird. Married Mary Ramsay. 1 daughter. | James of Oykhorne and 3rd of Auchmacoy. Married Jean Fraser of Tyrie. | General Thomas. Married Elizabeth, daughter of Patrick Urquhart of Meldrum. | Col. John, died 1728. Thomas. |

| Alexander, a priest, d. 1716. | James, 4th. Married Mary Forbes of Craigievar in 1707. James died 1726. | Jean. | Mary. | Isabel. |

| Thomas, 5th of Auchmacoy. | Mary. Married James Gordon of Banchory. | Jean. Married W. Brebner of Learney. | Margaret. Married Peter Ochterlony of Tilliefroskie. | Charles, R.N. | Besides 7 others, died young. |

—*Auchmacoy Papers.*

[1] *Aberdeen Sasines.*

[2] *A Short Memorandum of quhat heath occurred in Aberdeen.*

succeeded him as 4th Laird, and died 1726, and three daughters, Jean, Mary, and Isobel.

Mary Forbes, spouse of James Buchan, 4th Laird (married in 1707), had sasine for her liferent on 30th December, 1713.[1]

She was the daughter of Sir John Forbes of Craigievar, and widow of John Ramsay of Barra and Laithers.

MEIKLE ARTROCHIE—D.

The Lairds of Artrochie were formerly Roman Catholics, as "Artrochy" was one of the houses of call of Father Gilbert Blakhall, who went round the County of Aberdeen in 1637 in spite of the penal laws.[2] In 1644 Spalding notes that "Lieut. James Forbes, son of Camphill, had orders from the Covenanting Committee of Aberdeen to plunder the estates of the good wife of Artrochie, she being ane excommunicat Papist."[3]

Artrochie formed at one time part of the estate of Auchmacoy, after the days of the Setons and the Forbeses.

In 1700 Katherine Ramsay, spouse to Thomas Forbes of Thornton, had sasine on Meikle Artrochie.[4] In 1664 Margaret Jamesone, relict of John Alexander, had had sasine on the town and lands of Meikle Artrochie; she was the daughter of the famous artist, George Jamesone, and her son, John, and her grandson, Cosmo, were also well-known painters.

In 1724 George Forbes of Artrochie was a Fiar's Juror.

Little Artrochie was liferented by two widows, one of Hugh McGhie, and the other of Alexander McGhie, his son, but in 1702 William Hay of Balbithan had sasine of these lands.

BIRNESS—D.

Robert Cumming (son of Alexander, 1st of Birness), with Jean Gordon, his lady, was there in 1696, with John and Elizabeth, their children. Elizabeth married in 1715 Alexander Gordon of Logie. A later child, Barbara, born in 1711, married, in 1731, James Gordon of Hilton, who represented the family of Straloch, and their son became eventually John Gordon-Cumming-Skene of Pitlurg. Robert and Jean had one other daughter, Mary, who married Alexander Fraser, younger of Powis.[5] By the second wife, Mary Skene, there were two others, Anna and Margaret.

RAINISTOUN (now RANNIESTON).

Seton of Rainystoun in 1688. By 1696 this property was in the hands of John Gordon, younger of Fechil (see Parish of Ellon), but the freeholder of 1690 was "Maitland of Raineston."[6]

[1] *Aberdeen Sasines.*   [2] *Blakhall's Brief narration.*   [3] *Trubles*, vol. ii, 322.
[4] *Aberdeen Sasines.*   [5] *Powis Papers.*   [6] Kennedy's *Annals of Aberdeen.*

In the early 18th century these lands were the property of Arthur Dingwall (of the family of Brucklay) and Laird of Brownhill, and were inherited by his son, John, the famous founder of the stocking manufacture of Aberdeen—(see Parish of Monquhitter).[1]

TURNERHALL, FOR MORTIFIED LANDS—see above.

PARISH OF ELLON.

EARL OF ERROLL—see PARISH OF CRUDEN.

EARL OF ABERDEEN—*D*—see PARISH OF METHLICK.

DRUMWHYNLE—*D* (NOW DRUMWHINDLE). [John Gordon.]

That is that the Earl of Aberdeen paid this double Cess for the owner of Drumwhynle.

In the *Poll Book* this place is written "Droumquickmelne," and the owner is not given. In the special service of heirs, under date 12th January, 1677, Jean Barclay, daughter of William Barclay of Auchreddie, is served nearest heir to Patrick Barclay, her grand uncle, in the town and lands of Auchredie in the parish of Ellon, barony of "Drumqhyndle," held in chief of the Laird of Towie in free blanch for yearly payment of one penny.[2] But 35 years later the lands had passed into the hands of Gordons. On 19th December, 1712, John Gordon "of Drumquhynle" was served heir to his father, Alexander Gordon "of Drumquhynle in Drumquhynle in Aberdeenshire," and portions of the muir of Coldhome in Banff.[3]

ARNAGE—UNLIFERENTED.

David Rickart, with his wife and son, and John Rickart, his brother.[4] He had a Tailzie of the Lands of Cotton and others, 17th August, 1706.

LIFERENTED LANDS OF ARNAGE.

TURNERHALL. [Ditto, for Unmortified Lands.]

In addition to what has been already stated (Parish of Logie-Buchan), a deed of renunciation is found in the particular register of sasines concerning money lent to Robert Turner of Turnerhall by Duncan Sievewright, who bought up so many small properties in Crathie and neighbourhood.

Robert Turner had also at the time a sasine on Drumachie.

[1] *Family of Dingwall-Fordyce.*
[2] In 1672 Margaret Donaldson had sasine on "Drumquhyndle."
[3] *Service of Heirs.*   [4] *Poll Book.*

COLDWELLS—*D*—UNLIFERENTED AND LIFERENTED.

Alexander Gordon, who succeeded in 1684, was of Coldwells in 1696 with his wife and two sons—Alexander and John, and two daughters— Jane and Margaret. Mary Lunan, wife of the above Alexander, had, on 25th September, 1711, sasine for her liferent.

Alexander had to pay double Cess on his own portion and single on hers.

The family of Coldwells descended from the Gordons of Nethermuir.

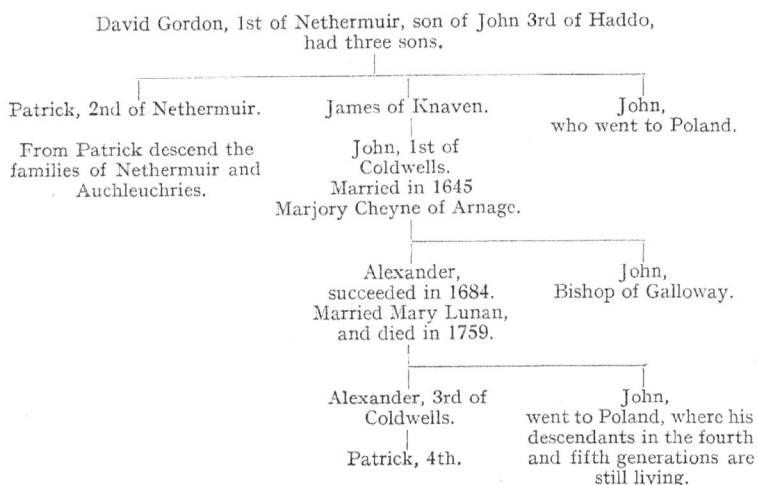

David Gordon, 1st of Nethermuir, son of John 3rd of Haddo, had three sons.

Patrick, 2nd of Nethermuir.	James of Knaven.	John, who went to Poland.
From Patrick descend the families of Nethermuir and Auchleuchries.	John, 1st of Coldwells. Married in 1645 Marjory Cheyne of Arnage.	

Alexander, succeeded in 1684. Married Mary Lunan, and died in 1759.	John, Bishop of Galloway.

Alexander, 3rd of Coldwells. Patrick, 4th.	John, went to Poland, where his descendants in the fourth and fifth generations are still living.

FORTRIE—LIFERENTED.   [Alexander Irvine of Fortrie.]

His son, the Rev. William, born about 1660 at Fortrie, was an ardent Jacobite. Fought at Killiecrankie, where he was taken prisoner, but escaped and went with Lord Dunfermline to France. Returned before the Rising of 1715, in which he took part, and Robert Patten, in his *History of the Late Rebellion*, narrates that Mr. William Irvine, a Scots Clergyman and Non-Juror, preached to the Troops at Kelso on Sunday 25th October the same sermon he had formerly preached "in the Highlands of Scotland to the Lord Viscount Dundee and his men when they were in arms against King William, a little before the battle of Gilley-cranky." [1]   William Irvine was taken prisoner for the second time at Preston and taken to the Fleet prison in London, but he again escaped.

He was consecrated Bishop in 1718 and died 1730.   A manuscript formerly at Slains Castle described him as "of rough and fiery temper."

[1] Patten's *History*, ed. 1717, p. 40.

DUDWICK. [Lady Auchterellon.]

John Fullarton (originally Udny) of Dudwick, second son of Robert Udny of Auchterellon (who died January, 1708) and his wife, Elizabeth Fullarton, only daughter of Colonel John Fullarton of Dudwick, took the name of Fullarton when he succeeded his grandfather in Dudwick. He married Mary, daughter of Sir David Falconer of Newton, Lord President of the Court of Session, and had a son, John, who was a Jacobite of the '45; Robert, who became a General in the service of the Empress of Russia; and three daughters. One was Agnes, who married John Forbes of Boyndlie (Middle Boyndlie, and *not* the compiler of the Cess Book).

John Fullarton took up arms for the Chevalier, though his name does not occur in connection with any of the actions. He is known to have "escaped from Banff in a ship loaded with meal for Norway on April 8th 1716" in company with his neighbours and friends, "Cumine of Pitullie, Stoneywood, elder and younger, Moir of Invernettie, Moir of Scotstown, and others." There is also some curious evidence given against him by John Patten, the Historian of the Rebellion. He stated "that the Defendant, John Fullerton (*sic*) had told him (Patten) that he was glad to see him concerned with the Earl of Mar before the battle of Sheriffmoor. That he (Patten) saw the Defend[t] at Lord Marr's lodgings talking with the Earl of Strathmore. That he saw him several times in a Highland habit. That he used to keep company with the Rebells, and that he saw him, with broad sword and pistol marching at the head of his Regiment."[1]

On 10th July, 1716, John Fullarton wrote to Mar from Paris : "Having escaped to Hamburg about 2 months ago, I came here yesterday, thinking to have gone to Avignon, but being informed that none go there without being called, I wait here for your orders. Had I lost my life as well as my fortune they both had been well spent, nor have I any regret for what has happened but only for his Majesty's disappointment."[2]

The Kirk Session of Ellon appears to have advanced him some money for his expenses, as a year later, May, 1717, his creditors met and the Session compounded for two-thirds of the sum as "the Laird still owed the principal with some arrears of interest."[3]

The Lady Auchterellon is, of course, his mother, Elizabeth Fullarton, Mrs. Udny; his father having died in 1708.

FECHILL.

John Gordon of Fechil, the second son of Robert Gordon, "the Great Straloch," died in 1698, aged 87. His son, John Gordon of Fechil, had

[1] *S.P.* 35.7.75. [2] *Stuart Papers.* [3] *Kirk Session Records.*

sasine on 3rd March, 1703.[1] He married (1) Rachel Sandilands, and (2) Jean Maitland. He died in 1730 (March 24th) but was predeceased by his only son, Dr. James Gordon, in whose favour he had resigned Fechil on the marriage of James with Anne, daughter of William Cumine of Pitullie, in 1711, for James writes: "My father hath denuded himself of the lands of Fechil in my favour, and renounced any rights of Fechil or power he had of redeeming me out of the same." [2]

Dr. James Gordon married (2) Margaret, daughter of James Baird, younger of Auchmedden. He died in 1723 and she in 1742.

The Wills of both are in the Commissariot of Aberdeen.

After the death of Dr. James, John Gordon resumed possession of Fechil.

WATERTOUN—see PARISH OF UDNY.

LAIRD OF ELLON.

The family of Gordon of Ellon descend from Alexander Gordon, a farmer in Bourtie in the year 1667, whose son, James Gordon, a merchant in Edinburgh, bought the property of Ellon from the Laird of Kermuck. He married Elizabeth Livingstone and died in 1732.

His son, James, succeeded as second of Ellon. The two younger brothers, John and Alexander, were murdered by their tutor in Edinburgh in 1717. The great grandson of James was Lord Balfour of Whittinghame.

"On 11th February, 1717 a Precept of sasine was granted by Sir William Keith of Ludquharn and William Keith younger, heritable proprietor of the lands under-written to *James* Gordon of Ellon, merchant in Edinburgh, of the lands of Boddom in Peterhead. Sic subscribitur. W. Keith, Will Keith Junior. Ja. Keith, witness, etc."

The grantors were Sir William Keith, 3rd Bart., and his son, the 4th Bart. (see page 146). This precept was apparently originally drawn up on 9th August, 1708.[3]

On 1st September, 1712, *James* Gordon of Ellon had sasine on Muirtack. (*Aberdeen Sasines.*)

"On 10th October 1715 Colonel Hay and Dr. Abercrombie sent ane expresse for James Gordon of Ellon who came immediately to them" at Aberdeen—they having come from the Camp at Perth.[4] He was therefore a Jacobite !

---

[1] In 1704 Marjorie, daughter of John Gordon, 2nd of Fechil, married John Rickart of Auchnacant.

[2] *Fordyce MS.*, quoted by J. M. Bulloch.

[3] *Aberdeen Sasines.*   [4] *Analecta Scotica*, vol. ii, p. 235.

PRESBYTERY OF TURRIFF.

PARISH OF FYVIE.

LORDSHIP OF FYVIE.

James, 4th Lord Fyvie and 4th Lord Dunfermline, who fought at Killiecrankie, was outlawed, and died at St. Germains in 1694, when the title became extinct and the estates forfeited to the Crown. Fyvie was purchased in 1726 by Lord Aberdeen.

It is not quite clear who can have been paying for the Lordship of Fyvie in 1715, it is entered as a single Cess ; in 1696, although the Earl was already dead, the valuation appears in *his* name in the *Poll Book*. His estate was then valued at £2,000.[1]

COWHILL AND KIRKTOUN AND HALF OF ARDLOGIE.

Cowhill and Ardlogie belonged later to Gight.

GIGHT AND MAINS OF ARDLOGIE.

The owner of all this in 1715 was Alexander Davidson of Newton, who had married, in 1701, Marie, only child and heiress of George Gordon, 9th of Gight, and his wife, Dame Elizabeth Urquhart of Meldrum, and eventually took the name of Gordon. His eldest surviving son, Alexander, 11th Laird, born 1710, married Margaret, one of the 36 children of Patrick Duff of Craigston, and their son, George, was the 12th Laird— the 13th and last Gordon who owned Gight being George's daughter, Catherine, who married Captain John Byron and was mother of the poet.

TOLQUHON (*Seq.*)—see TARVES.

TOWIE—see AUCHTERLESS.

MONKSHILL—*D*.

This estate belonged in 1715 to Alexander Dunbar, who had been in 1700 served heir to his father, Robert Dunbar, in this property. Alexander's mother was Marjorie Leslie of Chapelton, and she appears in the *Poll Book* of 1696 as "relict of Robert Dunbar" ; she was then residing at Monkshill with her son, Alexander, two daughters, Anna and Mary, and two female servants. A memorial panel to her and her husband is in Fyvie Parish Church ; it bears a coat of arms with the date 1671 and

---

[1] From an extract from a letter from Captain Straiton to the Earl of Mar in 1718 it appears that some relative of the 4th Earl bore the title in Jacobite circles. He says : "Lord Dunfermline is in so hard circumstances and his case among the most favourable that I could not well decline to represent it."

initials R.D. and M.L.   The estate of the "Airs of Robert Dunbar" was valued at £80 in 1696.

Alexander Dunbar married Elizabeth Smith, daughter of William Smith, Mill of Tiftie, and sister of "Tiftie's Annie," whose real name was Agnes Smith.

Alexander Dunbar and Elizabeth Smith had sasine on Monkshill, 5th May, 1711.   An assignation of some moneys to Alexander Dunbar of Monkshill by John Urquhart is in the charter chest at Meldrum.[1]

Monkshill was originally part of the Priory of Fyvie, the superior of which was the Abbey of Arbroath.   Alexander Dunbar was of Monkshill, 1700–1735.   In 1702 he had a precept of Clare Constat from George Gordon of Gight, by which the lands were redeemable by Gordon for 3,000 merks, but Dunbar's son was served heir and the wadset not redeemed by the Gordons till after that date. [2]

On 23rd August, 1710, Mr. Wm. Smith, Regent of Marischal College, had an arent on Monkshill.[3]

LITTLE FOLLA.

The Leslies of Little Folla were descended from the Leslies of Wardes and Warthill.   The third Laird of Warthill, William Leslie, bought the lands of Little Folla in Fyvie from " Gordon of Tilliechoudie," and left them to his second son, William, whose descendants enjoyed them for six generations and then, in 1799, succeeded to the estates of the parent stem—Warthill.

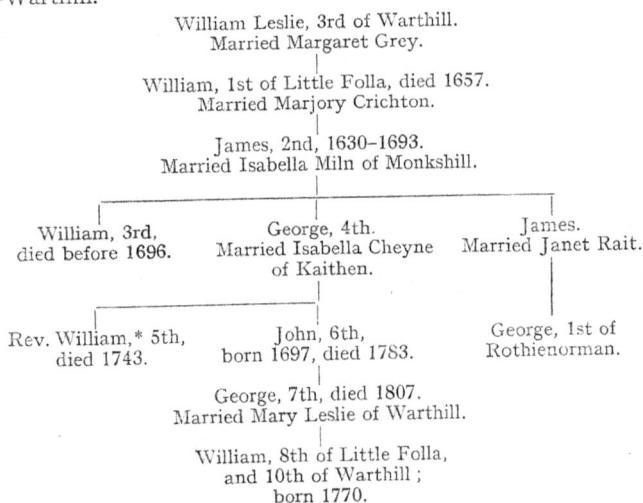

William Leslie, 3rd of Warthill.
Married Margaret Grey.

William, 1st of Little Folla, died 1657.
Married Marjory Crichton.

James, 2nd, 1630–1693.
Married Isabella Miln of Monkshill.

| William, 3rd, died before 1696. | George, 4th. Married Isabella Cheyne of Kaithen. | James. Married Janet Rait. |

| Rev. William,* 5th, died 1743. | John, 6th, born 1697, died 1783. | George, 1st of Rothienorman. |

George, 7th, died 1807.
Married Mary Leslie of Warthill.

William, 8th of Little Folla,
and 10th of Warthill ;
born 1770.

The owner appearing in the Cess Roll is shown by an asterisk.

[1] *Meldrum Papers.* [2] Temple's *Thanage of Fermareyn*, p. 79.
[3] *Aberdeen Sasines.*

The owner in 1715 was thus the Rev. William Leslie, eldest son of George Leslie, 4th Laird of Little Folla, and his wife, Isabella, daughter of William Cheyne of Kaithen. William Leslie was for some time schoolmaster at Auchterless, but went to Ireland to assist his uncle, who held the living of Aquareagh in County Fermanagh. On his return he was ordained in the Scottish Episcopal Church and became in 1710 pastor of Ellon till 1713, when the Rev. J. Burnett was appointed ; Leslie's adherents built a meeting-house near, where he continued to officiate till it was burnt in 1715. After the Rising was over he settled down in his own house of Little Folla, and ministered to the Episcopal congregation till his death, 31st July, 1743, in his 64th year. He was succeeded by his brother, John, as 6th Laird. This brother was born subsequent to 1696, for the entry in the *Poll Book* of that date is "George Lesley, heretor and gentleman, lives on his own land of his own labouring with Isobel Cheyne, his spouse, and William, Agnes, Jannet and Margaret Leslies their children, all under 16 years of age."

Mieckle Folla—*D*.

The Rait family were portioners of Mickle Folla in 1696. The owners in 1715 were Hanoverians. Janet Rait, daughter of John Rait, portioner of Mickle Folla, was wife of James Leslie, third son of James Leslie, 2nd Laird of Little Folla, and mother of George Leslie, who bought Rothienorman in 1723.

Blackfoord.

Alexander Gellie was of Blackfoord in 1696 and Alexander Forbes in 1715. He had married Helen Gellie, heiress of Blackford ; her mother, Margaret Gordon, relict of Alex. Gellie, had sasine for liferent on 3rd July, 1714. John Forbes of "Auquhortis in Tarves" was at the same time "Pror" for "Alexander Forbes of Blackfoord." [1] Hellen Gellie was relict of Alexander Forbes in 1719.[2]

Jackstown.

Mr. Thomas Alexander in 1696.

Margaret Alexander, wife of Mr. Thomas Alexander, Minister of the Gospel in Coldstone, had sasine of liferent, 28th February, 1710.[3]

Laird of Meldrum—*D*—see Parish of Meldrum.

Crichie.

William Grant of Crichie in 1696, with "Katharine Gordon, his spouse, William, James and Lodwick Grants, his sons, and Anna, his daughter."

---

[1] *Aberdeen Sasines.*   [2] *Pitcaple Papers.*   [3] *Aberdeen Sasines.*

Crichie was formerly in the hands of the Urquharts of Meldrum, but by 1690 "Grant of Crichie" appears among the freeholders of Aberdeenshire.[1] He was the son of William Grant of Conglas and Elizabeth Leslie of Balquhain (see page 91).

SAVOCH AND BOGHEADS—*D.*

Part of the lands belonging to Lethenty in this Parish.

WARTLE, FOR MIDAPLE—*D.*

The heritable possessor of "Miduple" in 1696 was Sophia Rait, with whom was "Magdalen Bryson her mother";[2] the superiority belonged to Wartle. On 14th July, 1709, Alexander Leslie of Wartle had "a writ out of the lairds of Kinbroom and Rothienorman."[3] But on 29th July, 1714, James Gordon, elder and younger of Rothienorman, had sasine.[4] This was Gordon of Badenscoth (see Parish of Auchterless).

LAW[5] FOR TERPERSIE'S VALUATION—see PARISH OF KEIG.

PARISH OF DRUMBLADE.

LESMORE—see RHYNIE.

LESSENDRUM.

James Bisset. In 1696 it was "Robert Bisset of Lessendrum, Alexander and James his sons, Anne, Jean and Margaret, his daughters, all under 16 years of age." Alexander, the elder son, died during the lifetime of his father, and James, the second son, succeeded. His mother was Agnes Abercromby of Birkenbog, who was married to Robert Bisset in 1681. James himself married Anne Dun of Tarty, and had a son, Robert, who died young; Alexander, who succeeded him, and six daughters, of whom *four* in turn owned Lessendrum.

James Bisset signed the roll of heritors of Aberdeenshire, 2nd April, 1700. He was on the Jacobite Council in Aberdeen in 1715,[6] and owing to his activities in the Rising was obliged to go abroad. A license to return to Great Britain in 1718, obtained for him and Alexander Irvine of Drum by the good offices of the 2nd Duke of Gordon, formerly Marquis of Huntly, has been given under Irvine of Drum.[7] Even after the Act of Indemnity of 1717 it was not safe for any known Jacobite to return to Great Britain

---

[1] Kennedy's *Annals of Aberdeen.* [2] *Poll Book.*

[3] *Aberdeen Sasines.* [4] *Ibid.*

[5] "Law" was John Gordon of Law and Wardhouse, who seems to have acted as a sub-collector.

[6] Allardyce, *Jacobite Papers*, vol. i, pp. 42, 51. [7] See page 32.

without a "license"; those who had been "overseas" being specially exempted from the Act.

James Bisset returned to Lessendrum and resided there quietly. In the Rising of the '45 he was more cautious, and seems merely to have been friendly to those who did "rise." He died in 1748.

CAMALEGY.

Following on the Lyons, there were Leslies of Camalegy early in the 17th century, before it was joined to Drumdollo. John Gordon of Pitlurg also owned part of it. In 1667 Alexander Anderson had been of Camalegy, and was succeeded by his son, George Anderson.

By 1715 it appears to have been sold in two portions. It is now part of the Lessendrum estate.

MINISTER OF RAINY (RHYNIE), FOR HALF CAMALEGY.

The Rev. James Gordon, who had been presented to the Charge in 1680.

He was deposed 30th May, 1716, for supporting the Jacobite cause.

He was the Laird of Chapelton, Drumblade, and appears in the *Poll Book*, 1696, with Christian Hacket, life rentrix, presumably his wife, three daughters, two house servants, and twenty-six tenants !

DRUMMUIRS HALF OF CAMALEGIE—*D.*

Alexander Duff of Drummuir, who was eldest son of William Duff, Provost of Inverness (William being the third son of Adam of Clunybeg, and brother of Alexander of Keithmore, who was ancestor of the Earls of Fife). William Duff was a merchant in Inverness, and as Baird, the early historian of the Duff family, says—"Made a great fortune with a fair"—that is unblemished—"character." He was Provost at the time of the taking of Inverness by Mackintosh of Borlum in 1715, and a declaration by him and his Town Council is still in the Record Office in which he says—"Wee are in no capacity to make the least opposition and if wee should draw the blood of one of them wee may expect our town to be burnt in a minute thereafter." [1] He died in the end of 1715, so had no occasion further to declare what he felt to be dangerous sympathy for the ruling House of Hanover.

His son, Alexander, married, in 1684, Katherine, the eldest daughter of the bankrupt Adam Duff of Drummuir, whose estate Alexander had acquired two years before, with the proceeds of the merchant business in which he had been engaged with his father. At the time of the marriage Alexander Duff was 27 and his bride, Katherine Duff, 15. They had a large family, of whom Anne, the eldest daughter, married Lachlan, 20th

[1] *S.P.* 54.8.57.

Laird of Mackintosh, who was in the Rising of 1715, made prisoner, condemned, and pardoned. She it was who entertained first Prince Charles and afterwards the Duke of Cumberland in her house in Inverness in April, 1746.[1]

Another daughter, Mary, married (1) Sir William Gordon, 7th Baronet of Lesmoir, and (2) Arthur Gordon of Carnousie.

Alexander Duff of Drummuir paid double Cess, thus showing clearly where *his* sympathies lay.

DALMUIE—*D*.

Also a double Cess. This name is sometimes written "Dumuoy," and "Dumuie." In the *Poll Book* the entry is "Westerton's lands of Dumuoy." In 1715 it was part of the lands belonging to Drummuir in this Parish.

COCKLARACHY. [James Gordon, 6th Laird.]

In 1696 it was John Gordon of Cocklarachie, with his wife, his sister Janet, George, Alexander, and James, his sons; Christian, Anne, and Isabel, his daughters—all under 16.

In 1715 it was his third son, James, 6th Laird, John Gordon having died in 1714, and George and Alexander predeceased him.

The wife of John, and mother of James, 6th Laird, was Anna, daughter of Sir James Baird of Auchmedden.[2]

PARISH OF KING EDWARD.

MOUNTCOFFER. [Alexander Russell of Montcoffer.]

These lands, which had been disponed by Sir Alexander Urquhart of Dunlugas (brother to Sir Thomas of Cromarty) to John Kinnaird and his wife, Violet Abercromby (she being daughter to George Abercromby of Birkenbog, and afterwards marrying Robert Grant of Dunlugas, formerly of Dalvey), were, in 1691 a subject of dispute between the heirs of Violet Abercromby and the heirs of Sir Colin Campbell of Lundie, who had given 10,000 merks for them, the right of Birkenbog to sell them being questioned. About this period, or shortly after, Patrick Russell bought the estate. Dr. Cramond gives the date as 1690, but that must be a mistake, as Russell's

---

[1] The famous "Colonel Anne" of the '45, wife of the 21st Laird of Mackintosh, was daughter-in-law of the above Anne Duff. She was born a Farquharson of Invercauld. Her husband was on the Government side.

[2] *Family of Baird.*

name is not mentioned in the MS. account of the disputes, in the Forglen charter chest, which is very curious. [1]

[1] At Banff, 6 May 1691 anent a Commission granted by Lords of Council and Session dated 9 Jan. at instance of Walter Kinnaird eldest lawful son to deceased John Kinnaird of Montcoffer and appt. heir to him, giving full power to Wm. Forbes of Tulloch, Alex. Duff of Braco and Robert Stewart of Inverchatt to take depositions at Banff concerning the custody of the writs.—compeared Sir Harie Guthrie of Kinedward, who deponed there was a heritable dispon. of Montcoffer, granted by decd. Sir Alex. Abercrombie of Birkenbog with consent of Sir Alex. Urquhart of Cromartie, to the said umquhile John Kinnaird and Violet Abercrombie, his spouse, and their heirs dated 27 July 1667. He declared that he has an oblin. granted him by sd. John Kinnaird mentioning the date thereof, and declared that sd. John Kinnaird died in possession of sd. lands, and that said Violet Abercrombie his relict, having been married to Robert Grant of Dalvey thereafter, did possess these lands as her jointure, and that James Kinnaird, brother to said John was entered factor thereto by Birkenbog.

Being asked what became of said disposin., he declared that he being with Mr. John Abercrombie of Glassaugh at his own house in Badintoull he did ask him for the sd. disposin. because it was clogged with some conditions in favour of his predecessor the Laird of Cromartie and he declared that he did see it burnt at the "Boatt of the Bogge" and promised that whenever he should be put to it, that he would give his oath before any judge that he did really see it burnt. And being asked what he knew of the selling of these lands : he declared that Mr. Robert Meldrum told him that he had offered £8,000 for said lands of Montcoffer, Corskie, and Inverichtnie, whereas the same were thereafter disponed by Birkenbog to the decd. Colin Campbell of Lundie for 10,000 marks as he was informed, and as to Papers, he declared that he knew the Lady Birkenbog had some relating to the bargaining of sd. lands, of which he had the doubles of some of them.

(Signed by Deponent and Commissioners.)

Compeared Robert Grant of Dunlugas and deponed that he knew nothing of the said disposin. except from hearsay, and that he married the sd. John Kinnaird's relict, and knew him in the possn. of the forenamed lands in his lifetime, and that he possessed the same as the relict's jointure, as long as she lived, and after her death, he knew James Kinnaird, her first Husband's brother possessed them, and as factor gathered up the rents. As to the sale to Colin Campbell of Lundie, he knew no more than the common report of the country.

(Signed by deponent and commissioners.)

At Auchmedden, 7 May 1691, the sd. Robert Stewart, one of the Commissioners went personally to Auchmedden because Sir James Baird of Auchmedden was not in a capacity to travel from his house and there examined the sd. Sir James on the matter.—Sir James deponed that he heard (although he never saw the disposin.) that Sir Alex. Abercrombie of Birkenbog with consent of Sir Alexr. Urquhart of Cromartie did dispone the sd. lands of Montcoffer, Corskie, and Inverichtnie to John Kinnaird — and that when Birkenbog and Mr Abercrombie of Glassaugh were about the settling of these lands to Colin Campbell of Lundie, he did forbid the sale and told them he wondered how they could presume to sell a minor's land and that they wd. find it a "black work" thereafter, — he only expostulated with Mr. John Abercrombie and thereafter concerned himself no more with that affair, except

Papers in the possession of Sidney Russell, Esq., of Aden, show that Patrick Russell became possessed of Inverichnie in 1680, and of Mont-coffer in 1696.

Patrick was the second son of Alexander Russell, Provost of Elgin. He married, first, Catherine Sharp, sister of the famous Archbishop of St. Andrews, and secondly, another Catherine, daughter and co-heiress of Sir Colin Campbell, above mentioned, and his wife, Helen Abercromby, daughter of Mr. John Abercromby of Glassaugh, who acted as factor for Birkenbog as well as for Drummuir. Russell's possession was confirmed, and he gave the estate, 8th September, 1708, to his son, Alexander, by his second wife. Patrick died in 1713; his Will is in the Commissariot of Aberdeen. Alexander married Catherine, daughter of Alexander, 15th Laird of Skene, and of Giles Adie, his wife; Catherine subsequently married Dr. Fotheringham.

Alexander Russell died in 1733 and was succeeded by his son, another Alexander, who married, in 1747, Peggy (Margaret), sister to Andrew Hay of Rannes. He sold Montcoffer in 1755 to William Duff of Braco, and his great-great-grandson is now the Laird of Aden. The son of the Alexander Russell who sold Montcoffer married, in 1792, the daughter of James Cumine of Kininmonth.

that he did inhibit Birkenbog, (whom he called a simple man) to meddle with the affair. As to the writs he knew nothing except the common report of the country.
(Signed by deponent and commissioner.)

At Banff 8 May 1691 compeared before sd. Robert Stewart, Dame Elizabeth Baird, relict of the sd. decd. Sir Alex. Abercrombie of Birkenbog, and deponed that she knows of only two Bonds granted by Thos. and Alex. Kinnaird, elder and younger of Culbin to the decd. Sir Alex. Abercrombie of Birkenbog, which she delivered to Sir James Abercrombie of Birkenbog her son.
(Signed by deponent and commissioner.)

Same day at Banff, compeared Sir James Abercrombie of Birkenbog, and deponed that he knows nothing except the Bonds which he received from his Mother, which he will deliver to Sir James Ogilvie, Advocate.
(Signed by deponent and commissioner.)

And Mr. Patrick Ogilvie of Pettibringain, son to Earl of Findlater and present husband to sd. Dame Elizabeth Baird, deponed that he knows nothing except by report.
(Signed by deponent and commissioner.)

" Sir Colin Campbell of Lundy in Angus son and heir of the Hon. Colin Campbell of Lundy which Colin was 2nd son of Colin 6th Earl of Argyll—served heir to his father 15 May 1619 and created a Baronet 13 Dec. 1627.

" Sir Colin Campbell son or grandson and heir appears to have succeeded to the Baronetcy and to have died without male heirs before 1696 when the title became dormant and vested in the Earls now Dukes of Argyll.

Catherine his eldest daughter and co-heir married in 1696 Alexander Russell of Moncoffer."—G.E.C. Complete Baronetage.

Alexander Russell,
purchased property in Moray in 1600 ;
died 1645. Provost of Elgin.

He had three sons, the second was Patrick,
who before 1630 had married
(1) Catherine, sister of James Sharp, Archbishop
of St. Andrews.
He married (2) Catherine, eldest daughter and co-heiress of
Sir Colin Campbell of Lundie and Helen,
daughter of John Abercrombie of Glassaugh.

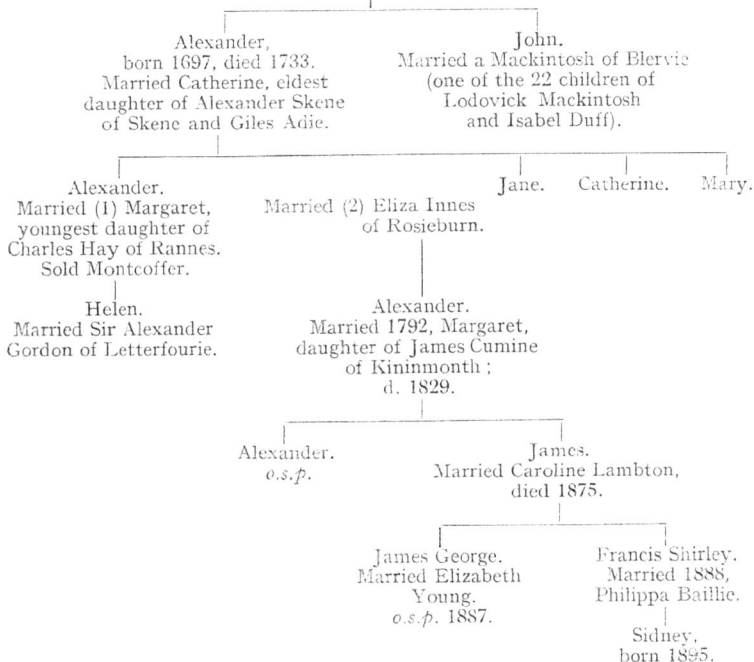

Alexander, born 1697, died 1733. Married Catherine, eldest daughter of Alexander Skene of Skene and Giles Adie.	John. Married a Mackintosh of Blervie (one of the 22 children of Lodovick Mackintosh and Isabel Duff).

Alexander. Married (1) Margaret, youngest daughter of Charles Hay of Rannes. Sold Montcoffer.	Married (2) Eliza Innes of Rosieburn.	Jane. Catherine. Mary.

Helen.
Married Sir Alexander
Gordon of Letterfourie.

Alexander.
Married 1792, Margaret,
daughter of James Cumine
of Kininmonth ;
d. 1829.

Alexander. *o.s.p.*	James. Married Caroline Lambton, died 1875.

James George. Married Elizabeth Young. *o.s.p.* 1887.	Francis Shirley. Married 1888, Philippa Baillie.

Sidney,
born 1895.

BALMAD, MORTIFIED TO YE KING'S COLLEGE.

This property, formerly belonging to the Gordons of Balmad, had been sold before 1672 to John Meldrum. In 1696 it belonged to William Cumine, Laird of Auchry, but on 16th July, 1703, it was sold by Sir Patrick Ogilvie of Boyne to "the Managers of the Reidhyth mortification" in connection with King's College, Aberdeen. In the following year, 5th June, 1704, Christian Guthrie, daughter of Sir Harie Guthrie, of King Edward, and wife of William Cumine of Pitullie, had sasine on part of these lands.[1]

[1] *Aberdeen Sasines.*

BRACCO, FOR IDEN. [William Duff of Braco—see PARISH OF GLASS, STRATHBOGIE.]

He left Eden to his only daughter, Margaret, the wife, first, of Patrick Duff of Premnay (her cousin, and "doer"), and afterwards of Alexander Udny of Udny. The property came eventually through the descendants of William's sister, Helen Gordon, to the late Sir Mountstuart Grant Duff of Eden, by whom it was sold in 1875. William Duff had purchased it from George Leslie, son of Sir Patrick Leslie, Provost of Aberdeen.[1]

BYTH. [James Urquhart.]

In 1696 James Leslie of Byth appears in the *Poll Book* with a wife and three children under 16, and John, his eldest son, "of 16 yeiris." James Leslie only bought the property from Baird of Auchmedden (who had succeeded the Forbeses of Byth) in 1681[2] and sold it again in 1711[3] to James Urquhart, second son of Adam Urquhart of Meldrum, who had been a captain in Dundee's Horse Guards, and his wife Lady Mary Gordon, sister of the first Duke.

James Urquhart was born *circa* 1670. He married Jane Porterfield of Commiston and had a son, James, 2nd of Byth, born 1711, who intended to join the Rising in 1745 but was dissuaded by his cousin of Meldrum. He died unmarried and was succeeded by his brother, Adam, who was gentleman of the bedchamber to Prince Charles (and "King Charles III"). In his latter days he was known as the "Chevalier Urquhart."

CRAIGSTOWN AND CASTLETOWN—*D.*

In the *Poll Book*, Craigston was the property of the Duke of Gordon (formerly that of John Lyon of Muiresk), but these lands had been purchased in 1705 by Patrick Duff of Castleton, henceforth known as Craigston, third son of Alexander Duff of Keithmore. Patrick Duff was twice married—(1) to Anne Innes, who had 13 children, and (2) to Mary Urquhart, who had 23—36 in all. He was a very successful man, who made a large fortune and was able to leave estates to many of his numerous sons, twelve of whom carried him to his grave. He was always on the side of the Government. He figures very often in the *Particular Register of Sasines*, Aberdeen, as he advanced money to many of the smaller proprietors in his neighbourhood on the security of their estates.[4]

---

[1] Later it was, appropriately, in the hands of a man named Adam, by whom it was sold to the late Sir Richard Nicholson.

[2] In the list of Freeholders of Aberdeenshire in 1690 it was "Leslie of Byth."

[3] On 28th August, 1711, Patrick Russell of Montcoffer advanced money to James Leslie of Byth—this was the year in which Leslie sold the estate.

—Aberdeen Sasines.

[4] On 1st March, 1712, he had sasine on two tenements in Fraserburgh.

23rd April, 1706, Patrick Duff of Castletown and Mary Urquhart, his second spouse, had a new sasine on Craigston.

In 1700 he had had sasine on "Overfulgie" and Moss of Eden, etc.

BLACKTOWN.   [William Forbes.]

Alexander Forbes was of Blackton in 1696, with his wife (who was Isobel Hacket, relict of Alexander Abernethy of Mayen), one son, and one daughter.   This Alexander was the son of Walter Forbes of Blackton and nephew of Arthur Forbes, who was at the "Trot of Turriff" in 1639. His mother, Helen Forbes of Balfluig, in 1696 had a "liferent on Blacktown."   She seems to have survived till 1715; Alexander, her son, until 1720.

Alexander's son, William, born 28th November, 1689 (therefore seven at the date of the *Poll Book*), was a Jacobite of the '15, having, as he stated at his trial, been summoned by his relative, the Earl Marischal, to Perth.   He had been in the British Army under Queen Anne, and on account of his experience was at once appointed to command a company under Lord Panmure.   He was taken at Sheriffmuir and imprisoned at Edinburgh, and subsequently at Carlisle.   He was eventually discharged on signing a declaration not to take up arms for the Stuarts again, and in 1745 he prepared a memorial to Prince Charles, giving the reason for his inability to join the second Rising.   He married on 31st August, 1714, Janet Brodie of Muiresk, sister of Joseph Brodie, and had one daughter. William Forbes survived until 1771.

Blackton was sold in 1725 to William Duff of Dipple, who had succeeded his nephew in Braco.

Helen Forbes, daughter of Alexander Forbes of Blackton, and sister of William, married, on 11th September, 1712, William Keith of Bruxie, in Deer, and had sasine on part of Blackton.   Later in the century, Keith of Bruxie and William Duff, son of William of Dipple, were involved in long feud.[1]

WALKERHILL—LIFERENT.

This very small estate was in 1696 in the hands of "Gilbert Gerard, Heretor thereof."   In the list of freeholders of 1690 appears "Gerard of Walkerhill."[2]

BRACO, FOR FISHERIE—*D*.

Fisherie, formerly the property of the Urquharts, had been granted by Charles II, in 1672, to Sir Henry Guthrie, who had married Barbara Urquhart, daughter of Sir Alexander of Dunlugas.

---

[1] *Duff House Papers.*   [2] Kennedy's *Annals of Aberdeen.*

It was sold to William Duff of Braco before 1715 by Sir John Guthrie, son of Sir Henry. The Complete Baronetage (G.E.C.) states that details are wanting of the creation of the Guthrie baronetcy ; in any case it only lasted three generations. Sir Alexander Guthrie of King Edward was served heir general to his father, Sir John, on 9th February, 1723, and the Will of Sir Alexander of Ludquharn (which estate Sir John had bought) is in the Commissariot, 18th January, 1762.

DUNLUGAS. [Peter Grant.]

Formerly the property of Sir Alexander Urquhart of Dunlugas. Robert Grant, formerly of Dalvey, married Violet Abercromby, widow of John Kinnaird of Dunlugas, and thus became possessed of the estate. Peter was his son, and step-brother to Walter Kinnaird.

TOLQUHON, FOR GAIRNISTOWN.

William Forbes, last of Tolquhon, was evicted by a band of soldiers, at the instance of his creditors in 1718 (see Parish of Tarves) ; but at this period William Forbes had already sold the greater part of his estates. Garniston was an estate of the Forbes' family (*not* that of Tolquhon), but the same purchaser held both in 1715.

BRACO, FOR BRAESIDE AND BOGSIDE.

Charles Gordon in 1696 owned these two small estates. They had been bought before 1715 by William Duff of Braco, or possibly by his father, Alexander, who died 1705, and was, like his brother, Patrick of Craigston, among the earliest of the lesser lairds of the North to amass large landed estates, now all again dispersed.[1]

BRACO, FOR PART OF FISHERIE, as above, but for this part he only pays single Cess.

PARISH OF TURRIFF.

EARL OF ERROLL—see PARISH OF ELLON.

CRAIGSTOWN—*D.* [Patrick Duff—see PARISH OF KING EDWARD.]

MUIRESK.

The owner in 1715 was Joseph Brodie, son of Alexander Brodie of Muiresk, who had been there also in 1696, with "Lilias Forbes (daughter

---

[1] It was Alexander of Braco who, looking at a number of little crofts, with their chimneys smoking in the evening, remarked, "I'll gar a' that reek gae thro' ae lum yet."

of William Forbes of Logie), his lady, and Jean Brodie his daughter."
Alexander Brodie was then said to be "a residenter in the Shire of Moray"
from which county and Nairn his family came, i.e. Brodie of Brodie.
They themselves were Brodies of Mayne, near Elgin, and Andrew Bennett
was the tenant of Muiresk. Joseph Brodie had a sasine from his father,
19th July, 1695; and on 21st April, 1710, he granted sasine to his four
children—"James, Joseph, Alexander, and Mary Brodies," on the lands
of Muiresk and others. His wife was Margaret Hunter. He died before
1727, as on 26th January his son, James, was served heir to him with a
general retour of the estate. Janet, the sister of Joseph Brodie, married
William Forbes of Blackton.

BALQUHOLLY, FOR OLD LANDS AND FOR LEASK'S VALUATION.

Alexander Duff of Hatton owned Balquholly in 1715. In 1696 it
was still in the hands of the Mowats, "Katherine Lauder, relict of the
deceist William Mowat," being there with her son, William, "under 16"
(he could only have been seven years old), who died young, when he was
succeeded by his great-uncle, George Mowat of Hamnave, Shetland,
whose grandson, John, sold the estate to Alexander Duff of Hatton in
1709. He had sasine thereon, 1st October, 1711.[1]

"Harie Gordon of Avachie" was tenant of the Mains of Balquholly
in 1696, he was son of John Gordon.

The valuation of Leask is not explained. In 1696 a Mr. Alexander
Leask of Smiddieseat, in the Parish of Turriff, is reported as being "out
of the kingdom."[2]

WOODEND.

George Wood of Woodend, the owner in 1667, had sold this estate
before 1696 to William Shand, who appears in the *Poll Book* with Elizabeth Simon, his wife, and James, Anna, and Elizabeth, their children.

HEIRS OF PROVOST ROSS.

Provost John Ross of Clochan, Arnage and Colp, Provost of Aberdeen,
died 15th September, 1714, of ague at Amsterdam, aged 50. He had
married, in 1704, Jean, only daughter of Arthur Forbes of Echt, and had
two sons, John and Arthur, and four daughters, of whom Christian,
the second, married Sir Arthur Forbes, 4th Baronet of Craigievar.

TOWIE—see PARISH OF AUCHTERLESS.

The "laird of Rothiemay" already had some rights over this estate
as early as 1696 for Elizabeth Barclay, heiress to her brother, Walter,

---

[1] *Aberdeen Sasines.*   [2] *Poll Book.*

who died before 1684. She married John Gordon of Rothiemay, and he took the name of Barclay.

TOLQUHON, FOR FINTRAY.

The lands of Fintray (Craigfintray) were disponed by John Urquhart of Craigfintray (with consent of Sir Robert Farquhar) in 1657 to John Lyon, and in 1674 John Lyon disponed them to Lord Banff. The position of the Laird of Tolquhon in the matter is unexplained, but before 1715 Forbes of Tolquhon was in pecuniary difficulties, and had parted with much of his estate to others, as shown in the *Register of Deeds*, so at this period the Laird was not a Forbes.

GASK—*D.*

John Forbes of Gask died in 1653, and is buried in Turriff with Isabel Urquhart, his spouse. After that date, the estate belonged to Mr. Arthur Mitchell, Minister of Turriff. In 1696 to the "airs of Mr. William Rires."

In the list of Freeholders of Aberdeen in 1690,[1] it is Ririe, but the name was really Rires; William Rires married Janet Seaton in 1675.

The Laird of Gask is given by the "Northern Diary," printed in *Banffshire Journal*, May 1931, as Mr. Fordyce in 1672.

THE FEUARS OF TURRIFF—pay single.

They included, in 1696, Mr. Arthur Mitchell, minister, late of Gask (above), and his wife, Marjory Lindsay.

LAITHERS.

Meldrum of Laithers. In 1696 it was Gilbert Meldrum, "factor for the laird of Laithers," his relative. The Laird of 1715 was Peter, son of John Meldrum and Jean Duff, Keithmore's daughter.

BALMELLIE (*Sequestrate*).

In the *Poll Book* of 1696 the lands of Balmellie belonged to Lord Banff, to whom Margaret Barclay, the tenant, paid rent.

The estate was bought on 5th February, 1700, by Alexander Garden of Troup, but in 1715 it appears to have been sequestrate, i.e. bankrupt.

PARISH OF MONQUHITTER.

AUCHRY—*D.*

John Cumine or Cumming and his wife, Anna Forbes, who had sasine, 25th January, 1706.

---

[1] Kennedy's *Annals of Aberdeen*, vol. ii, p. 492.

Provost William Cumming of Auchry died in 1707, aged 74. He had had three wives, Isabel Gordon, Jean Sandilands, and Christian Guthrie of King Edward, daughter of Sir Henry Guthrie. He was the largest heritor in the parish of Monquhitter, which was formed out of part of Turriff. He built the church in which he was afterwards buried ; he also owned Pitullie, in the parish of Pitsligo. In 1715 the Laird of Auchry was his son by his first marriage, John Cumine. George, the only son by Christian Guthrie, succeeded to Pitullie (*q.v.*).

In 1696 William Cumine had two other sons, William and Robert (but these must have died young), and five daughters—Margaret, Anna, Maria, Jean, and Barbara.[1]

JOHN BROWN, FOR NETHERASLEED—*D.*

Mr. Adam Brown of Nether Asleed was dead in 1696, and his widow, Marjorie Horne, was in possession, with two brothers (apparently) of the late Adam—"James and Andrew Browns." John was presumably son of one of them.

TOLQUHON, FOR LITTLE AUCHRY.

This had belonged to Thomas Forbes (brother of the Laird of Tolquhon), who died in 1671. His wife was Henrietta Erskine, and he had two sons, William, "the last laird," and Thomas. The estate had passed with Tolquhon from the Forbes family by 1715.

TUCKER—(TOUCHER).

In 1696 Isobel Hay was liferentrix of this estate, with her son, Alexander Grant.

EARL OF ERROL (SLAINES).

MR. ADAM HAY.

Mr. Adam Hay, minister of Monquhitter, had in 1696 the estate of Asleed, of the value of £363 17s. 10d. His wife, whom he married in 1691, was Anna Forbes, daughter of Alexander Forbes of Boyndlie, and their children were John, Andrew, Anna, and Jean. Adam Hay, who died in 1729, bequeathed two Communion Cups to the Parish.

Andrew, the second son, married Christian Cumine ("Lady Asleid"), as appears from a claim made after the '45 by James Hay, W.S., brother to Andrew (born after 1696, as he does not appear in the *Poll Book*), against the forfeiture of the estate by Adam, son of Andrew, who was a

---

[1] In 1673 Elizabeth Morison, spouse of John Gordon, Provost of Banff, had an arent on the lands of Auchry.—*Aberdeen Sasines.*

Jacobite and made prisoner at Culloden. James claimed that the estate fell to him and not to his nephew, and was, therefore, not forfeited. This claim failed. Young Adam was banished and Asleed taken possession of by the barons of the Exchequer. In the Will of Adam Hay of Monquhitter Mr. James Hay, W.S., is mentioned first, but he was the third son. He became a W.S. in 1728, having been apprenticed to Andrew Hay of Mountblairy. He married (1) Anna Farquharson and (2) Agnes Moodie.

Mr. Adam Hay was, with one exception, the last Episcopal minister under the Synod of Aberdeen.

FOVERAN, FOR BACKLANDS OF BALQUHOLLY—D.

Sir Samuel Forbes (Foveran) had purchased a portion of the Mowat estate in this parish. He was a Hanoverian. His eldest son, Alexander, succeeded him (see Parish of Foveran).

THOMAS MOWAT'S WADSET—D.

The holder of this Wadset, a member of the family of Balquholly, who was similarly entered in 1667, is not known. He was a Government adherent.

BROWNHILL.

Arthur Dingwall (eldest son of William Dingwall of Seilscrook and Barbara Barclay) married Lucretia, daughter of John Irvine of Brucklay, in Buchan. They had two sons, the eldest, William, became the progenitor of the family of Dingwall-Fordyce of Brucklay, to which estate he succeeded in 1706. He married Anna Gordon of Nethermuir and died 1733.

Arthur, the second son of William and Lucretia, inherited Brownhill ; he was born 1678 and died 1729. His first wife was Sarah Murray, daughter of the minister of Inverurie, and their fourth son, John Dingwall of Rannieston, in Logie-Buchan, acquired the estate of Ardo about 1750. He was the successful stocking merchant of Aberdeen, and his son, John, one of ten, was Provost of Aberdeen in 1799.

In 1721 Arthur Dingwall married, secondly, Jean Chalmers, daughter of a merchant in Aberdeen.

HAIRMOSS—(HAREMOSS).

James Panton owned this small estate in 1672, and in 1696 he was a *tenant* of the same, the owner being " John Thomsone residenter in Turriff."

It was originally part of the Barony of Delgaty.

The Panton family seems to have resumed possession of the estate, for on 20th December, 1709, Jean and Barbara Panton, daughters of the above James, and their respective husbands, had sasine thereon—James Ross for Jean, and Andrew Mackie for Barbara.

KEATHEN.

John Cheyne, who died 1st April, 1716. He was son of James Cheyne of 1696 (*Poll Book*) and grandson of William Cheyne of 1667 (see page 194).

BALQUHYNACHY.[1]

Part of the estates of Lord Erroll. Once the property of Walter Simpson of Idoch, in 1681 it had belonged to "Dominus Carolus Maitland of Pittrichie, miles baronatus, haeres masculus Domini Ricardi Maitland, junioris fratris,"[2] and in 1697 to Major George Simpson.[3]

In 1696 the *tenant* was Margaret Chalmer.

FOVERAN, FOR GREENS OF ALLATHEN.

John Forbes of Greens, with Jean Collison, his spouse, was the owner in 1696. "Foveran" was Alexander Forbes, eldest son of Sir Samuel, who bought the estate.

PARISH OF AUCHTERLESS.

HATTOUN AND FOR WILLIAM WHITE—*D*.

"Hatton" was Alexander Duff, eldest son of the 36 children of Patrick Duff of Craigston (born in 1688), to whom his father made over the estate of Hatton on his marriage with his cousin, Catherine Duff of Dipple, in 1709. William White was in Newmiln of Auchterless in 1696.[4]

BADENSCOTH.

In 1715 the owner was William Gordon, 3rd of Badenscoth.

George Gordon, 2nd of Badenscoth (son of Patrick of Badenscoth,

---

[1] Balquhynachy. These lands were held in 1699 by Mr. William Hay, parson of Crimond, and his son, William Hay of Crimondmogate. His sasine was witnessed by

> "WILLIAM MELDRUM of Strathwherie,
> ALEX. FARQUHAR of Mounie,
> DAV. RICKART of Arnadge, and
> GEORGE KEITH of Crichie."
>
> *—Pitcaple Papers.*

[2] *Aberdeen Sasines.*   [3] *Ibid.*

[4] William Smith, elder and younger at myln of Tiftie, and Elizabeth Smith, daughter to the said William Smith, younger, had an arent out of the lands of the barony of Hatton, 15 July, 1700.—*Aberdeen Sasines.*

who was fourth son of George Gordon, 2nd of Terpersie), died in 1713. In 1696 he was "of Badenscoth with Helen Keith, his lady; Jean, his daughter; and Alexander, George, and William, his sons."

(George Gordon had a brother, James, who married one of the Moirs of Barnes. See page 71.)

His third son, William, was served heir to him in 1713, married Mary, daughter of William Baird of Auchmedden, and was the father of James Gordon, 4th and last of Badenscoth, whose sisters, Jane and Catherine, inherited the property. Jane married James Leslie of Rothienorman, and Catherine married Alexander Forbes of Blackford. James Leslie bought the share of his sister-in-law and united the properties of Rothienorman and Badenscoth; he was of the family of Little Folla (see page 194).

THE LADY BADENSCOTH.

Either the mother of George Gordon, who was a daughter of Lord Banff, or his wife, Helen Keith, as above.

Alexander, the eldest son of George, known as younger of Badenscoth, died before 1710 without succeeding, as in that year Mrs. Anne Gordon of Coynach appears as his "relict." [1]

LAITHERS.

Peter Meldrum had been of Laithers in 1667 (see Valuation, Parish of Turriff). Later it came into the hands of the Lyons of Muiresk.

BLACKFORD—LIFERENT.

Alexander Gellie in 1696. He was then resident in Aberdeen, with his wife, two sons, John and William, and five daughters, "Rachel, Helen, Margaret, Mary and Jean Gellies." He also owned land in the parish of Fyvie.

The Cess in this case was a liferent to his widow, Margaret Gordon. [2]

Margaret Forbes, the heiress of Blackford in a later generation, married John Leith, a younger son of Rannes and Leith Hall, and was the mother of Lord Leith of Fyvie (see parishes of Oyne and Fyvie).

TEMPLAND (*Sup.*).

This had been a property of the Meldrum family, but subsequently belonged to the Viscount Frendraught, and then to Theodore Morison of Bognie, who sold it in 1719 to Alexander Duff of Hatton.

---

[1] *Aberdeen Sasines.*   [2] *Ibid., 5 May, 1714.*

KIRKTOWNHILL.

The Kirktown of Auchterless was part of the Meldrum's estate of Hatton—the superiority of this portion had apparently not passed to Alexander Duff, as only a single Cess was being demanded.

TOWIE.

The lands and barony of Towie, in Auchterless, belonged at this period to Alexander Innes, 1st Baronet of Coxton. He had married Elizabeth Gordon, daughter of Elizabeth Barclay of Towie, heiress of Towie, and John Gordon of Rothiemay. Elizabeth Gordon's brother, Patrick of Towie and Rothiemay, had, like his parents, assumed the name of Barclay with the estate, but he being mentally deficient, the lands of Towie came to his sister and her husband, Alexander Innes, who was "seized in the lands and Barony of Towie, 24th September, 1713." After the death, without issue, of the wife who brought him the estate, Sir Alexander (who had also taken the name of Barclay) married, secondly, Helen Duff of Crombie, daughter of James Duff and Jean Meldrum. Their second daughter, Isabel, and her husband, the Hon. Charles Maitland of Lauderdale, sold Towie in 1753.

TREE OF BARCLAYS.

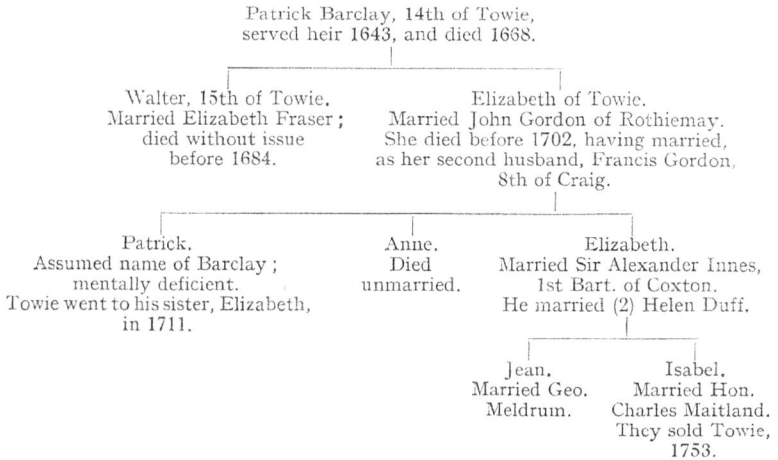

Patrick Barclay, 14th of Towie,
served heir 1643, and died 1668.

Walter, 15th of Towie. Married Elizabeth Fraser ; died without issue before 1684.	Elizabeth of Towie. Married John Gordon of Rothiemay. She died before 1702, having married, as her second husband, Francis Gordon, 8th of Craig.

Patrick. Assumed name of Barclay ; mentally deficient. Towie went to his sister, Elizabeth, in 1711.	Anne. Died unmarried.	Elizabeth. Married Sir Alexander Innes, 1st Bart. of Coxton. He married (2) Helen Duff.

Jean. Married Geo. Meldrum.	Isabel. Married Hon. Charles Maitland. They sold Towie, 1753.

PARISH OF FORGUE.

BOGNY.

This was Theodore Morison, son of George Morison of Bognie, and Christian, widow of Viscount Frendraught, who brought the estates of Frendraught into the family. (The *Complete Peerage* says she also brought the estate of Bognie, but that was previously Morison property.)

Theodore was born in 1685, succeeding his father in 1699, and in 1718 married Katherine, daughter and co-heiress of Sir Charles Maitland of Pitrichie and his wife.[1]

They had Alexander, who succeeded, George of Haddo, and Jane, who married John Forbes-Leith, son of the last Laird of Tolquhon. Theodore had two sisters—Elizabeth, who married a Grant of Grant, and Susanna, who married, in 1704, John Forbes of Upper Boyndlie, the collector of Cess in 1715.

Theodore Morison died on June 4, 1766, and in the obituary notice in the *Aberdeen Journal* of the period it is said that "He lived without an enemy and died without a groan."

BOGNY FOR THREE-QUARTERS OF CONLAND, GEORGE LESLIE OF NORTH LESLY—D. FOR A QUARTER OF CONLAND.

Conland had been disponed in 1625 to Robert Crichton with the consent of Sir James Crichton of Frendraught. In 1707 Lewis Crichton sold the "wadset of the sun plough of the town and lands of Condland to George Leslie of North Leslie" (who paid double Cess for his portion).

The wadsetter of the rest of the lands which had come to Bognie with the Crichton estates, was in 1696 William Davidson. The "sun plough" was afterwards adjudicated to George Ellice for a debt due to him by George Leslie, and Ellice sold it in 1726 to Sir James Gordon of Park. Twelve years after this period, North Leslie had been in prison, presumably for debt, as is shown by the following extracts from a letter to Sir James Gordon of Park from his wife (North Leslie's wife was Helen, Sir James' sister) :—

PARK, 5. June 1727.

North Leslie was taken out of prison Tuesday last, is at Arradoul, but so very ill that I fear she will find it a hard enough taske to keep him. I had a letter from her asking my advice what to do, for she says he is relly worse than when she saw him in Banff and to see if I would advise her to call Doctor Stewart. . . . No doubt Knokorth will write you how he was oblige to pay everything for him att Banff. . . . I have here inclosed what Knockorth thinks his Mother caused draw up at Banff — but I am posietive it has been wrot ere she went there, for it is in my opinion wrott by Westhal own hand.

Horn of Westhall had apparently advanced money here also.

George Leslie of North Leslie had bought a portion of Conland in 1709.

In 1721 George Ellice of Nether-third obtained a decree of adjudication against George Leslie for debt, and the whole estate passed to *him*. He sold it in 1726 to Sir James Gordon, above.

[1] Sir Charles' only son, Charles, died in 1703 without heirs, leaving five sisters (see page 180).

BOGNY, FOR LITTLE FORGUE.

John Watt of Little Forgue had sold his estate before 1696 to George Morison, the father of Theodore.

FRENDRAUGHT.

Lady Christian Urquhart, daughter of Sir Alexander Urquhart of Dunlugas, widow of Lord Rutherford and of the 2nd Viscount Frendraught. Her first husband died in 1668 and her second in 1674. She married, thirdly, George Morison of Bognie, and *after* the death of her son, the 3rd Viscount (as a minor between 1680 and 1686), she conveyed to her third husband (who already owned Bognie) the estate of Frendraught (see previous page).

In 1696 the estate of Frendraught was all liferented by the Viscountess Dowager of Frendraught, the title having passed to her late husband's brother, Lewis, "who obtained from the Privy Council 6 hundred merks of rent for the Mains." Lewis, 4th Viscount, was attained in 1693.[1] George Crichton, a distant kinsman, married the widow of Lewis and assumed the title, but died before 1702. His son and heir, James Crichton, a Jacobite of 1715, is sometimes styled the 6th Viscount.

HEIRS OF THOMAS CUSHNY.

The Glass-worker and Burgess of Aberdeen who married Christian, sister of Dr. William Guild, was dead before 1667. But in 1696 his estate in the Parish of Forgue was still an entity of £350 annual value, of which £210 is stated to belong to the liferent of the Viscountess Dowager of Frendraught, and £140 to James Anderson, glazier in Aberdeen, who may have succeeded to the business of Thomas Cushny. Part of the estate which had belonged to Thomas Cushny was called Auchaber.

CRICHTOWN'S HALF OF COMISTY.

Mr. George Crichton in 1696 was the owner and Alexander Shand the tenant. Probably the father of James Crichton of Auchingoul, and afterwards 6th Viscount ; James Crichton's son was a Jacobite of 1745.

SHAND'S HALF OF COMISTY—see above.

DRUMDOLLO—*D.* [Walter Leslie (as representing John Leslie of Drumdollo in 1715).]

In 1696 the owner was Lachlan Leslie, whose great-grandfather, James Leslie, or an earlier ancestor, was the natural son of a Leslie of Balquhain.

---

[1] It was with *him* that John Duff, messenger, was in arms, when both were taken prisoner at the Castle of Fedderat (see page 29).

James had a son, Walter, who had a son, James, the father or brother of Lachlan. Lachlan's wife was Elizabeth Leslie, and his son, John, the owner in 1715 (who was born before 1696, as he appears in the *Poll Book*) died in 1771, leaving a son, James, who married Margaret, daughter of James Chalmers of Cairnwhelp. Walter was his brother.

On 4th June, 1703, Elizabeth Leslie, spouse of Lachlan Leslie of Drumdollo, had a sasine of liferent. The deed was witnessed by her son, John Leslie.[1]

CORNYHAUGH, FOR ROBERT IRVING.

Robert Irvine, with his wife, three sons and one daughter, was there in 1696. He was son of William Irvine, elder of the Kirk of Forgue in 1663. Robert married Elizabeth, daughter of George Crichton of Auchingoul, father of James, a Roman Catholic, as is already shown in the minutes of the Presbytery of Turriff. Robert died before 1737.

MY LADY FRENDRAUGHT, FOR GLENMELLIN.

The estate of Glenmellin belonged in 1696 to George Morison of Bognie, either as part of his *own* estate or his wife's, and she had sasine on it. Half of it was wadset to John Cruickshank.

In 1719 Theodore Morison sold it to Alexander Duff of Hatton.

DITTO, FOR BOGFONTEIN.

This was wadset in 1696 to William Cruickshank. It was part of the estate of Bognie, and was sold in 1719 by Theodore Morison to Alexander Duff of Hatton.

AUCHINTENDER, which was on the Frendraught estate, was occupied in 1696 by Alexander Morison, gentleman. It was afterwards sold in 1719 to Alexander Duff of Hatton.

PARKDARGUE.[2] [Theodore Morison.]

This was a wadset to John Davidson in 1696. It had been sold by David Gregory to George Morison of Bognie in 1677. At one time this small place had an Episcopal church of its own. Aucharnie, Parkdargue, and Little Forgue were sold by Theodore Morison, son of George, to Alexander Duff of Hatton in 1719, and the lease to William Stuart in Boynsmill continued to his son.

---

[1] *Aberdeen Sasines.*

[2] On 4th January, 1710, Alexander Charles, Advocate, Aberdeen, advanced money on Parkdargue to Theodore Morison.

Alexander Charles, Procurator, was a Jacobite and a prisoner at Carlisle. He also appears to have been a money-lender.

GARRIESFORD, also part of the dominical lands of Frendraught, and included in the sale in 1719 by Theodore Morison of Bognie to Alexander Duff of Hatton.

MONELLIE—WISCHART—*D.*

James Wischart, "sometime of Cowbairdie," owned Monellie in 1696 with Elspet Massie, his spouse, but on 31st March, 1711, Anne Dunbar, spouse to George Cruickshank of Monellie, had sasine. (*Aberdeen Sasines.*) Later it belonged to Thomas Innes of Monellie, who bought it in 1730 from the family of Cruickshank, to whom it had been sold by James Wischart. Thomas Innes also bought Muirs of Fyvie from William Urquhart of Meldrum. Innes was a W.S. and son of Thomas Innes, a younger son of Edingight. His only daughter, Elizabeth, inherited from her uncle, John Innes of Muiryfold, factor to Lord Fife, the estate of Netherdale, obtained in excambion. She married, in 1797, James Rose, eldest son of William Rose, factor to Lord Fife—hence the family of Rose-Innes.[1]

LARGUE AND DRUMBLAIR.

Parts of Frendraught. Largue is now Largie.

NORTHLESSLY—*D.*

As above, George Leslie of North Leslie pays double Cess.

On 19th February, 1706, George Leslie of North Leslie had sasine on the lands "of Balthevy, Garrisfoord," etc., as heir of Alexander Leslie of Boynsmill (his uncle), who appears in the *Poll Book.*[2]

George Leslie of North Leslie was the eldest son of Walter Leslie of Tulloch and Christian, daughter of Alexander Douglas, Sheriff of Banffshire. Walter was the sixth son of Lauchlan Leslie, fourth son of the first Leslie Laird of Rudderie, who was himself a younger son of Alexander Leslie, first Laird of Kininvie, who descended through the Leslies of New Leslie from the family of Balquhain.

George Leslie married, first, Christina Gordon of Aberlour, and secondly, Helen Gordon of Park, and had a son, George.

He inherited from his uncle, Adam, a fortune of £20,000 Scots, but seems to have dissipated the whole.

On the 5th July, 1710, George Leslie of North Leslie and Helen Gordon, his spouse, and Alexander Leslie, their son, had sasine of the lands of North Leslie, a Barony which included Cobairdy, Bogniehead, Todhillock, Broomefold, etc.,[3] but lost it in 1721.

ASCHALLON (ASCHALLOCH).

Part of the lands of Frendraught.

[1] *Family Papers, Rose MSS.*   [2] *Aberdeen Sasines.*   [3] *Ibid.*

PRESBYTERY OF STRATHBOGIE.

PARISH OF DUNBENNAN.

Duke Gordon.

Nearly the whole of the Presbytery of Strathbogie appears in this Cess Roll under the heading of "the Duke of Gordon," and the lesser owners who figured in the Valuation Roll of 1667 have, with few exceptions, become merged in the "superiority of the great landlord."

Many of these lairds, when prisoners after the collapse of the Rising, urged as a plea for pardon the terms on which they held their lands, which included the accompanying of their chief "in hunting and hosting," (one, indeed, forwarded his actual "tack" (lease) to the Secretary of State's office to show that he could not help himself. . . . He was pardoned).[1]

It seems, therefore, quite fair that the Superior who wielded such power should also pay the greater part of the Cess.

The Duke had also large holdings in the neighbouring county of Moray, and a letter from an anonymous spy, now in the Public Record Office, notes in September, 1715, "Huntly (eldest son of the Duke) is gone with all his vassals and following, which is a great many, to joyn Mar, and in his retinue of Gentleman from this county are Sir Robert Gordon, Cluny his curator, Altyre, Sir Thomas Calder, Tannachy, Innes of Dunkindy and many others."[2]

The Duke of Gordon himself, who was suspect as being a Roman Catholic, had been taken prisoner after the abortive attempt at a Jacobite rising in 1708, when the main part of the expedition, under Admiral Claude de Forbin, beat a strategic retreat from the Forth. Three vessels, however, got as far as Speymouth and Buckie, where some of the French officers landed, and according to a laconic message sent by the Laird of

---

[1] This was John Hamilton of Gibston, Strathbogie, who, after his pardon, lived to take part in the Rising of 1745, and be made prisoner at Carlisle. He was again tried and subsequently hanged at Kennington. His spouse was Jean Forbes.

His petition in 1716, enclosing his "tack," is to be found in *S.P.* 35.12.14. For his subsequent history see *Jacobites of Aberdeenshire and Banffshire in the '45.*

Sir Thomas Calder of Muirtown, Morayshire, in his petition to Lord Townshend, 4th December, 1716, encloses Huntly's letter to him, dated Gordon Castle, September 26th, 1715, in which Huntly reminds him that "being my tenant you are bound to attend me at hosting and hunting. I recommend this and what you had formerly in command to your particular care and manadgment, and am your assured friend—Huntly."—*S.P. Entry Book,* 6.87.

[2] *S.P.* 54.9.46.

Reddite Medal, 1708, *rare*.

Obverse. Bust of James.
    Legend. CVIVS EST ("Whose (image) is this?" The King's). Monogram : NR, Norbert Rottier.
Reverse. Map of Great Britain and Ireland, showing the three capitals. The sea is dotted with ships.
    Legend. REDDITE IGITVR ("Render then to the King these islands, which are his").
        (In 1714 several of these medals were distributed among the Jacobites who had assembled at
        Lochmaben under plea of attending the races.)

From the British Museum.

Forglen to Lord Seafield in London, "they dined, paid well and went aboard." The Duke and his son, the Marquis of Huntly, with some others, were sent to London, but liberated not long after. On the outbreak of the Rising of 1715 the Duke was again imprisoned in Edinburgh, being afterwards transferred to the Citadel of Leith, where he died 7th December, 1716, having thus taken no actual part in the Rising.

He was George, 1st Duke of Gordon, 4th Marquis of Huntly, raised to Ducal rank on 1st November, 1684. He had married in 1676 Lady Elizabeth Howard, second daughter of the Duke of Norfolk. The Duchess of Gordon sent on 30th July, 1711, one of James' medals with *Cujus est* and *Reddite* to the Faculty of Advocates in Edinburgh. Of the 75 Advocates present only twelve voted against its acceptance, and the minutes of the meeting were immediately published in London. After Mr. Robert Bennett, the Dean of the Faculty, had proposed that the medal be accepted and thanks returned to the Duchess of Gordon, and Mr. Alexander Stevenson, Mr. Robert Alexander of Black House, and Mr. Duncan Forbes, with one or two more, had, in more or less vehement terms, demanded that it should be rejected, Mr. Dundas of Arniston rose and made the following speech : "Dean of Faculty, whatever these Gentlemen may say of their honour, I think they affront the Queen whom they pretend to honour, in disgracing her brother, who is not only a Prince of the Blood, but the first thereof, and if blood can give any right he is our undoubted sovereign. . . . Medals are the documents of history. . . . But, Dean of Faculty, what need further speeches. None oppose receiving the Medal but a few pitiful scoundrel Vermin and Mushrooms, not worthy our notice. Let us therefore proceed to name some of our number to return our hearty thanks to the Duchess of Gordon."

Dundas himself and Mr. Horn of Westhall were deputed to carry the Faculty's thanks to the Duchess of Gordon, who was at that time living in Flanders apart from her husband.

He was a Roman Catholic and had been a good soldier in foreign wars, but was cautious and anxious not to embroil himself in the politics of Scotland.

He was succeeded by his son, Alexander, who was Marquis of Huntly at the time of the Rising, whose activities his father, the Duke, seems to have made no efforts to control.

Huntly was not one of the earliest nor of the most loyal and consistent of the followers of the Old Chevalier. He was said both by friends and enemies to have been very much chagrined at the fact that the Earl of Mar was at the head of the Rising. Mar assumed this headship sometime before the arrival of his commission from Bar-le-duc, which was brought by James Ogilvie of Boyne on the 3rd of October, and delivered to Mar on the 6th, as he wrote to General Alexander Gordon. An anonymous correspondent says, "Huntly was surprised to see such an appearance for his master." [1]

Huntly's dislike to serving under Mar prevented his joining among the very first, but by 20th September he had decided to throw in his lot with the Jacobite cause and to force all those over whom he had authority to do the same, as the following two letters, among many others, prove :—

GORDON CASTLE, 22nd September 1715.

To the much honoured the Laird of Carnousie.[2]

Sir,

You gave me such assurance of your good wil when I saw you last that I can make no question of it if your health does not allow of yr venturing yr selfe with me, I expect you wil contribute as far as you can, particularly by giving your best hors and all the arms you can spare . . . I expect your company and concurrence as a true Scotchman and Gordon and am

Yr. affec^ate. friend and servant to oblige you

HUNTLY.

—*S.P.*54.12.338.

On 10th January, 1716, to the same :—

I entreat you to be at this place (Gordon Castle) upon Thursday next the 19th Curr. or the day after at the latest. Now we have the wished assurance of his Matie's landing I have reason to expect our numbers will augment, but no ground to fear that you and others who gave evident proof of their zeal to the Prince when matters stood upon a far greater uncertainty, will be slack upon this occasion.

—*S.P.*54.12.357.

According to Rae's History, Huntly joined Mar at Perth on 6th October with 500 horse and 2,000 foot. The Master of Sinclair, whose numbers are likely to be more nearly correct (though he belittles the services of his contemporaries whenever possible), gives them as 160 horse and 1,400 foot. Patten states that "the Duke of Gordon could put in the field 3,000 men, he himself is neutral, but the most of the men go with his son who is against the Government and in the Rebellion." The Master of Sinclair further adds that "after Mar's army marched south from Perth" (i.e. before Sheriffmuir) "two hundred of my Lord Huntlie's best men under the command of Glenbucket, deserted us, as his lordship said, because they had been designedlie more oppressed with dutie than any others."

Argyll, in a letter to Lord Townshend, now in the Public Record Office, says that "Huntly was made prisoner at Sheriffmuir," but escaped. There is, however, no Jacobite corroboration of this statement. He was certainly with Mar in the retreat from Perth.

[1] *S.P.* 54.9.100.

[2] George Gordon of Carnousie was the grandson of Sir John Gordon of Park, being son of his second son, Sir George Gordon of Edinglassie. He was a Banffshire vassal of the Duke of Gordon.

Early in 1716 Lord Huntly, with Lord Rollo and others, made over-
tures to Argyll, and offered categorically to "come over, if he could
assure them they would not be confined." This Argyll, to his own
chagrin, was not authorised to promise, and eventually Huntly surrendered to Lord Lovat on 27th February, 1716, and was imprisoned in
Edinburgh Castle.[1] His mother had made several applications for favour
to be shown to him, to which Argyll replied "that his Lordship has done
nothing as yet which could be made use of as argument for him."[2] He
remained in Edinburgh Castle until August, when the transference of all
prisoners to Carlisle was ordered. General Carpenter wrote to Lord
Townshend on 28th August : "The prisoners are to set out on Monday.
The Marquis of Huntly is still in hopes of an order from the Court for his
release and little expected to be sent or treated like the other prisoners
but I can say nothing in his case of my own knowledge." He forwarded
a letter from Huntly himself, begging for delay in going to Carlisle.[3]
But the order came that "The Marquis of Huntly's father being alive,
he is *not* a Peer, so is to march to Carlisle at which he is extremely mortified,
having daily expected orders to be sett at liberty."[4] He was included
in the third party, which left Edinburgh on 6th September. "After the
prisoners had started, orders came to keep Huntly in Edinburgh Castle,
so General Carpenter's son rode hard after him, and brought him back,"
and General Carpenter says he feels after discourse with Huntly, that
"he both can and will be very serviceable in suppressing the Highland
party with Keppoch and others about Badenoch."[5] Huntly remained
in Edinburgh, whence he was allowed to go to Leith to see his father.
On 27th October Carpenter wrote again that "the Marquis of Huntly
is advysed that his Maj : designs to extend his clemency to him in a
pardon which is passing the proper forms requisite and begs to be granted
his liberty in the meantime."[6] On 6th November Carpenter says : " The
Marquis of Huntly's remission was brought hither on Saturday night
last and on Sunday he was sett at Liberty. After going North he designs
to go to London and kiss H.R.H.'s hands."[7]

On 7th December, 1716, Huntly's father died, when he became 2nd
Duke of Gordon, and effectually made his peace with the Government.
His unfortunate tenants, languishing in Carlisle, confidently hoped
that he would be able to procure pardon for some of them. It proved
to be beyond his power. He sent money to relieve their necessities, and
two years later obtained a "licence" for three of those who had gone
"beyond the seas," viz.—Alexander Irvine of Drum, James Bisset of

---

[1] *S.P.* 54.11. [2] *Ibid.* 54.10.139. [3] *Ibid.* 54.12.135–144.
[4] *Ibid.* 54.12.152. [5] *Ibid.* 160. [6] *Ibid.* 226.
[7] *Ibid.* 232.

Lessendrum, and Robert Gordon of Cluny, to return to Scotland (see page 31).

He had married, in 1706, Lady Henrietta Mordaunt, daughter of the Earl of Peterborough, and died in 1728, leaving four sons—Cosmo, 3rd Duke, who played in 1745 the same cautious part that his grandfather had played in 1715 ; Lord Charles and Lord Adam, who were Hanoverian soldiers; and Lord Lewis, an ardent adherent of Prince Charles Stuart ; as well as seven daughters, of whom Anne married William, 3rd Earl of Aberdeen, Elizabeth married the Rev. John Skelly, and Catherine married Francis, 5th Earl of Wemyss ; while Henrietta, Mary, Jean, and Charlotte died unmarried.

PARISH OF KINOIR.

Duke of Gordon—see above.

Avachie.

Harry Gordon of Avochie, eldest of John Gordon of Avochie, a cadet of Cairnborrow, to whom he was served heir 1687.

His mother was Isobel Farquharson, and his wife was Elizabeth, sister to John Gordon of Glenbucket ; their son, John, being an ardent Jacobite of the '45 and a trusted leader under his famous uncle.

Harry or Hendry Gordon appears in the *Poll Book*, but he must have been young at the time ; his two sisters, Anna, 15 years, and Elizabeth, 12 years, are also mentioned.

William Gordon, gentleman, with two sons, James and William, and two daughters, Penelope and Jean, seemed to have lived at Avochie in 1696, while Henry was tenant of Balquholly.[1]   William was probably uncle to the young Henry.

PARISH OF RUTHEN.

Duke Gordon.

PARISH OF BOTARIE.

Duke Gordon.

PARISH OF GARTLY.

Duke Gordon.

---

[1] *Poll Book.*

PARISH OF RHYNIE, PARISH OF ESSIE.

DUKE GORDON—as above.

LESMORE.

Sir William Gordon, 6th Baronet of Lesmoir, succeeded his grand-father, Sir James Gordon, 5th Baronet, about 1712.

At the date of the *Poll Book*, 1696, Sir James Gordon was in possession with his lady (who was Jean Gordon of Haddo), and five sons—William, George, Alexander, John, and Robert, and three daughters, Anne, Jean, and Margaret. William, the eldest of these sons, married, in 1709, Mary, daughter of Alexander and Katharine Duff of Drummuir (the *Complete Peerage* calls this lady, Margaret, but her marriage contract at Drummuir gives her name as Mary). In this contract, dated 22nd November, 1709, Sir James Gordon dispones to his eldest son, William, the barony of " Newton Garie." William died before his father, Sir James, and William, son of William and Mary Duff, succeeded to his grandfather while still an infant. (His mother, Mary Duff, subsequently married Arthur Gordon

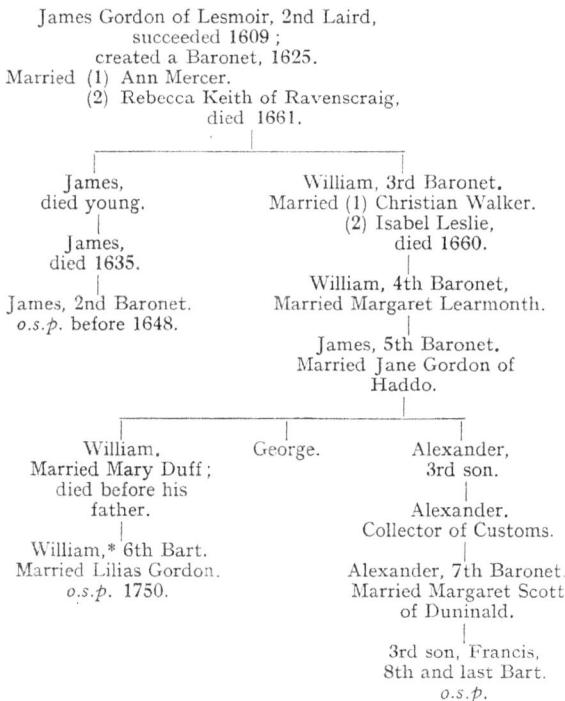

James Gordon of Lesmoir, 2nd Laird,
succeeded 1609 ;
created a Baronet, 1625.
Married (1) Ann Mercer.
(2) Rebecca Keith of Ravenscraig,
died 1661.

James, died young.	William, 3rd Baronet. Married (1) Christian Walker. (2) Isabel Leslie, died 1660.
James, died 1635.	William, 4th Baronet, Married Margaret Learmonth.
James, 2nd Baronet. *o.s.p.* before 1648.	James, 5th Baronet. Married Jane Gordon of Haddo.

William. Married Mary Duff; died before his father.	George.	Alexander, 3rd son.
William,* 6th Bart. Married Lilias Gordon. *o.s.p.* 1750.		Alexander. Collector of Customs.
		Alexander, 7th Baronet. Married Margaret Scott of Duninald.
		3rd son, Francis, 8th and last Bart. *o.s.p.*

The owner in 1715 is shown by an asterisk.

of Carnousie.) William, the Laird of 1715, and 6th Bart., married many years later Lilias Gordon (half-sister of his step-father, being daughter of John Gordon of Carnousie). He died September, 1750, without issue, and was succeeded by his cousin, Sir Alexander, as 7th Baronet.

Two of the uncles of the infant baronet took part in the Rising of '15. They were John and Robert Gordons, the 4th and 5th sons of Sir James, the 5th Baronet, who were, according to Maidment's *Analecta Scotica*, among the persons who came into Aberdeen with the Earl Marischal and were present at the Proclamation of King James VIII. John afterwards bought Kinellar, and married Henrietta, daughter of William, 11th Lord Saltoun, and sister of the 12th Lord. They had ten children, the youngest of whom, Eleanor, married her cousin, George, 14th Lord Saltoun.

Robert is said to have become an officer in the Hanoverian Army—he died unmarried.

The 7th Baronet was "the son of Alexander, collector of Customs at Aberdeen, which Alexander was 3rd son of the 5th Baronet," and therefore first cousin to the 6th, so that the new Baronet was first cousin once removed to the late one.

PARISH OF GLASS.

Bracco, for Edenglassie.

In 1737 William Duff bought the *whole* estate of Glenbucket, and with the funds derived from this sale, it is surmised that old Glenbucket proceeded to Rome to join in the plans for the Rising of 1745.[1]

Bracco, for Cairnburrow.

William Duff of Braco, only son of Alexander Duff of Braco, and born about 1686 (as he was not of age at his father's death in 1705). He owned large estates in Banffshire and Aberdeenshire, which, after his death by suicide in 1718, went to his uncle, William Duff of Dipple, father of the 1st Lord Fife. Braco was not an avowed Jacobite—the rest of his family, an uncle, Patrick Duff of Craigston, a cousin, Patrick Duff of Premnay, etc., were on the Hanoverian side—though the husband of his sister Margaret, Charles Gordon of Glengerrack, was concerned in the Rising ; but it is to be noted that William pays only the single Cess (in John Forbes' list), so he must have made his sympathies clear. More tangible proofs were, however, required, and in the *State Papers*

---

[1] See Blaikie's *Origins of the '45.*

in the Public Record Office [1] there exists a letter from Mar to George Gordon of Carnousie, dated

CAMP AT PERTH, 28 October 1715 :

You are to demand of the Lady Braco the sum of five hundred pounds. She refusing to pay it, you are to require it from Dipple, and in case he also refuses you are hereby ordered to uplift that sum out of the first and readiest effects of Braco's tenants, and you are directed to give receipt for what you receive. Upon payment of the 500 you are to deliver the passport to Braco, and the protection to his lady and tenants, and to demand of him and his tenants 6 months cess only. You are to transmit the money when received to Mr. Forbes, Collector at Aberdeen, and take his receipt and he is desired to send it hither.

MAR.

The passport is also among the *State Papers* (which may argue that it was never delivered to William Duff !)

John Earl of Mar Commander in Chief of His Majesty's forces in Scotland— Permit William Duff of Braco to ship on board any ship or vessell bound for any port in France, Holland, or Flanders from any seaport town in Scotland And that free of any troubling stop or Impediment and this to endure for three months after date. Given at the Camp Att Perth the 28th October 1715. MAR.

To all Magistrates of Seaport towns and Masters of Ships in Scotland. [2]

A letter was also sent of the same date—

To All commanders and parties of His Majesty's Forces
in Scotland.

John Earl of Mar — Whereas we have thought fitt to give our protection to William Duff of Braco, his lady and tenants, these are therefore discharging you to doe any manner of hurt to the persons of the said William Duff of Braco his lady and family or to the servants, houses, tennents or estates pertaining to the said William Duff as you shall be answerable at your highest peril. [3]

The actual attitude of William Duff in the Rising is somewhat perplexing, and may, perhaps, have been similar to that of his uncle and ultimate successor, William Duff of Dipple, who said to an inquirer that "William Duff would have gone out, but that Dipple would behold the event," [4] i.e., wait and see how things turned out. There is a letter from William Duff of Braco to his brother-in-law, Alexander Abercromby of Tilliebody, in which he speaks of Garrisoning Balvenie "on behalf of the Government, and as a good subject of King George." [5]

"From a letter from a gentleman in Murray to his correspondent in Edinburgh, 1716," it is known that "At the beginning of the troubles William Duff of Braco had garrisoned his house of Balvenie, provided it with a competent number of arms and abundance of ammunition, but upon Braco's leaving it (after a meeting with Earl of Huntly) it was

[1] *S.P.* 54.12.343.   [2] *Ibid.* 54.12.347.   [3] *Ibid.* 54.12.348.
[4] *Family Papers.*   [5] *Ibid.*

within a Hair-breadth of falling in the Earl of Huntly's hands, whose order to send the arms and ammunition therein under a Guard of 100 men, to Gordon Castle, was already lodged in hands capable effectually to execute it, but was prevented by Colonel Grant's diligence who by a handsome stratagem got a sufficient number conveyed to it who turned out Braco's men. . . ."

William Duff, taking advantage of Mar's pass, appears to have gone abroad, and was not heard of again during the Rising. He certainly went to Holland in the year 1716, but the date is not known. He joined the army of Prince Eugene in Hungary and was at the siege of Belgrade in 1717, after which he returned to Scotland, and died by his own hand at Balvenie in January, 1718, having an only child, Margaret, aged 8, who was three years later married to Patrick Duff of Premnay, the Hanoverian cousin already mentioned. His widow, Helen Taylor, Lady Braco, survived to the age of 112.[1]

ASWANLY. [Alexander Calder.]

George Calder, who married Isobel Skene, daughter of Alexander, 16th Laird of Skene, erected a gate at Aswanley in 1692 with the initials of himself and his wife carved on it. The Laird of 1710 was his son, another George, who married his cousin, Barbara Skene of Skene. He had sasine on Aswanley, 18th April, 1710. He was succeeded in 1711 by his son, Alexander Calder, who, with his wife, "Katharine Forbes, 2nd lawful daughter to John Forbes of Balfluig, had sasine, 4th January, 1711." [2]

George Calder, who married Barbara Skene, father of Alexander, the Laird of 1715, had a second wife, as on "4th February, 1713, sasine was taken on the Maynes of Aswanley for liferent for Elizabeth Innes, Lady Aswanley, relict of Mr. George Gordon of Cairnburrow, now spouse to George Calder, with consent of Alexander, his eldest son." [3]

There is at Castle Forbes a copy of an order from the Duke of Gordon to John Hamilton, his chamberlain, dated 15th May, 1715, "to pay to Alexander Calder, yr. of Aswanley the sum of 53 pounds, eighteen and ten pence for Elizabeth Calder, only lawfull Daughter to the sd. Alex. Calder and failing of her by decease to the said Alex. his other children—The money to be paid to Elizabeth herself at her comeing to the age of twenty one years compleat, or after she shall be a year and a day married or have a liveing child." [4]

The obligation was incurred in 1715, but the actual document is dated 6th July, 1725, which shows that the Duke concerned was Alexander, 2nd Duke, who had been Marquis of Huntly in 1715.

[1] *Family Papers.*
[2] *Aberdeen Sasines.*
[3] *Ibid.*
[4] *Castle Forbes Papers.*

PRESBYTERY OF ABERDEEN.

PARISH OF PETERCULTER AND HALF OF BANCHORY.

THE LAIRD OF DRUM—see PARISH OF TARLAND.

THE LAIRD OF CULTER.

Sir Alexander Cumming, born 1670, first Baronet of Culter, and 14th Laird, was the son of Alexander Cumming, 13th Laird, and Helen Allardyce. Alexander, the elder, was alive in 1709, as his son, the Baronet, was then still "younger of Culter." Alexander, younger, was made a Baronet of Nova Scotia on 28th February, 1695, being then 25 years old. He was M.P. for Aberdeenshire from 1710 to 1722.

He engaged largely and unsuccessfully in speculation at the time of the South Sea Bubble and mortgaged his estate to Patrick Duff of Premnay ; after Cumming's death, which occurred in 1725, the estate passed into the hands of Patrick Duff by decree of the Court of Session. He resided there for many years and is buried in Culter churchyard.

Sir Alexander married twice—(1) Elizabeth Swinton (daughter of Alexander Swinton, Lord Messington), who died in 1709, and (2) Elizabeth, daughter of William Dennis of Pucklechurch.

By his first wife he had a son, Captain Sir Alexander Cumming, who died in poverty, after parting with the estate (1726). He went, in 1729, to North America, and became very friendly with the Red Indians, by

Alexander Cumming of Culter, 10th Laird.
Married Helen, daughter of Walter Wood of Balbegno.
|
(Sir) Alexander Cumming, 11th Laird.
Married Margaret Gordon of Terpersie.
|
Alexander Cumming, 12th Laird.
Married (1) Jean Wood of Bonnington.
(2) Isobel Irvine.
|
Alexander Cumming, 13th Laird.
Alive 1709. Married Helen Allardyce.
(Was curator of Will of Sir Thos. Burnett, 1652.)
|
Sir Alexander Cumming, 14th Laird, 1st Baronet in 1695 ;
born 1670, died 1725.
Married (1) Elizabeth Swinton.
(2) Elizabeth Dennis.
(He took the oath of allegiance, 1696.)
|
Capt. Sir Alexander Cumming, 15th Laird,
Chief of the Cherokees.
Married Anna Whitehall.
Lost the estate.
|
Sir Alexander Cumming, 16th and last Laird,
born about 1742, died 1793.
Line extinct.

whom he was nominated Chief of the Cherokees. Returning to England, he laid his chief's crown at the feet of George II, accompanied by four scalps! His latter years were spent in London, and he died in the Charterhouse in 1775 at an advanced age (his first Commission being dated 1703) and is buried at Barnet.

(It was in 1766 that he became a pensioner of the Charterhouse; for more than 25 years before that he had been a frequent inmate of the Fleet prison for debtors.)

His son, and grandson of the 1st Baronet, was another Sir Alexander, 3rd and last Baronet, who died in 1793 and is buried at Culter.

COULTER, FOR GLASTERBERRIE—above.

WILLIAM MENZIES OF PITFODDELS.

He was a distinguished adherent of the Jacobite cause in 1715, as his grandfather, Sir Gilbert, had been of the Royalist Cause under Montrose. William was at Sheriffmuir, surrendered himself afterwards on 22nd February, 1716 (according to a letter from the Lord Justice-Clerk Cockburn),[1] and was confined in "Winton's House in the Canongate," prior to being transferred to Carlisle with the other prisoners (since it was considered useless to try Scottish Jacobites in Edinburgh before a Scottish jury!). He escaped from thence on 31st August, and the event is thus recorded in a letter now among the State Papers, *P.R.O.*, 1st September, 1716 :—

"James Beaton of Balfour, William Menzies of Pitfoddels and John Hutchinson, Merchant in Aberbrothick, have made their escape from Winton's house in the Canongate, by procuring a hole to be picked for them through a thick stone wall into a contiguous house. The woman that possessed the house from which the hole was made, is commit to prison."—*S.P.* 54.18.147.

General Carpenter, who was in charge of the transference of prisoners, calls it "the Winton House prison in the suburbs," and adds that he has now doubled the military guard. Previously the Town authorities had been responsible for these prisoners, and Carpenter wished, very naturally, to be exonerated from blame for the escape.

William Menzies was born in 1688, and married Mary Urquhart of Meldrum. He was the eldest son of William Menzies of Pitfodels (second son of Sir Gilbert) and William's first wife, Beatrix Fletcher, daughter of Andrew Fletcher, Lord Inverpeffer.

He survived until 1780, being then 92 years of age, and his wife, Mary, died 1771, aged 80.

[1] *S.P.* 54.11.143.

They had six sons—all educated at Douai and Ratisbon, and all Jacobites of 1745.

The Menzies family had been originally Protestants, as Thomas Menzies of Pitfoddels is mentioned in John Knox's *History of the Reformation* as "one of six deputes of the Kirk of Scotland" in 1561, but by the 17th century they were ardent Catholics, and various members of the family are "given up" in different parishes as "Papists." When the last John Menzies died in 1843 he left his estates to the Catholic Church, the old house of Blairs in Maryculter being now the Roman Catholic Seminary of St. Mary's.[1]

Various genealogical works give long family trees of Menzies of Pitfodels, *without dates*, but the following has been compiled from the Sasines, College Registers, etc. :—

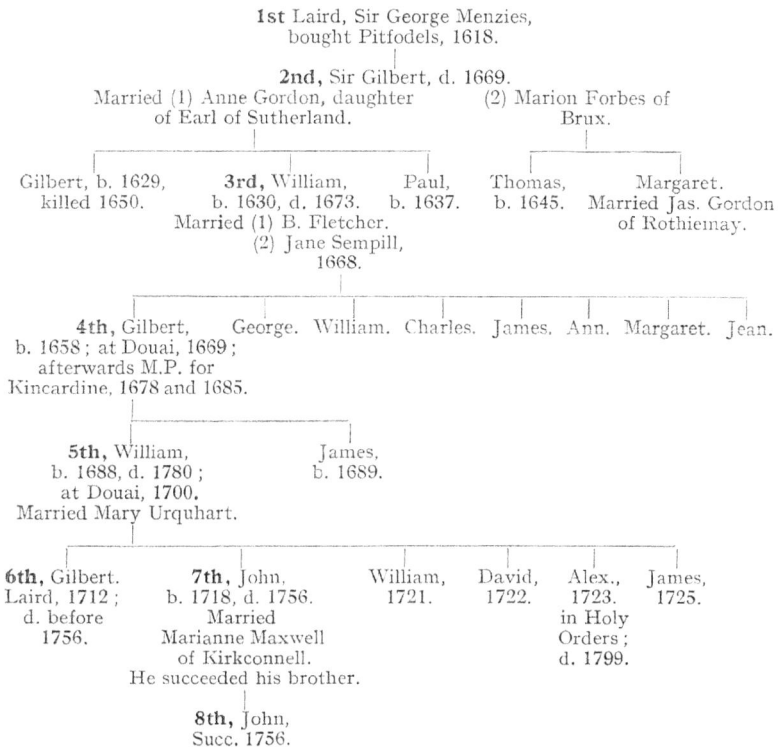

1st Laird, Sir George Menzies,
bought Pitfodels, 1618.

2nd, Sir Gilbert, d. 1669.
Married (1) Anne Gordon, daughter   (2) Marion Forbes of
of Earl of Sutherland.   Brux.

Gilbert, b. 1629,   **3rd,** William,   Paul,   Thomas,   Margaret.
killed 1650.   b. 1630, d. 1673.   b. 1637.   b. 1645.   Married Jas. Gordon
Married (1) B. Fletcher.   of Rothiemay.
(2) Jane Sempill,
1668.

4th, Gilbert,   George.   William.   Charles.   James.   Ann.   Margaret.   Jean.
b. 1658; at Douai, 1669;
afterwards M.P. for
Kincardine, 1678 and 1685.

5th, William,   James,
b. 1688, d. 1780;   b. 1689.
at Douai, 1700.
Married Mary Urquhart.

6th, Gilbert.   **7th,** John,   William,   David,   Alex.,   James,
Laird, 1712;   b. 1718, d. 1756.   1721.   1722.   1723.   1725.
d. before   Married   in Holy
1756.   Marianne Maxwell   Orders;
of Kirkconnell.   d. 1799.
He succeeded his brother.

8th, John,
Succ. 1756.

THE TOWN OF ABERDEEN, FOR MURTHILL.

John Irvine succeeded, in 1704, to his father, Alexander Irvine of Murthill. This branch of the Irvines of Drum had been in possession

[1] The remains of Pitfodels Castle are within the grounds of Norwood, Cults.

since after the battle of Pinkie, 1547. The fourth son of Alexander Irving, who was killed there, was Gilbert of Collairlie and Murthill.

CULTS AND BIELDSIDE.

In 1715 the owner of Cults was Robert Irvine, whose first wife, Jean Irvine, died, aged 32, in 1678 ; his second wife, Margaret Coutts, is buried in Peterculter churchyard. She died in 1710, aged 40. He himself died 10th April, 1728, aged 89, and was succeeded by his son, Charles.

PARISH OF DRUMOAK.

DRUM.

The House of Drum lies in this parish, but Alexander Irvine of Drum had estates in Tarland and Logiemar (see page 31).

PARISH OF SKENE.

FORNET—*D.*

The family of Irvine of Fornet became extinct in the end of the 17th century. The last note of them in the book of the *Irvines of Drum*, by Colonel Jonathan Forbes Leslie, is a receipt for money paid to Robert Irvine, younger of Fornet, by Alexander Irvine of Murthill, as administrator for "Alexander Irvine, now of Drum," 8th July, 1688.

Thereafter the estate was sold to Cumming of Culter, and later to the Earl of Kintore, who was the owner in 1715. But the tenant, who in 1696 was James Chessor, must, in 1715, have been a Hanoverian and paid double.

CONCRAIG.

This was Patrick Simpson, whose father was Alexander Simpson, brother to Robert Simpson of Thornton, Chamberlain to the Earl of Kintore. He built the house of Concraig. His son, Patrick, on 13th May, 1714, had a contract of marriage with Margaret, daughter of the deceased Robert Udny of Auchterellon.[1]

THE TOWN OF ABERDEEN, FOR LANDS IN THE PARISH OF SKENE.

THE LAIRD OF SKEEN—*D.*

Alexander, 16th Laird of Skene—from 1680 to 1724.

John Skene of Skene, the 15th Laird, died in 1680. Alexander, his eldest son by his wife, Jean (daughter of Alexander Burnett, eldest son of Sir Thomas, first baronet of Leys), was born in 1665, succeeded in 1680,

---

[1] *Aberdeen Sasines.*

and was served heir six years later, when he came of age. He married, in 1690, Giles, daughter of Mr. David Adie of Newark and Katherine Skene, niece of Sir George Skene of Wester Fintray and Rubislaw, who settled the latter estate on Giles, his great-niece, revoking a former disposition of it to his nephews, George and Alexander, sons of David Skene of Poland, who had displeased him.

Alexander and Giles Skene had nine children, and the eldest son, George, succeeded. He married (1) Elizabeth Skene of "Caraldstone" (Careston), and (2) Sarah Simpson. One daughter, Katharine, married Alexander Russell, second of Montcoffer; and another, Barbara, married George Calder of Aswanley.

PARISH OF KINELLAR.

The Town of Aberdeen.

Kinellar and Mieckle Kinaldie.

John, son of Provost Paton.

Provost Alexander Paton was eldest son of Alexander Paton of Kinaldie and his wife, Isobel Keith, born 1673. In 1686 he was served heir to his father in the town and lands of Kinellar, and of "Miekle and Little Kinaldies." He became a Burgess of Aberdeen, 20th October, 1698.

In the *Poll Book* of 1696 his mother was still living with him, with his two sisters, Isobel and Marjorie, and two nieces, Isobel and Marjorie Forbes.

The Provost died in 1705 and is buried with two of his children in Saint Nicholas Church, Aberdeen—the name of his wife is not given there, but her grave is in Dyce churchyard: "Here lyes Janet Forbes, spouse was to Alexander Paton of Kinaldie," also "Here lies Lilias Forbes, daughter was to John Forbes of Leslie." They were probably sisters—the date is 1752.

The Patons of Kinaldie were of the family of Grandhome.

Concraig, for Nether Auchorsk—D.

Concraig belonged to Alexander Simpson, brother to Robert Simpson of Thornton.

Auchorsk—D. [George Keith.]

It belonged in 1696 to "Mr. Gilbert Keith." This Gilbert Keith was the minister of Dunnottar, who bought the lands from his kinsman, James Keith of Auquhorsk, W.S., and Sheriff-Depute of the Mearns, who was also a Magistrate of Old Aberdeen. Gilbert died May, 1710, and his brother, George, succeeded him in one half of Auquhorsk in Aberdeen-shire, and in Coldham in Kincardineshire, being served heir, 22nd March, 1712.

On 17th November, 1713, George Keith has sasine on Auquhorsk.[1]

It would appear that Alexander Simpson bought the other half of Auquhorsk. Both of these estates pay double Cess.

GLASGOWEGO.

This estate belonged in 1696 to John Keith, described as a Cadet of the Keiths of Auquhorsk, and afterwards to Robert Keith, the son of John and his wife, "Isobel Skein" (Skene), who was the owner in 1715. In 1720 he sold it to Alexander Mollyson in Old Aberdeen.

PARISH OF DYCE.

KINALDY—LIFERENTED.

Alexander Paton, Laird of Kinaldie, died in 1705. His widow, who had liferent on part of the estate, was Janet Forbes of Leslie, who died 1752, and is buried in the Parish of Dyce.

WILLIAM JOHNSTON OF CRAIG.

The estate of Craig of Dyce belonged in 1655 to William Shand, and after him to his son, Thomas (Treasurer of the City), and to his grandson, William, who was in possession in 1696, and subsequently sold it to William Johnston.

This Craig is now Caskieben, from the estate formerly owned by the Johnstons in the Garioch, sold to Lord Kintore and now called Keith-Hall.

SIR JOHN JOHNSTON.

Sir John Johnston of New Place, 4th Baronet, succeeded his cousin, Sir John, the 3rd Baronet, who was in 1690 hanged for assisting a brother officer, the Hon. James Campbell of Burnbank, to abduct and marry Miss Mary Wharton, an heiress of 16. Campbell escaped scot-free and afterwards became a Member of Parliament!

Sir John Johnston, 4th Baronet, had a charter of the estate of Craig of Dyce and transferred to it the name of Caskieben—see above.

On 22nd June, 1711, William Gordon of Goval granted sasine to Sir John Johnston of Caskieben on the lands of Overtown of Dyce.

Sir John fought at Sheriffmuir, where his only son, John, born 1690, was killed by his side. His wife was Janet, daughter of Thomas Mitchell of Thainston.

[1] *Aberdeen Sasines.*

Marjory Johnston, his daughter, had sasine on the lands of Mony-cabock, 1st June, 1708. She married Andrew Burnett of Elrick, and her sister, Janet, married Charles Forbes of Shiels. The property of Caskieben, etc., was all sold about 1730 to the Burnett family, Sir John having died without male heirs in 1724. Thomas Burnett of Kirkhill, Dyce, died in 1722, and was succeeded by his son, another Thomas Burnett who had married, in 1716, Margaret, daughter of Robert Turner of Turnerhall. He died 3rd November, 1763.

LAIRD OF DYCE—*D*.

John Skene of Dyce, 5th Laird, who was in possession from 1704 to 1729. He married Margaret Farquharson.

THE HEIRS OF PROVOST JOHNSTOUN.

Provost John Johnston was elected in 1697 by the agency of his father-in-law, the retiring Provost, Robert Cruickshank, but the election was considered invalid and to have been obtained by force, the small number of Town Councillors present having been reinforced by "Burghers off the streets."[1] A decree of the Privy Council set the election aside after a few weeks, and Provost Alexander Walker reigned in his stead, December, 1697.

John Johnston died in November of the following year. He left a widow, Elspet Cruickshank, daughter of the former Provost, but his heir in the fishings on the Don was Alexander Johnston of Pettens, to whom he conveyed the rights by writ on 8th November, 1698, three weeks before his death.

PARISH OF FINTRAY.

CRAIGIVAR—PARISH OF LEOCHEL—*D*.

DYCE—JOHN SKENE—as above—*D*.

SKEEN, FOR WESTERFINTRAY—*D*.

Sir George Skene, the Provost, who bought Wester Fintray in 1666, had died on 9th April, 1707. He had settled Wester Fintray in 1690 on his great-niece, Giles Adie, who married the Laird of Skene.

DISBLAIR.

This estate, which had been long in the hands of the family of Rolland, was sold in 1695 to Thomas Burnett.

---

[1] Munro's *Provosts of Aberdeen*, p. 193.

Early in the following year Burnett resold it to William Forbes, formerly of Rubislaw, who was in possession at the date of the *Poll Book* with his lady and two children (though James Rolland still styled himself "younger of Disblair"). Forbes was succeeded by three daughters :—

(1) Ann, who married John Farquharson of Allanaquoich.

(2) Elizabeth, who married George Gordon, Professor of Hebrew in King's College.

(3) Lilias, who married Thomas Gordon, Professor of Greek in the same place.

In 1744 the lands were purchased by James Dyce, a merchant in Aberdeen, and from his hands passed into those of his grandson, Thomas Morison, M.D.

WILLIAM REID—*D.*

"John Reed," reader at Fintray, Clerk and Collector nominated by Sir John Forbes of Craigievar and William Forbes of Disblair, appears in the *Poll Book,* 1696. No other Reid in this parish is known as a heritor.

PARISH OF BELHELVIE.

EARL OF PANMURE.

This title lasted in its first creation for a very brief period. Patrick Maule of Panmure, in Forfar, was one of the few Scots who accompanied James VI when he went from Scotland in April, 1603, to take possession of the English throne. He became later a personal friend of the young Prince of Wales, and the latter, when Charles I, created him Earl of Panmure and Baron Maule of Brechin in the Peerage of Scotland on 3rd August, 1646. He was one of the King's most faithful adherents, and remained with him when he was a prisoner at Holdenby and Carisbrooke till forced to leave. Cromwell's Government afterwards ordered him to be fined £10,000 sterling and £2,500 on account of his second son, Henry, who commanded a regiment at Dunbar. These fines were eventually reduced to £4,000 and £1,000. The first Lord Panmure died 22nd December, 1661. George, the 2nd Earl, had also commanded his regiment at Dunbar, but after the final defeat of the cause at Worcester he made his peace with General Monk, and died 24th March, 1671.

The 3rd Earl, George, was a Privy Councillor to Charles II and James II. He died 1st February, 1686. The 4th Earl, James, with his brother, The Hon. Harry Maule of Kelly, a member of Convention, left the Scottish Parliament on the proclamation of the Accession of William and Mary, and both joined the Jacobite Rising of 1715 from the very beginning.

The Earl commanded a battalion of Foot at Sheriffmuir, where he was taken prisoner. but rescued by his brother.[1]

The Master of Sinclair gives the incident more dramatically: "The Earl of Panmure was taken, walking at his own leisure and so very ill cut in the head that he was left for dead in a house by the ennemie. Whence he was retaken by his brother."

He fled to France, and later to Avignon, where the old Chevalier bestowed on him the Order of the Thistle. [2] He was attainted and died in Paris, 11th April, 1723.

His estates, valued at £316,896, were sold to the York Building Society for £60,400. Later, the Society sold the Aberdeenshire lands to various small proprietors, the estates of Parkhill, Balmedie, Muirton, Belhelvie, Ardo, and Potterton, all being formed out of the Panmure lands. A considerable portion was bought by Harry Lumsden, Advocate, Aberdeen, for his family (see page 97).

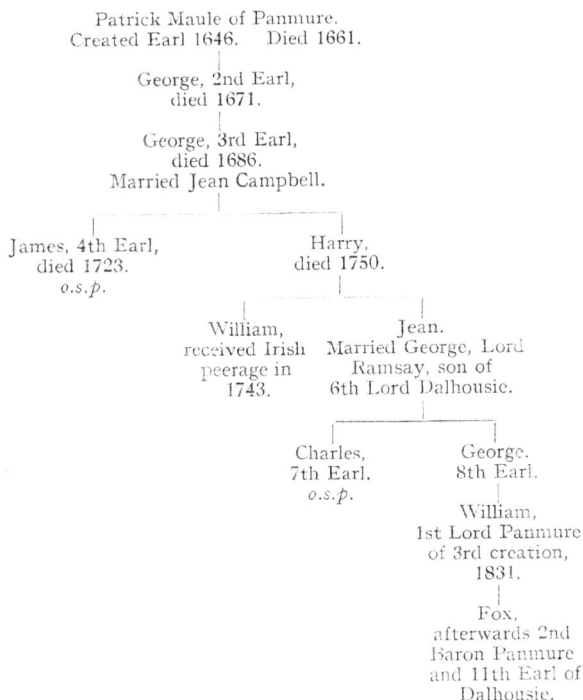

Patrick Maule of Panmure.
Created Earl 1646.   Died 1661.

George, 2nd Earl,
died 1671.

George, 3rd Earl,
died 1686.
Married Jean Campbell.

James, 4th Earl,
died 1723.
o.s.p.

Harry,
died 1750.

William,
received Irish
peerage in
1743.

Jean.
Married George, Lord
Ramsay, son of
6th Lord Dalhousie.

Charles,
7th Earl.
o.s.p.

George.
8th Earl.

William,
1st Lord Panmure
of 3rd creation,
1831.

Fox,
afterwards 2nd
Baron Panmure
and 11th Earl of
Dalhousie.

[1] According to a letter from Argyll to Lord Townshend, now in the Record Office, "Panmure was wounded and left in charge of a dragoon in a cottage, whence he was rescued."

[2] *Bibliothèque du Musée Calvet MSS.*

Of his five sons, Hugh became Laird of Pitcaple; Henry, of Tilquhilly; Clements, an Advocate; and William, of Balmedie; while Thomas, the third, retained Belhelvie and was father of Sir Harry Lumsden of Belhelvie (and "the Guides") and of Sir Peter Lumsden of Buchromb (see page 113). William, son of Lord Panmure's brother, Harry, was made Earl Panmure in the Irish Peerage in 1743, and purchased the Forfarshire portion of the estates from the York Building Society in 1764. This title also became extinct.

The third creation, of 9th September, 1831, was on behalf of the Hon. William Maule, formerly Ramsay, second son of the 8th Earl of Dalhousie, and grandson of Jean Maule, daughter of the Hon. Harry Maule (above), and grand-nephew of the Irish peer. His son, the Hon. Fox Maule, was Member of Parliament for the Elgin Burghs, 1828–41, and afterwards Secretary for War during the Crimean War, when Kinglake describes him as "the rhinoceros of Palmerston's Cabinet." In 1852 he succeeded his father as Lord Panmure, and in 1860 his uncle as Earl of Dalhousie, in which title that of Panmure is now merged.

The Hon. Harry Maule (above), second son of George, 3rd Earl of Panmure, and Jean Campbell of Loudon, was a convinced Jacobite to the date of his death. He retired to Holland (where he amassed a large collection of documents relative to Scotland) and died in 1750.

BLAIRTON.

This property, which in 1667 was in the hands of Walter Stewart, was bought before 1684 by James Milne, Burgess of Aberdeen, son of James Milne, merchant, and Elspet Donaldson. He appears in the *Poll Book* of 1696. He had two daughters—(1) Janet, married, in 1714, the Rev. Henry Likly, minister of Meldrum, and (2) Margaret, who married, 8th August, 1716, Alexander Gordon, Commissary Clerk of Aberdeen, second son of James Gordon of Seaton; this Alexander Gordon was a Jacobite of 1715.

Later, the estate of Blairtown belonged to Alexander Walker, a prominent agriculturist.

MENIE.

Alexander Ker of Menie, second son of Robert Ker, who acquired it in 1667, succeeded in 1678 to his brother, Robert, in the "lands of Meanie, Legtane, Cothill, Cowhill, and Alterseat, all in the parish of Belhelvie." He was in possession in 1696, and appears in the *Poll Book* with his wife and two sons, Robert and Alexander, and four daughters, Elizabeth, Margaret, Jane, and Susanna.

Colpnay.

John Leslie, who was of South Colpnay in 1667 was still there in 1696, with his wife and two children, Thomas and Anna.

The owner in 1715 was Walter, the son of Thomas, who married Anna Forbes, and together they had sasine on 1st May, 1707.[1]

Walter Leslie had sasine 10th July, 1713.[2]

Town of Aberdeen, for Pettens.

In the lands of "Pettenes and Wastbourne," belonging to the town of Aberdeen from donation by George Davidson, there were in 1696 ten separate tenants.[3]

PARISH OF NEW MACHAR.

The Earl of Panmuir (Belhelvie).

Mr. George Gordon of Rainieshill.

Rainieshill, in Peterculter Parish, was in 1676 in the possession of Cumming of Culter. In 1696 "Upper Rheniehill" is entered as belonging to "Mr. Patrick Harvey who resides in Forgue parish." George Gordon of Rainieshill, with John Paton of Grandhome, was granted in 1720 "the freedom and use for themselves and families of the Mort Cloths of the Trades and that gratis without paying any dues thereof."

Boddams (*sequestrate*).

"Boddoms" appears in the *Poll Book*, but without an owner! It was actually part of the estate of William Forbes of Tolquhon (who was in great financial difficulties at this period) and was at one time the family residence.

Hiltoun—*D.*

In 1696 the lands of "Hiltoune, Boghill and Swelend" were owned by Henry Panton, who had married Anna Irvine, daughter of Francis Irvine, the laird, in 1667. They had then two sons, James and Alexander, and four daughters, Anna, Margaret, Katherine, and Marjorie Panton.

In 1715 it was in the hands of Dr. John Gordon of Hilton, a great-grandson of "the great Straloch" (see Parish of Old Machar). Dr. John was a Doctor of Medicine. His son, Dr. James Gordon, married in 1731 Barbara Cumming, heiress of Birness. In 1744 he was served heir to his younger brother, Ludovick,[4] and in 1748 he also succeeded to the estate of his cousin, Alexander Gordon of Straloch.

---

[1] *Aberdeen Sasines.* [2] *Ibid.* [3] *Poll Book.* [4] *Service of Heirs.*

KINMUNDIE (*sequestrate*).

In 1696 Thomas Menzies of Kinmundy, the heritor, was under age, his father, Alexander Menzies, son of Sir Paul Menzies, being dead. His mother resided with him ; she was Anna Hamilton, and there were three daughters—Helen, Barbara, and Jean Menzies. The tutor was John Hamilton, his uncle.

In 1711 Charles Menzies of Kinmundy was the owner.

In 1715 the estate was apparently bankrupt, or at least taken possession of by Government.

There is an interesting petition from Charles Menzies among some MSS. in the City Chambers, Edinburgh, dated *1716*.

He says he was Solicitor for the Earl of Wintoun, and had resided in London since the death of Queen Anne. "Yet to his great surprise he learns that his Majesty's officers and soldiers have thought proper to riffle and plunder his country house and to ruin and plunder all his tenants and to commit many disorders on his grounds. He himself prays to be heard at the Bar of the House of Commons, and that the honourable house in their great wisdom and Justice may fall upon some proper method for repairing the loss sustained by Innocent persons."

No answer is recorded.

SMALEND—LIFERENTED (SWAILEND).

Part of the estate of Hilton in 1667. It was probably the portion of Anna Hamilton, wife of Alexander Menzies of Kinmundy (above).

ROSEHALL OR BOGHALL.

Also belonging to Hilton, formerly in the hands of William Thomson.

GUOVELL—*D*.

William Gordon in 1696 in the *Poll Book*. He also had sasine on Goval, November, 1713.

William Gordon, 1st of Goval, was a Burgess of Guild, Aberdeen, 1687. His first wife was Christian Wylie, and his second, Elizabeth Cruickshank of Banchory. He was second son of James Gordon, 1st of Seaton, his elder brother being John Gordon, 2nd of Seaton. William's eldest son, William, 2nd of Goval, was an Ensign in Lord Shannon's Regiment, 1715. The second son, Nathaniel, went to Poland in 1701. His daughter, Janet, married George Middleton, Principal of King's College. Although he paid double Cess, William Gordon of Goval's name appears surprisingly in the list of Jacobites who met at Mistress Hepburn's.[1]

ELRICK—*D*.

[1] *A Short Memorial of quhat heath occurred, etc.*

ALEX. GARDEN OF TROUP.

Andrew Burnet of Elrick had been served heir to his father, John (who was the owner in 1696 and died 28th March, 1697), in the lands of Elrick, Monycabok, etc., on 16th August, 1706.

He married, 1707, Marjorie, elder daughter of Sir John Johnston, 4th Baronet of Caskieben. She died, 1723, and is buried in St. Nicholas.

Andrew Burnet himself was "out" in the '15 and died before 1721, as his son, Robert, was served heir to him 11th February in that year, and a younger brother, John, was also served heir on 3rd September, 1737.

But the estate of Elrick had been sold before the '15 to Alexander Garden of Troup, who, on 2nd January, 1710, had sasine on Elrick, Annachie, and Blackhill.[1]

PARISH OF OLD MACHAR.

EARL OF PANMUIR—see BELHELVIE.

TOWN OF ABERDEEN, FOR GIKINSTOUN (GILCOMSTON).

In 1696 the valued rent of these lands had been £501 1s. 2d. They were in the hands of the town of Aberdeen, Jean Wauchope, relict of Robert Menzies, being the principal tenant.

In 1715 William Souper was of Gilcomston, Merchant Burgess of Aberdeen. He had married Jean Byres, daughter of James Byres of Coates, in 1685. He was Master of Mortification in 1689 and Master of Kirkwork in 1693.[2] His Will is in the Commissariot Records, 30th June, 1725. He was a Jacobite of 1715.[3]

LADY STONYWOOD'S JOINTURE LANDS.

Jean Abernethy, daughter of James Abernethy of Mayen, widow of Dr. William Moir, 3rd Laird of Scotstown, and second wife of James Moir, 2nd of Stoneywood.

SCOTSTOUN.

Alexander Moir, 5th Laird of Scotstown, son of Dr. William, the 4th Laird, and Jean Abernethy (above). He was served heir to his father in 1695, but in the *Poll Book* of 1696 the entry is "the relict of Dr. Moir," that is Jean Abernethy (above), before her second marriage to James Moir. Alexander Moir was a Jacobite of 1715 with his relative of Stoneywood, and a member of the Jacobite council as well as a Jacobite magistrate. He married Mary Chalmers and had a son, George, who succeeded him in 1752.

[1] *Aberdeen Sasines.*   [2] *House of Moir and Byres.*   [3] *Analecta Scotica.*

Mr. William Moir, Burgess of Aberdeen, 1st of Scotstown.
Married Janet Rae.
Sasines on Scotstown, 1602 and 1620.

Mr. William Moir, Principal of Marischal College, 1649–1661,
2nd of Scotstown.
Married Jean, daughter and co-heiress of Patrick Gordon of Gordon's Mills.
(John Moir of Barnes was his nephew.)

Dr. William Moir, 3rd of Scotstown.
Married, 1656, Margaret, daughter of Gilbert Skene of Dyce.

Dr. William Moir, 4th of Scotstown, M.D., died 1695.
Married Jean Abernethy.

Alexander Moir, 5th, died 1752.
Married Mary Chalmers.

George, 6th Laird.

EARL PANMUIR—PARISH OF BELHELVIE.

GEORGE CRUICKSHANK, FOR BERRIEHILL AND WATER.

Berriehill, with the Fishings on the Don.

Samuel Middleton of Berriehillock was served heir to his brother, David, in 1652. Afterwards the lands were bought by George Cruickshank of Berriehillock, who was one of those who had a warrant from General Monk to elect a Commissioner in 1659.[1] He was Dean of Guild of Aberdeen in 1664, in which year there was a deposition of the lands of Gordon's Mills by Robert Irvine to George Cruickshank and his successors in office. (In 1666 he had been succeeded by John Smith.) He married Barbara Hervie,[2] and had at least two sons—George, a baillie of Aberdeen and a Jacobite, and William, Provost in 1728 ; George Cruickshank was still alive in 1696.

On 2nd January, 1667, George Cruickshank of Berriehillock had sasine on " ane tenement in Old Aberdeen, called ' Monymusk Manse.' "[3]

NEWTOUN, FOR BERRIEHILL AND FISHING—*D*.

Berryhillock had been long in the possession of the family of Cruickshank. George Cruickshank, son of Robert Cruickshank, in Banchory, was a Baillie and Dean of Guild at the time he was one of the Aberdeenshire heritors convened by General Monk in 1659. He was twice married— (1) to Barbara Hervie, and (2) to Anna Gordon, daughter of Provost Gordon, and left two sons, George and William.

By 1696 Berryhill and the fishings on the Don were in the possession

---

[1] *Records of Aboyne*, p. 319.

[2] "Barbara Hervie, spouse to George Cruickshank, at the Bridge of Don, died in childbed, 19. July 1669."—*John Row's Diary.*

[3] *Aberdeen Sasines.*

of Mr. Alexander Davidson of Newton, who lived in Aberdeen, and also owned the estates in Culsalmond, from which he took his designation. The reason why Davidson of Newton should have paid double Cess on his holding of Berryhill and fishings is not known.

He was a Jacobite, and appears as such in the Parish of Culsamond (in the present roll), where he is entered as paying single.

On 29th July, 1715, " Mr. George Cruickshank, younger of Banchory, Advocate, heritable proprietor of the lands, mylne, salmon fishing," etc., belonging to his father, Robert Cruickshank of Banchory, had sasine on "Mains of Banchory, Bransmyres, Berriehillock," etc. Robert Cruickshank of Banchory died in May, 1717, and is buried in St. Nicholas churchyard, Aberdeen.

On 27th July, 1715, George Cruickshank, elder, merchant in Old Aberdeen, and George Cruickshank, younger, had sasine on a house in Old Aberdeen. The wife of this George Cruickshank, elder, was Barbara Finnie. The relationship between the two pairs of George Cruickshanks is not known.

THOMAS CASSIE.

The family of Cassie owned Whitestripes : Andrew Cassie being served heir to his father in Whitestripes, a pendicle of Scotstown, in 1640. Thomas (above) was the son of Andrew and his wife, Jean Henderson. In 1696 John Leslie seems to have owned the larger part of the estate, but Andrew Cassie had still a valuation of £58 0s. 0d., and was residing on his property with his wife and five children—Thomas, Duncan, Margaret, Elizabeth, and Janet. His relict resided subsequently in the town of Old Aberdeen. The wife of Thomas Cassie was Rachel Walker, for on 7th June, 1712, Thomas Cassie, merchant in Old Aberdeen, and Rachel Walker, his spouse, had an arent on Torrieleith in Udny, the property of Andrew Walker, her father, and subsequently of Patrick Walker, her brother.[1]

Andrew Cassie, son of Thomas, was Town Clerk of Aberdeen, 1738. James Cassie, the artist, is believed to have been of this family.

KING'S COLLEGE MORTIFIED LANDS.

WILLIAM THOMSON, FOR PART OF CASSIE'S VALUATION.

William Thomson in Old Aberdeen appears as one of Andrew Cassie's tenants in the *Poll Book*, 1696.

HILTON—*D*.

Hilton was owned in 1715 by Dr. John Gordon, an M.D. of King's College, 1712. He was the eldest son of Dr. John Gordon of Collieston,

[1] *Aberdeen Sasines.*

who was grandson of "the great Straloch," being second son of Straloch's eldest son, Robert, and his wife, Katherine Burnett. Dr. John Gordon of Collieston married Katharine Fullarton. The son, John, married Margaret Dowell, and was father of Dr. James Gordon (see *Seaton*, page 243).

Dr. John Gordon sold Collieston and bought Hilton.

He had in all 14 children. His second son, John, a Doctor of Divinity, married his cousin, Jane, daughter of the last Gordon of Fechil.

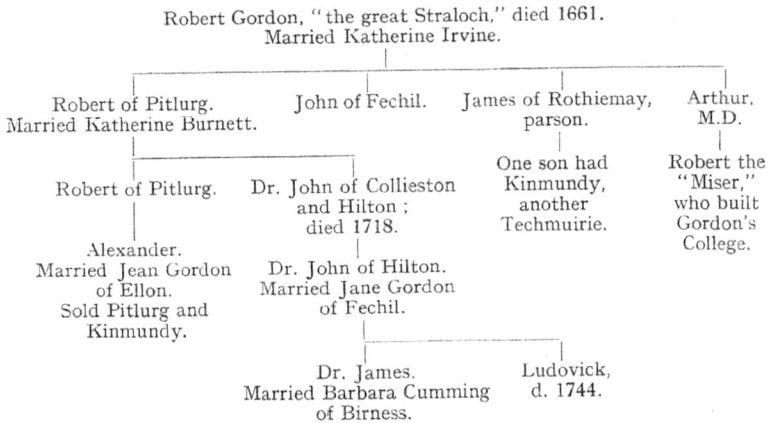

Robert Gordon, "the great Straloch," died 1661.
Married Katherine Irvine.

Robert of Pitlurg. Married Katherine Burnett.	John of Fechil.	James of Rothiemay, parson.	Arthur, M.D.
Robert of Pitlurg.	Dr. John of Collieston and Hilton ; died 1718.	One son had Kinmundy, another Techmuirie.	Robert the "Miser," who built Gordon's College.
Alexander. Married Jean Gordon of Ellon. Sold Pitlurg and Kinmundy.	Dr. John of Hilton. Married Jane Gordon of Fechil.		

Dr. James.   Ludovick,
Married Barbara Cumming   d. 1744.
of Birness.

SUNNYSIDE.

This small estate, lying between Old and New Aberdeen, was owned in 1696 by the heirs of John Moir of Barnes. Christian Moir became, in 1691, the wife of Mr. Alexander Fraser of Powis, and Sunnyside became absorbed in that estate ; but on 11th July, 1700, the Principal, Masters, and Members of King's College (the Superiors), granted a feu charter of these lands to Dr. George Chalmers, Rector of "Foord," in England, and on 14th February, 1724, Mr. Francis Chalmers, only son and heir of the deceased Dr. George Chalmers, executed a disposition in favour of Alexander Moir of Scotstown.[1]

BALGOWNY, LORD GRAY.

John, 9th Lord Gray, had, in 1707, a charter from the Crown of the Lands of Balgownie. He had in that year succeeded to the title and estates of the 8th Lord Gray, his uncle and father-in-law. He was the second son of John Gray of Crichie and Alison, daughter of James Troup, Merchant Burgess of Edinburgh. He married before 20th February, 1683, Marjorie, "Mistress of Gray" (only child and heiress of the 8th Lord Gray, who therefore took the place of the "Master").

[1] *Powis Papers.*

The charter of 1707 comprised "the whole lands of Balgowny with Westfield, Murcor and Cathick's Mill (Kethock's Mill) fishing rights," etc.[1]

Balgownie was formerly Menzies property, and in 1696 had been in the hands of Mr. John Gray of Balgownie, with Margaret Menzies his lady, two sons, John and James, and two daughters. He was grandfather to the 9th Lord Gray.

Grandham and Densfield. John Paton.

Densfield was a temporary name for Upper Grandhome, formerly "Dilspro." John Paton was the owner in 1715. In 1696 George Paton, his father, was there with three sons—John, George, and James, and four daughters—Janet, Katherine, Margaret, and Anna.

This George, who had a fresh sasine in 1700, married Isabella Christie, died in 1711, and was succeeded by his eldest son, John (above), who was an Advocate. He was twice married—(1) in 1710 to Margaret, eldest daughter of Alexander Garden of Troup (on 29th May in that year she had a liferent on Grandhome), and (2) to Christian, daughter of John Forbes of Leslie.[2]

John Paton joined the Jacobite Rising of 1715 in October, but according to his depositions, prepared for his trial at Carlisle on 15th August, 1716, and the evidence of the witnesses called, he did so only on compulsion. The witnesses included Sir William Forbes of Craigievar ; his own father-in-law, Garden of Troup,[3] a noted Whig, and two servants. Paton was one of 34 prisoners set at liberty without trial. He had surrendered himself, 17th February, 1716 (*vide* the letter of James Cockburn, son to the Lord Justice-Clerk), to Mr. Robert Pringle,[4] and pleaded guilty—two points in his favour. On being set free, he made a famous speech extolling the "mercifull disposition of King George." In the next Jacobite Rising, John Paton's son was found on the Government side.[5]

Mr. Peacock, Pitmuckston.

George Peacock, Regent of Marischal College from 1673. In 1715 he showed plainly his Jacobite sympathies, as indeed did most of his colleagues, for after the Rising was over, one, Thomas Blackwell, Professor of Divinity, sent a memorial (now in the Record Office) to Lord

---

[1] John, Lord Gray, had also sasine on Torrieleith, 29th August, 1712.

—Aberdeen Sasines.

[2] *Ibid.*

[3] His wife, Margaret Garden, "died 6 March 1715 aged 28 years," and is buried in Old Machar. His parents—"that worthie good man, George Paton of Grandholm who dyed 15 Feb. 1711" and Isabella Christie are also buried there. George Paton was a Burgess of Aberdeen.

[4] *S.P.* 54.11.127.   [5] See Blaikie's *Origins of the Forty-five*, pp. 124, 147.

Townshend, the Secretary for Scotland, in which he says that he is the "only member of the College whose circumstances allow him to address your Lordship," that "other members, viz. :—

Mr. Robert Paterson, Principal.

Dr. Patrick Chalmers, Professor of Medicine.

Mr. George Liddell, Professor of Mathematics.

Mr. George Peacock, Mr. Alexander Moir, Mr. William Smith and Mr. William Meston were guilty of the following crimes, viz. :—

Paterson, Peacock, Moir and Smith were present at the electing of the Jacobite Magistrates. Meston came riding in with the Earl Marischal, sword in hand. Peacock, Moir, Smith, and Meston delivered an address to the Pretender at Fetteresso under the title of King James, which address being from the College, it is highly probable it was signed by the Principal who was aged and infirm and unable to travel."

The Memorial goes on to request that the Government will speedily appoint new Masters in their places—"Lest the time of opening of the College now approaching and parents not seeing the College timeously supplied with masters shall lye under a great temptation to send their children privately to the old masters, which would be prejudicial to the Government." [1] Blackwell had been "put out of his charge for some months" by the Jacobites, but considered himself at this time still (or again) in office. George Peacock was finally deprived of his office in 1717. "He did not pretend to justify his conduct during the late Rebellion." [2]

WHYTESTRIPES, JOHN ANDERSON.

As has been already seen, Whitestripes belonged to the family of Cassie until 1696, when John Leslie owned a large part of it. On 4th August, 1690, Gilbert Anderson (father of John), a merchant in Aberdeen, had sasine on a portion. [3]

On 4th January, 1710, Alexander Charles, Advocate in Aberdeen, advanced money on the estate. He was a Jacobite and described (when a prisoner) as "Procurator of Aberdeen." He seems to have made a practice also of money-lending (see Parish of Forgue, Parkdargue).

RUTHRIESTOUN, MORTIFIED.

These were lands which had been made over to the town of Aberdeen ; they had formerly belonged to a family of Skene, Merchant Burgesses of Aberdeen.

STONEYWOOD, FOR SALMON FISHING—see NEWHILLS PARISH.

[1] *State Papers*, 54.12.39.
[2] *Report of Royal Commission*, 21st December, 1716.   [3] *Aberdeen Sasines*.

SEATOWN—*D.*

John Gordon, 2nd Laird of Seaton, who married Elizabeth Irvine. He had succeeded his father, James, who died in 1714. In 1696 (*Poll Book*) it is "James Gordon of Seatown with Marjorie Forbes his lady and Margaret Scougall, his grandchild."

The second son of John Gordon and Elizabeth Irvine was Alexander Gordon, Commissary Clerk, who married Marjory Milne of Blairton.

Alexander was a Jacobite, but his father appears to have been on the opposite side.

The second son of James Gordon, 1st of Seaton and brother of John, was William, 1st of Goval, who died in 1733.[1]

MR. GEORGE KEITH, WRITER, FOR FISHING—*D.*

The family of Keith of Auquhorsk (Kinellar) held Lower Grandhome during part of the 18th century and retained their fishing rights. George Keith was the famous Advocate (see page 158).

COTTOUN.

"Master Patrick Sandilands," 2nd Laird of Cotton, succeeded his father, the Town Clerk, who died in 1660, in the estate of Cotton, while the next brother, John, had the estate of Countesswells, which came from their mother, Marjorie Burnett. Patrick Sandilands was the founder of the Aberdeen paper-making industry. He was twice married—(1) to Margaret Orr of Carnbee, the mother of his family of six, and (2) to Margaret Boyes, widow of Alexander Davidson of Newton (who did not die till after 1696).

The children of Patrick Sandilands were Patrick, William, and George, Jean, Rachel, and Magdalen; the last-named was born 1688, married Thomas Paul, merchant, and died in 1778, aged 90.

PATRICK SANDILANDS, the eldest son of "Mr. Patrick," took his degree of M.A. at Marischal College, 8th June, 1699, and was, therefore, born about 1682. He became a member of the Society of Advocates in 1705; Sheriff-Substitute, 1710–12; and Sheriff-Depute, 1712—the Commission for which was issued at Whitehall on 22nd April and signed by John, Earl of Mar, when Secretary for Scotland under Queen Anne.

Sandilands afterwards joined the Rising under Mar, being one of those who met at Mistress Hepburn's in Aberdeen, and was also at the meeting to elect Magistrates, 29th September, 1715. He married Barbara Cumine of Pitullie, but died without issue, as did his next brother, William.

---

[1] Dr. George Middleton, Principal of King's College, with Janet Gordon, his wife, and Helen, Margaret, Elizabeth, and Janet, their daughters, had sasine on part of the lands of Seaton and Mill of Ardoch, 7th December, 1710.

George, the third brother, sold Cotton and settled as a wine merchant at Bordeaux. Jean Sandilands, his eldest sister (according to the *Poll Book*, second according to the *Annals of Woodside*), married Robert Byres of Dublin, and was the mother of Patrick Byres of Tonley.

The first James Sandilands came to Aberdeen from Midlothian about 1606, and shortly afterwards bought the lands of Craibstone. His second son, James, Town Clerk of Aberdeen, married the heiress of Cotton.

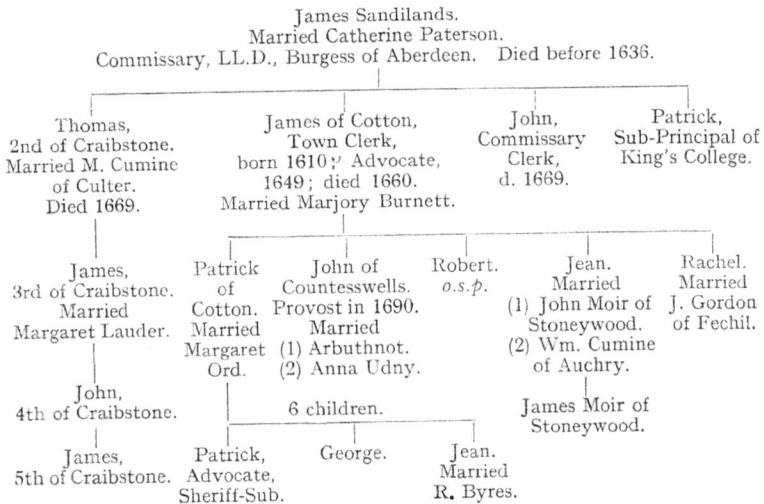

James Sandilands.
Married Catherine Paterson.
Commissary, LL.D., Burgess of Aberdeen. Died before 1636.

| Thomas, 2nd of Craibstone. Married M. Cumine of Culter. Died 1669. | James of Cotton, Town Clerk, born 1610 ? Advocate, 1649; died 1660. Married Marjory Burnett. | John, Commissary Clerk, d. 1669. | Patrick, Sub-Principal of King's College. |

| James, 3rd of Craibstone. Married Margaret Lauder. | Patrick of Cotton. Married Margaret Ord. | John of Countesswells. Provost in 1690. Married (1) Arbuthnot. (2) Anna Udny. | Robert. *o.s.p.* | Jean. Married (1) John Moir of Stoneywood. (2) Wm. Cumine of Auchry. | Rachel. Married J. Gordon of Fechil. |

| John, 4th of Craibstone. | | 6 children. | | James Moir of Stoneywood. | |

| James, 5th of Craibstone. | Patrick, Advocate, Sheriff-Sub. | George. | Jean. Married R. Byres. |

Mr. Alex. Fraser, for Lands and Fishing.

The subject of the above entry was "Alexander Fraser, Regent of King's College, who in 1699 had a Sasine of a ½ net Salmon fishing." [1] He was Laird of Powis. [2] His youngest son, also Alexander Fraser, became Professor of Civil Law, and the latter's widow, Mary Cumming, subsequently married Donald Farquharson, merchant in Aberdeen, in 1754.

A great deal more about Mr. Alexander Fraser, Regent of King's College and afterwards Sub-Principal, can be gathered from Papers kindly supplied by Mr. J. G. Burnett, M.P., of Powis House, Old Aberdeen, his descendant.

---

[1] *Aberdeen Sasines.*

[2] On 27th April, 1715, Christian Moir granted to her husband, Mr. Alexander Fraser, discharge of her life-rent on the 12 roods called Powis "seeing that the said Mr. Alexander Fraser my husband hath by ane obliedgement of the date of these presents secured me in the equivalent life-rent provision furth of ane half nets salmond fishing upon the water of Done and ane tenement of land belonging to him."

—Powis Papers.

A disposition, 25th March, 1691, by the family of Anderson, grants to "Mr. Alexander Fraser, one of the Regents of King's College (*Probus adolescens*) those twelve roods of land with their pertinents, lying within the bounds of the City of Aberdeen on the West side of the same, between the lands of Mr. Robert Gray, mediciner, on the north part, the King's Common-way of the City on the East, the hill called Broyn hill towards the West, and a certain piece of land, waste, watery, and almost uninhabitable toward the South." In 1697 he had another sasine "of a piece of land called Powis." For the 12 roods of Powis and the waste and watery land he paid 12/- Scots to the superiors.

He was the son of Mr. Donald Fraser, minister of Urquhart, and he married, in 1691, Christian, daughter and co-heiress of John Moir of Barnes and Mary, daughter of Walter Cochrane of Dumbreck. He was infeft in one-sixth of the lands of Barnes, and she in 15,000 merks Scots. She died in 1702 and he, 15th January, 1742. They had six sons and eight daughters. The fifth son, Capt. Hugh Fraser, became 2nd Laird of Powis, and seems to have been a notable farmer who greatly improved his lands. The youngest son, Mr. Alexander Fraser, was Civilist of King's College. He married Mary, 2nd daughter of Robert Cumming of Birness. He died in 1741.

For some reason, during the lifetime of his father and his elder brother, Hugh, Mr. Alexander Fraser, younger of Powis, had a Royal Charter of the lands of Powis for himself and his wife, "including the two big Tenements recently built by Mr. Alexander Fraser elder of Powis and the half nets salmon fishing recently belonging to the deceased Mr. William Johnston of Forrester hall," reserving certain revenues for his father, and power "to burden the land and fishings with the sum of 17,000 merks for the satisfaction of Mr. Alex. Fraser elder's creditors, and for the provision for his younger children." The date of the Charter was 26th July, 1729.

Mr. Alexander Fraser of Powis also obtained, in 1711, from John Paton of Grandhome the small estate of Peterstown (adjoining his own), part of the lands belonging to the Hospital of St. Peter. The crofts of Peterstown were also included, viz. Cuikiscroft, Broadhill, and Southcroft, the Masters and Members of King's College being superiors of the whole.

In 1746 a Charter was granted to Capt. Hugh Fraser, son of Alexander Fraser, and another in 1773 to Hugh Leslie, grandson of Hugh Fraser, son of Mr. John Leslie, Professor of Greek at King's College, and the deceased Christian Fraser, eldest daughter to the said Capt. Hugh Fraser.

In 1805 these lands belonged to Robert Baron, shoemaker.

On 24th March, 1705, George Gordon of Kirktown of Dyce disponed Calsieseat to Mr. Alexander Fraser of Powis, followed by an instrument of Resignation of the same, 21st May, 1718, and a Charter, 29th May.

On 5th July, 1729, Mr. Alexander Fraser, elder, resigned "Causey seat" (*sic*) to his youngest son, Alexander Fraser, Advocate.

In 1747 these lands were adjudged from Capt. Hugh Fraser as heir of line to Mr. Alexander Fraser to James Dyce, etc., for several sums of money.

Mr. Alexander Fraser at different times had sasines on tenements and closes in Old Aberdeen, all of which go to make up the modern estate of Powis. He had also other fishings at Midshingle, which came to him through his wife from Walter Cochrane.

Christian, sister of Hugh Leslie, married Alexander Burnett of Kemnay (died 1802), whose great-grandson, Mr. John George Burnett of Powis, M.P., son of George Burnett, Lyon King at Arms, succeeded to Powis under entail, June, 1894, and became 7th Laird.

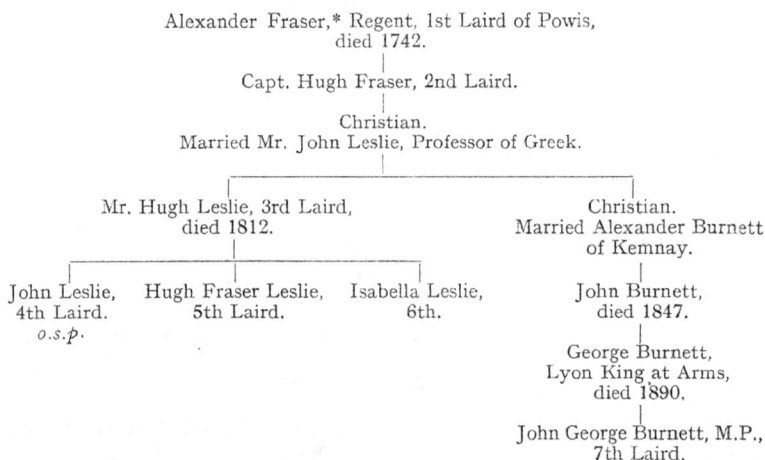

Alexander Fraser,* Regent, 1st Laird of Powis,
died 1742.

Capt. Hugh Fraser, 2nd Laird.

Christian.
Married Mr. John Leslie, Professor of Greek.

Mr. Hugh Leslie, 3rd Laird,
died 1812.

Christian.
Married Alexander Burnett
of Kemnay.

John Leslie,   Hugh Fraser Leslie,   Isabella Leslie,
4th Laird.   5th Laird.   6th.
o.s.p.

John Burnett,
died 1847.

George Burnett,
Lyon King at Arms,
died 1890.

John George Burnett, M.P.,
7th Laird.

The name appearing in the Cess Roll is shown by an asterisk.

WILLIAM MOIR, FOR FISHING HALF-NET.

William Moir, 3rd of Scotstown, son of Dr. William Moir and Margaret Dyce. He married Jean Abernethy of Mayen and had a son, Alexander, 4th of Scotstown, who married Mary Chalmers.

In 1696 it was the mother of this William, "Relict of Dr. Moir."

KING'S COLLEGE, FOR FISHING FOR HALF-NET.

PARISH OF NEWHILLS.

WILLIAM JOHNSTON, FOR BISHOPS CLINTERTY.

William Johnston of Foresterhill (Foresterhall), one of the Regents of King's College. He was eldest son of Dr. Arthur Johnston, the poet, and married, in 1662, Helen, daughter of Provost Cullen, whose sister, Isabel, was the wife of Gilbert Gray, Provost in 1660.

In the *Poll Book* of 1696 William Johnston of Bishops Clinterty is said to be polled in Banffshire !

STONEYWOOD, ELDER.

James Moir, 2nd of Stoneywood, born 1659, the eldest son of John Moir, 1st of Stoneywood, who died 1674, and his wife, Jean Sandilands, who died 1687 (she married, secondly, William Cumine of Auchry). James, 2nd of Stoneywood, married (1) Mary Scroggie, by whom he had James, 3rd of Stoneywood, three other sons and three daughters ; and (2) Jean Abernethy of Mayen, widow of William Moir, by whom he had William of Lonmay, two other sons (one of whom, John, died 19th April, 1720), and two daughters. James, 2nd of Stoneywood, died 22nd November, 1739.

STONEYWOOD, YOUNGER.

James Moir, 3rd of Stoneywood, born about 1685, married Jean Erskine of Pittodrie,[1] and was father of the famous James Moir, 4th of Stoneywood, who commanded a regiment under Prince Charles in 1745, escaped after Culloden, and after hiding for some time in his own country, set sail for Norway and became a successful merchant in Sweden. He returned in 1762 and lived until 1784. James, 3rd of Stoneywood, died before 1745.

CRABSTOUN—*D.* (CRAIBSTONE.)

Mr. James Sandilands, 3rd of Craibstone, son of Thomas, the eldest son of the original James Sandilands, who came to Aberdeen in 1606 and purchased the estate. The wife of Thomas was Margaret "Cuming" (Cumming) of Culter. Thomas died in 1669, leaving an only son, the "Mr. James Sandilands" (above), who married and had, in 1696, seven children : four sons—John, Alexander, Thomas, and Robert ; and three daughters—Jean, Anna, and Elizabeth. He kept a Chaplain and Governor, to whom he paid £20 per annum !

He appears to have had Hanoverian sympathies.

SCLETY.

In 1696 Sclatie was "part of Craibstoun," occupied by William Bruce, James Thom, Alexander Fettis, and other smaller tenants.

---

[1] On 13th July, 1710, Jean Erskine, spouse to James Moir, younger of Stoneywood, had sasine of the lands of Stoneywood and others, William Erskine of Pittodrie, her father, appearing for her.—*Aberdeen Sasines.*

On 8th August, 1706, John Sandilands of Craibstone and Janet Gordon, his spouse, had sasine "on the lands of Sclattie and Craibstoun."[1]

AUCHMULL.

In 1669 Northfield and Auchmull, with salmon fishing, belonged to Alexander Alexander, Baillie of Aberdeen. In 1715 Auchmull belonged to Mr. William Alexander.

In the *Poll Book*, Auchmull is in the parish of Kinellar, former part of the estate of Midmar.

In 1733 Jean, daughter and co-heir of Alexander Alexander of Auch-mull, married Alexander Forbes, son of "Black Jock" of Inverernan; she died 1787.

Seaton and Jackstown also belonged to Alexander Alexander. The estate of Auchmull is now part of Seaton.

PARISH OF NEW ABERDEEN.

EARL OF ABERDEEN—*D*.

See Parish of Meldrum.

MR. ALEX. MOIR.

In the *Poll Book* of 1696 "Mr. Alexander Moir, regent, resident in Aberdeen, no wife, child nor servants," pays "rent for Waters, under £200." He was brother-german to James Moir, 2nd of Stoneywood, and was described as "a gentleman of great erudition and primitive simplicity of manners."

On 15th December, 1712, Alexander Moir had sasine "on Spytall."[2]

He was one of those Jacobites who met at Mistress Hepburn's and elected Jacobite Magistrates on 29th September, 1715.

In the report of the Royal Commission, 21st September, 1716, it is stated that "Alexander Moir, Regent, Marischal College, did not pretend to vindicate his conduct during the late Rebellion further than by pleading the necessity of the times." He was "deprived" in 1717, when he went to Edinburgh and "kept an Academy for the sons of the Jacobite nobility and gentry."[3]

KIRKLANDS.

THE ARCHBISHOPRICK OF ST. ANDREWS.

George Wilson of Finzeauch was factor for the Archbishop of St. Andrews, and on 9th January, 1674, had granted a discharge to Sir John Forbes of Monymusk for £144 17s. 4d. as two years' feu-duty "for the

---

[1] *Aberdeen Sasines.*   [2] *Ibid.*   [3] *Family of Moir and Byres.*

lands of Dullab, Coullie, Inzean, Todlachie, Auchrevie, and Tillafourie, held by the said Sir John from the Marquis of Huntly and by the Marquis of Huntly of the Archbishop of St. Andrews." [1]

On the 5th October, 1706, another discharge was granted by Mr. William Smith, Regent in Marischal College, Aberdeen, of the rents payable to the Archbishopric of St. Andrews.[2]

THE PARSONAGE OF AUCHTERLESS.

THE PARSONAGE OF INVERNOCHTIE.

THE PARSONAGE OF TURREFF (EARL OF ERROL).

THE PARSONAGE OF KINCAIRDEN.

These amounts, which were all *single*, were levied, *not* on the individual incumbent, but on the heritors of the parish who paid his stipend.

As already stated, the ministers of Aberdeenshire were for the most part Jacobite and Episcopalian in sympathy both in 1715 and 1745. Those who were not openly so, busied themselves afterwards in procuring petitions in favour of captive Jacobites, as in the case of young Alexander Hay of Arnbath, Alex. Forbes of Balfluig, and others. The Jacobite tradition had, perhaps, a firmer hold in this county than anywhere else in Scotland.

[1] *Aberdeen Sasines.*   [2] *Ibid.*

BIBLIOGRAPHY

LIST OF BOOKS which have been specially helpful in compiling the notes to the present volume.

The following publications of the SPALDING CLUB and the NEW SPALDING CLUB :—

"Antiquities of the Shires of Aberdeen and Banff."
"Cartularium Ecclesiæ Sancti Nicholai Aberdonensis."
"Family of Burnett of Leys."
"Fasti Aberdonenses."
"Fasti Academiæ Mariscallanæ."
"Historical Papers Relating to the Jacobite Period."
"Memorials of the Family of Skene of Skene."
"Miscellany of the New Spalding Club."
"Records of Aboyne."
"Records of Invercauld."
"Records of the Scots Colleges at Douai, Rome, Madrid, Valladolid, and Ratisbon."

List of Pollable Persons within the Shire of Aberdeen, 1696.
The Privy Council Records and other State Papers.
Stuart Papers (Hist. MSS. Commission).

J. ARBUTHNOTT . .	"Historic Account of Peterhead."
P. HUME BROWN . .	"History of Scotland."
P. BUCHAN . . .	"Annals of Peterhead."
G. BRUNTON and D. HAIG	"Historical Account of the Senators of the College of Justice."
J. DAVIDSON . . .	"Inverurie and the Earldom of the Garioch."
J. A. HENDERSON . .	"Aberdeenshire Epitaphs and Inscriptions."
J. A. HENDERSON . .	"Annals of Lower Deeside."
A. JERVISE . . .	"Epitaphs and Inscriptions of the North-East of Scotland."
A. LAING . . .	"Donean Tourist."
W. FORBES LEITH	"Memoirs of Scottish Catholics during the XVIIth and XVIIIth Centuries."
C. LESLIE . . .	"Historical Records of the Family of Leslie."
J. FORBES LESLIE .	"The Irvines of Drum."
J. L. MICHIE . .	"History of Logie Coldstone."
R. PATTEN . . .	"History of the Late Rebellion, 1715."
J. B. PRATT . . .	"Buchan."
D. W. RANNIE . .	"Student's History of Scotland."
J. ROBERTSON . .	"Book of Bon-Accord."
J. ROBERTSON . .	"A Short Memorandum of quhat heath occurred in Aberdeen since XX September, MD CCXV."
A. FRANCIS STEUART .	"News Letters of 1715."
J. STIRTON . . .	"Crathie and Braemar."
J. F. TOCHER . .	"Book of Buchan."

The bulk of the researches have been conducted from Family Papers, from Birth Brieves, Parish Records, and various Manuscripts, in London, Edinburgh, Aberdeen, Paris, and Avignon.

INDEX

When John Forbes's spelling is so peculiar that the places might not be recognised, both his own and the correct spelling are given.
Where his error is only of one letter, the modern spelling is substituted.
The figures in black type denote where the long account of family or place may be found.

254

255

THE ABERDEEN UNIVERSITY PRESS LIMITED

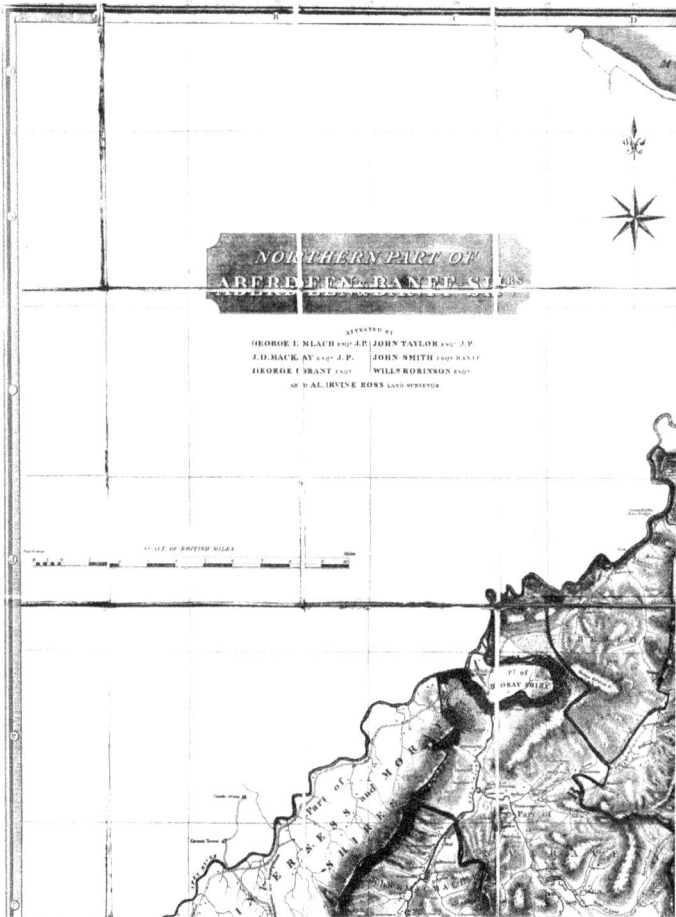

Upper left portion of the original map of the shires of
Aberdeen and Banff, divided into parishes, date 1826

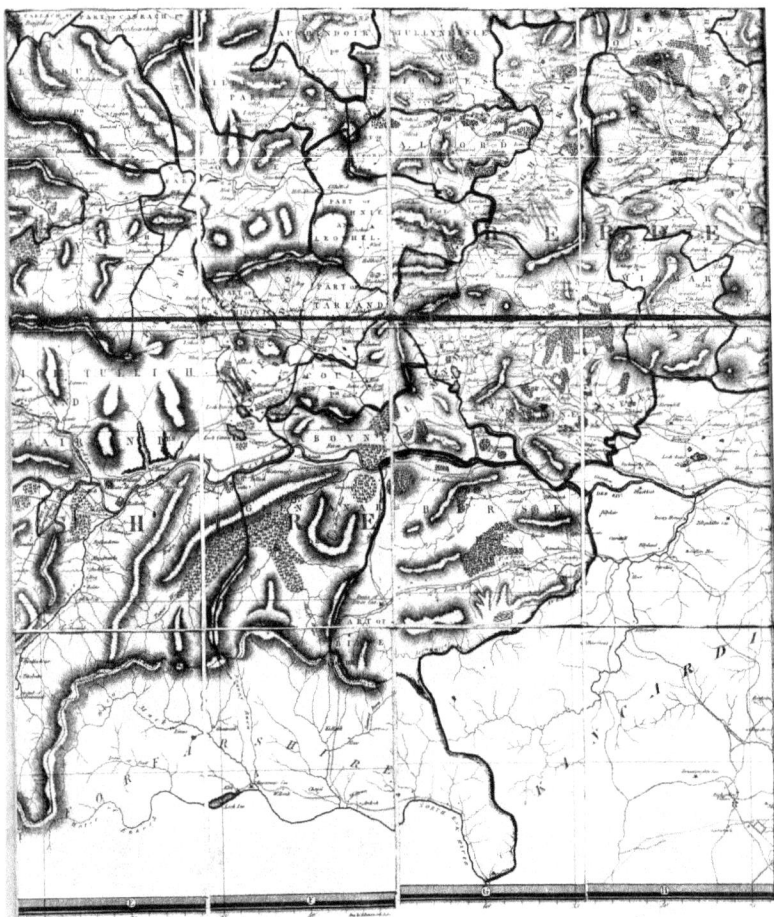

Lower middle portion of the original map of the shires of
Aberdeen and Banff, divided into parishes, date 1826

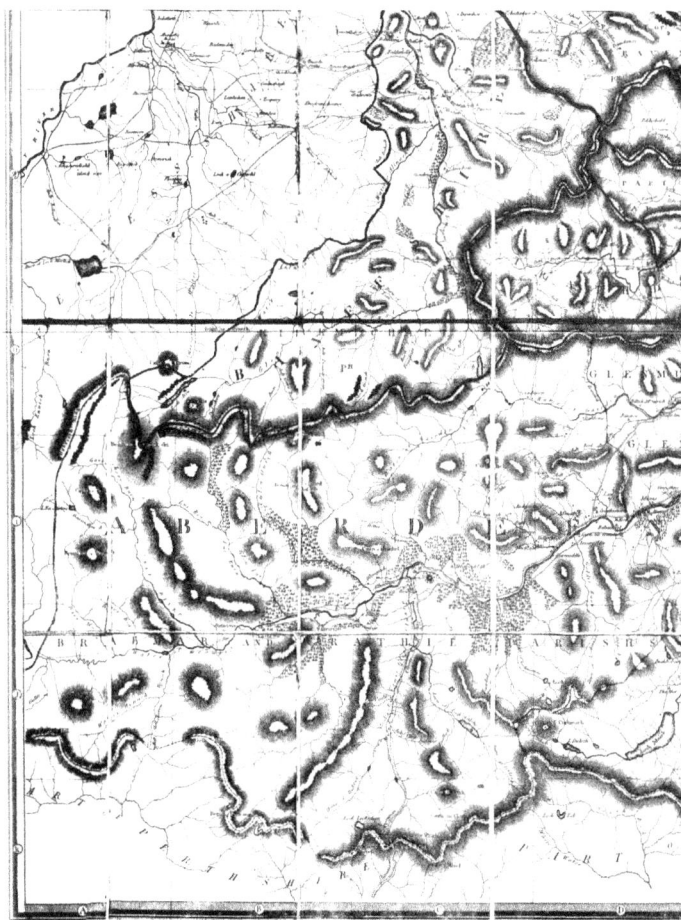

Lower left portion of the original map of the shires of
Aberdeen and Banff, divided into parishes, date 1826

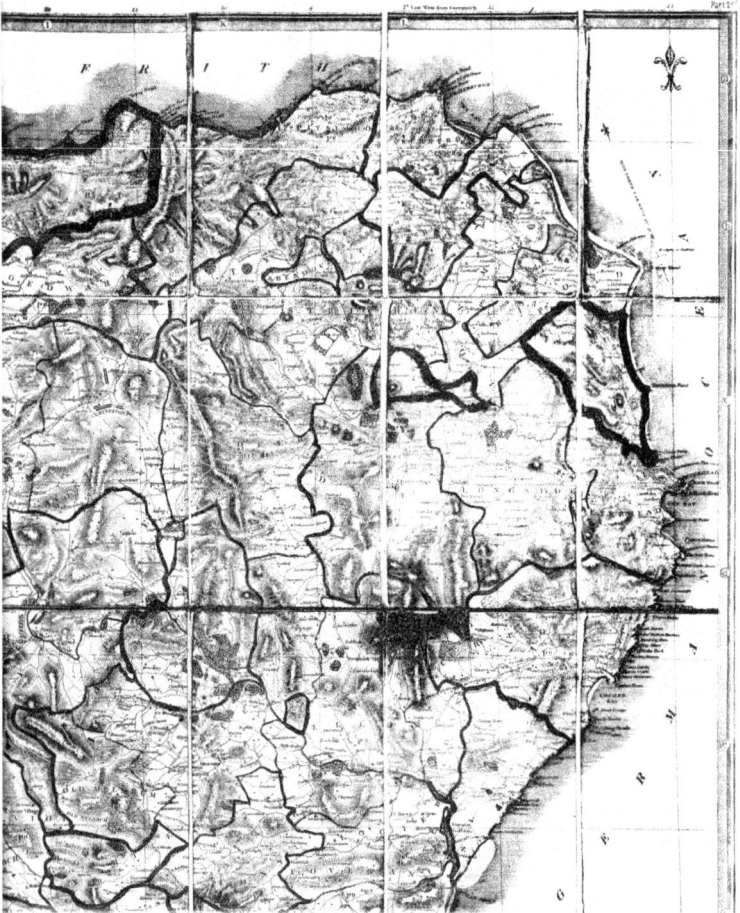

Upper right portion of the original map of the shires of
Aberdeen and Banff, divided into parishes, date 1826

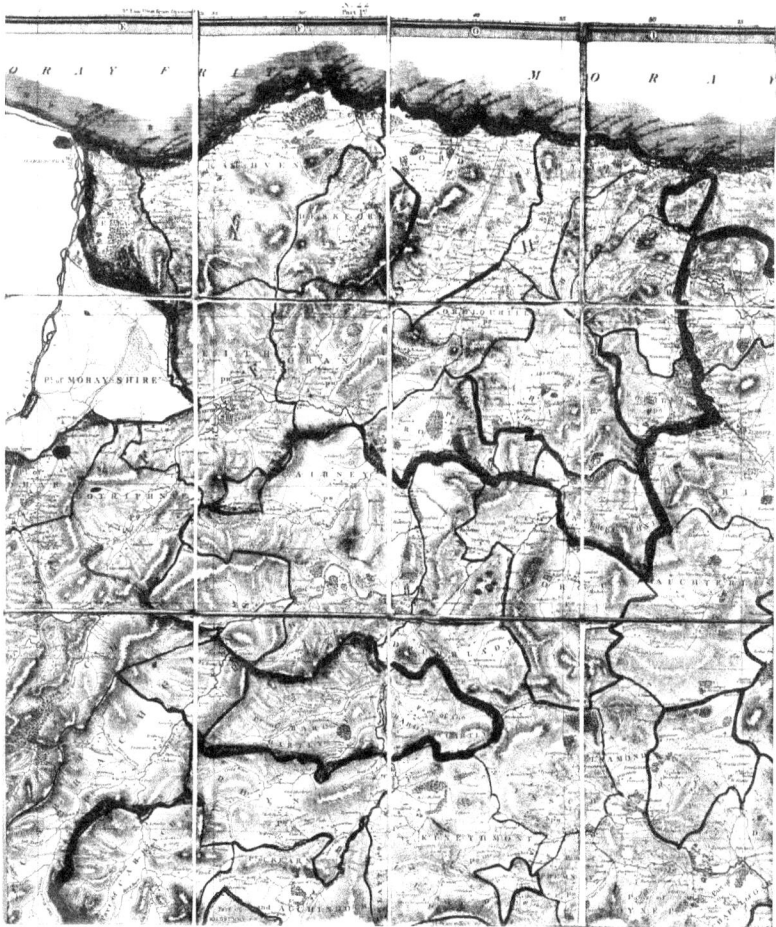

Upper middle portion of the original map of the shires of
Aberdeen and Banff, divided into parishes, date 1826

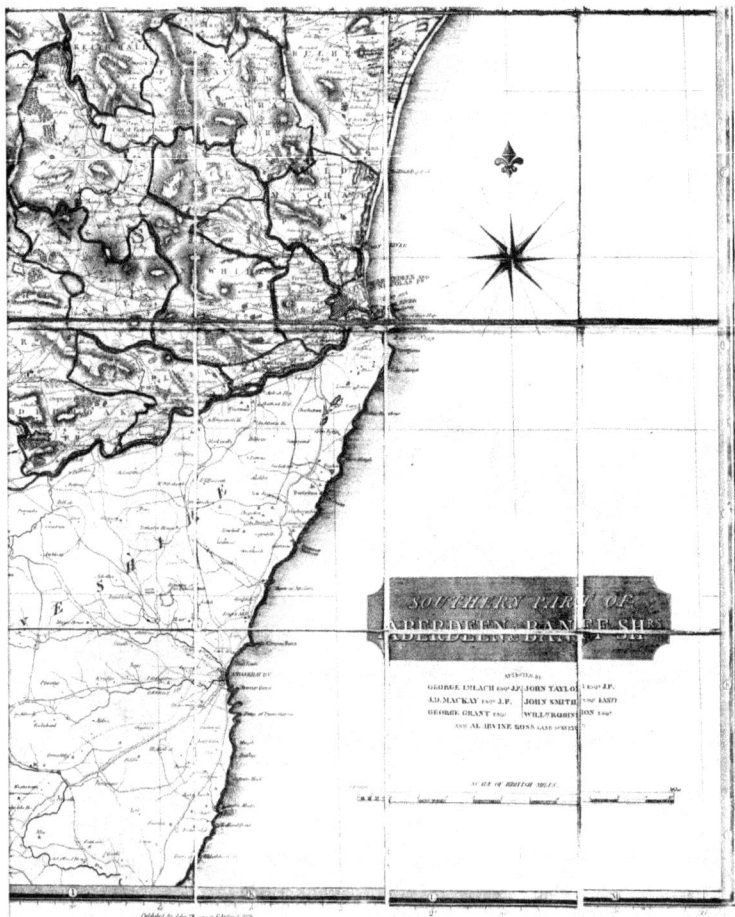

Lower right portion of the original map of the shires of
Aberdeen and Banff, divided into parishes, date 1826

www.ingramcontent.com/pod-product-compliance
Lightning Source LLC
Chambersburg PA
CBHW050700280326
41926CB00088B/2413